# Java™ Network Programming and Distributed Computing

# JAVA™ NETWORK PROGRAMMING AND DISTRIBUTED COMPUTING

David Reilly and Michael Reilly

✦▾Addison-Wesley

Boston • San Francisco • New York • Toronto • Montreal
London • Munich • Paris • Madrid
Capetown • Sydney • Tokyo • Singapore • Mexico City

The publisher offers discounts on this book when ordered in quantity for special sales. For more information, please contact:

Pearson Education Corporate Sales Division
201 W. 103rd Street
Indianapolis, IN 46290
(800) 428-5331
corpsales@pearsoned.com

Visit Addison-Wesley on the Web: www.awl.com/cseng/

Library of Congress Control Number:
2002101206

ISBN 0-201-71037-4
Text printed on recycled paper
12345678910—CRS—0605040302
First printing, March 2002

*To the memory of Countess Ada Lovelace, the world's first computer programmer, and to Myrtle Irene Daley, my beloved grandmother. A gracious thanks goes out to two former instructors, Mr. Terry Bell and Dr. Zheng da Wu, whose encouragement and faith in writing and networking, respectively, guided me to what I am today.*

*—David Reilly*

# CONTENTS

# PREFACE

Welcome to *Java Network Programming and Distributed Computing*. The goal of this book is to introduce and explain the basic concepts of networking and discuss the practical aspects of Java network programming.

This book will help readers get up to speed with network programming and employ the techniques learned in software development. If you've had some networking experience in another language and want to apply your existing skills to Java, you'll find the book to be an accelerated guide and a comprehensive reference to the networking API. This book does not require you to be a networking guru, however, as Chapters 1–4 provide a gentle introduction to networking theory, Java, and the most basic elements of the Java networking API. In later chapters, the Java API is covered in greater detail, with a discussion supplementing the documentation that Sun Microsystems provides as a reference.

## What You'll Learn

In this book, readers will learn how to write applications in Java that make use of network programming. The Java API provides many ways to communicate over the Internet, from sending packets and streams of data to employing higher-level application protocols such as HTTP and distributed computing mechanisms.

Along the way, you'll read about:

- How the Internet works, its architecture and the TCP/IP protocol stack
- The Java programming language, including a refresher course on topics such as exception handling
- Java's input/output system and how it works
- How to write clients and servers using the User Datagram Protocol (UDP) and the Transport Control Protocol (TCP)

- The advantages of multi-threaded applications, which allow network applications to perform multiple tasks concurrently
- How to implement network protocols, including examples of client/server implementations
- The HyperText Transfer Protocol (HTTP) and how to access the World Wide Web using Java
- How to write server-side Java applications for the WWW
- Distributed computing technologies including remote method invocation (RMI) and CORBA
- How to access e-mail using the extensive JavaMail API

## What You'll Need

A reasonable familiarity with Java programming is required to get the most out of this book. You'll need to be able to compile and run Java applications and to understand basic concepts such as classes, objects, and the Java API. However, you don't need to be an expert with respect to the more advanced topics covered herein, such as I/O streams and multi-threading. All examples use a text interface, so there's no need to have GUI experience.

You'll also need to install the Java SDK, available for free from Sun Microsystems (http://java.sun.com/j2se/). Java programmers will no doubt already have access to the SDK, but readers should be aware that some examples in this text will require JDK 1.1, and the advanced sections on servlets, RMI and CORBA, and JavaMail will require Java 2.

A minimal amount of additional software is required, and most of the tools for Java programming are available for free and downloadable via the WWW. Chapter 2 includes an overview of Java development tools, but readers can also use their existing code editor. Readers will be advised when examples feature additional Sun Microsystems software.

## Companion Web Site

As a companion to the material covered in this book, the book's Web site offers the source code in downloadable form (no need to wear out your fingers!), as well as a list of Frequently Asked Questions about Java Networking, links to networking resources, and additional information about the book. The site can be found at

http://www.davidreilly.com/jnpbook/.

## Contacting the Authors

We welcome feedback from readers, be it comments on specific chapters or sections or an evaluation of the book as a whole. In particular, reader input about whether topics were clearly conveyed and sufficiently comprehensive would be appreciated. While we'd love to receive only praise, honest opinions are valued (as well as suggestions about coverage of new networking topics).

Feel free to contact us directly. While we can't guarantee an individual reply, we'll do our best to respond to your query. Please send questions and feedback via e-mail to: jnpbook@davidreilly.com.

David Reilly and Michael Reilly
September 2001

# ACKNOWLEDGMENTS

This book would not have been possible without the assistance of our peer reviewers, who contributed greatly to improving its quality and allowing us to deliver a guide to Java network programming that is both clear and comprehensive. Our thanks go to Michael Brundage, Elisabeth Freeman, Bob Kitzberge, Lak Ming Lam, Ian Lance Taylor, and John J. Wegis.

We'd like to make special mention of two reviewers who contributed detailed reviews and offered insightful recommendations: Howard Lee Harkness and D. Jay Newman. Most of all, we would like to thank Amy Fong, whose thoroughness and invaluable suggestions, including questions that the inquisitive reader might have about TCP/IP and Java, helped shape the book that you are reading today.

We'd also like to thank our editorial team at Addison-Wesley, including Karen Gettman, whose initial encouragement and persistence convinced us to take on the project, Mary Hart, Marcy Barnes-Henrie, Melissa Dobson, and Emily Frey. Their support throughout the process of writing, editing, and preparing this book for publication is most heartily appreciated.

# CHAPTER 1

## Networking Theory

This chapter provides an overview of the basic concepts of networking and discusses essential topics of networking theory. Readers experienced with networking may choose to skip over some of these preliminary sections, although a refresher course on basic networking concepts will be useful, as later chapters presume a knowledge of this theory on the part of the reader. A solid understanding of the relationship between the various protocols that make up the TCP/IP suite is required for network programming.

## 1.1   What Is a Network?

Put simply, a network is a collection of devices that share a common communication protocol and a common communication medium (such as network cables, dial-up connections, and wireless links). We use the term *devices* in this definition rather than *computers*, even though most people think of a network as being a collection of computers; certainly the basic concept of a network in most peoples' mind is of an assembly of network servers and desktop machines.

However, to say that networks are merely a collection of computers is to limit the range of hardware that can use them. For example, printers may be shared across a network, allowing more than one machine to gain access to their services. Other types of devices can also be connected to a network; these devices can provide access to information, or offer services that may be controlled remotely. Indeed, there is a growing movement toward connecting non-computing devices to networks. While the technology is still evolving, we're moving toward a network-centric as opposed to a computing-centric model. Services and devices can be distributed across a network rather than being bound to individual machines. In the same way, users can move from machine to machine, logging on as if they were sitting at their own familiar terminal.

1

One fun and popular example from very early on in the history of networking is the soda machine connected to the Internet, allowing people around the world to see how many cans of a certain flavor of drink were available. While a trivial application, it served to demonstrate the power of networking devices. Indeed, as home networks become easier to use and more affordable, we may even see regular household appliances such as telephones, televisions, and home stereo systems connected to local networks or even to the Internet.

Network and software standards such as Sun's Jini already exist to help devices and hardware talk to each other over networks and to allow instant plug-and-play functionality. Devices and services can be added and removed from the network (as, for example, when you unplug your printer and take it to the next room) without the need for complex administration and configuration. It is anticipated that over the course of the next few years, users will become just as comfortable and familiar with network-centric computing as they are with the Internet.

In addition to devices that provide services are devices that keep the network going. Depending on the complexity of a network and its physical architecture, elements forming it may include network cards, routers, hubs, and gateways. These terms are defined below.

- *Network cards* are hardware devices added to a computer to allow it to talk to a network. The most common network card in use today is the Ethernet card. Network cards usually connect to a network cable, which is the link to the network and the medium through which data is transmitted. However, other media exist, such as dial-up connections through a phone line, and wireless links.
- *Routers* are machines that act as switches. These machines direct packets of data to the next "hop" in their journey across a network.
- *Hubs* provide connections that allow multiple computers to access a network (for example, allowing two desktop machines to access a local area network).
- *Gateways* connect one network to another—for example, a local area network to the Internet. While routers and gateways are similar, a router does not have to bridge multiple networks. In some cases, routers are also gateways.

While it is useful to understand such networking terminology as it is widely used in networking texts and protocol specifications, programmers do not generally need to be concerned with the implementation details of a network and its underlying architecture. However, it is important for programmers to be aware of the various elements making up the network.

## 1.2    How Do Networks Communicate?

Networks consist of connections between computers and devices. These connections are most commonly physical connections, such as wires and cables, through which electricity is sent. However, many other media exist. For example, it is possible to use infrared and radio as a communication medium for transmitting data wirelessly, or fiber-optic cables that use light rather than electricity.

Such connections carry data between one point in the network and another. This data is represented as bits of information (either "on" or "off," a "zero" or a "one"). Whether through a physical medium such as a cable, through the air, or using light, this raw data is passed across various points in the network called nodes; a node could represent a computer, another type of hardware device such as a printer, or a piece of networking equipment that relays this information onward to other nodes in the network or to an entirely different network. Of course, for data to be successfully delivered to individual nodes, these nodes must be clearly identifiable.

### 1.2.1    Addressing

Each node in a network is typically represented by an address, just as a street name and number, town or city, and zip code identifies individual homes and offices. The manufacturer of the network interface card (NIC) installed in such devices is responsible for ensuring that no two card addresses are alike, and chooses a suitable addressing scheme. Each card will have this address stored permanently, so that it remains fixed—it cannot be manually assigned or modified, although some operating systems will allow these addresses to be faked in the event of an accidental conflict with another card's address.

Because of the wide variety of NICs, many addressing schemes are used. For example, Ethernet network cards are assigned a unique 48-bit number to distinguish one card from another. Usually, a numerical number is assigned to each card, and manufacturers are allocated batches of numbers. This system must be strictly regulated by industry, of course—two cards with the same address would cause headaches for network administrators. The physical address is referred to by many names (some of which are specific to a certain type of card, while others are general terms), including:

- Hardware address
- Ethernet address
- Media Access Control (MAC) address
- NIC address

These addresses are used to send information to the appropriate node. If two nodes shared the same address, they would be competing for the same information and one would inevitably lose out, or both would receive the same data. Often, machines are known by more than one type of address. A network server may have a physical Ethernet address as well as an Internet Protocol (IP) address that distinguishes it from other hosts on the Internet, or it may have more than one network card.

Within a local area network, machines can use physical addresses to communicate. However, since there are many types of these addresses, they are not appropriate for internetwork communication. As discussed later in this chapter, the IP address is used for this purpose.

### 1.2.2   Data Transmission Using Packets

Sending individual bits of data from node to node is not very cost effective, as a fair bit of overhead is involved in relaying the necessary address information every time a byte of data is transmitted. Most networks, instead, group data into packets. Packets consist of a header and data segment, as shown in Figure 1-1. The header contains addressing information (such as the sender and the recipient), checksums to ensure that a packet has not been corrupted, as well as other useful information that is needed for transmission across the network. The data segment contains sequences of bytes, comprising the actual data being sent from one node to another. Since the header information is needed only for transmission, applications are interested only in the data segment. Ideally, as much data as possible would be combined into a packet, in order to minimize the overhead of the headers. However, if information needs to be sent quickly, packets may be dispatched when nearly empty. Depending on the type of packet and protocol being used, packets may also be padded out to fit a fixed length of bytes.

When a node on the network is ready to transmit a packet, a direct connection to the destination node is usually not available. Instead, intermediary nodes carry packets from one location to another, and this process is repeated indefinitely until the packet reaches its destination. Due to network conditions (such as congestion or network failures), packets may take arbitrary routes, and sometimes they may be lost in transit or arrive out of sequence. This may seem like a chaotic way of communicating, but as will be seen in later chapters, there are ways to guarantee delivery and sequencing. Indeed, the properties of guaranteed delivery and sequential order are often irrelevant to certain types of applications (such as streaming video and audio, where it is more important to present current video frames and audio segments than to retransmit lost ones). When these properties are necessary, networking software can keep track of lost packets and out-of-sequence data for applications.

| Header fields | Data     1101011111001010101101111101 |
|---------------|----------------------------------------|

**Figure 1-1**   Pictorial representation of a packet header

Packet transmission and transmission of raw bits of information are low-level processes, while most network programming deals with high-level transmission of data. Rather than simultaneously covering the gamut of transmission from raw bytes to packets and then to actual program data, it is helpful to conceive of these different types of communication as comprising individual layers.

## 1.3   Communication across Layers

The concept of layers was introduced to acknowledge and address the complexity of networking theory. The most popular approach to network layering is the Open Systems Interconnection (OSI) model, created by the International Standards Organization (ISO). This model groups network operations into seven parts, from the most basic physical layer through to the application layer, where software applications such as Web clients and e-mail servers communicate.

Under the OSI model, each of the seven layers into which communication is grouped can be referred to by a number or by a descriptive name. Generally, when network programmers refer to a particular layer (e.g., Layer $n$), they are referring to the $n$th layer of the OSI model. Each of the seven layers is illustrated in Figure 1-2.

Each of the layers is responsible for some form of communication task, but each task is narrowly defined and usually relies on the services of one or more layers beneath it. In some systems, one or more layers may be absent, while in other systems all layers are used. Frequently, though, only a subset of the seven layers is employed by an operating system. Generally, programmers limit themselves to working with one layer at a time; details of the layers below are thus hidden from view. When writing software for one layer—say, for communicating across the Internet—we as programmers don't need to concern ourselves with issues such as initiating a modem connection and sending data to and from the communications port to the modem. Breaking the network into layers leads to a much simpler system.

### 1.3.1   Layer 1—Physical Layer

The physical layer is networking communication at its most basic level. The physical layer governs the very lowest form of communication between network nodes. At this level, networking hardware, such as cards and cables,

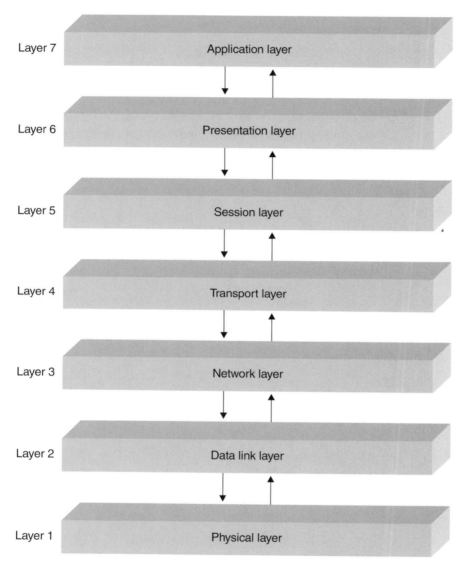

**Figure 1-2**   Seven layers of the OSI Reference Model

transmit a sequence of bits between two nodes. Java programmers do not work at this level—it is the domain of hardware driver developers and electrical engineers. At this layer, no real attempt is made to ensure error-free data transmission. Errors can occur for a variety of reasons, such as a spike in voltage due to interference from an outside source, or line noise in networks that use analog transmission media.

### *1.3.2 Layer 2—Data Link Layer*

The data link layer is responsible for providing a more reliable transfer of data, and for grouping data together into frames. Frames are similar to data packets, but are blocks of data specific to a single type of hardware architecture (whereas data packets are used at a higher level and can move from one type of network to another). Frames have checksums to detect errors in transmission, and typically a "start" and "end" marker to alert hardware to the division between one frame and another. Sequences of frames are transmitted between network nodes, and if a frame is corrupted it will be discarded. The data link layer helps to ensure that garbled data frames will not be passed to higher layers, confusing applications. However, the data link layer does not normally guarantee retransmission of corrupted frames; higher layers normally handle this behavior.

### *1.3.3 Layer 3—Network Layer*

Moving up from the data link layer, which sends frames over a network, we reach the network layer. The network layer deals with data packets, rather than frames, and introduces several important concepts, such as the network address and routing. Packets are sent across the network, and in the case of the Internet, all around the world. Unless traveling to a node in an adjacent network where there is only one choice, these packets will often take alternative routes (the route is determined by routers). Communication at this level is still very low-level; network programmers are rarely required to write software services for this layer.

### *1.3.4 Layer 4—Transport Layer*

The fourth layer, the transport layer, is concerned with controlling how data is transmitted. This layer deals with issues such as automatic error detection and correction, and flow control (limiting the amount of data sent to prevent overload).

### *1.3.5 Layer 5—Session Layer*

The purpose of the session layer is to facilitate application-to-application data exchange, and the establishment and termination of communication sessions. Session management involves a variety of tasks, including establishing a session, synchronizing a session, and reestablishing a session that has been abruptly terminated. Not every type of application will require this type of service, as the additional overhead of connection-oriented communication can increase network delays and bandwidth consumption. Some applications will instead choose to use a connectionless form of communication.

### 1.3.6   Layer 6—Presentation Layer

The sixth layer deals with data representation and data conversion. Different machines use different types of data representation (an integer might be represented by 8 bits on one system and 16 bits on another). Some protocols may want to compress data, or encrypt it. Whenever data types are being converted from one format to another, the presentation layer handles these types of tasks.

### 1.3.7   Layer 7—Application Layer

The final OSI layer is the application layer, which is where the vast majority of programmers write code. Application layer protocols dictate the semantics of how requests for services are made, such as requesting a file or checking for e-mail. In Java, almost all network software written will be for the application layer, although the services of some lower layers may also be called upon.

## 1.4   Advantages of Layering

The division of network protocols and services into layers not only helps simplify networking protocols by breaking them into smaller, more manageable units, but also offers greater flexibility. By dividing protocols into layers, protocols can be designed for interoperability. Software that uses Layer $n$ can communicate with software running on another machine that supports Layer $n$, regardless of the details of Layer $n$-1, Layer $n$-2, and so on. Lower-level layers, for example, can be substituted and replaced without having to modify or redesign higher-level layers, or recompile application software. For example, a network layer protocol can work with an Ethernet network and a token ring network, even though at the physical and data link layers, two different protocols and hardware devices are being used. In a world of heterogeneous networks, this is an important quality, as it makes networks interoperable.

## 1.5   Internet Architecture

The most important revolution in networking history has been the evolution of the Internet, a worldwide collection of smaller networks that share a common communication suite (TCP/IP). The term *evolution* rather than *creation* is used here, as the Internet did not simply come into existence one day and start running. Over the years, the Internet has been extended to include what we have today; it has evolved from a defense communications project called ARPANET into a worldwide collection of networks that spans both the commercial and noncommercial domains. Contributions to the design of the Internet came from both the original ARPANET developers and from academic and commercial researchers who offered suggestions and improvements that helped shape what it is today.

The Internet is an open system, built on common network, transport, and application layer protocols, while granting the flexibility to connect a variety of computers, devices, and operating systems to it. Whether an individual is running a PC, Unix, Macintosh, or Palm handheld computer, the complexities of communication and translation are handled transparently for users by the TCP/IP suite of protocols.

**NOTE:** The history of the Internet is a fascinating topic, but one that some readers will find rather dry. Those interested in learning more about the history of the Internet and the people involved in its evolution can consult a variety of resources online. One of the best resources is from the Internet Society, at http://www.isoc.org/internet/history/.

## 1.5.1 Design of the Internet

The Internet as we know it today is the result of many decades of innovation and experimentation. The protocols that make up the TCP/IP suite have been carefully designed, tested, and improved upon over the years. Some of the major goals (expressed in RFC 871[1]) were to achieve:

- *Resource sharing between networks,* by creating network protocols that support internetwork communication or "internetting." The various protocols that make up the Internet must support a variety of networking gateways.
- *Hardware and software independence,* by creating network protocols that would be interoperable with any CPU architecture, operating system, and networking card.
- *Reliability and robustness,* by creating network protocols that would be fault tolerant, so that regardless of the state of intermediary networks, data could be rerouted if necessary in order to reach its destination. Because the Internet started as a defense research project, robustness in the event of catastrophic network failure was extremely important. Damaged networks can be circumvented so that the Internet at large remains accessible.

---

[1] Request for Comment (RFC) specifications, described in more detail in Chapter 8, Section 8.2.

- *"Good" protocols that are efficient and simple,* by creating network protocols that exhibited quality design principles, such as the concepts of communication sockets, network ports, and so on. Though such a design goal seems intuitive now, designers had to make a conscious effort to develop TCP/IP for long-term and high-volume use, and to make it as simple as possible to use.

The ease of interconnection between computers and networks connected to the Internet has been brought about by common protocols that are independent of specific hardware and software architectures, are robust and fault tolerant, and are efficient and simple to learn. As a result, we have the TCP/IP protocol suite. Each of the major protocols involved are detailed below.

### 1.5.1.1 Internet Protocol (IP)

The Internet Protocol (IP) is a Layer 3 protocol (network layer) that is used to transmit data packets over the Internet. It is undoubtedly the most widely used networking protocol in the world, and has spread prolifically. Regardless of what type of networking hardware is used, it will almost certainly support IP networking. IP acts as a bridge between networks of different types, forming a worldwide network of computers and smaller subnetworks (see Figure 1-3). Indeed, many organizations use the IP and related protocols within their local area networks, as it can be applied equally well internally as externally.

The Internet Protocol is a packet-switching network protocol. Information is exchanged between two hosts in the form of IP packets, also known as IP datagrams. Each datagram is treated as a discrete unit, unrelated to any other previously sent packet—there are no "connections" between machines at the network layer. Instead, a series of datagrams are sent and higher-level protocols at the transport layer provide connection services.

### IP Datagram Format

The IP datagram carries with it essential information for controlling how it will be delivered. This information is stored inside the datagram header, which is followed by the actual data being sent. The various header fields, and their sizes, are shown in Figure 1-4.

**NOTE:** Full coverage of the design and implementation details of the Internet Protocol would require extremely complex theory, well beyond the scope of this book. For those readers interested in learning more, full details of the Internet Protocol version 4 are available in RFC 791. Chapter 8 outlines how to retrieve RFCs.

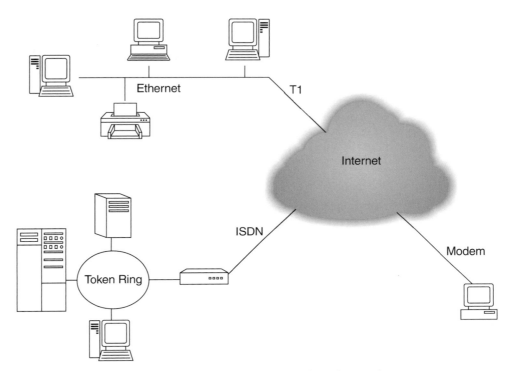

**Figure 1-3** Support for IP networking among various physical networks

A thorough knowledge of each individual IP datagram header field is not required for everyday programming. Nonetheless, a rough understanding of how IP datagrams work will assist readers in understanding how Internet communication takes place; therefore a brief description of these header fields is offered.

The *version* field describes which version of the Internet Protocol is being used. Currently, Internet Protocol version 4 (referred to as IPv4) is in common use, but the next generation of the Internet Protocol is already in testing. Future versions of the Internet Protocol will feature additional security, and include an expanded IP address space (greater than the current 32-bit address range) to allow more devices to have their own addresses.

The *header length* field specifies the length of the header, in multiples of 32 bits. When no datagram options are specified, the minimum value for this will be 5 (leaving a minimum header length of 160 bits). However, when additional options are used, this value can be greater.

The *type of service* field requests that a specific level of service be offered to the datagram. Some applications may require quick responses to reduce network delays, greater reliability, or higher throughput.

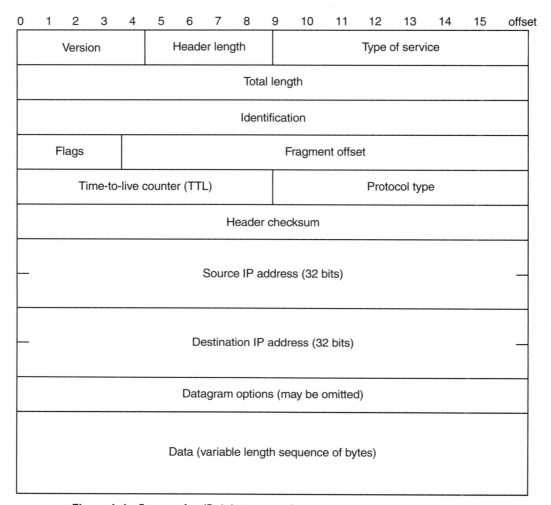

**Figure 1-4**   Format of an IPv4 datagram packet

The *total length* field states the total length of the datagram (including both header and data). A maximum value of 65,536 bytes is usually imposed, but many networks may only support smaller sizes. All networks are guaranteed to support a minimum of 576 bytes.

The *identification* field allows datagrams that are part of a sequence to be uniquely identified. This field can be thought of as a sequence number, allowing ordering of datagrams that arrive out of sequence.

Sometimes when packets are sent between network gateways, one gateway will support only smaller packets. The *flags* field controls whether these datagrams may be fragmented (sent as smaller pieces and later reassembled). Fields marked "do not fragment" are discarded and are undeliverable.

As datagrams are routed across the Internet, congestion throughout the network or faults in intermediate gateways may cause a datagram to be routed through long and winding paths. So that datagrams don't get caught in infinite loops and congest the network even further, the *time-to-live counter* (TTL) field is included. The value of this field is decremented every time it is routed by a gateway, and when it reaches zero the datagram is discarded. It can be thought of as a self-destruct mechanism to prevent network overload.

The *protocol type* field identifies the transport level protocol that is using a datagram for information transmission. Higher-level transport protocols rely on IP for sending messages across a network. Each transport protocol has a unique protocol number, defined in RFC 790. For example, if TCP is used, the protocol field will have a value of 6.

To safeguard against incorrect transmission of a datagram, a *header checksum* is used to detect whether data has been scrambled. If any of the bits within the header have been modified in transit, the checksum is designed to detect this, and the datagram is discarded. Not only can datagrams become lost if their TTL reaches zero, they can also fail to reach their destination if an error occurs in transmission.

The next two fields contain addressing information. The *source IP address* field and *destination IP address* fields are stored as two separate 32-bit values. Note that there is no authentication mechanism to prove that a datagram originated from the specified source address. Though not common, it is possible to use the technique of "IP spoofing" to make it appear that a datagram originated from a specific address, such as a trusted host.

The final field within the datagram header is an optional field that is not always present. The *datagram options* field is of variable length, and contains flags to control security settings, routing information, and time stamping of individual datagrams. The length of the options field must be a multiple of 32— if not, extra bits are added as padding.

## IP Address

The addressing of IP datagrams is an important issue, as applications require a way to deliver packets to specific machines and to identify the sender. Each host machine under the Internet Protocol has a unique address, the IP address.

The IP address is a four-byte (32-bit) address, which is usually expressed in dotted decimal format (e.g., 192.168.0.6). Although a physical address will normally be issued to a machine, once outside the local network in which it resides, the physical address is not very useful. Even if somehow every machine could be located by its physical address, if the address changed for any reason (such as installation of a new networking connection, or reassignment of the network interface by the administrator), then the machine would no longer be locatable.

Instead, a new type of address is introduced, that is not bound to a particular physical location. The details of this address format are described in more detail in Chapter 3, but for the moment, think of the IP address as a numerical number that uniquely identifies a machine on the Internet.

Typically, one machine has a single IP address, but it can have multiple addresses. A machine could, for example, have more than one network card, or could be assigned multiple IP addresses (known as virtual addresses) so that it can appear to the outside world as many different machines.

Machines connected to the Internet can send data to that IP address, and routers and gateways ensure delivery of the message. To map between a physical network address and an IP address, host machines and routers on a local network can use the Address Resolution Protocol (ARP) and Reverse Address Resolution Protocol (RARP). Such details, however, are more the domain of network administrators than of programmers. In normal programming, only the IP address is needed—the physical address is neither useful nor accessible in Java.

### Host Name

While numerical address values serve the purposes of computers, they are not designed with people in mind. Users who can remember thousands of 32-bit IP addresses in dotted decimal format and store them in their head are few and far between. A much simpler addressing mechanism is to associate an easy-to-remember textual name with an IP address. This text name is known as the hostname. For example, companies on the Internet usually choose a .com address, such as www.microsoft.com, or java.sun.com. The details of this addressing scheme are covered further in Chapter 3.

### 1.5.1.2 Internet Control Message Protocol (ICMP)

Though the IP might seem to be an ineffectual means of transmitting information, it is actually highly efficient (leaving the provision of an error-control mechanism to other protocols if they require it). Since the Internet Protocol provides absolutely no guarantee of datagram delivery, there is an obvious need for error-control mechanisms in many situations. One such mechanism is the Internet Control Message Protocol (ICMP), which is used in conjunction with the Internet Protocol to report errors when and if they occur.

The relationship between these two protocols is strong. When IP must notify another host of an error, it uses ICMP. ICMP, on the other hand, uses IP to send the error message. When minor errors occur, such as a corrupt header in a datagram, the datagram will be discarded without warning since the sender address in the header cannot be trusted. Therefore a host cannot rely solely upon ICMP to guarantee delivery—the services of ICMP are more informational, to prevent wasted bandwidth if errors are likely to be repeated. No guarantee is offered that ICMP messages will be sent, or that they will reach their intended destination.

The ICMP defines five error messages:

1. *Destination Unreachable.* As datagrams are passed from gateway to gateway, they will (it is hoped!) travel closer and closer to their final destination. If a fault in the network occurs, a gateway may be unable to pass the datagram on to its destination. In this case, the "destination unreachable" ICMP message is sent back to the original host.

2. *Parameter Problem.* When a gateway determines that there is a problem with any of the header parameters of an IP datagram and is unable to process them, the datagram is discarded and the sending host may be notified via a "parameter problem" ICMP message.

3. *Redirect.* When a shorter path, or alternate route, is available, a gateway may send a "redirect" ICMP message to the router that passed on a datagram.

4. *Source Quench.* When too many datagram packets hit a router, gateway, or host, it may become overloaded and be unable to accept more packets. This occurs when the buffer allocated for datagram storage becomes full, and datagrams can't be removed from the buffer as fast as they are coming in. Rather than allowing datagrams to be discarded, an attempt is made to reduce the number of incoming datagrams, by sending a "source quench" ICMP message.

5. *Time Exceeded.* Whenever the TTL value of a datagram reaches zero, it is discarded. When this occurs, a "time exceeded" ICMP message may be sent.

In addition to error messages, ICMP supports several informational messages. These are not generated in response to error conditions, and are instead used to pass control information. Additional ICMP messages include:

- *Echo Request/Echo Reply.* Used to determine whether a host is alive and can be reached. In response to an "echo request" ICMP message, the recipient sends back an "echo reply" ICMP message. Although no guarantee of message delivery is offered, repeated requests can be made if no response is received. If the host is unreachable, then the last gateway dealing with the message should send back a "destination unreachable" ICMP message. The "echo request" and "echo reply" messages are used by the "ping" application to test if a remote host is accessible.

- *Address Mask Request/Address Mask Reply.* Though not part of the original ICMP specification, functionality to determine the address mask (also known as a subnet mask) is added to the protocol in RFC 950. The address mask controls which bits of an IP address correspond to a host, and which bits determine the network/subnet portion. A host can send an "address mask request" ICMP message, and receive an "address mask reply" ICMP message.

While ICMP is a useful protocol to be aware of, only a few network applications will make use of it, as its functionality is limited to diagnostic and error notification. One of the most well known applications that use ICMP is the ping network application, used to determine if a host is active and what the delay is between sending a packet and receiving a response.

**NOTE:** Java does not support ICMP access, so ping applications are impossible to write in Java. Some Java textbooks include a UDP example called ping, but it is important to remember that this is not the real ping application. The only way to write a true ping application in Java would be to use the Java Native Interface (JNI) to access native code; such a discussion is beyond the scope of this book.

### 1.5.1.3 Transmission Control Protocol

The Transmission Control Protocol (TCP) is a Layer 4 protocol (transport layer) that provides guaranteed delivery and ordering of bytes. TCP uses the Internet Protocol to send TCP segments, which contain additional information that allows it to order packets and resend them if they go astray. TCP also adds an extra layer of abstraction, by using a communications port.

A communications port is a numerical value (usually in the range 0–65,535) that can be used to distinguish one application or service from another. An IP address can be thought of as the location of a block of apartments, and the port as the apartment number. One host machine can have many applications connected to one or more ports. An application could connect to a Web server running on a particular host, and also to an e-mail server to check for new mail. Ports make all of this possible.

The Transmission Control Protocol is discussed further in Chapter 6. TCP's main advantage is that it guarantees delivery and ordering of data, providing a simpler programming interface. However, this simplicity comes at a cost, reducing network performance. For faster communication, the User Datagram Protocol may be used.

### 1.5.1.4 User Datagram Protocol

The User Datagram Protocol (UDP) is a Layer 4 protocol (transport layer) that applications can use to send packets of data across the Internet (as opposed to TCP, which sends a sequence of bytes). Raw access to IP datagrams is not very useful, as there is no easy way to determine which application a packet is for. Like TCP, UDP supports a port number, so it can be used to send datagrams to specific applications and services. Unlike TCP, UDP does not guarantee delivery of packets, or that they will arrive in the correct order.

In fact, UDP differs very little from IP datagrams, save for the introduction of a port number. It may seem puzzling why anyone would want to use an unreliable packet delivery system. The additional error checking of TCP adds overhead and delays, so UDP might be seen to offer better performance. The pros and cons of UDP are discussed further in Chapter 5, but for now, it is sufficient to realize that error-free transmission comes at a cost, and UDP can be used as an alternative.

## 1.6 Internet Application Protocols

While network and transport layer protocols are certainly interesting, for network programmers the real excitement lies in the application layer. At the application layer are network protocols that do real work, rather than just facilitating communication. Here you'll find protocols for accessing and sending e-mail, transferring files, reading Web pages, and much more.

**NOTE:** Application protocols generally run on a specific port number (also referred to as a well-defined port). However, these services can be configured to run on a nonstandard port (for example, if two Web servers are operating on one machine).

Some of the more commonly used application protocols are examined below.

### 1.6.1 *Telnet*

Telnet is a service that allows users to open a remote-terminal session to a specific machine. This allows Unix users, for example, to access their account from terminal servers or desktop machines. Since Unix servers are intended to support multiple users, a telnet session is often used, as only one person can access the machine from the local terminal (using a keyboard and monitor). Telnet allows many users to connect over the network and to access their accounts as if they were doing so locally. Telnet services use TCP port 23.

### 1.6.2   File Transfer Protocol (FTP)

The ability to transfer files is extremely important. Even before the World Wide Web, people distributed images, documents, and software using the File Transfer Protocol (FTP). FTP allows a user to log in (using a special username and password), or to attempt an anonymous log-in (by using the username of "anonymous"). FTP servers will often grant different access permissions depending on the user. For example, an anonymous account might be unable to write a file to the server, but may be able to read all files. FTP uses two TCP ports for communication—port 21 is used to control sessions and port 20 is used for the actual transfer of file contents.

### 1.6.3   Post Office Protocol Version 3 (POP3)

E-mail has become a vital part of modern life. With the exception of Web-based e-mail or specialized accounts, the majority of people access their e-mail using the Post Office Protocol, version 3 (POP3), which uses TCP port 110. Messages are stored on a server, retrieved by an e-mail client, and then deleted from the server. This allows users to read mail offline, without being connected to the Internet.

### 1.6.4   Internet Message Access Protocol (IMAP)

While many browsers and e-mail clients support only POP3, some also support the Internet Message Access Protocol (IMAP). This protocol is less popular, as it requires a continual connection to the mail server, and thus increases bandwidth consumption and disk usage since messages are not stored on the user's system. IMAP allows users to create folders on the mail server, and also allows online searching of mail. IMAP uses TCP port 143.

### 1.6.5   Simple Mail Transfer Protocol (SMTP)

The Simple Mail Transfer Protocol allows messages to be delivered over the Internet. The separation between retrieving mail and sending mail might be perceived as a bit strange. However, separation actually simplifies the process considerably, allowing different mail-retrieval protocols to be used and enabling custom mail accounts. SMTP uses TCP port 25.

### 1.6.6   HyperText Transfer Protocol (HTTP)

HTTP is one of the most popular protocols in use on the Internet today; it made the World Wide Web possible. HTTP is an extremely important protocol, and

Java includes good HTTP support. Detailed information about HTTP and accessing Web resources from Java will be given in Chapter 9. HTTP uses TCP port 80.

### 1.6.7 Finger

Finger is a handy protocol that allows someone to look up a person's account and find out certain information, such as when they last logged in and checked their mail. Typically, only Unix servers support finger. Unfortunately, many administrators disable finger access for security reasons, and so it is no longer as prevalent as it was. Finger uses TCP port 79.

### 1.6.8 Network News Transport Protocol (NNTP)

The Network News Transport Protocol allows users to access Usenet newsgroups. Usenet is a collection of discussion forums on a colorful and diverse number of topics, ranging from political and social commentary, to fan discussions about television programs, movies, and actors, to computing and business. Online services such as DejaNews (http://www.dejanews.com/usenet/) provide a Web-based interface, but newsgroups can also be accessed via newsreader software that uses NNTP. NNTP uses TCP port 119.

### 1.6.9 WHOIS

The WHOIS protocol allows users to look up information about a domain name (such as awl.com, or microsoft.com). You can find some surprisingly useful information by doing this, such as the address of a company, who registered the domain name, and contact details for the registration. WHOIS uses TCP port 43.

## 1.7 TCP/IP Protocol Suite Layers

Earlier in the chapter, the seven OSI network layers were discussed. However, not all of these layers are used in Internet programming. The TCP/IP suite of protocols can be mapped to a subset of the OSI layers, as shown in Figure 1-5.

Each layer is stacked upon another layer, using encapsulation. Data passes from the top application layer, down to the transport layer, and then flows on to the network layer. At this stage, the data is sent across the Internet, and will reach a local area network or dial-up connection. Below the network layer, the data will flow to the data link layer and finally to the physical layer. Starting from the higher-level layers, protocol requests are encapsulated into the container of the previous layer.

To illustrate this process (see Figure 1-6), consider the example of a POP3 command to retrieve the first message in a mailbox. POP3 uses TCP as its

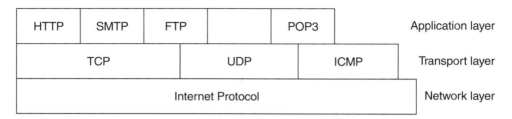

**Figure 1-5**   TCP/IP stack divided by layers

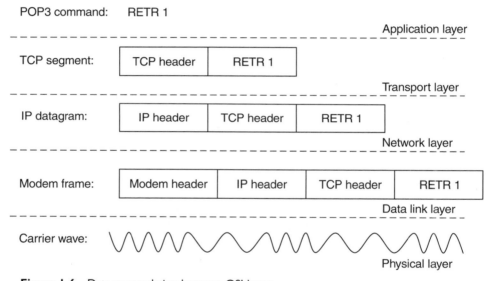

**Figure 1-6**   Data encapsulation between OSI layers

transport mechanism, and the command is encapsulated within a TCP segment. IP datagrams are used to transmit these segments across the Internet, and to send these datagrams a user might rely on a dial-up modem connection. The modem can send data across the phone line using sound waves (if you've ever listened to a fax machine, you'll know what these sound like). At each layer, the request is encapsulated—but we as application programmers do not normally write a direct modem interface. That's the domain of operating system and device driver developers, who work with low-level assembly language and operating system calls. Instead, programmers use standard Internet services, and let the operating system and device drivers handle such complexities. This is one of the perks of being a network programmer.

## 1.8　Security Issues: Firewalls and Proxy Servers

Network security is an important topic, both for network administrators charged with protecting the computer systems of companies and organizations and for developers producing network software. Even if that software is fairly innocuous and not worth fitting out with sophisticated security mechanisms such as passwords and encryption, it is still important to take security issues into consideration, for the simple reason that network security restrictions on some local area networks may prevent software from working.

In an ideal world, we could implicitly trust incoming data from machines connected to the Internet, as well as the actions of colleagues sending outgoing data from within a local area network. Indeed, in many ways the Internet is an open and trusting collection of hosts, allowing public access to information and services. However, companies holding sensitive commercial information need to protect the integrity of their data to prevent access or modification by unauthorized individuals. The solution adopted by most organizations is to draw a line in the sand, across which no machine outside of the private network can cross without authorization. This barrier is called a firewall.

### 1.8.1　*Firewalls*

The firewall is a special machine that has been configured specifically to prohibit harmful (or as is sometimes the case in the business world, distracting) incoming or outgoing data. Usually, but not always, the firewall system will be a stripped-down computer, with all nonessential services removed to minimize the potential for cracking/hacking. The firewall is the first line of defense against intrusions from outside, and so any software that might assist in compromising the firewall should be removed, and all security patches for the operating system installed. There are many commercial firewall packages available, and some are even designed for use on desktop machines by individuals. Firewalls are most commonly separate machines except when used in companies and organizations where more than one or two individual machines are connected by, for example, a dial-up connection.

The firewall works by intercepting incoming communication from machines on the Internet, and outgoing communication from machines within a local area network, as shown in Figure 1-7. It operates at the packet level, intercepting IP datagrams that reach it. By examining the header fields of these datagrams, the firewall can tell where the datagram is heading and from where it was sent. An outgoing datagram, for example, would have a source address from a machine within the firewall and a destination address from outside the firewall, whereas an incoming datagram would have a destination address of

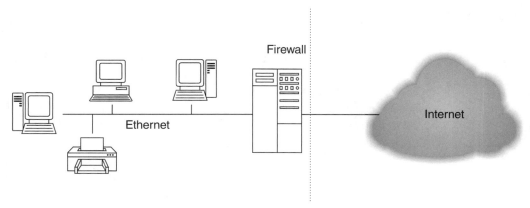

**Figure 1-7**    The firewall draws a line in the sand, insulating internal computers from the Internet.

an internal machine and a source address external to the firewall. Firewalls can also help prevent a hacking technique known as masquerading, whereby an external host fakes the IP address of an internal machine to appear to be a legitimate machine, thus gaining access to resources. While there are legitimate uses for the masquerading of IP addresses (such as within an intranet), incoming datagrams from the Internet that use masquerading are suspect, and a firewall can make the distinction to filter them out.

Firewalls offer administrators very powerful security and fine-grained control of the network. Various permissions can be assigned to firewall filters. For example, outgoing data may be given greater access than incoming, and perhaps only certain machines within the network will be allowed Internet access, or only at certain times. Certain protocols, for example, might be allowed through (blocking UDP packets to certain machines and not others, or TCP access to certain port ranges). Many network administrators configure their firewalls to block all access by default, and then allow only limited network access through a proxy server.

### 1.8.2  Proxy Servers

A proxy server is a machine that acts as a proxy for application protocols. The server accepts incoming connections from machines within a local network, and makes requests on their behalf to machines connected to the Internet. This has two advantages: direct access to internal machines is never established, and the proxy server can control the transaction. This means that popular protocols such as HTTP may be permitted or perhaps limited to certain Web sites. However, newer protocols such as RealAudio, or custom applications including games and application software, are not always permitted. Most proxy servers also log networking events, to allow network administrators to track unusual communications and their origin—in this way, employees visiting inappropriate sites or goofing off during work can be easily monitored. This might sound worrisome, and introduce some very serious legal and privacy issues, but there are legitimate security concerns addressed by logging, such as identifying disloyal employees who are visiting job-search sites or sending information to competitors.

### 1.8.3  Firewalls for Developers

While the firewall is an excellent tool for network administrators, it is frequently the developer's worst enemy. Most corporate firewalls, for example, block direct UDP and TCP access, making these protocols (and any applications that use them for communication) unusable. There is always a tradeoff between functionality and security—developers who have users behind firewalls become keenly aware of just what that tradeoff costs. This means that developers must make a choice—either use standard Internet protocols and ignore users who work within a firewall, or adapt software to proxy requests using protocols such as HTTP (piggybacking the request to a Web server, which performs the operation). Neither choice is preferable, as one eliminates a portion of the potential user base and the other involves considerably more work for the developer, and significantly greater overhead in data transmission. Java does support HTTP proxy servers, which means that users within a firewall will normally be able to communicate using that protocol. Where possible, however, direct use of UDP or TCP is a much better choice for communication, as they both offer a simpler interface and better performance. Interposing a proxy server and HTTP between direct network communications can add delays that are several orders of magnitude greater.

**NOTE:** To manually specify a proxy server for Java to use for HTTP communication, a value can be assigned to the proxyHost and proxyPort system properties. System properties are Java-specific, and are covered in more detail in Chapter 2.

## 1.9    Summary

An understanding of the basics of networking theory is essential for network programmers, as this theory provides the foundation on which the practical side of networking is based. To assist in this regard, networking communication is broken into seven layers (forming the Open Systems Interconnection, or OSI, Reference Model).

At the most basic level, communication deals with individual bits of information. There are a wide variety of network mediums, ranging from dial-up modems to local area networks. At the physical and data link layers, various hardware types and network protocols can be used, making networks interoperable. We as Java programmers do not need to concern ourselves with such issues, however, and in fact are unable to access such low-level network devices. TCP/IP communication uses a subset of the OSI model, dealing only with the network, transport, and application layers. It is these layers, more than any others, that Java programmers must be familiar with.

As one moves higher and higher up the OSI levels, hardware issues are put aside and more and more levels of abstraction are introduced. First there is the network layer, which deals with the dispatch of packets over a network and the issue of addresses. The Internet Protocol (IP) is used for this purpose, and machines are identified by an IP address. At the transport layer, protocols offer different characteristics, such as high-speed transmission or guaranteed delivery. The same machine can provide many services, and a client can access many services concurrently. For this reason, an address is not sufficient, and the concept of a port is added. The two main transport protocols in use are TCP and UDP, both of which Java supports. In addition, ICMP is used by IP to handle network errors—Java, however, does not support ICMP access.

Finally, at the application layer, networking software uses application protocols to communicate with remote software services. The range of application protocols is vast, and new protocols are continuously being designed. Some, such as HTTP and e-mail, are destined to become extremely popular, while others are custom protocols used by a very small community. Much network programming involves the implementation of these network protocols, although fortunately Java provides classes that implement HTTP for Web access for convenience.

Network programmers should also be aware of security issues. The term security covers a wide spectrum, but in this context we mean network security, and most importantly the firewall. Network administrators normally protect critical systems by using a firewall; the firewall is a benevolent dictator that protects systems but restricts network access to users and hence to software applications.

**Chapter Highlights**

In this chapter, you have learned:

- What a network is
- How networks transmit information using packets and addresses
- The layers of the OSI Reference Model
- The major protocols of the Internet, including the Internet Protocol (IP), Internet Control Message Protocol (ICMP), Transmission Control Protocol (TCP), and User Datagram Protocol (UDP)
- The effect of firewalls and proxy servers on users and developers

# CHAPTER 2

## *Java Overview*

This chapter provides an introduction to the Java programming language and the Java platform. The information presented here is expected to benefit both novice and experienced Java practitioners; Java programmers with experience writing applets may be unaware of the range of Java programming environments available, including stand-alone applications, JavaBean software components, and Java servlets. Readers will also learn some of the finer points of the Java language, including exception handling, and be given an overview of the various networking Application Program Interfaces (APIs) of Java.

## 2.1   What Is Java?

The name *Java* is applied to a variety of technologies created by Sun Microsystems. While the reader will instantly associate Java with a programming language (which it most certainly is), in actuality Java is also much more. There are three main components of Java:

- *The Java programming language*—a programming language used to write software for the Java platform
- *The Java platform*—a range of runtime environments that support execution of software written in Java
- *The Java API*—a rich, fully featured class library that provides graphical user interface, data storage, data processing, I/O, and networking support

Each of these parts is equally important, and is discussed individually below.

## 2.2   The Java Programming Language

The Java programming language has an interesting history, and draws heavily from earlier object-oriented languages such as C++ and Smalltalk. While the success of Java has been phenomenal, it is important to remember that as of 2002, Java was still the "new kid on the block."

### 2.2.1   History and Origins of Java

Java had very humble beginnings. In the early 1990s a team at Sun Microsystems began work on a language for the embedded systems market. This language would be used to develop the software that would power consumer electronics products such as handheld PDA units. The language, when completed, was called Oak, named after the type of tree outside the project leader's window.

James Gosling, affectionately known as the father of the Java language, originally modified a C++ compiler, but rather than adapt C++, a new language was created. As many C++ developers will attest, the language is powerful, but includes many features that, when used improperly, can have unpleasant side effects, such as memory leaks and runtime errors including cross pointers. Instead, a language that carried many of the benefits of C++ and other object-oriented languages, but few of the disadvantages, was born.

But what does a language called Oak have to do with the language we know today as Java? After a change in focus from consumer electronics to online services, the Oak team incorporated their programming language into a Web browser. The name of the language was changed, and soon after, the first Web browser capable of running Java software was produced. This browser was named HotJava, and when released in March 1995 it changed the way people looked at the Web. Instead of static pages, or dynamically generated pages created at the server end, the Web now had active documents that executed Java applets. Both Netscape and Microsoft licensed this technology for use in their respective Web browsers, and the language became a runaway success.

**NOTE:** Further information about the history of Java can be found in the article at http://java.sun.com/features/1998/05/birthday.html.

### 2.2.2   Properties of the Java Language

Java is a unique language. While many of its properties are present in other languages, the sheer popularity and rapid adoption of Java by programmers indicate that Sun Microsystems found the right mix of functionality and sophistication. Many of the so-called features of C++, such as multiple inheritance, dramatically increased the complexity of the software. While Java has its origins in C++, many of the hang-ups of C++ and of the original C language have been removed, such as multiple inheritance, pointers, and direct memory access. In addition, Java was designed from the ground up to support the World Wide Web and the Internet, making it an attractive choice for network programming.

Some of the most important properties of Java are its

- Object orientation
- Simplicity
- Automatic garbage collection
- Portability
- Multi-threaded programming
- Security
- Internet awareness

### 2.2.2.1 Object Orientation

Older languages such as C, Pascal, and Basic are procedural languages. While it is certainly possible to produce software using procedural languages, such languages do not offer the most efficient way to do so, nor are they robust. Rather than thinking of software in terms of procedures and data structures, in an object-oriented language we think in terms of classes and objects. Classes have member variables, which store data and methods that act on that data. In an object-oriented language, procedures are replaced with methods, leading to more cohesive software. This can be thought of as combining a data structure with procedures that act upon the data structure.

Java is an object-oriented language. There are many other object-oriented languages, including C++, Visual Basic, Delphi, and Smalltalk. Object-oriented languages offer many advantages for programmers. Most programmers find objects simpler to work with than procedures, and find that writing code in an object-oriented language is more productive. By applying good object-oriented design principles, it becomes easier to integrate different parts of a software project, and object orientation makes large projects more manageable, by dividing large modules of code into small classes. Other features such as class inheritance and visibility modifiers (the public, private, and protected keywords of Java) make object-oriented languages much easier and safer to work with than older procedural languages.

Procedural languages can be used to develop networking software, and indeed C remains a popular choice today for Unix networking software. However, network programming in any language is not a walk in the park. When designing large and complex systems such as network servers, any technique that can minimize the complexity of software development is important, and in this respect an object-oriented language such as Java is exceedingly preferable to procedural languages.

### 2.2.2.2 Simplicity

Object-oriented languages may make software development easier, but object orientation alone is not the answer. Indeed, some object-oriented languages such as C++ are renowned for their complexity. This is not to disparage C++, of course, but features such as direct memory access through pointers (a throwback from C), and the need for programmers to explicitly allocate and deallocate memory regions for the storage of objects and data structures, as well as multiple inheritance, make it a complex language.

Although Java shares a common heritage with C++, it is a far simpler language to learn. In Java, there are no pointers through which memory can be accessed. Only through object references can a programmer access another object. Also, multiple inheritance is not allowed by Java. While classes can inherit from one class, they cannot inherit from a second. This keeps coding simpler, which is important for any type of application but particularly so in the case of networking. Of course, simplicity is a relative thing—Java is far simpler than many other object-oriented languages, but many first-time programmers still find it a steep learning curve due to the power of the language.

### 2.2.2.3 Automatic Garbage Collection

In languages such as C and C++, programmers must explicitly request that a memory region be set aside for data structures and classes. In most software, variables are used for short-term storage, and memory is allocated and deallocated frequently. This amounts to more work for developers, as memory must be set aside and then reclaimed when it is no longer needed. If this is not done, the application will consume more memory than is needed, affecting system performance. If memory is not reclaimed and the application terminates, it may become permanently reserved, leading to a memory leak.

Java, however, takes a different approach. When a new instance of an object is declared, the Java Virtual Machine (JVM) allocates the appropriate amount of memory for it automatically. When the object is no longer needed, a null value can be assigned to the object reference, and the automatic garbage collection thread will silently reclaim the memory for later use, without the programmer having to worry about how or when this occurs (such as when the application is idle and waiting for input). If a reference to an object is not maintained, and not explicitly assigned a null value, the garbage collector will still reclaim the memory (for example, if a temporary object is created by a method, and the method terminates). This has two big advantages: (1) less work for programmers and (2) elimination of memory leaks.

Since networking servers will service many different clients over the course of their lifetime, memory is frequently allocated and deallocated. Even a network client benefits from automatic garbage collection—any nontrivial network protocol will require a client to set aside memory for data storage and processing. By preventing memory leaks, such software will offer better performance during the course of its execution.

### 2.2.2.4 Portability

Java's main claim to fame is that it is operating system and hardware neutral—Java software is capable of running on a wide variety of platforms without the need for recompilation of software by programmers, or modification of source code. For programmers used to writing software for a single platform, this might not seem very efficient. For commercial software developers, however, portability amounts to big cost and time savings, as software can be written for a single environment: the Java platform. Software written for Java can then be executed on any CPU type and operating system that supports Java, without the need to modify and convert source code (a process known as porting). Whether a programmer is writing for one operating system or a hundred, the amount of work required is the same. For networking applications, this is an attractive feature. Though C++ networking software can be written for both Unix and Wintel systems, networking system calls are vastly different (even between Unix variants). Java provides a standard interface to sockets that is operating system neutral.

Of course, this portability comes at a cost. Java source code is compiled into bytecode, which is executed by the JVM. This means that Java code does not run as fast as native code compiled to machine language instructions. While some attempts have been made to increase the performance of Java software, such as just-in-time (JIT) compilers that convert Java bytecode to native code, developers and users will find that performance is not as fast as comparable C++ code, and that a greater amount of memory is consumed.

There are also, of course, operating-system-specific differences between Java applications. A Macintosh applet or application will have a different GUI than that of a Windows or Unix system. Glitches in initial releases caused problems when running software on different platforms due to defects in early JVM implementations, but for the most part, the promise of Java portability remains strong.

### 2.2.2.5 Multi-threaded Programming

Programmers working in languages such as C or PERL may have come across the concept of multiple processes. In operating systems such as Unix, processes are used quite heavily by software. A process can split itself into many parts, which execute concurrently, by using the fork() command. Of course, this involves extra overhead, as the memory for application code and variables is duplicated among each process.

A much better alternative is multi-threaded programming. A multi-threaded language supports concurrent processing, but with shared memory for application code and data. This allows threads to conserve memory and interact with each other to work collaboratively if required. The importance of a multi-threaded language for network programming cannot be overstated. Though it is possible to write trivial client and server applications without using multiple threads of execution, even a moderately complex server will typically use the technique of multi-threading. Having this support within Java is useful, and makes it an attractive choice for almost any type of programming. Other languages, too, have multi-threaded support (often in the form of an add-on API or operating system calls), but Java has been designed from the ground up to support such programming, and provides language keywords to simplify writing thread-safe code.

### 2.2.2.6 Security

In a networked world, security is an extremely important issue for software developers. After all, systems connected to a public network are far more vulnerable to attack than a system connected to a closed private network. When systems contain sensitive data, they are prime targets for attacks, but even systems with little or no useful data can be compromised and used to hijack other systems. Because of such risks, developers must take the issue of security very seriously.

Of course, while many developers write their own security mechanisms, it is often useful if a language enforces some form of security of its own. This can save developers both time and effort, and it is reassuring to know that users will have an equitable level of security installed by default. Java is often billed as a "secure" language, and while it is impossible for a language to guarantee absolute security (much of this must be the responsibility of individual programmers, and the implementers of the JVM), the Java security model makes it an attractive choice for network developers.

In an ideal world, Java code could be implicitly trusted to execute without causing damage or a security breach. In the real world, Java uses the "sandbox" approach, wherein untrusted code, which includes classes downloaded

over a network within a Web browser, is placed within the sandbox and required to meet certain expectations. In addition, the new Java 2 security model
makes it possible to sandbox other classes, whether downloaded over the network or loaded locally (such as in an application). Using default settings, however, only applet code is placed in the sandbox.

When a Java class is placed in the sandbox, it must "play fairly," and it
finds its actions severely restricted. Prior to the Java 2 security model, digitally
signed classes, or classes loaded from the user's hard drive, such as a stand-
alone application, did not need to be placed in the sandbox and had free reign
over the JVM. With the introduction of the Java 2 security model, however, it
is possible to change almost any aspect of the security settings, giving greater
or lesser privileges to classes running inside and outside of the browser.

During a browser session, applets are faced with several significant
limitations.

- Network access is restricted to a single machine, namely the machine
  from which the applet was loaded.
- Applets cannot bind to local ports, to masquerade as a legitimate
  service.
- No file access is permitted, either reading or writing.
- While threads may be used freely, no external processes may be started
  (such as launching external programs like format.exe).

The browser security manager imposes these restrictions. A custom security
manager can impose additional restrictions, or relax some of them if need be.
However, once assigned a security manager, the JVM will not permit a second
manager to be appointed. Thus it is not possible to override browser security
restrictions, but in a custom network application, developers can customize
their security settings. Additionally, the Java 2 platform supports security policies that give finer-grained control over security settings. An example is given
in Chapter 11, in which a security policy is defined that restricts file access
to prevent code downloaded over a network from accessing or modifying the
hard drive.

### 2.2.2.7 Internet Awareness

Obviously, there are many advantages to network programming of a language
being Internet aware. While other languages such as C and C++ can be used to
write Internet applications, they rely on special libraries that must be imported,
and change from operating system to operating system. The Java language
provides a rich, fully featured networking API that offers a consistent interface
for Java developers no matter what platform they are running. The networking

API is also well designed, and is certainly easier to pick up than those of other languages. The combination that Java offers of networking classes and input/output streams makes it easy to use and efficient to program in.

In particular, Java offers classes for the following network resources:

- IP addresses
- User Datagram Protocol packets
- Transmission Control Protocol streams
- HyperText Transfer Protocol requests
- Multicasting of data packets

However, Java's networking support is not limited to the above. Java software can be written to execute within a Web browser (the applet), as well as within a Web server (the servlet). Java also supports higher-level network communication, in the form of two distributed systems technologies:

- Remote method invocation (RMI)
- Common Object Request Broker Architecture (CORBA)

Each of these technologies allows methods of an object to be invoked from a remote application executing in a separate JVM. Both are covered in more detail in later chapters.

## 2.3    The Java Platform

Certainly the language is an important part of Java technology, but the story doesn't end there. As a third-generation language, the source code instructions written in Java must be compiled to a form that the computer is capable of understanding. Most languages would be compiled to native machine code, capable of running on a specific CPU architecture. The problem with that approach, however, is that code must be compiled for all the likely CPU architectures that the user may want (resulting in many software builds, as well as issues of distribution for developers), or for a single architecture that the user must adapt to the software—neither are optimum solutions.

 **NOTE:** For those unfamiliar with the term *third-generation language,* this refers to a language that must be converted to a machine-readable format before it can be executed. A second-generation language is written in assembly language, which is a very low-level form of programming that is best suited to those who are "at one with the computer," and not ordinary programmers. A first-generation language is raw machine code, capable of being read and executed only by the CPU.

The Java platform takes a different approach. Instead of creating machine code for particular pieces of hardware, Java source code is compiled to execute on a single CPU architecture. Now this may seem, at first, counterproductive for achieving portability. In fact, it sounds no different to the approach a C++ or Visual Basic compiler might take. There is, however, a big difference: in most cases there isn't an actual hardware chip that runs the Java machine code. Java machine code, referred to as Java bytecode, is executed by a special piece of software that mimics a CPU chip capable of understanding bytecode. We call this piece of software the Java Virtual Machine, or JVM. Only a few types of CPUs capable of executing bytecode natively exist at present (though this will change within the near future as the demand for high-performance Java devices increases), and they are typically used in embedded systems in which the overhead of translation is prohibitive.

### 2.3.1 The Java Virtual Machine

The JVM is an emulation of a hardware device. The concept of emulation isn't new—emulation is often used to re-create older CPU systems such as long-dead gaming consoles or mainframe systems. This provides access to software that, while aged, is still very useful. While there are a growing number of chips capable of running Java bytecode, they remain specialized systems not yet found on a PC motherboard. The vision of Java is to "Write Once, Run Anywhere," or WORA. The average computer must be capable of running Java code without new chips, so a "virtual" machine is emulated. For any CPU architecture, and any operating system that needs to run Java, a JVM is written. This allows Java software to run on Unix as well as Windows systems. Portable devices such as palmtop computers and some mobile phones can also run Java software, and there are even plans to run Java on set-top boxes for television.

Of course, this flexibility is not without cost. Software emulation of a hardware device suffers from a moderately serious drawback—performance. Java software runs far slower than comparable code written in a language that supports native compilation. While many techniques can be applied to speed up performance, such as just-in-time (JIT) compilation (which converts Java code to native code when it is first loaded), Java is still not as fast as its C++ cousin. With continuing advances in CPU performance, the speed of Java becomes less and less of an issue.

### 2.3.2 Java Runtime Environments

While the JVM is capable of running Java bytecode, it is not a software application that can itself be run. Usually, the JVM is hosted within a Java runtime environment (JRE). The JRE will also include the core classes from the Java API (see Section 2.4), and other supporting files. There are many types of JREs, from many vendors. Some of the most important categories today are:

- *Java 2 Platform, Standard Edition (J2SE)*—used to run Java software as stand-alone applications, either in a user console or as a windowed application with a GUI interface.
- *Java 2 Platform, Enterprise Edition (J2EE)*—used to run Java software within large enterprises, using a diverse suite of Java technologies for distributed systems, transaction management, and electronic commerce.
- *Java 2 Platform, Micro Edition (J2ME)*—fulfilling the original Java goal of consumer electronics, such as phones, palmtop computers, and set-top television boxes. This is a cut-down version of the Java 2 plat-form, with the emphasis on a lightweight implementation suitable for use on low-memory systems.
- *Browser runtime environments*—allowing Java code to execute within the browser, to serve up interactive content that is downloaded from a Web site. This form of Java software is called an applet. Applets can be used to write user interfaces, games, and even entire software appli-cations, but are subject to necessary security restrictions to prevent "harmful" applets from compromising security.
- *Web-server runtime environments*—allowing Java code to run within a Web server, to dynamically generate Web pages and con-tent. In the early days of the Web, pages were static and unchanging—they required manual intervention by a Web master to change their content. The arrival of dynamically generated Web pages changed com-pletely what could be done with a Web site, through Common Gate-way Interface (CGI) scripts written in languages like PERL. Java, of course, has not been left behind. Server-side Java can generate cus-tomized pages, based on user interaction, and access other content such as databases or networking resources. This type of Java software is called servlets. Servlets are much faster than applets, as they don't need to be downloaded to the user's browser; only their output is downloaded. Of course, servlets must send data as HTML, or as a custom file-type, so the user can't interact with them in the same way as an applet. A second type of Java application for the Web server is Java Server Pages (JSP), a script-like version of Java that is compiled into a servlet.

Many third-party vendors, including IBM and Microsoft, provide runtime environments. It is important to note that some vendors provide support only for early Java versions, such as JDK1.1 or JDK1.02, and some support only a subset of the Java API. For example, by default, the implementation for the Java remote method invocation packages (which allow objects hosted by a remote JVM to be used as if they were local) is missing from the Microsoft JVM. An additional download is required for the Microsoft JVM to support RMI. The latest runtime environment from Sun Microsystems is guaranteed to support the full API, but that is not to say that third-party runtime environments do not have their place. Many offer better performance, or are the only runtime environment available for a particular operating system or CPU architecture.

## 2.4    The Java Application Program Interface

If a programming language is viewed as the mind of software, and the JVM as the heart that keeps that software beating, then the Application Program Interface (API) must surely be Java's arms and legs. The API provides a rich suite of classes and components that allow Java to do real work, such as:

- Reading from and writing to files on the local hard drive
- Creating graphical user interfaces with menus, buttons, text fields, and drop-down lists
- Drawing pictures from graphical primitives such as lines, circles, squares, and ellipses
- Accessing network resources, such as Web sites or network servers
- Storing data in data structures such as linked lists and arrays
- Manipulating and processing data such as text and numbers
- Retrieving information from databases or modifying records

Of course, the above list constitutes only a sampling of the power of Java. The API consists of a set of packages that are collections of commonly related classes offering specific features. While the Java packages are extremely interesting, and readers who have not previously done so are urged to investigate the API documentation that Sun provides to see what functionality is offered, the coverage of this book is limited to network programming. Of most interest to readers will be the various networking packages that allow Java developers to create network applications and services.

**NOTE:** An online version of Sun's API documentation can be found at Sun's Web site at http://java.sun.com/docs/. Readers are advised, however, to download a copy of the documentation and view it locally, as this will mean reduced Internet access charges and faster access to documentation.

The following is a list of the major networking packages that form the Java API.

- *Package java.net*—comprises the majority of classes that deal with Internet programming. This package provides the basic building blocks needed to write network applications and services, such as UDP packets, TCP sockets, IP addresses, URLs, and HTTP connections.
- *Package java.rmi.*\*—a set of packages that support remote method invocation (RMI), allowing objects hosted by a remote JVM to be used as if they were local objects.
- *Package org.omg.*\*—a set of packages that support the Common Object Request Broker Architecture (CORBA), allowing objects hosted by a remote JVM, or written in a language like C++ or Ada that provides a CORBA mapping, to be used as if they were local objects. CORBA has the added advantage over RMI of not being limited to objects written in Java.

In addition, several other packages are available to developers in the form of a Java extension. Java extensions are add-ons that don't ship with the core Java API but may be installed separately by users, developers, and administrators. Examples of popular networking extensions for Java include:

- *JavaMail*—an extension that provides access to e-mail services, allowing Java software to send and receive electronic mail.
- *Java Servlets*—an extension that allows Java software to produce dynamic content for a Web site, by executing within a Web server.

Each of these packages and extensions are covered in later chapters; interested readers may want to consult the API documentation to gain an understanding of the scope of the networking classes that the API provides.

## 2.5  Java Networking Considerations

The range of networking classes provided by Java makes it an ideal language for network programming. Having been designed from the ground up to support networking, developers will find Java a far easier language to work with than, for example, C or C++. There are no annoying data structures and pointers to worry about, nor is there a need to change networking libraries when moving from a Wintel platform to Unix. That said, there are some unique considerations and restrictions relative to Java of which developers must be mindful.

First, readers should be aware that Java does not provide low-level access to Internet protocols. Some languages make it possible to write raw IP datagrams and to send ICMP messages. Java does not provide this functionality. While this will not affect many developers, it does mean that Java can't be used to write, for example, a ping application that sends ICMP echo request messages. It also means that developers can't create custom transport protocols that run on IP datagrams (for example, creating a substitute for TCP).

Second, Java imposes severe security restrictions on Java applets. While stand-alone applications and servlets have free reign when it comes to network access, applets will find their actions limited. This is, of course, justified. Consider the risk to users if applets—which are downloaded automatically and may not be visible to the user if the size of the applet is set very small, say a few pixels in size—could connect to any machine on the Internet to send data, or could connect to machines within a local area network (LAN). They would undoubtedly be used to compromise the security of machines. The ability to bypass a firewall and run from within a LAN would make them a severe security risk.

The designers of Java, and browser manufacturers, sought to balance the need for functionality against the need for security. Rather than running the risk of network administrators barring the use of Java (either through firewall filters, or the configuration of browsers to disable access to Java applets), a decision was made to limit applets' network access.

The restrictions are fairly simple.

1. No applet may bind to a local port, to prevent an applet masquerading as a legitimate service (such as a Web server).

2. An applet may connect only to the machine from which its codebase[1] was loaded (usually, but not always, the same Web server of the page that hosts the applet), to prevent applets from accessing internal servers or covertly sending data to another site.

Now, these conditions may seem quite severe, and the reader may be wondering what use Java is for networking if an applet is limited to a single machine. Rest assured, however, that the restrictions apply only to applets (which make up a small part of the world of Java programming), and that they help safeguard users and the reputation of Java. But sometimes restrictions must be overcome. A digitally signed applet may be granted greater network privileges (as well as access to other resources, such as files and printers). However, digitally signing code is a complex task, and acquiring a digital certificate with which to sign involves great expense for the average Java developer (though large corporations will obviously find it less of a financial burden). There are many code-signing mechanisms and they vary from browser to

---

[1] The location or directory from where classes are loaded.

browser. Code signing is beyond the scope of this book, and not the domain of network programming; readers requiring applets with greater network privileges should further investigate code signing on their own.

## 2.6   Applications of Java Network Programming

Network programming adds a new dimension to software applications. Instead of dealing with a single user, or the resources of a single machine (such as files and database connections), network programming gives software the ability to communicate with machines scattered around the globe. This gives software access to potentially millions of external resources, as well as millions of users. The applications of such connectivity are limited only by the imagination—and the bandwidth of a network connection.

What follows is a brief overview of the practical applications of network programming. This discussion is by no means exhaustive—one of the wonders of the Internet is the creativity and imagination that it inspires in individuals to drive it forward, with the design of new protocols and new networking applications.

### 2.6.1   Network Clients

With the wide variety of networking protocols used today on the Internet, and the prolific rate at which new ones are developed, a common use for Java is to create network clients, such as mail readers, remote file transfer applications, and software that browses the Web. Of course, users can download existing software for these purposes off the Internet, most of which is freely available for noncommercial use. However, it is always possible to improve upon software and provide new features. Furthermore, most existing software is compiled to run on a specific CPU and operating system, so portable network clients written in Java offer an advantage over their compiled cousins.

Another important use for Java is in the design of new network protocols for which no client yet exists. Whether you are prototyping a client for testing a protocol or building a commercial-strength client, Java can be used to create network clients in much less time than a C++ counterpart.

### 2.6.2   Games

Traditionally, computer games involve a challenge against computer opponents, with a single player (or perhaps two players if an alternate input device such as a joystick is available) battling to overcome challenges and obstacles controlled by some simple game logic. In some games, more sophisticated game logic is employed, to create more complex behavior that is more challenging. Despite even the most sophisticated artificial intelligence algorithms, such games lack the intelligence of human players, and often exhibit predictable patterns that can be exploited. For novice gamers this may actually be advantageous, but more advanced gamers prefer the challenge of human players.

Playing against human opponents, then, is preferable to playing against computer-generated ones. One major application of network communication in practice is multiplayer games that run over a LAN, or online gaming that runs over the Internet.

Java is ideally suited to this, due in part to its built-in support for Internet programming and to the ease with which games can be distributed to users. Rather than downloading and installing special software (something that many users are wary of for security reasons), games can be played from within a Web browser, in the form of a Java applet. A full discussion of the merits and intricacies of game programming for the Internet is well beyond the scope of a networking text, but the theory and skills of network programming in Java can be applied to create online games.

### 2.6.3  Software Agents

The term *software agent* is used in many different ways, to encompass a variety of software applications. Indeed, a precise definition that everyone can agree upon is hard to come by, as programmers, journalists, and authors use the term to refer to different things. Some people think of agents as intelligent programs that can think for themselves, while others believe agents to be mobile programs that zip across networks searching for information. In actual fact, such descriptions apply only to certain types of agents—software does not have to be either intelligent or mobile to qualify as a software agent.

Simply put, a software agent is a software process that acts on the behalf of one or more users, to perform specific commands and tasks or to fulfill a set of goals. An agent may use predefined logic, or may be flexible enough to modify itself as it learns about its environment and the user, and may even exhibit signs of intelligent programming (hence the term *intelligent agents*). Some agents will use network protocols to search for information or resources on a network, while other agents can transfer themselves from one machine to another (hence the term *mobile agents*). Many people think of agents as either intelligent, mobile, or both. Indeed, very few agents could be said to exhibit significant degrees of intelligence, and few agents are actually mobile—most rely instead on established network protocols to gather information or access resources rather than jumping from host to host themselves.

Theories and definitions aside, let's look at some examples of software agents in practice.

- An agent that sorts through e-mail messages and filters out unsolicited commercial e-mail commonly known as spam.
- An agent that searches for information on the Web, either directly by looking at Web sites, or by sending queries to one or more search engines.
- An agent that learns what type of news stories a user is interested in, and fetches suitable content from news sources such as CNN, MSNBC, and other major media sites.
- An agent that compares prices on products for users across a variety of sites, and offers "comparison shopping" through a Web interface.
- Mobile agents that send themselves to a central meeting site to exchange information and barter for prices on products or services, and then return to their users with prices and costs.
- An agent that monitors a source of information (such as a store catalog), for changes relating to the interest of a user, such as movie releases starring a particular actor or actress, or new novels by a particular author. Such an agent might e-mail one or more users to alert them to this change.

Of course, software agents can be written to perform all sorts of tasks, limited only by one's imagination. For some time, artificial intelligence researchers have been predicting that software agents will be the next "killer application," and that we'll see agents roaming the Web and working for us. While such a vision may be overly optimistic, software agents are likely to be a significant growth area in the future.

As a language, Java is ideally suited to the development of software agents. With its built-in support for HTTP communication, agent developers can easily make their agents "Web aware," without the need to write a custom HTTP implementation. This helps agent developers concentrate on the application, without being overly burdened by developing the network code.

Another major challenge for software agent developers is making them mobile. While an agent does not need to be mobile, and can rely on network protocols for communication, sometimes it is advantageous for an agent to relocate to another machine. For example, when agents are working together cooperatively, it may be cheaper for them to move to a single environment (a meeting place), rather than communicating individually with each other across the Internet. This conserves bandwidth and reduces the time taken to send messages.

Few languages were designed with mobile code in mind, however. Here is where Java really shines—not only is Java bytecode portable from one machine to another regardless of the underlying operating system or CPU architecture, but the designers of Java recognized the need for developers to transmit code over a network. Java's support for this comes in the form of remote method invocation (RMI), which supports dynamic loading of new classes downloaded from the Internet. This makes mobile agents easier to deploy.

### 2.6.4 Web Applications

One of the most important areas for Java network programming is the Web. The rapid growth of the Internet, and the popularity of the browser, has made Web surfing a pastime. Whether it is searching for information, communicating and exchanging ideas, or shopping, people find the Web entertaining, and it has become a popular medium. Java applets executing within a browser can provide amusement, but they also have practical applications, such as performing calculations or displaying information in a more interactive form than static HTML pages. However, the real power of Java on the Web lies not on the client side, where it is hindered by security restrictions, but inside the Web server.

Within the Web server, Java code can perform a variety of tasks such as accessing databases and interacting with other systems. For example, a shopping cart servlet might track a user's order and then verify credit card details before accepting an order. Server-side Java is very powerful, and an important topic in its own right. However, as there is an overlap between Java network programming and server-side Java Web development, we'll be covering this in a later chapter.

Readers should be aware, however, that programming Web applications for Java no longer means just simple applets that run client-side. Many programmers who learned Java when it was first released may not have made the transition yet to server-side Java development. Indeed, most textbooks covering Web programming continue to overemphasize the importance of the applet, and omit server-side Java programming altogether.

Server-side Java already is an important area of Java development, and thus a useful skill for the Java network programmer. More and more portal and e-commerce sites are adopting server-side Java, and those who want to write Web applications need to understand this area.

### 2.6.5 Distributed Systems

It is sometimes impractical to run large and complex systems on a single machine. The reasons for this are many and varied. For example, a task may be so complex that it requires many CPUs working on it concurrently in order to be completed in a reasonable amount of time. Sometimes, resources will be distributed across an organization, and distributed systems technologies are used to integrate them (for example, databases and inventory systems from different departments). With its choice of two distributed systems technologies (RMI and CORBA), developers can create systems that span many computers.

**NOTE:** There are many large distributed systems, using a variety of languages and technologies that work cooperatively to complete tasks. The most well known is the SETI@Home project, which harnesses the idle CPU power to process signal data obtained from observatories listening for signs of extraterrestrial intelligence. Massive parallel processing systems that are composed of systems distributed over a network offer a very cost-effective way of performing highly complex calculations. While certainly not the only language suitable for distributed systems, Java does make an excellent platform for it.

Another use for distributed systems is connecting older "legacy" systems within an organization to newer systems or to a Web interface. The use of technologies like CORBA as middleware is very important in organizations with many systems written in many languages. Java and CORBA can act as the glue that binds all these disparate machines and services together.

## 2.7    Java Language Issues

While readers should be familiar with at least the basics of the Java programming language and will likely be proficient with the language, there are some issues, delineated below, that all readers should be aware of.

### 2.7.1   Exception Handling in Java

Exception handling is a mechanism for dealing with errors that occur in software at runtime. Anyone who has done programming is familiar with errors in source code (often due to typing errors, or breaking the rules of the language) that occur at compile time, but the notion of runtime error-handling may be new to some readers; some may instead be familiar with badly written software that simply crashes. Even if source code is perfectly correct in syntax, errors can occur when running the software. For example, while attempting to read from a file, an application may be unable to proceed because the file is missing. This is an example of an error that occurs at runtime.

In languages such as C, the onus for error checking was placed on the programmer but was not rigidly enforced. An application could, for example, obtain a handle to read from a file, but if the file were not found, a null value would be returned. Good programmers would check for the null value and output an appropriate error message, but there was no obligation to do so. While checking to see if a file was opened seems to be a fairly obvious practice, it is easy to overlook a potential error condition such as this. In more complex applications, where third-party libraries are used that can exhibit unpredictable errors, a program can run into serious problems at runtime that aren't detected and handled appropriately.

The solution is to rigidly enforce error handling, through exception handling.

### 2.7.1.1 What Are Exceptions?

Exceptions are unusual conditions (usually, but not always, errors) that occur at runtime and are represented as objects. These exception objects contain member variables that track information about the error condition, making it possible to diagnose the cause of a problem or at least to provide clues as to why it occurred. When an exception occurs, the method in which it occurs will "throw" the exception and pass it up to the calling method. The calling method may choose to handle the error condition and thus "catch" the exception, or it may throw the exception to its calling method (and so on, as the exception propagates up the stack), as shown in Figure 2-1.

Methods that are likely to generate exceptions will indicate the type of exception that will be thrown. A calling method must catch the exception and provide error-handling code or indicate that it throws that type of exception. This means that at some point in the code, the exception must be caught and dealt with. Without exception handling, it would be easy to miss errors that could occur at runtime. While developers might never see them in testing, users most certainly would.

### 2.7.1.2 Types of Exceptions

There are many different types of exceptions, to suit the many different types of errors that can occur in software. However, all exceptions share a common class inheritance, from the java.lang.Throwable class. In Java, exceptions are grouped into two categories, represented by the class tree in Figure 2-2.

Exceptions that are extended from the Error class are serious errors that typical Java software should not encounter, and which in any case the developer will have no control over. While methods may certainly attempt to catch these errors, they are not required to do so. This may seem contrary to the reasoning behind exceptions (to force developers to handle errors), but as they are almost always beyond the control of the programmer and extremely rare, it is

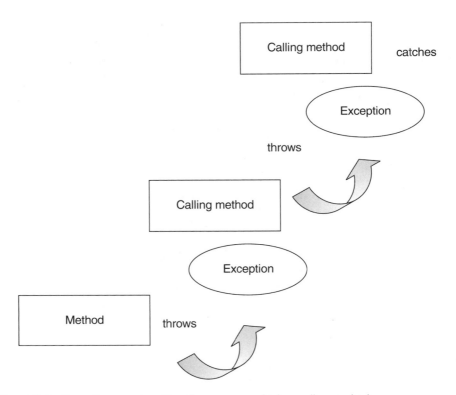

**Figure 2-1**   Exceptions may be either thrown, or caught, by a calling method.

certainly understandable for compilers to enforce handling of them. Some examples of these errors include:

- `AWTError`—thrown when a serious error occurs in the Abstract Windowing Toolkit
- `NoClassDefFoundError`—thrown when the JVM is unable to locate the class definition file (.class) for a class, as for example when the JVM tries to run a stand-alone application but the class file is missing.
- `OutOfMemoryError`—thrown when the JVM can no longer allocate memory to objects and the garbage collector can free no further objects.

Exceptions that are extended from the `Exception` class, on the other hand, should nearly always be dealt with by calling methods. Omitted from this rule are subclasses of the `RuntimeException` class. These types of exceptions are usually fairly serious errors, which are difficult to recover from. Nonetheless, if there is a good reason for encountering them and dealing with them, programmers are free to add exception-handling code even though a

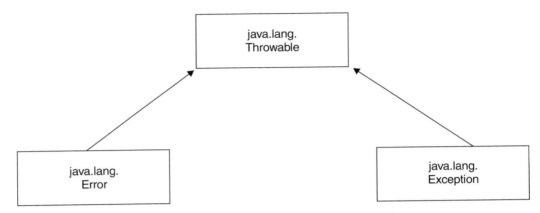

**Figure 2-2**  Exception class tree and categories

compiler will not require it. Some examples of exceptions that fall into this category are:

- NoSuchElementException—thrown when an attempt is made to access the next element of an enumeration, but all elements have been exhausted.
- NullPointerException—thrown when an attempt to reference an object has been made, but the reference was null.
- SecurityException—thrown by the current security manager when an attempt to access a resource, object, or method has been made but not permitted.

Dealing with exceptions can involve either catching them or throwing the exception to a calling method. There are many different types of exceptions, and many of these have subclasses of exceptions. For example, when dealing with TCP sockets, it is possible for a SocketException to be thrown. The SocketException class has several subclasses, however, that indicate more specific error conditions. A ConnectException may have been thrown, to indicate that the connection was refused, or a NoRouteToHost connection may have been thrown, to indicate that the network connection to the host is down or blocked by a firewall.

As readers work through the various classes that make up the Java API, and their methods, an enormous range of exceptions will be encountered. Rather than provide an exhaustive list here, when methods of a class are discussed in later chapters, the methods likely to be thrown will be covered.

### 2.7.1.3 Handling Exceptions

To deal with errors that occur at runtime, programmers must write an exception handler. This is a special section of code that catches any thrown exceptions. How programmers choose to handle such code is not prescribed (for example, an error message could be output to the user or the exception ignored), but an exception must be caught and dealt with, unless a method indicates that it will throw an exception itself.

Java provides three statements for handling exceptions.

1. The `try` statement indicates a block of code that can generate exceptions. Unless a method that throws a specific type of exception instead of handling it is being written, any code that generates an exception within a `try` block must be enclosed. For example, if the programmer is dealing with network I/O and his or her method doesn't declare that it throws an `IOException`, then the network I/O code must be enclosed within a `try` statement.

2. The `catch` statement is used to catch exceptions thrown within a `try` block of code. A `catch` statement must specify which exception it is dealing with; many `catch` statements can be applied to a single `try` statement.

3. The `finally` statement is a generic catchall for cleaning up after a `try` block. Whether exceptions were thrown or not, the code within a `finally` statement will be executed.

### Exceptions: Try Statements

Unless a method indicates that it throws an exception, the compiler will enforce exception handling. Any code that uses a method that indicates it throws an exception must be enclosed within a `try` block. If an exception does occur, execution of the code within the `try` block stops immediately, and the exception will be caught by a `catch` block or `calling` method.

```
// Code outside of try block should not throw an exception

try {
        // do something that could generate an exception....
}
// Handle exception  .....
```

### Exceptions: Catch Statements

The purpose of the `catch` statement is to provide error-handling code that handles an error gracefully. One or more `catch` statements may follow a `try` block, dealing with specific types of exceptions.

```
// Try block can generate exceptions
try {
        // generate an exception
}
```

```
catch (SocketException se)
{
        System.err.println ("Socket error reading from host : " + se);
         System.exit(2);
}
catch (Exception e)
{
        System.err.println ("Error : " + e);
        System.exit(1);
}
```

### Exceptions: Finally Statements

Sometimes the programmer will want to execute statements regardless of whether or not an error occurs. Putting cleanup code within a `try` block is not appropriate, as it will not be executed if an exception is thrown. Instead, the `finally` statement should be used; it comes after any `catch` statements and the try block.

```
// Try block can generate exceptions
try {
        // generate an exception
}
catch (SomeException some)
{
        // handle some exception
}
finally
{
        // clean up after try block, regardless of any
        // exceptions that are thrown
}
```

### 2.7.1.4 Causes of Exceptions

Despite the best-laid plans, no application is foolproof and exceptions will be encountered at runtime. This will, it is hoped, occur during debugging, rather than exceptions being accidentally discovered by users. By catching and handling exceptions, applications will be robust enough to recover, and if not, to retire gracefully with an appropriate message.

In networking, the most common cause of exceptions is related to the state of the network connection. Users connect to network services over a variety of communication mechanisms, of varying degrees of speed and quality. When a network loses its connection to the Internet, or that connection becomes highly congested with traffic, it may be impossible to connect to a particular host and thus to its network services. Or the user may be behind a firewall, preventing a direct connection from being established. In our experience, these are the two most common causes of exceptions in network applications.

The next most likely cause is a security restriction, either imposed by the browser on applets or by a Java security policy or security manager. When writing applets or software that uses security (such as distributed clients and servers), programmers may want to consider trying to catch any Security-Exception that is thrown. Though not mandatory, in that the compiler does not enforce it, it may be advantageous to do so if users are likely to change their security settings or run software within restricted environments. However, a SecurityException is thrown only if code attempts to do something prohibited by the JVM—external security measures such as firewalls will simply result in an inability to connect to certain hosts.

## 2.8    System Properties

The notion of system properties will be recognizable to readers, as most operating systems support a similar concept in the form of environmental variables. Environmental variables contain control information, such as the path that dictates where an operating system will look for executable files. Indeed, as part of the reader's installation of Java, an environmental variable was probably independently set: the classpath, which controls where the JVM will look for class files.

System properties, within the context of Java, are specific to a JVM rather than an operating system (so two different JVMs can be assigned two different sets of properties). They can be used for a variety of purposes, such as controlling the configuration parameters of an application. The most important use for network programmers involves the specification of a proxy server (covered in Chapter 1), to defeat firewalls that stop network software from working.

A value can be assigned to a system property in two ways:

1. By passing a system property from the command line
2. By programmatically assigning a new system property

### 2.8.1    *Passing a System Property from the Command Line*

When invoking a JVM, command-line parameters can be passed to it for the purpose of changing system settings. There are a wide range of parameters that the JVM supports, controlling things such as memory allocation and whether just-in-time (JIT) compilation is enabled. For the programmer's purposes, the most important thing is setting a system property, using the –D flag.

For example, to set a proxy server from the command line, the following command (modifying, of course, the application name and proxy settings) could be executed:

```
java -DproxyHost=firewall.mynetwork.net -DproxyPort=80
MyApplication
```

Setting a system property in this manner is, of course, dependent upon the user. It also allows the user to "proxy-enable" his or her existing applications without modifying the original code.

### 2.8.2 Programmatically Assigning a New System Property

To give the application control of the setting of system properties rather than relying on users, it is possible to modify system properties at runtime. Accessing or modifying system properties is accomplished through the `java.lang.System` class. To assign a new property, the `System.setProperty` method can be used. For example, to set a proxy host and port the following could be done:

```
// Set proxy host
System.setProperty ( "proxyHost" , "firewall.mynetwork.net" );


// Set proxy port
System.setProperty ( "proxyPort" , "80" );
```

A complex network application intended for use in a commercial environment might offer a dialog box that allows users to customize proxy settings for their own firewall environment. If a security manager is installed, however, it may not allow modification of settings.

## 2.9 Development Tools

When writing software for the Java platform, developers will need to rely on a variety of tools. The choice of exactly which tools to use is largely personal. The user interface of a tool that one developer likes might be frustrating to another developer. For some projects, a particular feature will be called for, necessitating the use of a particular tool or development suite. Rather than advocating a particular development tool for network programming, we leave it to the reader to evaluate which tools best suit him or her. Below is a brief overview of some of the tools available for editing, compiling, and debugging Java software.

### 2.9.1 Integrated Development Environments

An integrated development environment (IDE) is a suite of tools that a developer uses to design, create, modify, compile, and test software. Each IDE has its own unique user interface and set of features. Before selecting an IDE, one should identify required features (such as JDK version) and download an evaluation copy to see if the user interface is amenable. Since the package will be used for a large amount of time, developers should be satisfied before making such a purchase.

The following is a selection of commercial IDE packages available.

### 2.9.1.1 Borland JBuilder

Borland JBuilder is a powerful and fully featured IDE that is available in both Windows and Unix editions. Much of JBuilder itself is actually written in Java, and it fully supports the Java 2 platform. With an easy-to-use visual form designer, code editor, and debugger, JBuilder is an extremely popular IDE. A "community" edition, downloadable for free, contains most of the functionality a developer will need. For more information, see http://www.borland.com/jbuilder/.

### 2.9.1.2 Symantec Visual Café

Visual Café, formerly a Symantec product but now produced by WebGain, is another popular IDE for Java. Like Borland JBuilder, it offers a visual form designer and combined code editor and debugger. However, Visual Café has the additional advantage of offering a variety of compilation options, including native machine code binaries for running on Windows machines. For more information, see http://www.webgain.com/.

### 2.9.1.3 Visual Age for Java

The Visual Age for Java product, produced by IBM, is a high-level tool for developing enterprise applications. As such, it carries with it a huge amount of functionality, ranging from servlet and Enterprise JavaBean components to more esoteric abilities such as support for IBM's WebSphere line. A free evaluation version of Visual Age is available, and it is certainly worth a look with respect to managing large software development projects. For more information, see http://www.ibm.com/software/ad/vajava/.

### 2.9.1.4 Visual J++

The earliest version of Visual J++ came with support only for JDK1.02 (although the JVM and compiler could be upgraded), and minimal support for visual designing of GUIs. With the release of Visual J++ 6.0 came much better GUI design tools, but also reliance on the Windows Foundation Classes (WFC), which violated the goal of Java's cross-platform portability. For this reason, many developers advocate not using Visual J++, as it is far too easy to lock your software into running only on Windows.

Microsoft Visual J++ is not included in the next release of the Visual Studio (7.0) suite, and is substituted by a new language, C# (pronounced "C-sharp"). Existing users of Visual J++ may still prefer to use these tools, however, and Microsoft has announced that it intends to offer a tool named Visual J# for migrating Visual J++ users to Visual Studio.NET. For more information, see http://msdn.microsoft.com/visualj/.

### 2.9.1.5 Forte for Java Community Edition

A relative newcomer in the IDE market, Forte for Java is an IDE from Sun Microsystems, based on an earlier product that Sun had acquired: NetBeans. Forte for Java stacks up well against products like Borland JBuilder, and has a fully featured API offering code editing, visual design, compiling, and debugging. It also has extra modules that can be incorporated, and a handy auto-update feature. The Forte line contains commercial products, but the community edition is freely downloadable. For more information, see http://www.sun.com/forte/ffj/ce/.

### 2.9.2 *Java System Development Kits*

The most important system development kit (SDK) available for Java developers is, obviously, the Java SDK, available from Sun Microsystems. This is a freely available product, which may be downloaded from the JavaSoft Web site at http://java.sun.com/j2se/.

Of course, there are additional development kits, from third parties and from Sun, that augment the existing tools and classes that ship with JDK. Full coverage is beyond the scope of this book, and most of these additional SDKs are not network related in nature. Where appropriate, however, they will be mentioned in later chapters, in discussing additional Java networking functionality.

## 2.10  **Summary**

Readers of this chapter will have gained a better understanding of the essential components of Java. Java is not just a computer programming language, nor is it just a software platform. Java is a rich and powerful computing language and software execution environment, with a fully featured API class library that includes excellent networking support. The many attributes of Java covered within this chapter make it a popular choice for network programming.

**Chapter Highlights**

In this chapter, you have learned:

- About the history, design goals, and properties of the Java language
- About compiled bytecode, the Java Virtual Machine, and the wide assortment of runtime environments available
- About the core Java API, and some of the Java extensions available for network programming
- About the important network and security considerations of applets
- About some of the practical areas in which Java can be applied
- About exception handling and system properties
- About some of the major Java development tools available

# CHAPTER 3

## *Internet Addressing*

Unlike local area networks (LANs), the Internet is a vast collection of machines and devices spread out across the nation and the world. When there are hundreds of millions (and eventually many billions) of computers and devices attached to a network, the need to identify and locate a specific one is obviously important. Indeed, one of the most fundamental concepts in network programming is that of the network address. Without it, there would be no way of identifying the sender of a data packet or where the packet must be sent.

Chapter 1 included a preliminary discussion of network addresses. The theory behind such addresses was covered in brief, so as to give the reader a basic understanding of how addresses work. This chapter will delve into greater detail, covering important topics such as IP addresses and domain names, and how these are represented in Java.

Readers with networking experience may be familiar with these topics, but likely will not have covered their representation in Java. A new class is introduced from the Java API to cover the representation of an IP address. Even readers comfortable with the theory will benefit from reading the practical sections of this chapter, as they form the foundation for the chapters that follow.

## 3.1 Local Area Network Addresses

Devices connected to a LAN have their own unique physical or hardware address. This assists other machines on the network in delivering data packets to the correct location. The address is useful only in the context of a LAN, however—a machine can't be located on the Internet by using its physical address, which does not indicate the location of the machine. Indeed, machines often move from location to location, in the case of laptop or palmtop computers.

Java network programmers do not need to be concerned with the details of how data is routed within a LAN. Indeed, Java does not provide access to the lower-level data link protocols used by LANs. Supporting the wide range of protocols available would be a mammoth task. Since each type of protocol uses a different type of address and has different characteristics, different code would need to be written for each and every type of network. Instead, Java provides support for TCP/IP, which can be thought of as the glue that binds networks together.

No matter what type of LAN is used—if one is used at all—software can be written for it in Java providing it supports TCP/IP. Individual machines have unique addresses for the transmission and receipt of IP datagrams, in addition to their normal network or physical addresses.

## 3.2    Internet Protocol Addresses

Devices having a direct Internet connection are allocated a unique identifier known as an IP address. IP addresses may be static (in that they are bound permanently to a certain machine or device), or dynamic (leased to a particular machine or device for a certain period, for example in the case of an Internet service provider [ISP] that offers a pool of modems for dial-up connections). Dynamically assigned IP addresses are typically used when many devices require Internet access for limited periods of time. Thus addresses can be allocated from a pool of remaining addresses on a case-by-case basis. However, an IP address can be bound to a single machine only; it cannot be shared concurrently. This address is used by the Internet Protocol to route IP datagrams to the correct location. Without an address, a machine cannot be contacted; hence, all machines must have a unique IP address.

**NOTE:** The only exception to this is the case of a TCP/IP LAN, also known as an intranet. Within the environment of an intranet, a shared range of IP addresses can be used, specially set aside for intranet use. Anyone may bind a machine to one of these addresses; as they are not exposed to the public Internet there is no conflict with an external machine. One must be careful, however, not to use the same IP address for multiple machines or devices within an intranet.

### 3.2.1    Structure of the IP Address

Under the Internet Protocol version 4, referred to as IPv4, the IP address is a 32-bit number made up of four octets (a series of 8 bits). While computers read an IP address as a sequence of bits, people see them in dotted decimal format (for example, 127.0.0.1). There are five classes of IP addresses (A through E), and each class is allocated an address range, as shown in Table 3-1.

Each class of IP addresses is structured differently, allowing for greater versatility in how private networks and host machines are allocated (see Figure 3-1). Private networks are allocated a network ID that is a unique identifier for a specific network. Control of and responsibility for how machines within a network are allocated falls to the network administrator, so that host IDs can be assigned as needed.

The reason for a division of IP address classes that gives greater or lesser weighting to the host ID field is simple: each private network needs its own block of IP addresses, but allocating too large a block means that these addresses will be wasted. With a finite range of addresses, this becomes particularly important as the number of allocated addresses increases. Class A addresses, for example, have a very small network ID field but a large host ID.

**Table 3-1**   Range of IP Addresses by Class

| Type | Address Range |
| --- | --- |
| Class A | 0. 0. 0. 0 – 127.255.255.255 |
| Class B | 128.0.0.0 – 191.255.255.255 |
| Class C | 192.0.0.0 – 223.255.255.255 |
| Class D | 224.0.0.0 – 239.255.255.255 |
| Class E | 240.0.0.0 – 247.255.255.255 |

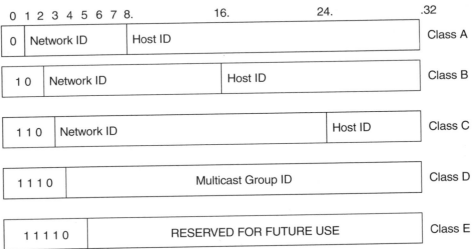

**Figure 3-1**   Address structures by class

This means that a private network with a Class A address can assign IP addresses to a large number of machines, whereas a Class C address can support a smaller number, but there are more network IDs available. Figure 3.1 shows the breakup of network and host ID fields by class.

Note that two address classes (D and E) are not allocated a network ID field. Class D is used for simultaneously broadcasting data to a large number of machines that are grouped together (a technique known as multicasting). Class E is reserved for future use and allocation.

### 3.2.2   Obtaining an IP Address

The central body responsible for allocating blocks of IP addresses is the Internet Corporation for Assigned Names and Numbers (ICANN), building on the work of an earlier organization, the Internet Assigned Numbers Authority (IANA). A person setting up a private network would be allocated either a Class A, B, or C address, and could then assign host IP addresses to the machines on that particular network. A discussion of the process of setting up a private network is beyond the scope of this book, of course, but readers interested in further information will find the ICANN and IANA organization Web sites useful, at http://www.icann.org/ and http://www.iana.org/.

The most common way to obtain an IP address is to have one assigned to you by a network administrator, ISP, or other network service. When you establish a dial-up connection, you will usually be assigned an IP address. This address is normally dynamically assigned from a pool of available addresses, and when you reconnect you'll usually get a different address. In an intranet, a network administrator may assign a specific address to your machine, or you may have a dynamically assigned address allocated by a Dynamic Host Control Protocol (DHCP) server. DHCP provides addresses on demand; if machines are going online and offline frequently, a smaller pool of addresses can be used.

### 3.2.3   Special IP Addresses

Programmers should be aware of some special IP addresses as well. The first, and most important from a network programming perspective, is known as the loopback or localhost address. When writing and debugging network software, programmers often want to connect to the local machine for testing purposes. Regardless of whether a connection to the Internet exists via a dial-up service or work is being done offline, the local machine may be accessed using the loopback address; this address is 127.0.0.1.

**NOTE:** Your machine may be known by many IP addresses in addition to the loopback address. For example, you may be assigned an IP address when you dial your ISP, or your network administrator may have assigned an address for your intranet. Programmers experimenting with writing networking software may find that it makes sense from a financial perspective to disconnect from their ISP and use the loopback address whenever possible.

Another set of useful IP addresses are those reserved for private networking. In an intranet environment, it may be desirable to configure all machines with a unique IP address, without having them exposed to the public Internet. The Internet Assigned Number Authority (IANA) has reserved three sets of addresses for use within a local intranet environment, as described in RFC 1918. If you plan on setting up a LAN of your own, you can pluck addresses from these ranges without worrying about a collision conflict with a host on the Internet. On the Internet, routers will not forward data for these addresses, so they can be safely used locally. It must be noted, however, that this is the only time when IP addresses can be safely picked, unless you are allocated a block of addresses. Table 3-2 shows the IP address ranges for Classes A through C.

## 3.3 Beyond IP Addresses: The Domain Name System

While IP addresses comprise an efficient system for network administrators, most people find memorizing them to be an impossible task. People generally find words much easier to recall than the dotted decimal format of an IP address. It is easier to remember a name such as Amazon or Sun than a set of numbers designating such a dotted decimal IP address.

### 3.3.1 What Is a Domain Name?

The domain name system (DNS) makes the Internet user-friendly, by associating a textual name with an IP address. Any entity, be it commercial,

**Table 3-2**  Class A, B, and C Address Ranges for Intranet Usage

| Type | Address Range |
| --- | --- |
| Class A | 10.0. 0.0 – 0.255.255.255 |
| Class B | 172.16.0.0 –172.31.255.255 |
| Class C | 192.168.0.0 –192.168.255.255 |

government, or private, can apply for a domain name, which can be used by people to locate that entity on the Internet. Simple text names, as opposed to arbitrary numbers, are used for identification. In addition, organizations can allocate their own hostnames, such as ftp.davidreilly.com and www.davidreilly.com, without having to register every host with an outside body. Once you have a domain name, you can control how it is used.

**NOTE:** Many registries perform the service of registering domain names, at variable prices. The original domain name registrar, Network Solutions, is located at http://www.networksolutions.com/.

### 3.3.2   How Does the Domain Name System Work?

Given the vast number of machines connected to the Internet, the number of domain-name-to-IP-address mappings is too great for any one system to handle. Even if there were a large enough system to store all of these mappings, it would be quickly overloaded by requests. Furthermore, in the event of a system breakdown, isolating the problem to a fraction of the Internet would be preferable to having the entire system grind to a shuddering halt. Ironically, however, when the Internet was originally conceived, host-to-IP-address mappings were stored in a single file, called hosts.txt, which was downloaded and mirrored across the Internet. This file still exists in many operating systems and can be used to override DNS mappings or cover up ones that are missing or unresolvable by the local DNS servers. In some cases, they can be used to cover up not having a local DNS server on an intranet.

The DNS (outlined in RFC 1034/1035) is a more sophisticated and robust system. It can be thought of as a distributed database, in which responsibility for accepting new registrations, and returning the addresses of existing registrations, is spread out across many different hosts. Different categories, such as commercial and educational, are handled by different registry servers. Furthermore, international registries handle their own mappings (called cou try-code top-level domains), and can be subdivided into further categories. This forms a hierarchical structure, a small subset of which is shown in Figure 3-2. Since the range of address categories changes rapidly, only a small number are shown.

This hierarchical structure is broken up by the type of address (either .net, .com, .gov, .edu, .mil, or one of the newer addresses such as .info or .biz) or by the country (.au, .uk, among many others). For example, to access the site www.davidreilly.com, a request to resolve this name would be sent to the .com DNS server. Some countries have their own way of organizing DNS

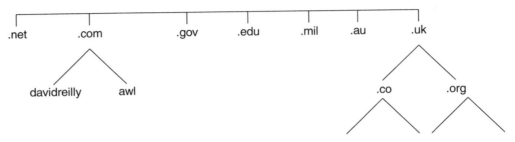

**Figure 3-2**   Subset of the DNS hierarchy

records for example, as seen in Figure 3-2, the United Kingdom (.uk) uses .co rather than .com.

### 3.3.3   *Domain Name Resolution*

When software applications need to look up a hostname (such as ftp.david reilly.com), they don't contact the .com registry directly. Your network administrator, or ISP, configures your system to access the application's DNS server, which handles the lookup process. Often, however, the DNS server doesn't even need to send out a query, as the same sites will be requested (-either by multiple users or a single one). This works much the same as a Web browser caching pages, and prevents excessive overload of the network.

When a request for a hostname (such as www.aol.com) is made, the operating system of the client computer contacts the local DNS server on the LAN. It is responsible for locating the domain server aol.com, and interrogating it to find the IP address of the hostname (www.aol.com). To do this, it must query the "root" level domain server, which refers it to the .com server. Finally, the IP address is returned to the user (see Figure 3-3).

As can be seen from the example in Figure 3-4, DNS requests can be cached. The LAN DNS server can maintain a cache of recently requested addresses, to prevent overloading of the root-level domains. Furthermore, this improves network performance, as the delay between requesting a domain name and receiving a response is diminished.

## 3.4   **Internet Addressing with Java**

By now it should be clear that a host on the Internet can be represented either in dotted decimal format as an IP address, or as a hostname such as ftp.david reilly.com. Under Java, such addresses are represented by the `java.net.Inet-Address` class. This class can fill a variety of tasks, from resoling an IP address to looking up the hostname. In the next section, this important class is examined in detail.

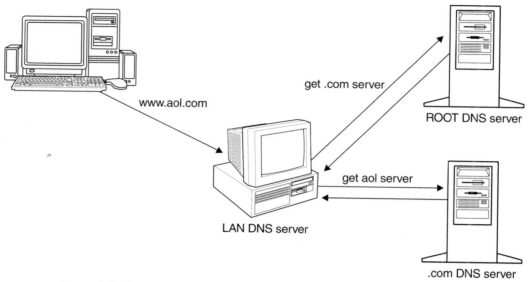

**Figure 3-3**   Request for www.aol.com reaches LAN DNS server and is resolved.

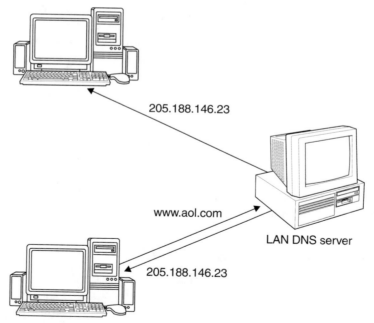

**Figure 3-4**   DNS server returns IP address, and caches query from another machine.

### 3.4.1   *The java.net.InetAddress Class*

The `InetAddress` class is used to represent IP addresses within a Java networking application. Unlike most other classes, there are no public constructors for that of `InetAddress`. Instead, there are two static methods that return `InetAddress` instances. Those and the other major methods of this class are covered in the list below; all are public unless otherwise noted.

- `boolean equals(Object obj)`—compares two IP addresses, and returns "true" if there is a match. Note, however, that some machines can be known by multiple IP addresses, so this is not an absolute test for equality; what is tested is only that the two addresses are equal, not that they are the same machine.
- `byte[] getAddress()`—returns the IP address in byte format (as opposed to dotted decimal notation). The bytes are returned in network byte order, with the highest byte as `bytearray[0]`.
- `static InetAddress[] getAllByName ( String hostname )` throws `java.net.UnknownHostException, java.lang.SecurityException`—returns, as a static method, an array of `InetAddress` instances representing the specified hostname. While most machines will have a single IP address, there are some situations in which one hostname can be mapped to many machines and/or a hostname can map to many addresses on one machine (virtual addresses). If the host cannot be resolved, or if resolving the host conflicts with the security manager, an exception will be thrown.
- `static InetAddress getByName ( String hostname )` throws `java.net.UnknownHostException, java.lang.SecurityException`—returns an `InetAddress` instance representing the specified hostname, which may be represented as either as a text hostname (e.g., davidreilly.com) or as an IP address in dotted decimal format. If the host cannot be resolved, or resolving the host conflicts with the security manager, an exception will be thrown.
- `String getHostAddress()`—returns the IP address of the `InetAddress` in dotted decimal format.
- `static InetAddress getLocalHost()` throws `java.net.UnknownHostException, java.lang.SecurityException`—returns, as a static method, the IP address of the localhost machine. If the IP address cannot be determined, or doing so conflicts with the security manager, then an exception will be thrown.
- `String getHostName()` throws `java.lang.SecurityManager`—returns the hostname of the `InetAddress`.
- `boolean isMulticastAddress()`—returns "true" if the `InetAddress` is a multicast address, also known as a Class D address.

- String toString()—returns a string representation of the InetAddress. Readers are advised to use the getHostName() and getHostAddress() methods, to control which type of data is being requested.

### 3.4.2  Using InetAddress to Determine Localhost Address

The first, and most simple, example of InetAddress is to find out the IP address of the current machine. If a direct connection to the Internet exists, a meaningful result will be obtained, but dial-up users and those without any Internet connection (such as in an intranet environment) may get the loopback address of 127.0.0.1. The short example program given below shows how it is possible to determine the address.

#### Code for LocalHostDemo

```
import java.net.*;

// Chapter 3, Listing 1
public class LocalHostDemo
{
    public static void main(String args[])
    {
        System.out.println ("Looking up local host");

        try
        {
            // Get the local host
            InetAddress localAddress =
            InetAddress.getLocalHost();

            System.out.println ("IP address : " +
                        localAddress.getHostAddress() );
        }
        catch (UnknownHostException uhe)
        {
            System.out.println ("Error - unable to resolve localhost");
        }
    }
}
```

#### How LocalHostDemo Works

The LocalHostDemo application starts by prompting the user that an IP address lookup will be performed (this is important if there is any delay in determining the IP address). The networking operation must be enclosed within a try/catch block, because it is possible that no IP address will be found and an exception will be thrown. Using the static method InetAddress.getLocalHost(), we obtain an object representing an IP address. To display the address in dotted decimal notation, the `InetAddress.getHostAddress()` method is used.

### Running LocalHostDemo

This application requires no command-line parameters. Running it will display information about the host machine. To run, type:

```
java LocalHostDemo
```

### 3.4.3 Using InetAddress to Find Out About Other Addresses

The previous example familiarized you with the `InetAddress` class. Below is a more complex example, which resolves hostnames to IP addresses and then attempts to perform a reverse lookup of the IP address.

### Code for NetworkResolverDemo

```java
import java.net.*;

// Chapter 3, Listing 2
public class NetworkResolverDemo
{
    public static void main(String args[])
    {
        if (args.length != 1)
        {
            System.err.println ("Syntax -
            NetworkResolverDemo host");
            System.exit(0);
        }

        System.out.println ("Resolving " + args[0]);

        try
        {
            // Resolve host and get InetAddress
            InetAddress addr = InetAddress.getByName
            ( args[0] );

            System.out.println ("IP address : " +
                            addr.getHostAddress() );

            System.out.println ("Hostname : " +
            addr.getHostName() );
        }
        catch (UnknownHostException uhe)
        {
            System.out.println ("Error - unable to resolve hostname"
);
        }
    }
}
```

### How NetworkResolverDemo Works

In the previous example, we used a static method of `InetAddress` to return the local address. Most commonly, however, we will be working with other systems on the network, so we need to learn how to use `InetAddress` to resolve their hostnames and obtain an IP address. In this example, we use the static method, `InetAddress.getByName()` to return an `InetAddress` instance. We then display the IP address and hostname, using the same methods in `LocalHostDemo`.

### Running NetworkResolverDemo

This application requires as a parameter either a hostname or an IP address. To run, type:

```
java NetworkResolverDemo hostname
```

## 3.4.4 Other Types of Addresses in Java

There are other types of networking addresses represented in Java, such as URLs and remote object references. To avoid confusion, discussion of these will be reserved for later chapters.

## 3.5 Summary

This chapter delved further into IP addresses and discussed domain names and how they are represented within Java software. The `InetAddress` cannot be directly instantiated, but provides several static methods that can be invoked to obtain an `InetAddress` representing a specific IP address or hostname.

**Chapter Highlights**

In this chapter, you have learned:

- About the Domain Name System (DNS) and domain name suffixes (such as .com)
- About the structure of an IP address and the various classes of IP addresses
- About the `InetAddress` class and its various methods

# CHAPTER 4

## *Data Streams*

## 4.1   Overview

Communication over networks, with files, and even between applications, is represented in Java by streams. Stream-based communication is central to almost any type of Java application. The concept of streams is especially important when dealing with networking applications. Almost all network communication (except UDP communication) is conducted over streams, so it is essential that programmers be familiar with this concept.

Readers with previous input/output (I/O) stream experience may choose to skim through this section, but will likely benefit from a revised look at the topic, as changes to streams were introduced in JDK1.1 to deal with text-based reading and writing. A thorough knowledge of I/O streams is critical for almost any type of Java programmer, and is required for an understanding of the later chapters of this book. In addition, since so much of network communication involves the transmission of text, knowledge of the new text readers and writers is also necessary.

### 4.1.2   *What Exactly Are Streams?*

Byte-level communication is represented in Java by data streams, which are conduits through which information—bytes of data—is sent and received. A simple analogy is a pipe through which material such as water may be moved from one location to another. Provided that the pipe is installed correctly, what goes in one end comes out the other (see Figure 4-1).

When designing a system, the correct stream must be selected; when building a system, the type of stream used is not important, as a consistent interface

**Figure 4-1**   Communication stream sends data from one point to another.

is provided. The end effect of the stream, not how it was constructed, is of interest. Streams may be chained together, to provide an easier and more manageable interface. If, for example, the data needed to be processed in a particular way, a second stream could connect to an existing stream, to provide for processing of the data. For example, bytes might be converted from one form into another (such as a number), or a stream of bytes may be interpreted as sequences of characters, as shown in Figure 4-2. In Java, streams take a flexible, one-size-fits-all approach—they are fairly interchangeable, and can be applied on top of another stream, or even several other streams.

Interchangeability is an extremely important attribute of streams, as it simplifies programming considerably. Streams are divided into two categories—input streams that may be read from and output streams that may be written to. Provided you don't try to read from an output stream, or write to an input stream, you can safely attach any "filter" stream (a stream that filters data in some fashion, such as processing it or converting it from bytes into a different form) to any low-level stream (such as a file or network stream). Readers should be aware that, although streams are usually one-way, multiple streams can be used together (e.g., an input stream and an output stream) for two-way communication.

### 4.1.3  How Streams Relate to Networking

At the heart of network programming is the transmission of data and the sending of sequences of bytes. A stream-based approach to communication simplifies programming, as a standard interface for data transmission is offered regardless of the type of data being sent and received, or of the mechanism by

**Figure 4-2**   Streams may be fitted together for additional functionality.

which data is sent across the network. Of course, streams are not limited to networking—they can read from and be written to data structures, files, and other applications. However, as will be seen in later chapters, there is more than one way to send data over a network, and I/O streams provide a consistent interface for working with network communication.

## 4.2 How Streams Work

As mentioned earlier, streams provide communication of data at the byte level, and are used for either reading or writing. Streams for reading inherit from a common superclass, the `java.io.InputStream` class, shown in Figure 4-3. Likewise, streams used for writing data inherit from the superclass `java.io.OutputStream`, shown in Figure 4-4. These are abstract classes; they cannot be instantiated. Instead, an appropriate subclass for the task at hand is created. Several streams inherit directly from either `InputStream` or `OutputStream`, but most inherit from a filter stream.

### 4.2.1 Reading from an Input Stream

Many input streams are provided by the `java.io` package, and choosing the right low-level stream is a fairly straightforward task, since the name of the stream matches the data source it will read from. As shown in Table 4-1, there are six low-level streams to choose from, each of which performs an entirely different task.

There are other streams that programmers cannot create directly but that are nonetheless low-level streams. A good example of such a stream is one that

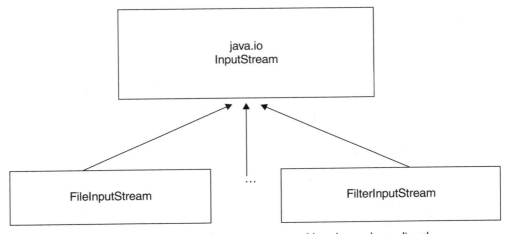

**Figure 4-3** Input streams inherit from `InputStream`, although not always directly.

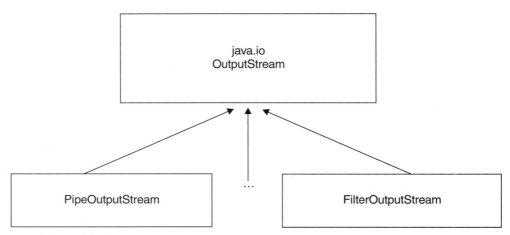

**Figure 4-4**   Output streams inherit from `OutputStream`, although not always directly.

**Table 4-1**   Low-Level Input Streams of the `java.io` Package

| Low-Level Input Stream | Purpose of Stream |
|---|---|
| `ByteArrayInputStream` | Reads bytes of data from an in-memory array |
| `FileInputStream` | Reads bytes of data from a file on the local file system |
| `PipedInputStream` | Reads bytes of data from a thread pipe |
| `StringBufferInputStream` | Reads bytes of data from a string |
| `SequenceInputStream` | Reads bytes of data from two or more low-level streams, switching from one stream to the next when the end of the stream is reached |
| `System.in` | Reads bytes of data from the user console |

represents a network connection to a TCP socket. You can create the socket, but not the input stream to read it. These types of streams will be discussed where appropriate throughout the text. Such streams are not directly instantiated by developers, and are instead returned by invoking a method of a networking object.

When a low-level input stream is created, it will read from a source of information that supplies it with data (see Figure 4-5). Input streams act as consumers of information—they devour bytes of information as they read them. That is, bytes are read from a file sequentially—subject to a few exceptions, once they have been read, you can't go back and read them again. They haven't been erased; the stream has simply moved on to the next byte of information.

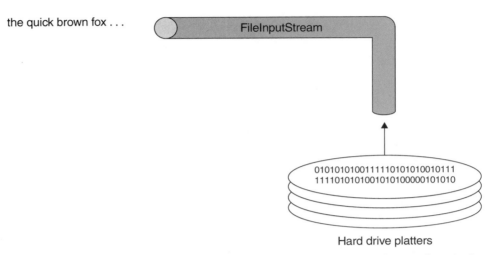

the quick brown fox . . .

FileInputStream

010101010011111010101010101111
11110101010010101010000101010

Hard drive platters

**Figure 4-5** Reading from a low-level stream is done sequentially—you can't normally go back to the beginning and read again.

Of course, the sequential nature of input streams isn't necessarily a bad thing. We wouldn't want to store the entire contents of a five-megabyte file in memory just so that a program had the option of going back to an earlier point in time. However, some high-level filter streams support a limited push-back ability, allowing you to jump back to a specific point in the stream, on the condition that the point is marked. This functionality is useful at times for looking ahead to see the contents of a stream, but is not supported by many filter streams.

A further point that readers should be aware of is that reading from an input stream uses blocking I/O. *Blocking I/O* is a term applied to any form of input or output that does not immediately return from an operation. For example, reading from a file will block indefinitely, until the hard drive is accessible and the drive read head moves to the correct location to retrieve a byte of data. This is usually fairly quick, but if you're reading a byte at a time (rather than, say, a chunk of 1,024 bytes, or a kilobyte) then the number of read operations that may block can add up to some significant delays. When reading from a network connection, where delays can range from milliseconds to tens of seconds—or, worse still, not at all—then blocking I/O can cause performance problems. This can be alleviated, but not eliminated, by using data buffering, discussed later in the chapter.

### 4.2.1.1 The java.io.InputStream Class

The abstract `InputStream` class defines methods, listed below, common to all input streams; all of them are public.

## Methods

- `int available()` throws `java.io.IOException`—returns the number of bytes currently available for reading. More bytes may be available in the future, but reading more than the number of available bytes will result in a read that will block indefinitely.
- `void close()` throws `java.io.IOException`—closes the input stream and frees any resources (such as file handles or file locks) associated with the input stream.
- `void mark(int readLimit)`—records the current position in the input stream, to allow an input stream to revisit the same sequence of bytes at a later point in the future, by invoking the `InputStream.reset()` method. Not every input stream will support this functionality.
- `boolean markSupported()`—returns "true" if an input stream supports the `mark()` and `reset()` methods, "false" if it does not. Unless overridden by a subclass of `InputStream`, the default value returned is false.
- `int read()` throws `java.io.IOException`—returns the next byte of data from the stream. Subclasses of `InputStream` usually override this method to provide custom functionality (such as reading from a file or a string). As mentioned earlier, input streams use blocking I/O, and will block indefinitely if no further bytes are yet available. When the end of the stream is reached, a value of −1 is returned.
- `int read(byte[] byteArray)` throws `java.io.IOException`—reads a sequence of bytes and places them in the specified byte array, by calling the `read()` method repeatedly until the array is filled or no more data can be obtained. This method returns the number of bytes successfully read, or −1 if the end of the stream has been reached.
- `int read(byte[] byteArray, int offset, int length)` throws `java.io.IOException, java.lang.IndexOutOfBoundsException`—reads a sequence of bytes, placing them in the specified array. Unlike the previous method, `read(byte[] byteArray)`, this method begins stuffing bytes into the array at the specified offset, and for the specified length, if possible. This allows developers to fill up only part of an array. Developers should be mindful that at runtime, out-of-bounds exceptions may be thrown if the array size, offset, and length exceed array capacity.
- `void reset()` throws `java.io.IOException`—moves the position of the input stream back to a preset mark, determined by the point in time when the `mark()` method was invoked. Few input streams support this functionality, and may cause an `IOException` to be thrown if called.
- `long skip(long amount)` throws `java.io.IOException`—reads, but ignores, the specified amount of bytes. These bytes are discarded, and

the position of the input stream is updated. Though unlikely, it is entirely possible that the specified number of bytes could not be skipped (for example, as stated in the Java API, if the end of the stream is reached). The skip method returns the number of bytes skipped over, which may be less than the requested amount.

### 4.2.1.2 Using a Low-Level Input Stream

Below we examine a practical application of using a low-level input stream to display the contents of a file. A byte at a time is read from the file and displayed to the screen. Though not the most efficient way to do this (performance could be sped up by buffering, for example), it is illustrative of how low-level streams can be read from.

*Code for FileInputStreamDemo*

```java
import java.io.*;

// Chapter 4, Listing 1
public class FileInputStreamDemo
{
    public static void main(String args[])
    {
        if (args.length != 1)
        {
            System.err.println ("Syntax - FileInputStreamDemo file");
            return;
        }

        try
        {
            // Create an input stream, reading from the
            // specified file

            InputStream fileInput = new FileInputStream ( args[0] );

            // Read the first byte of data
            int data = fileInput.read();

            // Repeat : until end of file (EOF) reached
            while (data != -1)
            {
                // Send byte to standard output
                System.out.write ( data );

                // Read next byte
                data = fileInput.read();
            }
```

```
                    // Close the file
                    fileInput.close();
            }
            catch (IOException ioe)
            {
                    System.err.println ("I/O error - " + ioe);
            }
    }
}
```

### How *FileInputStreamDemo* Works

The code for this example is quite simple to follow, and shows just how easy it is to use input streams in Java. Aside from error checking (such as the presence of a command-line parameter and exception handling), very little code is required to work with streams. There is a single line of code to create the initial `FileInputStream` object, which takes as a parameter a string representation of the location of a file.

```
// Create an input stream, reading from the specified file
InputStream fileInput = new FileInputStream ( args[0] );
```

Once the stream is created, the source of the data is not important—it may be treated as an `InputStream` object. That's the power behind object inheritance—because all of the input stream classes share a common superclass, they inherit the same method signatures to read and work with input streams. The next step is to read the first byte of data and then enter a while loop. The loop terminates when the end of the file is reached, and displays each byte of data to the user console.

```
// Read the first byte of data
int data = fileInput.read();

// Repeat : until end of file (EOF) reached
while (data != -1)
{
        // Send byte to standard output
        System.out.write ( data );

        // Read next byte
        data = fileInput.read();
}
```

Finally, the program closes the input stream and then terminates. The power of streams in Java is clearly conveyed by this small number of lines of code.

### Running *FileInputStreamDemo*

Running the example is easy. Simply pass the name of a file to the program as a command-line parameter, and the contents of the file will be displayed.

For example, to display the file document.txt that is located in the current directory, the following command would be executed:

```
java FileInputStreamDemo document.txt
```

### 4.2.2 Writing to an Output Stream

A number of output streams are available in the java.io package for a variety of tasks, such as writing to data structures including strings and arrays, or to files or communication pipes. As seen in Table 4.2, six important low-level output streams may be written to (in addition to filter streams that may be connected to these low-level streams).

As mentioned earlier, there are other streams which may be written to that developers cannot create and instantiate directly, but that nonetheless will be encountered. For example, a networking stream such as a connection to a TCP service is not created directly, but is provided by invoking the appropriate method on a socket. These types of streams will be covered in later chapters, as appropriate.

Output streams work somewhat differently from input streams, as might reasonably be expected due to their different purposes. While an input stream is a data consumer, an output stream is a data producer—it literally creates bytes of information and transmits them to something else (such as a file or data structure or network connection). Like input streams, data is communicated sequentially; that is, the first byte in will be the first byte out (see Figure 4-6). This

**Table 4-2** Low-Level Output Streams of the java.io Package

| Low-Level Output Stream | Purpose of Stream |
| --- | --- |
| ByteArrayOutputStream | Writes bytes of data to an array of bytes. |
| FileOutputStream | Writes bytes of data to a local file. |
| PipedOutputStream | Writes bytes of data to a communications pipe, which will be connected to a java.io.PipedInputStream. |
| StringBufferOutputStream | Writes bytes to a string buffer (a substitute data structure for the fixed-length string). |
| System.err | Writes bytes of data to the error stream of the user console, also known as standard error. In addition, this stream is cast to a PrintStream. |
| System.out | Writes bytes of data to the user console, also known as standard output. In addition, this stream is cast to a PrintStream. |

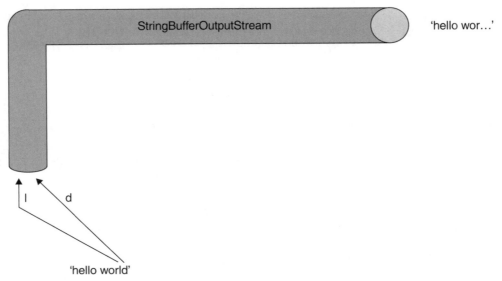

**Figure 4-6**   Output streams send data one byte at a time, sequentially.

approach is analogous to a FIFO queue, in which data that is sent may be read back in order, without regard to sequencing. Unlike some specialized filter input streams, which allow you to "go back *n*" bytes within a sequence, once data is sent to an output stream it cannot be undone. Consider it as like an e-mail message—once sent you cannot (no matter how much you may want to) take it back.

Bytes may be sent one at a time or as part of an array. However, when bytes are read one at a time, individual byte writes may affect system performance. Reading information can block indefinitely, but writing information may also block for small amounts of time. This is not normally as significant an issue as the case of blocking read operations, however, as the bytes are ready to send. Bytes to be read may not be immediately available, and are several orders of magnitude slower. This problem can be avoided by using buffering, discussed later in the chapter.

### 4.2.2.1 The java.io.OutputStream Class

The java.io.OutputStream class is an abstract class, from which all output streams (be they low-level streams or filter streams) are inherited. The following methods are defined by the OutputStream class (all are public).

*Methods*

- void close() throws java.io.IOException—closes the output stream, notifying the other side that the stream has ended. Pending data that has not yet been sent will be sent, but no more data will be delivered.

- void flush() throws java.io.IOException—performs a "flush" of any unsent data and sends it to the recipient of the output stream. To improve performance, streams will often be buffered, so data remains unsent. This is useful at times, but obstructive at others. The method is particularly important for OutputStream subclasses that represent network operations, as flushing should always occur after a request or response is sent so that the remote side isn't left waiting for data.
- void write(int byte) throws java.io.IOException—writes the specified byte. This is an abstract method, overridden by OutputStream subclasses.
- void write(byte[] byteArray) throws java.io.IOException—writes the contents of the byte array to the output stream. The entire contents of the array (barring any error) will be written.
- void write(byte[] byteArray, int offset, int length) throws java.io.IOException—writes the contents of a subset of the byte array to the output stream. This method allows developers to specify just how much of an array is sent, and which part, as opposed to the OutputStream.write(byte[] byteArray) method, which sends the entire contents of an array.

### 4.2.2.2 Using a Low-Level Output Stream

Each output stream operates differently; for specific details, the Java API documentation should be consulted for the relevant class. The simple example given below is sufficient to show how output streams are used. It concerns an application that copies a file by reading the contents of the file and writing it, one byte at a time, to a new file.

*Code for FileOutputStreamDemo*

```
import java.io.*;

// Chapter 4, Listing 2
public class FileOutputStreamDemo
{
    public static void main(String args[])
    {
    // Two parameters are required, the source and destination
        if (args.length != 2)
        {
            System.err.println
          ("Syntax - FileOutputStreamDemo src dest");
            return;
        }
```

```
String source = args[0];
String destination = args[1];

try
{
    // Open source file for input
    InputStream input = new FileInputStream( source );

    System.out.println ("Opened " +
            source + " for reading.");

    // Output file for output
    OutputStream output = new FileOutputStream
    ( destination );

    System.out.println ("Opened " +
            destination + " for writing.");

    int data = input.read();

    while ( data != -1)
    {
        // Write byte of data to our file
        output.write (data);

        // Read next byte
        data=input.read();
    }

    // Close both streams
    input.close();
    output.close();

    System.out.println ("I/O streams closed");
}
catch (IOException ioe)
{
    System.err.println ("I/O error - " + ioe);
}
}
}
```

## How FileOutputStreamDemo Works

Writing to an output stream involves little more effort than reading from one (particularly if only bytes are being sent). This example reads from a file and writes to another. To open a file for writing, a FileOutputStream is used. This class will create a file, if one does not already exist, or override the contents of the file (unless opened in append mode).

```
// Output file for output
OutputStream output = new FileOutputStream ( destination );
```

Once opened, it can be written to by invoking the `OutputStream.write()` method. This method is called repeatedly by the application, to write the contents of a file that it is reading.

```
while ( data != -1)
{
        // Write byte of data to our file
        output.write (data);

        // Read next byte
        data=input.read();
}
```

Finally, both of the files are closed, and the copied file may now be read or modified by other applications.

### Running FileOutputStreamDemo

This example copies a file. Two parameters are required: the first represents the source file, and the second the destination for the duplicate.

For example, to copy the file document.txt that is located in the current directory to mybackup.txt, the following command would be executed:

```
java FileOutputStreamDemo document.txt mybackup.txt
```

## 4.3   Filter Streams

While the basic low-level streams provide a simple mechanism to read and write bytes of information, their flexibility is limited. After all, reading bytes is complex (for people, at least), and there's more to the world that just bytes of data. Text, for example, is a sequence of characters, and other forms of data like numbers take up more than a single byte. Byte-level communication can also be inefficient, and data buffering can improve performance. To overcome these limitations, filter streams are used.

Filter streams add additional functionality to an existing stream, by processing data in some form (such as buffering for performance) or offering additional methods that allow data to be accessed in a different manner (for example, reading a line of text rather than a sequence of bytes). Filters make life easier for programmers, as they can work with familiar constructs such as strings, lines of text, and numbers, rather than individual bytes. Instead of the programmer writing a string one character at a time and converting each character to an int value for the `OutputStream.write(int)` method, the filter stream does this for them.

### 4.3.1   Connecting a Filter Stream to an Existing Stream

Filter streams can be connected to any other stream, to a low-level stream or even another filter stream. Filter streams are extended from the java.io. FilterInputStream and java.io.FilterOutputStream classes. Each filter stream supports one or more constructors that accept either an InputStream, in the case of an input filter, or an OutputStream, in the case of an output filter. Connecting a filter stream is as simple as creating a new instance of a filter, passing an instance of an existing stream, and using the filter from then on to read or write.

For example, suppose you wanted to connect a PrintStream (used to print text to an OutputStream subclass) to a stream that wrote to a file. The following code may be used to connect the filter stream and write a message using the new filter.

```
FileOutputStream fout = new FileOutputStream ( somefile );
PrintStream pout = new PrintStream (fout);
pout.println ("hello world");
```

This process is fairly simple as long as the programmer remembers two things:

1. Read and write operations must take place on the new filter stream.
2. Read and write operations on the underlying stream can still take place, but not at the same time as an operation on the filter stream.

### 4.3.2   Useful Filter Input Streams

There are many useful filter streams, some of which are present in all versions of Java; others (such as streams for data compression) are available only in JDK1.1 or Java 2. The most common, and most useful, are shown in Table 4-3. These streams are discussed in detail below.

#### 4.3.2.1 BufferedInputStream Class

The purpose of I/O buffering is to improve system performance. Rather than reading a byte at a time, a large number of bytes are read together the first time the read() method is invoked. When an attempt is made to read subsequent bytes, they are taken from the buffer, not the underlying input stream. This improves data access time and can reduce the number of times an application blocks for input.

#### Constructors

- BufferedInputStream (InputStream input)—creates a buffered stream that will read from the specified InputStream object.

**Table 4-3** Filter Input Streams of the `java.io` Package

| Filter Input Stream | Purpose of Stream |
| --- | --- |
| BufferedInputStream | Buffers access to data, to improve efficiency. |
| DataInputStream | Reads primitive data types, such as an int, a float, a double, or even a line of text, from an input stream. |
| LineNumberInputStream | Maintains a count of which line is being read, based on interpretation of end-of-line characters. Handles both Unix and Windows end-of-line sequences. |
| PushBackInputStream | Allows a byte of data to be pushed into the head of the stream. |

- `BufferedInputStream (InputStream input, int bufferSize)` throws `java.lang.IllegalArgumentException`—creates a buffered stream, of the specified size, which reads from the `InputStream` object passed as a parameter. This allows developers to specify a size, which can improve efficiency if large amounts of data are going to be read. The buffer size specified must be greater than or equal to one.

### Methods

No additional methods are provided by the `BufferedInputStream` class. However, it does override the `markSupported()` method, indicating that it supports the `mark(int)` and `reset()` methods.

### 4.3.2.2 DataInputStream Class

A frequent task in any programming language is reading and writing primitive data types such as numbers and characters. These information types are not easily represented as bytes (for example, some data types take up more than one byte of information). Developers should not be concerned, however, with the way in which representation occurs. Instead, the data types can be read simply by invoking methods of the `DataInputStream` class, which handles the translation automatically. This class implements the `java.io.DataInput` interface.

**NOTE:** Readers should be aware that only conversion from byte(s) to a data type is performed. Reading a character by invoking the `readChar()` method won't convert a byte value into a number. It is a common mistake to think that a byte value, for example 0009, will be converted into the numerical character 9.

## Constructors

- `DataInputStream (InputStream input)`—creates a data input stream, reading from the specified input stream.

## Methods

Many methods are added to the `DataInputStream` class, in order to facilitate access to new data types.

- `boolean readBoolean()` throws `java.io.EOFException, java.io.IOException`—reads a byte from the input stream, and returns "true" if the byte is nonzero. If no more data is available, an exception will be thrown to indicate that the end of the stream has been reached.
- `byte readByte()` throws `java.io.EOFException, java.io.IOException`—reads a byte value from the input stream. This byte is an actual byte datatype, as opposed to the byte returned by the `InputStream.read()` method, which is represented by an `int` value. An exception may be thrown to indicate the end of the stream.
- `char readChar()` throws `java.io.EOFException, java.io.IOException`—reads a character from the underlying input stream. If no more data is available, an exception will be thrown.
- `double readDouble()` throws `java.io.EOFException, java.io.IOException`—reads eight bytes from the input stream and returns a double value. If the end of stream has been reached, an exception will be thrown.
- `float readFloat()` throws `java.io.EOFException, java.io.IOException`—reads four bytes from the input stream and converts this to a float value. If the end of the stream has been reached, an exception will be thrown to indicate the end of the stream.
- `void readFully(byte[] byteArray)` throws `java.io.EOFException, java.io.IOException`—fills the specified `byteArray` with bytes, read from the underlying input stream. Unlike the `InputStream.read(byte[] byteArray)` method, which returns an `int` value containing the number of bytes read, this method will throw an exception if the byte array could not be filled.
- `void readFully(byte[] byteArray, int offset, int length)` throws `java.io.EOFException, java.io.IOException`—overloaded version of the `DataInputStream.readFully(byte[] array)` method, which allows the offset within an array and the length of data read to be specified.
- `float readInt()` throws `java.io.EOFException, java.io.IOException`—reads four bytes from the input stream and converts this to an `int` value. Unlike the `InputStream.read()` method, which

returns −1 if no more data can be read, an exception is thrown to indicate the end of a stream.

- `String readLine()` throws `java.io.IOException`—reads an entire line of text from the underlying input stream and converts it to a string. If no data at all could be read, a null value is returned. Note that this method is deprecated as of JDK1.1, and if only text is being read, the programmer is advised to use a reader object (discussed later in the chapter) rather than an input stream.

- `long readLong` throws `java.io.EOFException, java.io.IOException`— reads eight bytes and converts them into a `long` value. If no data could be read, an exception will be thrown.

- `short readShort()` throws `java.io.EOFException, java.io.IOException`—reads two bytes and converts them into a `short` value. If the two bytes could not be read, an exception is thrown to indicate the end of the stream.

- `int readUnsignedByte()` throws `java.io.EOFException, java.io.IOException`—reads an unsigned byte and converts it to an `int` value. Bytes are in the range −128 to 127, but an unsigned byte will be in the range 0 to 255. If the end of the input stream was reached, an exception is thrown.

- `int readUnsignedShort()` throws `java.io.EOFException, java.io.IOException`—reads two bytes and converts them to an `int` value between 0 and 65535. If the two bytes were not read, an exception will be thrown.

- `String readUTF()` throws `java.io.EOFException, java.io.IOException`—reads a string from the underlying input stream using a modified Universal Transfer Format (UTF). UTF doesn't use a carriage return to indicate the end of a string, and so this character can be safely included within a string written to a file or other such stream using UTF notation. If the end of the stream is encountered, an exception will be thrown.

- `static String readUTF(DataInputStream input)` throws `java.io.EOFException, java.io.IOException`—returns a string read using UTF from the specified input stream. This is a static method, and will throw an exception if the end of the stream is reached.

- `int skipBytes(int number)` throws `java.io.IOException`—attempts to skip over the specified number of bytes. If this is not possible (for example, if the end of the stream has been reached), an exception is not thrown. Instead, the number of bytes read and discarded is returned as an int value. Unlike the `InputStream.skip(long)` method, this method takes an `int` as a parameter.

### 4.3.2.3 LineNumberInputStream Class

This class provides helpful functionality by tracking the number of lines read from an input stream. It is deprecated as of JDK1.1, however, since the preferred way to process text data is to use a reader class. Also, line numbers are not very serviceable in terms of a stream of bytes. Nonetheless, if writing for JDK1.02 systems, it may be useful.

*Constructors*

- `LineNumberInputStream(InputStream input)`—creates a line number stream, reading from the specified input stream.

*Methods*

- `int getLineNumber()`—returns the number of lines that have been read by this input stream.
- `void setLineNumber(int number)`—modifies the line number counter to the specified value.

### 4.3.2.4 PushBackInputStream Class

The `PushBackInputStream` class allows a single byte to be read and then "pushed back" into the stream for later reading. An internal buffer is maintained that allows data to be pushed back into the front of the input stream buffer, or added if the data had never been read from it. This is useful when the programmer needs to take a "sneak peek" at what's coming—for example in a text parser or to determine what the next command in a communications protocol is going to be.

*Constructors*

- `PushBackInputStream(InputStream input)`—creates a `PushBackInput-Stream` that will read from the specified input stream.
- `PushBackInputStream(InputStream input, int bufferSize)` throws `java.lang.IllegalArgumentException`—creates a `PushBackInput-Stream` that will read from an input stream and use a buffer of the specified size. If a value of less than one is specified for the buffer size, an exception will be thrown.

*Methods*

- `void unread(byte[] byteArray)` throws `java.io.IOException`—pushes back the contents of the specified array. If a buffer overrun occurs, an exception is thrown.
- `void unread(byte[] byteArray, int offset, int length)` throws `java.io.IOException`—pushes back a subset of the contents of the

specified array, starting at the specified offset and lasting for the specified duration. If a buffer overrun occurs, an exception is thrown.

- `void unread(int byte) throws java.io.IOException`—pushes back the specified byte into the front of the buffer. If a buffer overrun occurs, an exception is thrown.

### *4.3.3 Useful Filter Output Streams*

While there are plenty of filter input streams, a few useful output streams are available as well. The most useful are presented in Table 4-4 and discussed in detail below.

#### 4.3.3.1 BufferedOutputStream Class

The `BufferedOutputStream` provides data buffering similar to the `BufferedInputStream`. As suggested by the name of the class, however, it buffers writes, not reads. An internal buffer is maintained, and when the buffer is complete (or earlier, if a request to flush the buffer is made), the buffer contents are dumped to the output stream to which the buffered stream is connected.

#### *Constructors*

- `BufferedOutputStream (OutputStream output)`—creates a buffer for writing to the specified output stream. The default size of this buffer is 512 bytes in length.
- `BufferedOutputStream (OutputStream output, int bufferSize)` throws `java.lang.IllegalArgumentException`—creates a buffer for writing to the specified output stream, overriding the default buffer sizing. The buffer is set to the specified buffer size, which must be greater than zero or an exception is thrown.

#### *Methods*

No extra methods have been added to this class. However, the `flush()` method is important to be aware of—this has been overridden, and will flush the

**Table 4-4**  Useful Filter Output Streams of the `java.io` Package

| Filter Output Stream | Purpose of Stream |
|---|---|
| `BufferedOutputStream` | Provides buffering of data writes, to improve efficiency |
| `DataOutputStream` | Writes primitive datatypes, such as bytes and numbers |
| `PrintStream` | Offers additional methods for writing lines of text, and other datatypes as text |

contents of a buffer, sending it immediately to the output stream it is connected to. This is particularly important in networking, as a protocol request can't be sent if it is still stuck in the buffer, and the remote program may be waiting for a response.

### 4.3.3.2 DataOutputStream Class

Like its sister class, `DataInputStream`, the `DataOutputStream` class is designed to deal with primitive datatypes, such as numbers or bytes. Most of the read methods of `DataInputStream` have a corresponding write method mirrored in `DataOutputStream`. This allows developers to write datatypes to a file or other type of stream, and to have them read back by another Java application without any compatibility issues over how primitive datatypes are represented by different hardware and software platforms. It implements the `java.io.DataOutput` interface, which provides additional methods for writing primitive datatypes.

#### Constructors

- `DataOutputStream (OutputStream output)`—creates a data output stream, which will write to the specified stream.

#### Methods

The class adds the following new methods, all of which are public unless otherwise noted.

- `int size()`—returns the number of bytes written to the data output stream at any given moment.
- `void writeBoolean (boolean value) throws java.io.IOException`— writes the specified boolean value, represented as a one-byte value. If the boolean value is "true," the value 1 is sent, and if "false," the value 0 is sent.
- `void writeByte (int byte) throws java.io.IOException`—writes the specified byte to the output stream.
- `void writeBytes (String string) throws java.io.IOException`—writes the entire contents of a string to the output stream a byte at a time.
- `void writeChar (int char) throws java.io.IOException`—writes the character (represented by an `int` value) to the output stream as a two-byte value.
- `void writeChars (String string) throws java.io.IOException`— writes the entire contents of a string to the output stream, represented as two-byte values.
- `void writeDouble(double doubleValue) throws java.io.IOException`—converts the specified double value to a long value, and then converts it to an eight-byte value.

- void writeFloat(float floatValue) throws java.io.IOException—converts the specified float value to an int, and then writes it as a four-byte value.
- void writeInt(int intValue) throws java.io.IOException—writes an int value as a four-byte value.
- void writeLong(long longValue) throws java.io.IOException—writes a long value as eight bytes.
- void writeShort(int intValue) throws java.io.IOException—writes a short value as two bytes.
- void writeUTF(String string) throws java.io.IOException—writes a string using UTF-8 encoding. This string may be read back by using the DataInputStream.readUTF() method, without worrying about issues of string termination and the presence of carriage returns or linefeeds.

### 4.3.3.3 PrintStream Class

The PrintStream is the most unusual of all filter output streams. Aside from the change in naming convention (PrintStream versus the expected PrintOutputStream), it is atypical in that it overrides methods inherited from FilterOutputStream without throwing the expected java.io.IOException class. The PrintStream adds additional methods as well, none of which may throw an IOException. No errors are overtly reported, and instead the presence of an error is determined by invoking the checkError() method—although no further details may be obtained as to the cause of the error. Despite its idiosyncrasies, the PrintStream is an extremely useful class, as it provides a convenient way to print primitive datatypes as text using the print(..) method, and to print these with line separators using the println(..) method.

### Constructors

- PrintStream (OutputStream output)—creates a print stream for printing of datatypes as text.
- PrintStream (OutputStream output, boolean flush)—creates a print stream for printing of datatypes as text. If the specified boolean flag is set to "true," whenever a byte array, println method, or newline character is sent, the underlying buffer will be automatically flushed.

### Methods

- boolean checkError()—automatically flushes the output stream and checks to see if an error has occurred. Instead of throwing an IOException, an internal flag is maintained that checks for errors.
- void print(boolean value)—prints a boolean value.

- void print(char character)—prints a character value.
- void print(char[] charArray)—prints an array of characters.
- void print(double doubleValue)—prints a double value.
- void print(float floatValue)—prints a float value.
- void print(int intValue)—prints an int value.
- void print(long longValue)—prints a long value.
- void print(Object obj)—prints the value of the specified object's toString() method.
- void print(String string)—prints a string's contents.
- void println()—sends a line separator (such as '\n'). This value is system dependent and determined by the value of the system property "line.separator."
- void println(char character)—prints a character value, followed by a println().
- void println(char[] charArray)—prints an array of characters, followed by a println().
- void println(double doubleValue)—prints a double value, followed by a println().
- void println(float floatValue)—prints a float value, followed by a println().
- void println(int intValue)—prints an int value, followed by a println().
- void println(long longValue)—prints a long value, followed by a println().
- void println(Object obj)—prints the specified object's toString() method, followed by a println().
- void println(String string)—prints a string followed by a line separator.
- protected void setError()—modifies the error flag to a value of "true."

## 4.4 Readers and Writers

While input streams and output streams may be used to read and write text as well as bytes of information and primitive data types, a better alternative is to use readers and writers. Readers and writers were introduced in JDK1.1 to better support Unicode character streams.

### 4.4.1 What Are Unicode Characters?

Unicode is an extended character set. Most people think of characters as being composed of 8 bits of data, offering a range of 256 possible characters. Low

ASCII (0–127) characters are followed by high ASCII characters (128–255). The high ASCII characters represent characters and symbols such as those used in foreign languages or punctuation. However, people quickly realized that even 256 characters were not enough to handle the many characters used in languages around the world. This is where Unicode came in.

Unicode characters are represented by 16 bits, allowing for a maximum of 65,536 possible characters—an enormous number. Unicode characters are supported by Java, although many developers are unaware of their use. Java also supports a modified form called UTF-8. This is a variable-width encoding format; some characters are a single byte and others multiple bytes.

**NOTE:** For those wanting to learn more about Unicode and the importance of an international standard for character representation, the Unicode Web site has an impressive amount of information available at http://www.unicode.org/.

### 4.4.2  The Importance of Readers and Writers

Readers and writers are a better alternative than input streams and output streams when used on text data. For those dealing solely with primitive data-types, use of input streams and output streams may by all means be continued. However, if applications are processing text information only, use of a reader and/or a writer, to better support Unicode characters, should be considered.

**NOTE:** Programmers may notice compilation warnings when compiling code that uses methods such as `DataInputStream.readLine()`. These are warnings, however, and not errors. If a good reason exists for use of a deprecated method like `DataInputStream.readLine()`, such as backward compatibility with older JDK1.02 virtual machines, then these warnings may be ignored. A better alternative, if possible, is to use a reader or writer such as `BufferedReader`, which also provides a `readLine()` method.

Readers and writers support Unicode character sequences. Internationalization may not seem like a significant concern for those of us with an English-speaking background. However, in a growing global economy, internationalization may become more important, and the Y2K bug (which, while overrated, required significant cost and effort to repair) certainly taught us that software should be written with an eye toward the future.

### 4.4.3   From Input Streams to Readers

The java.io.InputStream class has a character-based equivalent in the form of the java.io.Reader class. The reader class has similar method signatures to that of the InputStream class, and existing code may be quickly converted to use it. However, some slight changes are made to the method signatures, to support character, and not byte, reading. Additionally, the available() method has been removed, and replaced by the ready() method.

#### 4.4.3.1   The java.io.Reader Class

*Constructors*

No public constructors are available for this class. Instead, a reader subclass should be instantiated.

*Methods*

The class includes the following methods, all of which are public:

- void close() throws java.io.IOException—closes the reader.
- void mark(int amount) throws java.io.IOException—marks the current position within the reader, and uses the specified amount of characters as a buffer. Not every reader will support the mark(int) and reset() methods.
- boolean markSupported()—returns "true" if the reader supports mark and reset operations.
- int read() throws java.io.IOException—reads and returns a character, blocking if no character is yet available. If the end of the reader's stream has been reached, a value of –1 is returned.
- int read(char[] characterArray) throws java.io.IOException— populates an array of characters with data. This method returns an int value, representing the number of bytes that were read. If the end of the reader's stream is reached, a value of –1 is returned and the array is not modified.
- int read(char[] characterArray, int offset, int length) throws java.io.IOException—populates a subset of the array with data, starting at the specified offset and lasting for the specified duration. This method returns an int value, representing the number of bytes read, or –1 if no bytes could be obtained.
- boolean ready() throws java.io.IOException—returns "true" if there is data available, or "false" if not. This is similar to the InputStream. available() method, except that the number of bytes/characters is not available.

- `void reset()` throws `java.io.IOException`—attempts to reset the reader's stream, by moving back to an earlier position. Not every reader supports either mark or reset, and an exception could be thrown or the request ignored.
- `long skip(long amount)` throws `java.io.IOException`—reads and discards the specified number of characters, unless the end of the input stream is reached or another error occurs. The skip method returns the number of characters successfully skipped.

### 4.4.4 Types of Low-Level Readers

Like input streams, there are a variety of low-level readers (which connect to a data source, such as a file or a data structure), and there are filter readers for high-level communication tasks. Table 4-5 shows the important low-level readers of the `java.io` package.

#### 4.4.4.1 CharArrayReader Class

The `CharArrayReader` class is a reader that (as is indicated by its name) obtains data by reading characters from an array.

*Constructors*

- `CharArrayReader(char[] charArray)`—creates a character array reader that will operate on the specified array.
- `CharArrayReader(char[] charArray, int offset, int length)`— creates a character array reader that will operate only on a subset of the specified array, starting at the specified offset and lasting for the specified length.

**Table 4-5**  Low-Level Reader Streams of the `java.io` Package

| Low-Level Reader | Purpose of Reader |
| --- | --- |
| CharArrayReader | Reads from a character array |
| FileReader | Reads from a file on the local file system, just like a `FileInputStream` |
| PipedReader | Reads a sequence of characters from a thread communications pipe, exactly like a `PipedInputStream` |
| StringReader | Reads a sequence of characters from a String, as if it were a `StringBufferInputStream` |
| InputStreamReader | Bridges the divide between an input stream and a reader, by reading from the input stream |

*Methods*

The CharArrayReader adds no new methods.

### 4.4.4.2 FileReader Class

This reader obtains its data directly from a local file, similar to the File-InputStream class. Care must be taken, as with the FileInputStream class, when creating an instance of it, as an exception will be thrown if the file could not be located (or if security access permissions restrict it from being read).

*Constructors*

- FileReader(File file) throws java.io.FileNotFoundException—creates a reader that will access the contents of the specified file object, if the file it represents exists.
- FileReader(String filename) throws java.io.FileNotFoundException—creates a reader that will access the contents of the specified filename, if it exists.
- FileReader(FileDescriptor descriptor)—creates a reader that will access the contents of the specified descriptor handle.

*Methods*

The FileReader class adds no new methods.

### 4.4.4.3 PipedReader Class

This reader class is used to establish a pipe between one thread and another (for further information on this topic, see Chapter 7, "Multi-threaded Applications"). It is the equivalent of the PipedInputStream class.

*Constructors*

- PipedReader()—creates an unconnected pipe reader.
- PipedReader(PipedWriter writer)—creates a connected pipe that will read the output of the specified writer.

*Methods*

A single (public) method is added by this class.

- void connect(PipedWriter writer) throws java.io.IOException—connects the reader to the specified writer. Any output that is sent by the piped writer may then be read by the piped reader.

### 4.4.4.4 StringReader Class

While it is sometimes useful to work with a character array, most programmers prefer to deal with strings. The `StringReader` class offers a substitute to the `CharArrayReader`, accepting a string as an input source.

#### Constructors

- `StringReader(String stringToBeRead)`—reads from the beginning of the specified string until the end.

#### Methods

No additional methods are added.

### 4.4.4.5 InputStreamReader Class

While readers are quite common, there is still a need for backward compatibility with older input streams, particularly those written by third parties for which there is no equivalent reader class. For example, the `System.in` member variable is an `InputStream` instance that can read input from a user. There is no comparable reader class for this. The solution is to connect an `InputStreamReader` to an `InputStream` instance, which will perform the necessary translation. Furthermore, specialized character encoding may be used.

#### Constructors

- `InputStreamReader(InputStream input)`—connects an input stream to the reader.
- `InputStreamReader(InputStream input, String encoding)` throws `java.io.UnsupportedEncodingException`—connects an input stream to the reader using the specified encoding form. If the encoding form isn't supported, an exception is thrown.

#### Methods

The `InputStreamReader` class adds the following public method:

- `String getEncoding()`—returns the name of the character encoding used by this stream.

### 4.4.4.6 Combining Streams and Readers

To illustrate the use of input streams and readers together, we'll examine how an input stream may be converted to a reader for easy character reading without using a `DataInputStream`.

### Code for InputStreamToReaderDemo

```java
import java.io.*;

// Chapter 4, Listing 3
public class InputStreamToReaderDemo
{
    public static void main(String args[])
    {
        try
        {
            System.out.print ("Please enter your name : ");

            // Get the input stream representing standard input
            InputStream input = System.in;

            // Create an InputStreamReader
            InputStreamReader reader = new
            InputStreamReader ( input );

            // Connect to a buffered reader, to use the
            // readLine() method
            BufferedReader bufReader = new BufferedReader
            ( reader );

            String name = bufReader.readLine();

            System.out.println ("Pleased to meet you, " +
            name);
        }
        catch (IOException ioe)
        {
            System.err.println ("I/O error : " + ioe);
        }
    }
}
```

### How InputStreamToReaderDemo Works

The code is fairly self-explanatory. We start by connecting an InputStream-Reader to standard input (represented by System.in). We connect a Buffered-Reader, to maximize performance, and then read a single line of text.

### Running InputStreamToReaderDemo

Running this example is straightforward. To run the application, type in your name at the prompt and hit enter. To run the example, use:

```java
java InputStreamToReaderDemo
```

### 4.4.5 Types of Filter Readers

Filter readers, just like filter input streams, provide additional functionality in the form of new methods, or process data in a different way (such as buffering). Generally, but not always, they are extended from the java.io. FilterReader class, and always connect to another reader. Filters may even be chained together (for example, connecting a BufferedReader to a custom reader, or vice versa). Some useful filter readers are listed in Table 4-6.

#### 4.4.5.1 BufferedReader

One of the most frustrating problems with reading data from a writer, as with an input stream, is that blocking I/O is used. When attempting to read, the application will block until data is available. This can last for a few milliseconds, a few seconds, or even worse, a few minutes. When this happens frequently, the performance and responsiveness of software suffers. An alternative is to buffer data so that reads are grouped together for better performance. Just as the BufferedInputStream buffers bytes of data, the BufferedReader buffers characters. Also, although one would not guess it from the name, the BufferedReader is a partial substitute for the DataInputStream class; it provides a readLine() method that is not deprecated.

#### Constructors

- BufferedReader (Reader reader)—reads data from the specified reader into a buffer.
- BufferedReader (Reader reader, int bufferSize) throws java.lang. IllegalArgumentException—reads data from the specified reader into a buffer, which is allocated to the specified size. The buffer size must be greater than zero.

**Table 4-6** Useful Filter Readers of the java.io Package

| Filter Reader | Purpose of Stream |
| --- | --- |
| BufferedReader | Buffers access to data, to improve efficiency |
| FilterReader | Provides a class to extend when creating filters |
| PushBackReader | Allows text data to be pushed back into the reader's stream |
| LineNumberReader | Buffered reader subclass, which maintains a count of which line it is on |

*Methods*

The following public method is added by `BufferedReader`, as a replacement for the deprecated `DataInputStream.readLine()` method. In addition, the reader overrides the `markSupported()` method, to indicate that it supports the mark and reset operations.

- `String readLine()` throws `java.io.IOException`—reads a line of text from the underlying stream. The line is terminated by a line separator sequence, such as a carriage return/linefeed.

### 4.4.5.2 FilterReader

Rather than perform a practical action, this class acts as a template on which other filters can be constructed. If a custom filter needs to be written, the class should be extended, and methods overridden or new ones added.

*Constructor*

The `FilterReader` class has been designed so that it cannot be instantiated by making its constructor protected; the class should instead be extended.

*Methods*

The `FilterReader` class defines no new methods, but subclasses are free to add additional methods or override existing ones.

### 4.4.5.3 PushBackReader

This class allows characters to be "pushed back" into the head of a reader's input queue, so that it may be read again. This allows programs to peek ahead at the next character and then push it back into the queue.

*Constructor*

- `PushBackReader(Reader reader)`—creates a push-back reader with a single character buffer.
- `PushBackReader(Reader reader, int bufferSize)` throws `java.lang.IllegalArgumentException`—creates a push-back reader with a larger buffer, of the specified size. The buffer size must be greater than zero, or an exception is thrown.

*Methods*

The following new methods (all public) are added in `PushBackReader`.

- `void unread(int character)` throws `java.io.IOException`—pushes the character back to the beginning of the queue. If the queue is full, an exception is thrown.

- `void unread(char[] charArray)` throws `java.io.IOException`—pushes every character in the specified array into the queue. If full, an exception is thrown.
- `void unread(char[] charArray, int offset, int length)` throws `java.io.IOException`—pushes a subset of the characters in the specified array into the queue, starting at the specified offset and lasting for the specified length. If full, an exception is thrown.

### 4.4.5.4 LineNumberReader

The `LineNumberReader` class provides a useful line counter, which measures how many lines have been read. It is the writer equivalent of the `LineNumberInputStream`. As it extends the `BufferedReader` class, it also supports the mark/reset operations.

*Constructors*

- `LineNumberReader (Reader reader)`—creates a new line-number reader.
- `LineNumberReader (Reader reader, int size)`—creates a new line-number reader and allocates a buffer of the specified size.

*Methods*

Two new methods, to determine and to modify the line-number counter, are offered.

- `int getLineNumber()`—returns the current line number.
- `void setLineNumber(int lineNumber)`—modifies the line-number counter.

## 4.4.6 From Output Streams to Writers

Going from an output stream to a writer is not a difficult task. An equivalent class to `java.io.OutputStream`, the `java.io.Writer` class has similar method signatures and supports Unicode characters.

### 4.4.6.1 The java.io.Writer Class

*Constructors*

There are no public constructors for this class. Instead, a writer subclass should be instantiated.

*Methods*

The following methods are included in this class; all are public.

- void close() throws java.io.IOException—invokes the flush() method to send any buffered data, and then closes the writer.
- void flush() throws java.io.IOException—flushes any unsent data, sending it immediately. A buffered writer might not yet have enough data to send, and may be storing it for later. Flushing sends this data immediately, and is particularly useful when working with networking streams, as a client might want to send data immediately when a command request is made.
- void write(int character) throws java.io.IOException—writes the specified character.
- void write(char[] charArray) throws java.io.IOException—reads the entire contents of the specified character array and writes it.
- void write(char[] charArray, int offset, int length) throws java.io.IOException—reads a subset of the character array, starting at the specified offset and lasting for the specified length, and writes it.
- void write(String string) throws java.io.IOException—writes the specified string.
- void write(String string, int offset, int length) throws java.io.IOException—writes a subset of the string, starting from the specified offset and lasting for the specified length.

### 4.4.7   Types of Low-Level Writers

There are many types of low-level writers (see Table 4-7). Some of these have an OutputStream equivalent; others are brand-new classes that write to new output targets such as a character array.

**Table 4-7**   Low-Level Writers of the java.io Package

| Low-Level Writer | Purpose of Writer |
|---|---|
| CharArrayWriter | Writes to a variable length character array (and resizes as characters are added) |
| FileWriter | Writes to a file on the local file system, just like a FileOutputStream |
| PipedWriter | Writes characters to a thread communications pipe, just like a PipedOutputStream |
| StringWriter | Writes characters to a string buffer (not a string, as the name might suggest), like a StringBufferOutputStream |
| OutputStreamWriter | Writes to a legacy output stream |

### 4.4.7.1 CharArrayWriter Class

The `CharArrayWriter` maintains an internal buffer that is added to each time a write request is made, and may be converted to a character array.

#### Constructors

- `CharArrayWriter()`—creates a character array writer that can be converted to a character array.
- `CharArrayWriter(int bufferSize)` throws `java.lang.Illegal-ArgumentException`—creates a character array writer using the specified initial buffer size (which must not be negative).

#### Methods

The `CharArrayWriter` adds the following public methods:

- `char[] toCharArray`—returns a character array, containing all characters written thus far.
- `String toString()`—returns a string containing all characters written thus far.

### 4.4.7.2 FileWriter Class

The `FileWriter` class extends the `OutputStreamWriter` class (discussed later in this section), and provides a convenient way to write characters to a local file. This class is equivalent to the `FileOutputStream` class discussed earlier.

#### Constructors

- `FileWriter (File file)` throws `java.io.IOException`—creates a writer connected to the resource represented by the specified file object, if not prevented by security permissions.
- `FileWriter (FileDescriptor)` throws `java.io.IOException`—creates a writer connected to the specified descriptor handle, if allowable.
- `FileWriter(String filename)` throws `java.io.IOException`—writes to the specified file location, creating a file if one does not already exist and overwriting an existing one. If not permitted by security access restrictions, an exception will be thrown.
- `FileWriter(String filename, boolean appendFlag)` throws `java.io.IOException`—writes to the specified file location. If the `appendFlag` is set to "true," the file will be opened in append mode and data will be written to the end of the file.

## Methods

The FileWriter class provides no new methods.

### 4.4.7.3 PipedWriter Class

The purpose of the PipedWriter class is to write data that will be read by a PipedReader. These two classes are reader/writer equivalents of the PipedInputStream and PipedOutputStream classes, but may not be interchanged.

### Constructors

- PipedWriter()—creates an unconnected pipe writer.
- PipedWriter(PipedReader reader) throws java.io.IOException—creates a piped writer connected to the specified reader. The reader may later read any data written to this writer.

### Methods

The PipedWriter class adds the following public method:

- void connect (PipedReader reader) throws java.io.IOException—attempts to connect to the specified pipe, so that any data written may be read by the reader. If the pipe is already connected to another pipe, an IOException will be thrown.

### 4.4.7.4 StringWriter Class

Judging by its name, you might expect that this class allowed for writing to a string. This is not technically the case, however. A string is of fixed length and is immutable (the contents of a string may not be modified). New strings can be composed, concatenated, and assigned to a variable, but the contents of a string cannot be changed. So the question is, how does one write to a string?

Writing to a string is accomplished by using a StringBuffer. The StringBuffer class is similar to a string, but may be modified. When the modifications are complete, the StringBuffer can be converted back to a string. This is how the StringWriter class works. It maintains a string buffer, and provides a method to access the buffer contents or to convert to a string.

### Constructors

- StringWriter()—creates a new string writer, using the default-sized buffer.
- StringWriter(int startingSize)—creates a new string writer and allocates a StringBuffer of the specified size.

### Methods

The StringWriter class adds two new methods, both of which are public.

- StringBuffer getBuffer()—returns the buffer used to store data sent to the writer.
- String toString()—converts the internal buffer into a string.

## 4.4.7.5 OutputStreamWriter Class

While there are many writer classes equivalent to output stream classes in the Java API, there is still a need to maintain compatibility with older output stream classes, as most of the networking API and some third-party libraries provide only stream interfaces. The OutputStreamWriter class handles the translation between a Writer and an OuputStream, allowing new writer classes to interact with older output streams.

### Constructors

- OutputStreamWriter(OutputStream output)—creates a writer that will translate between characters and bytes, using the default character encoding.
- OutputStreamWriter(OutputStream output, String encoding) throws java.io.UnsupportedEncodingException—creates a writer that translates between characters and bytes, using the specified character encoding. If the specified encoding form is not supported, an exception is thrown.

### Methods

The OutputStreamWriter class adds the following public method:

- String getEncoding()—returns the character encoding used by the writer.

### OutputStreamToWriter Example

The example below demonstrates how a writer may be connected to an output stream by using the OutputStreamWriter class. The code to convert from an output stream to a writer is extremely compact, and doesn't require much effort.

### Code for OutputStreamToWriterDemo

```
import java.io.*;

// Chapter 4, Listing 4
public class OutputStreamToWriterDemo
{
```

```
public static void main(String args[])
{
    try
    {
        // Get the output stream representing standard
        // output
        OutputStream output = System.out;

        // Create an OutputStreamWriter
        OutputStreamWriter writer = new
        OutputStreamWriter (output);

        // Write to standard output using a writer
        writer.write ("Hello world");

        // Flush and close the writer, to ensure it is
        // written
        writer.flush(); writer.close();
    }
    catch (IOException ioe)
    {
        System.err.println ("I/O error : " + ioe);
    }
}
}
```

### How OutputStreamToWriterDemo Works

The code is fairly self-explanatory. We start by connecting an OutputStream-Writer to standard output (represented by System.out). Next, we write a line of text using our writer, and then flush the buffer so it is written to the user's screen.

### Running OutputStreamToWriterDemo

Running this example is simple. To run the example, use:

```
java OutputStreamToWriterDemo
```

## 4.4.8   Types of Filtered Writers

Table 4-8 shows writers that act as a filter, by connecting to an existing writer stream and providing different functionality. Strangely enough, there are no FilterWriter subclasses, but as the other classes perform filter-like functionality, they have been grouped together in the table.

### 4.4.8.1  BufferedWriter Class

The BufferedWriter is used to improve system performance, by buffering write requests together. This can make for a more efficient system, as I/O-bound

**Table 4-8** Filter Writers of the `java.io` Package

| Filter Writer | Purpose of Writer |
|---|---|
| `BufferedWriter` | Buffers write requests, like a `BufferedOutputStream` |
| `FilterWriter` | Abstract class for developing filter writers |
| `PrintWriter` | Provides convenient `PrintStream`-like functionality |

operations are notoriously slow (particularly when dealing with networking streams, which are several orders of magnitude slower than, say, a file stream). By reducing the number of writes and grouping them together, I/O efficiency is improved.

### Constructors

- `BufferedWriter(Writer writer)`—creates a buffered writer, connected to the specified writer. Write requests will be buffered, to improve efficiency. To send all queued data, the `flush()` method should be invoked.
- `BufferedWriter(Writer writer, int bufferSize)` throws `java.lang.IllegalArgumentException`—creates a buffered writer, with a buffer of the specified size. The size must be greater than or equal to 1.

### Methods

The `BufferedWriter` class defines no new methods.

## 4.4.8.2 FilterWriter Class

Developers creating custom filter classes should extend this class, rather than extending the `java.io.Writer` class. It provides no additional functionality, but may be used as a template on which filters can be constructed.

### Constructors

- `protected FilterWriter(Writer writer)`—creates a filter writer instance.

### Methods

The `FilterWriter` class defines no new methods, but subclasses are free to add additional methods or override existing ones.

## 4.4.8.3 PrintWriter Class

`PrintWriter` is the sister class of `PrintStream`, and provides the same methods for writing datatypes as text. Like `PrintStream`, none of the methods may throw an IOException—rather, the error state is determined by invoking the checkError() method, which returns a boolean value.

### Constructors

The constructors for this class include:

- PrintWriter(Writer writer)—creates a print writer, writing to the specified writer.
- PrintWriter(Writer writer, boolean flushFlag)—creates a print writer, the output of which may or may not be automatically flushed whenever a println() method or a line separator is sent, based on the state of the specified boolean flag. A value of "true" will flush when a println method is executed.

### Methods

The PrintWriter class implements new methods to match the signatures of the PrintStream class (see Section 4.3.3.3).

## 4.5    Object Persistence and Object Serialization

Data that can be read or written ranges from individual bytes to primitive datatypes and strings. If you wanted to, for example, write a data structure (such as a sequence of data records, composed of individual fields) out to a file, you could do so. But what if you wanted to store an entire object, composed of a series of member variables?

To do this would require that each field of the object be written individually; then at a later time, each field would be read back and assigned to an object. This is a complicated process, particularly if some member variables are marked as private or protected. Yet saving data is one of the most important functions of software—unless you're writing trivial applications, state information must be saved for a later time (and even games save data, such as high scores or save games). The solution is to use object persistence.

### 4.5.1    *What Is Object Persistence?*

Object persistence is the ability of an object to persist over time (and, if moved to a different computer or JVM, over space). Most objects in a Java Virtual Machine are fairly short-lived. When there are no references to an object, the memory space allocated to it is reclaimed by the automatic garbage collector thread. If an object is frequently used, and does not lose references to it, it will still die at some point in time—after all, even in daemon processes that run for days or weeks on end, the JVM will terminate eventually and the object will be destroyed.

Object persistence allows an object to outlive the JVM that hosts it. A custom class representing a key component of a system, a `java.util.Vector` list containing state data, or even a `java.util.Properties` object containing system settings, are all good examples of objects that might be important enough to be needed every time a program is run. While the memory address space that is allocated to an object cannot be locked away for later use, the data stored there comprising the essence of an object may be stored elsewhere to be read and reconstructed at another date. The technique in Java is known as object serialization.

### 4.5.2 *What Is Object Serialization?*

Object serialization is the technique by which object persistence is realized. Basically, object serialization controls how the data that comprises an object's state information (the individual member variables, whether public, private, or protected) is written as a sequence of bytes. The serialized object might be sent over a network (enabling technologies such as remote method invocation, discussed in Chapter 11), or saved to a disk so that it can be accessed at some point in the future. This allows objects to move from one JVM to another, whether located on the same machine or a remote one.

Serialization works by examining the variables of an object and writing primitive datatypes like numbers and characters to a byte stream. But if an object contains an object as a member variable (as opposed to a primitive datatype), the story is somewhat different. The object member variable would cease to function correctly if the object was left out, so the variable must be serialized as well. If it contains an object or a collection of objects (such as an array or a vector), then they too must be serialized. This must be done recursively, so that if an object has a reference to an object, which has a reference to another object (and so on), they are all saved together. This happens transparently—developers do not need to manually specify which objects are to be written. The set of all objects referenced is called a graph of objects, and object serialization converts entire graphs to byte form (as shown in Figure 4-7).

### 4.5.3 *How Serialization Works*

Support for serialization was introduced in JDK1.1. Prior to this, no support for object persistence was offered, and developers had to write the contents of an object themselves. This was an arduous process, as the developer would normally have to come up with a proprietary data structure, save all the wanted

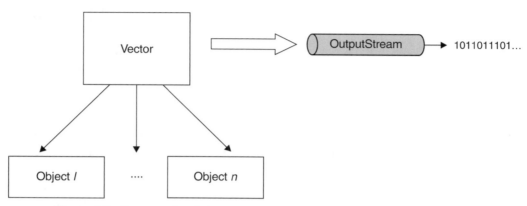

**Figure 4-7**   Entire graphs of objects may be serialized to an output stream.

objects (recursively if necessary), and write code to restore the objects at a later date. This was not a fun task, and any change to the objects (such as adding new member variables) required a change to the code to save and restore an object. Now, however, any object that implements the `java.io.Serializable` interface may be serialized with only a few lines of code (along with any other object referenced by a serialized object).

Implementing the `java.io.Serializable` interface requires no additional effort on the part of developers, other than adding the appropriate "implements" statement during the class declaration and declaring a no-argument constructor (also referred to as the default constructor). The interface serves only as an indication that the developer endorses serialization—no methods need to be implemented to support serialization. The constructor is required so that the class may be instantiated later by the JVM, and then deserialized by assigning new values to member variables. For example, the following class declaration identifies a serializable object.

```
public class SomeClass extends SomeOtherClass implements
java.io.Serializable {
        public class SomeClass()
        {
        }

                . . . . . . . . .

}
```

**NOTE:** Failure to declare a default constructor is, as the Java API documents state, an error in programming, and will result in an exception being thrown at runtime.

There are some legitimate reasons, too, for not supporting serialization. For example, if an object contained very sensitive information, it might be unwise to serialize it and save it to disk or send it over a network. Developers should be aware that no special care is taken to protect the contents of a serialized object from scrutiny or modification, and that any class in any JVM may choose to deserialize an object at a later time.

Of course, boycotting the serializable interface entirely isn't always an option. For example, suppose a class stored password data that could be easily obtained elsewhere and would be dangerous to serialize. To prevent individual member variables being serialized, they can be marked with the *transient* keyword, which indicates that the object or primitive datatype must not be serialized. Consider the following class, which models a user's personal account that can be serialized but whose password field may not.

```
public class UserAccount implements java.io.Serializable {
        protected String username;
        protected transient String password;

        public UserAccount()
        {
                . . . . . .
        }
}
```

Other uses for the *transient* keyword are for fields that are being continuously updated by some means, such as a timer, and hence do not make sense to serialize, or for stopping the serialization of fields that store GUI displays of data. The GUI display could be dynamically created, and hence there is no need to serialize it.

### 4.5.4  *Reading and Writing Objects to Streams*

The main point of serialization is to write an object out to a stream and to read it back. This is accomplished by using the `java.io.ObjectOutputStream` and `java.io.ObjectInputStream` classes, which can write serializable objects out to an output stream and read them back from an input stream.

#### 4.5.4.1 ObjectInputStream Class

The `ObjectInputStream` class is used to read a serialized object from a byte stream, to allow an object to be reconstituted back to its original form, providing the object's class can be loaded by the JVM's class loader. The `ObjectInputStream` class implements the `ObjectInput` interface, which extends the `DataInput` interface. This means that the `ObjectInputStream` class provides many methods with the same signature as DataInputStream, in addition to extra methods responsible for reading objects.

### Constructors

- protected ObjectInputStream() throws java.io.IOException, java.lang.SecurityException—provides a default constructor for ObjectInputStream subclasses. Few developers will want to override the ObjectInputStream class and create a nonstandard implementation.
- ObjectInputStream(InputStream input) throws java.io.IOException—creates an object input stream connected to the specified input stream, which is capable of restoring serialized objects.

### Methods

Many of the methods of ObjectInputStream were covered in the discussion of the DataInputStream class (see Section 4.3.2.2). The reader is reminded that the ObjectInputStream can read primitive datatypes just like the DataInputStream class. There are also several methods that pertain to the construction of ObjectInputStream subclasses. Creating such a subclass is an extremely complex task, and not a normal part of Java programming. For this reason, only the most important method of the ObjectInput interface is covered—for further information consult the Java API documentation.

- public final Object readObject() throws java.io.OptionalDataException, java.io.IOException, java.lang.ClassNotFoundException—reads a serialized object from the stream and reconstructs it to its original state (save for transient and static fields). If the object contains references to other objects, these objects are also reconstructed. During the deserialization process, notification is given to any registered validation listeners of the success or failure of the process; however, the details of validation are beyond the scope of this book. It is sufficient to say here that if an object cannot be read, the application will be notified by the method throwing an exception. An Object instance is returned. If required, this object can be cast to a specific class type before it is used.

### 4.5.4.2 ObjectOutputStream Class

The ObjectOutputStream class serializes an object to a byte stream, for the purpose of object persistence. It may be connected to any existing output stream, such as a file or a networking stream, for transmission over the Internet. Objects written to an ObjectOutputStream have all their member variables (such as primitive data types and objects) written. If the object contains references to other objects, they too will be written, so an ObjectOutputStream can write entire object graphs. A sequence of objects can be written or wrapped in a collection (such as an array or a vector) whose entire contents could be serialized with one call to the `ObjectOutputStream.writeObject` method.

### Constructors

- `protected ObjectOutputStream ()` throws `java.io.IOException`, `java.lang.SecurityException`—default constructor, provided for the benefit of subclasses of the `ObjectOutputStream`. Overriding `ObjectOutputStream` is not necessary, and readers are advised not to create subclasses.
- `ObjectOutputStream (OutputStream output)` throws `java.io.IOException`—creates an object output stream capable of serializing objects to the specified output stream.

### Methods

Like the `ObjectInputStream` class, `ObjectOutputStream` offers extra methods that may be used by subclasses to implement object serialization. However, this is a complex task and is rarely done. For this reason, only the most important method, used for writing objects, is covered here—for further information, the Java API documentation should be consulted. Readers are reminded that the `ObjectOutputStream` class also provides method implementations for the `DataOutput` interface—these methods are covered in Section 4.3.3.2 on `DataOutputStream`, and may be used to write primitive data types to a stream.

- `void writeObject (Object object)` throws `java.io.IOException`, `java.io.InvalidClassException`, `java.io.NotSerializable-Exception`—writes the specified object to the output stream, through object serialization. All variables that are not marked as transient or `static` will be written, providing the specified class is an instance of the `java.io.Serializable` interface.

### 4.5.4.3 Serialization Example

Let's look at an example of an application that can save and restore state information by using the Java serialization classes.

### Code for SerializationDemo

```
import java.io.*;
import java.util.*;

// Chapter 4, Listing 5
public class SerializationDemo
{
```

```java
public static void main(String args[])
{
    try
    {
        Vector list;

        // Create a buffered reader for easy input
        BufferedReader reader = new BufferedReader
                ( new InputStreamReader ( System.in ) );

        System.out.println ("Checking for previous serialized list");

        // Check to see if serialized list exists
        try
        {
            FileInputStream fin = new FileInputStream
                    ("list.out");

            // Connect an object input stream to the
            // list
            ObjectInputStream oin = new ObjectInputStream ( fin );

            try
            {
                // Read the vector back from the list
                Object obj = oin.readObject();

                // Cast back to a vector
                list = (Vector) obj;
            }
            catch (ClassCastException cce)
            {
                // Can't read it, create a blank one
                list = new Vector();
            }
            catch (ClassNotFoundException cnfe)
            {
                // Can't read it, create a blank one
                list = new Vector();
            }

            fin.close();
        }
        catch (FileNotFoundException fnfe)
        {
            // Create a blank vector
            list = new Vector();
        }
```

```java
// Repeat indefinitely
for (;;)
{
    // Now, display menu
    System.out.println ("Menu :-");
    System.out.println ("1.. Add item");
    System.out.println ("2.. Delete item");
    System.out.println ("3.. List items");
    System.out.println ("4.. Save and quit");
    System.out.print   ("Choice : ");

    // Read choice
    String response = reader.readLine();

    // Convert to an int
    int choice = Integer.parseInt (response);

    switch (choice)
    {
case 1 :
    // Add the item to list
    System.out.print
    ("Enter item : ");
    String item = reader.readLine();
    list.addElement(item);
    break;
case 2 :
    // Delete the item from list
    System.out.print
    ("Enter item : ");
    String deadItem =
    reader.readLine();
    list.removeElement(deadItem);
    break;
case 3 :
    // List the elements of the list
    for (Enumeration e =
    list.elements();
         e.hasMoreElements();)
    {
         System.out.println
         (e.nextElement());
    }
    break;
case 4 :
    // Save list and terminate
    System.out.println
    ("Saving list");
    FileOutputStream fout =
    new FileOutputStream
         ( "list.out" );
```

```
                                   // Construct an object output stream
                                   ObjectOutputStream oout = new
                                           ObjectOutputStream ( fout );

                                   // Write the object to the stream
                                   oout.writeObject (list);
                                   fout.close();
                                   System.exit(0);
                               }
                          }
                   }
                   catch (IOException ioe)
                   {
                          System.err.println ("I/O error");
                   }
            }
       }
```

### How SerializationDemo Works

This example is longer than other I/O programs from this chapter, as it presents a text-based user interface that allows items to be added to, or removed from, a java.util.Vector list. Such code is fairly simple, but what is not so easy to understand is the serialization process. The main difference between this example and other programs is that the list doesn't die when the application terminates—it is serialized to a FileOutputStream for later access.

```
// Save list and terminate
System.out.println ("Saving list");
FileOutputStream fout = new FileOutputStream ( "list.out" );

// Construct an object output stream
ObjectOutputStream oout = new ObjectOutputStream ( fout );

// Write the object to the stream
oout.writeObject (list);
fout.close();
System.exit(0);
```

When the application first starts, it checks to see whether the serialized file exists. If so, the vector list is read back from the file, along with any object references by the vector list, by using an ObjectInputStream connected to a FileInputStream. The ObjectInputStream.readObject() method returns an Object instance, and must be cast back to the original form of a Vector. Just in case the object wasn't an actual vector (for example, if another application had modified the file), a ClassCastException is caught.

```
FileInputStream fin = new FileInputStream    ("list.out");

// Connect an object input stream to the list
ObjectInputStream oin = new ObjectInputStream ( fin );

try
{
    // Read the vector back from the list
    Object obj = oin.readObject();

    // Cast back to a vector
    list = (Vector) obj;
}
catch (ClassCastException cce)
{
    // Can't read it, create a blank one
    list = new Vector();
}
catch (ClassNotFoundException cnfe)
{
    // Can't read it, create a blank one
    list = new Vector();
}
```

### Running SerializationDemo

This example demonstrates the use of serialization to save program state. You can follow the menu prompts to add data, and then exit the program. Run the program a second time, and you'll notice that it "remembers" the original state of the list. Deleting the file list.out will erase the program's memory again.

To run the example, the following command would be executed:

```
java SerializationDemo
```

## 4.5.5 Securing Serialization of Objects

The need for secure serialization becomes an important concern in systems that deal with sensitive data, control access to other resources, or transmit data over insecure network communications (such as the Internet, as opposed to a corporate intranet). Some of the security risks can be identified as follows:

- Interception of serialized object
- Access to the contents of a serialized object
- Modification of a serialized object, and then transmission to intended recipient

Each of these scenarios can be risky, depending on the nature of the program. Changing the high score on a game might not be too serious, but changing a bank account PIN number or balance is very serious, and allows a system to be compromised. When developing a system—any system—the seriousness of possible security breaches should always be considered. In some systems such risks can be disregarded, but if not, there is a solution. Transmission of sensitive objects (either to disk or across a network) could occur over an encrypted stream, providing an added layer of security. Security and encryption are complex topics worthy in their own right of book-length discussions, and are beyond the scope of this book.

### 4.5.6   Object Serialization and Versioning

When an object is written to an `ObjectOutputStream`, an extra member variable is sent that developers may otherwise be unaware of. This variable is a stream unique identifier (SUID), which serves as an object version number. For example, the following is the SUID for a particular class, and is represented as a long value:

```
static final long serialVersionUID = 11847310353484904134L;
```

The `serialVersionUID` field is used to determine whether a compatible class definition was found during deserialization that matches that of a serialized object. In large systems, it might be possible for two versions of the same class to be used, and one of them may be incompatible. For this reason, a SUID is added as a field, to enable a deserializing `ObjectInputStream` to check for a match. The version number is a 64-bit number, based on a variety of class-specific factors such as the name of a class, methods, and fields. This provides for a fair degree of certainty that no two numbers will be alike, even if classes are similarly named.

**NOTE:** For more information on the exact composition of the SUID, consult the Java Object Serialization specification, available at http://java.sun.com/products/jdk/1.2/docs/guide/serialization/.

Now, however, consider the problems that would occur if a class was modified and methods or member variables added or removed. Since the object version number is based upon the methods and member variables of a class, the object's `serialVersionUID` field, generated automatically by `ObjectInputStream`, will change, rendering it incompatible. Maintenance is an important part of any software development project, and if an application's save files are suddenly unusable because the developer decided to add an extra method or two, users of the application are not going to be happy.

The solution is for the developer to work out the `serialUID` field independently, and add it as a member variable of the appropriate class, to keep things compatible. Of course, calculating such a long number oneself might be a little tricky. That's why the Serial Version Command tool ships as part of JDK. It analyzes a class file and displays the value of its `serialVersionUID` field. There are two ways to use the tool, and the easiest is the GUI version, which allows the field to be copied and pasted into the application.

To invoke the serial version tool, simply type the following (presuming you have added the correct path statement to point to Java's bin directory, per the JDK installation instructions):

```
serialver -show
```

You should see a window like that in Figure 4-8, which shows the serial version inspector in action. Simply specify the classpath of each class you're interested in, and copy and paste the `serialVersionUID` field into your applications.

By adding the `serialVersionUID` field, you can make future versions somewhat compatible, as they share the same SUID. Changes to method names can then be made, without invalidating previously serialized objects. However, adding or removing member variables will still cause incompatibility problems.

## 4.6   Summary

The Java input and output package (`java.io`) provides developers with a comprehensive range of options for reading and writing bytes of data, as well as characters. Once mastered, streams play an important part in application development, and particularly so in the case of network programming. By applying filter streams, or filter readers and writers, to low-level streams, developers can read numbers, arrays, characters, strings, and other datatypes from a sequence of bytes, or write such datatypes to a new sequence of bytes.

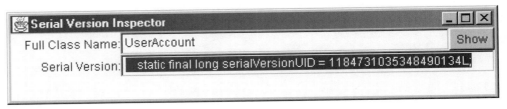

**Figure 4-8**   Serial version inspector displays the `serialVersionUID` field.

**Chapter Highlights**

In this chapter, you have learned:

- What streams are, and how they work
- What readers and writers are, and how they work
- How to connect filter streams to low-level streams
- How to connect readers and writers to streams
- About object serialization and how to read and write objects

# CHAPTER 5

## User Datagram Protocol

### 5.1    Overview

The User Datagram Protocol (UDP) is a commonly used transport protocol employed by many types of applications. UDP is a connectionless transport protocol, meaning that it doesn't guarantee either packet delivery or that packets arrive in sequential order. Rather than reading from, and writing to, an ordered sequence of bytes (using I/O streams, as discussed in Chapter 4), bytes of data are grouped together in discrete packets, which are sent over the network. Although control over the ultimate destination of a UDP packet rests with the computer that sends it, how it reaches that destination is an arbitrary process (see Figure 5-1).

The packets may travel along different paths, as selected by the various network routers that distribute traffic flow seemingly whimsically—depending on factors such as network congestion, priority of routes, and cost of transmission. (For example, for one packet a cheaper network route might be selected, even though it is slower, but another might travel along a superfast pipeline if the cheaper alternative becomes too congested.) This means that a packet can arrive out of sequence, if it encounters a faster route than the previous packet (or if the previous packet encounters some other form of delay). No two packets are guaranteed the same route, and if a particular route is heavily congested, the packet may be discarded entirely. Each packet has a time-to-live (TTL) counter, which is updated when the packet is routed along to the next point in the network. When the timer expires, it will be discarded, and the recipient of the packet will not be notified. If a packet does arrive, however, it will always arrive intact. Packets that are corrupt or only partially delivered are discarded.

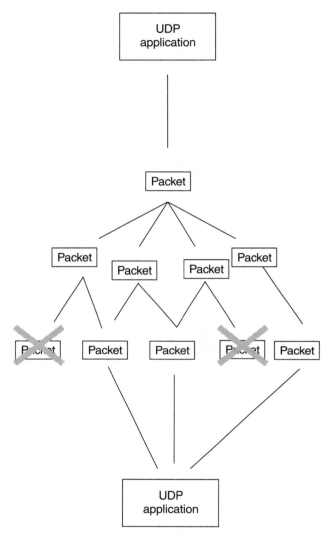

**Figure 5-1**   UDP packet transport over a network can be unreliable.

**NOTE:** Testing UDP applications in an intranet environment will yield various rates of packet loss (or none at all), due to the small number of hops a packet must make, and high bandwidth. Internet-based UDP transmission is more likely to result in dropped packets, and testing only in an intranet environment is dangerous, as developers may be unaware of the effects of lost packets.

Given the potential for loss of data packets, it may seem odd that anyone would even consider using such an unreliable, seemingly anarchical system. In fact, there are many advantages to using UDP that may not be apparent at first glance.

- UDP communication can be more efficient than guaranteed-delivery data streams. If the amount of data is small and the data is sent frequently (such as in the case of a counter whose previous value is irrelevant), it may make sense to avoid the overhead of guaranteed delivery.
- Unlike TCP streams, which establish a connection, UDP causes fewer overheads. If the amount of data being sent is small and the data is sent infrequently, the overhead of establishing a connection might not be worth it. UDP may be preferable in this case, particularly if data is being sent from a large number of machines to one central one, in which case the sum total of all these connections might cause significant overload.
- Real-time applications that demand up-to-the-second or better performance may be candidates for UDP, as there are fewer delays due to the error checking and flow control of TCP. UDP packets can be used to saturate available network bandwidth to deliver large amounts of data (such as streaming video/audio, or telemetry data for a multi-player network game). In addition, if some data is lost, it can be replaced by the next set of packets with updated information, eliminating the need to resend old data that is now out of date.
- UDP sockets can receive data from more than one host machine. If several machines must be communicated with, then UDP may be more convenient than other mechanisms such as TCP (discussed in Chapter 6).
- Some network protocols specify UDP as the transport mechanism, requiring its use.

Java supports the User Datagram Protocol in the form of two classes:

- `java.net.DatagramPacket`
- `java.net.DatagramSocket`

## 5.2 DatagramPacket Class

The `DatagramPacket` class represents a data packet intended for transmission using the User Datagram Protocol (see Figure 5-2). Packets are containers for a small sequence of bytes, and include addressing information such as an IP address and a port.

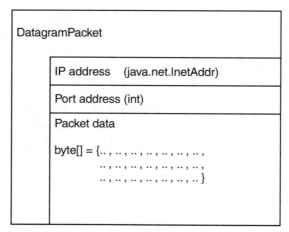

**Figure 5-2**   `DatagramPacket` representation of a UDP packet

The meaning of the data stored in a `DatagramPacket` is determined by its context. When a `DatagramPacket` has been read from a UDP socket, the IP address of the packet represents the address of the sender (likewise with the port number). However, when a `DatagramPacket` is used to send a UDP packet, the IP address stored in `DatagramPacket` represents the address of the recipient (likewise with the port number). This reversal of meaning is important to remember—one wouldn't want to send a packet back to oneself!

### 5.2.1  Creating a DatagramPacket

There are two reasons to create a new `DatagramPacket`:

1. To send data to a remote machine using UDP
2. To receive data sent by a remote machine using UDP

#### Constructors

The choice of which `DatagramPacket` constructor to use is determined by its intended purpose. Either constructor requires the specification of a byte array, which will be used to store the UDP packet contents, and the length of the data packet.

To create a `DatagramPacket` for receiving incoming UDP packets, the following constructor should be used: `DatagramPacket(byte[] buffer, int length)`. For example:

```
DatagramPacket packet = new DatagramPacket(new byte[256], 256);
```

To send a `DatagramPacket` to a remote machine, it is preferable to use the following constructor: `DatagramPacket(byte[] buffer, int length, Inet-Address dest_addr, int dest_port)`. For example:

```
InetAddress addr = InetAddress.getByName("192.168.0.1");
DatagramPacket packet = new DatagramPacket ( new byte[128],
128, addr, 2000);
```

## 5.2.2  Using a DatagramPacket

The `DatagramPacket` class provides some important methods that allow the remote address, remote port, data (as a byte array), and length of the packet to be retrieved. As of JDK1.1, there are also methods to modify these, via a corresponding set method. This means that a received packet can be reused. For example, a packet's contents can be replaced and then sent back to the sender. This saves having to reset addressing information—the address and port of the packet are already set to those of the sender.

### Methods

- `InetAddress getAddress()`—returns the IP address from which a `DatagramPacket` was sent, or (if the packet is going to be sent to a remote machine), the destination IP address.
- `byte[] getData()`—returns the contents of the `DatagramPacket`, represented as an array of bytes.
- `int getLength()`—returns the length of the data stored in a `Datagram-Packet`. This can be less than the actual size of the data buffer.
- `int getPort()`—returns the port number from which a `Datagram-Packet` was sent, or (if the packet is going to be sent to a remote machine), the destination port number.
- `void setAddress(InetAddress addr)`—assigns a new destination address to a `DatagramPacket`.
- `void setData(byte[] buffer)`—assigns a new data buffer to the `DatagramPacket`. Remember to make the buffer long enough, to prevent data loss.
- `void setLength(int length)`—assigns a new length to the `Datagram-Packet`. Remember that the length must be less than or equal to the maximum size of the data buffer, or an `IllegalArgumentException` will be thrown. When sending a smaller amount of data, you can adjust the length to fit—you do not need to resize the data buffer.
- `void setPort(int port)`—assigns a new destination port to a `DatagramPacket`.

## 5.3    DatagramSocket Class

The `DatagramSocket` class provides access to a UDP socket, which allows UDP packets to be sent and received. A `DatagramPacket` is used to represent a UDP packet, and must be created prior to receiving any packets. The same `DatagramSocket` can be used to receive packets as well as to send them. However, read operations are blocking, meaning that the application will continue to wait until a packet arrives. Since UDP packets do not guarantee delivery, this can cause an application to stall if the sender does not resubmit packets. You can use multiple threads of execution, discussed in Chapter 7, or as of JDK1.1, you can use nonblocking I/O to avoid this problem, as shown in the `EchoClient` example discussed in Section 5.7.2.

### 5.3.1    Creating a DatagramSocket

A `DatagramSocket` can be used to both send and receive packets. Each `DatagramSocket` binds to a port on the local machine, which is used for addressing packets. The port number need not match the port number of the remote machine, but if the application is a UDP server, it will usually choose a specific port number. If the `DatagramSocket` is intended to be a client, and doesn't need to bind to a specific port number, a blank constructor can be specified.

#### Constructors

To create a client `DatagramSocket`, the following constructor is used: `DatagramSocket() throws java.net.SocketException`. To create a server `DatagramSocket`, the following constructor is used, which takes as a parameter the port to which the UDP service will be bound: `DatagramSocket(int port) throws java.net.SocketException`.

Although rarely used, there is a third constructor for `DatagramSocket`, introduced in JDK1.1. If a machine is known by several IP addresses (referred to as multihomed), you can specify the IP address and port to which a UDP service should be bound. It takes as parameters the port to which the UDP service will be bound, as well as the `InetAddress` of the service. This constructor is: `DatagramSocket (int port, InetAddress addr) throws java.net.SocketException`.

### 5.3.2    Using a DatagramSocket

`DatagramSocket` is used to receive incoming UDP packets and to send outgoing UDP packets. It provides methods to send and receive packets, as well as to specify a timeout value when nonblocking I/O is being used, to inspect and modify maximum UDP packet sizes, and to close the socket.

## *Methods*

- void close()—closes a socket, and unbinds it from the local port.
- void connect(InetAddress remote_addr, int remote_port)—restricts access to the specified remote address and port. The designation is a misnomer, as UDP doesn't actually create a "connection" between one machine and another. However, if this method is used, it causes exceptions to be thrown if an attempt is made to send packets to, or read packets from, any other host and port than those specified.
- void disconnect()—disconnects the DatagramSocket and removes any restrictions imposed on it by an earlier connect operation.
- InetAddress getInetAddress()—returns the remote address to which the socket is connected, or null if no such connection exists.
- int getPort()—returns the remote port to which the socket is connected, or −1 if no such connection exists.
- InetAddress getLocalAddress()—returns the local address to which the socket is bound.
- int getLocalPort()—returns the local port to which the socket is bound.
- int getReceiveBufferSize() throws java.net.SocketException—returns the maximum buffer size used for incoming UDP packets.
- int getSendBufferSize() throws java.net.SocketException—returns the maximum buffer size used for outgoing UDP packets.
- int getSoTimeout() throws java.net.SocketException—returns the value of the timeout socket option. This value is used to determine the number of milliseconds a read operation will block before throwing a java.io.InterruptedIOException. By default, this value will be zero, indicating that blocking I/O will be used.
- void receive(DatagramPacket packet) throws java.io.IOException—reads a UDP packet and stores the contents in the specified packet. The address and port fields of the packet will be overwritten with the sender address and port fields, and the length field of the packet will contain the length of the original packet, which can be less than the size of the packet's byte-array. If a timeout value hasn't been specified by using DatagramSocket.setSoTimeout(int duration), this method will block indefinitely. If a timeout value has been specified, a java.io.InterruptedIOException will be thrown if the time is exceeded.
- void send(DatagramPacket packet) throws java.io.IOException—sends a UDP packet, represented by the specified packet parameter.
- void setReceiveBufferSize(int length) throws java.net.SocketException—sets the maximum buffer size used for incoming UDP packets. Whether the specified length will be adhered to is dependent on the operating system.

- void setSendBufferSize(int length) throws java.net.Socket-Exception—sets the maximum buffer size used for outgoing UDP packets. Whether the specified length will be adhered to is dependent on the operating system.
- void setSoTimeout(int duration) throws java.net.SocketException—sets the value of the timeout socket option. This value is the number of milliseconds a read operation will block before throwing a java.io.InterruptedIOException.

## 5.4   Listening for UDP Packets

Before an application can read UDP packets sent to it by remote machines, it must bind a socket to a local UDP port using DatagramSocket, and create a DatagramPacket that will act as a container for the UDP packet's data. Figure 5-3 shows the relationship between a UDP packet, the various Java classes used to process it, and the actual application.

When an application wishes to read UDP packets, it calls the Datagram-Socket.receive method, which copies a UDP packet into the specified Data-gramPacket. The contents of the DatagramPacket are processed, and the process is repeated as needed.

The following code snippet illustrates this process:

```
DatagramPacket packet = new DatagramPacket (new byte[256], 256);
DatagramSocket socket = new DatagramSocket(2000);
boolean finished = false;

while (! finished )
{
      socket.receive (packet);

      // process the packet
}
socket.close();
```

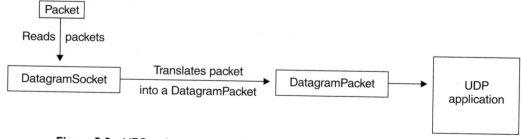

**Figure 5-3**   UDP packets are received by a DatagramSocket and translated into a DatagramPacket object.

When processing the packet, the application must work directly with an array of bytes. If, however, your application is better suited to reading text, you can use classes from the Java I/O package to convert between a byte array and another type of stream or reader. By hooking a `ByteArrayInputStream` to the contents of a datagram and then to another type of `InputStream` or an `InputStreamReader`, you can access the contents of UDP packets relatively easily (see Figure 5-4). Many developers prefer to use Java I/O streams to process data, using a `DataInputStream` or a `BufferedReader` to access the contents of byte arrays.

For example, to hook up a `DataInputStream` to the contents of a `Datagram-Packet`, the following code can be used:

```
ByteArrayInputStream bin =  new ByteArrayInputStream(
packet.getData() );
DataInputStream din = new DataInputStream (bin);

// Read the contents of the UDP packet
.......
```

## 5.5    Sending UDP packets

The same interface (`DatagramSocket`) employed to receive UDP packets is also used to send them. When sending a packet, the application must create a `DatagramPacket`, set the address and port information, and write the data intended for transmission to its byte array. If replying to a received packet, the address and port information will already be stored, and only the data need be overwritten. Once the packet is ready for transmission, the send method of `DatagramSocket` is invoked, and a UDP packet is sent (see Figure 5-5).

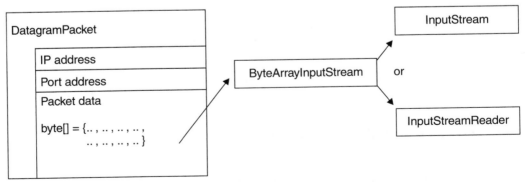

**Figure 5-4**  Reading from a UDP packet is simplified by applying input streams.

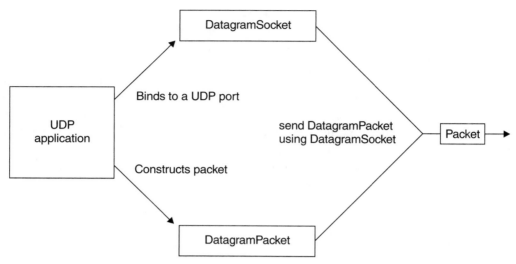

**Figure 5-5**   Packets are sent using a `DatagramSocket`.

The following code snippet illustrates this process:

```
DatagramSocket socket = new DatagramSocket(2000);
DatagramPacket packet = new DatagramPacket (new byte[256], 256);

packet.setAddress ( InetAddress.getByName ( somehost ) );
packet.setPort ( 2000 );

boolean finished = false;

while !finished )
{
    // Write data to packet buffer
    .........
    socket.send (packet);

    // Do something else, like read other packets, or check to
    // see if no more packets to send
    .........
}

socket.close();
```

## 5.6   User Datagram Protocol Example

To demonstrate how UDP packets are sent and received, we'll compile and run two small examples. The first will bind to a local port, read a packet, and display its contents and addressing information. The second example will send the packet read by the first.

## Code for PacketReceiveDemo

```java
import java.net.*;
import java.io.*;

// Chapter 5, Listing 1
public class PacketReceiveDemo
{
    public static void main (String args[])
    {
        try
        {
            System.out.println ("Binding to local port
            2000");

            // Create a datagram socket, bound to the
            // specific port 2000
            DatagramSocket socket = new
            DatagramSocket(2000);

            System.out.println ("Bound to local port "
            + socket.getLocalPort());

            // Create a datagram packet, containing a
            // maximum buffer of 256 bytes
            DatagramPacket packet = new
            DatagramPacket( new byte[256], 256 );

            // Receive a packet - remember by default
            //this is a blocking operation
            socket.receive(packet);

            System.out.println ("Packet received!");

            // Display packet information
            InetAddress remote_addr =
            packet.getAddress();
            System.out.println ("Sent by  : " +
            remote_addr.getHostAddress() );
            System.out.println ("Sent from: " +
            packet.getPort());

            // Display packet contents, by reading
            // from byte array
            ByteArrayInputStream bin = new
            ByteArrayInputStream  (packet.getData());

            // Display only up to the length of the
            // original UDP packet
            for (int i=0; i < packet.getLength(); i++)
            {
                int data = bin.read();
                if (data == -1)
                    break;
```

```
                                        else
                                            System.out.print ( (char)
                                            data) ;
                            }

                            socket.close();
                }
                catch (IOException ioe)
                {
                            System.err.println ("Error - " + ioe);
                }

        }
    }
```

### How PacketReceiveDemo Works

Most of the code is self-explanatory, or is similar to code snippets shown earlier. However, readers may benefit from a closer examination.

The application starts by binding to a specific port, 2000. Applications offering a service generally bind to a specific port. When acting as a receiver, your application should choose a specific port number, so that a sender can send UDP packets to this port. Next, the application prepares a `DatagramPacket` for storing UDP packets, and creates a new buffer for storing packet data.

```
// Create a datagram socket, bound to the specific port 2000
DatagramSocket socket = new DatagramSocket(2000);

System.out.println ("Bound to local port " +
socket.getLocalPort());

// Create a datagram packet, containing a maximum buffer of 256
// bytes
DatagramPacket packet = new DatagramPacket( new byte[256], 256 );
```

Now the application is ready to read a packet. The read operation is blocking, so until a packet arrives, the server will wait. When a packet is successfully delivered to the application, the addressing information for the packet is displayed so that it can be determined where it came from.

```
// Receive a packet - remember by default this is a blocking
// operation
socket.receive(packet);

// Display packet information
InetAddress remote_addr = packet.getAddress();
System.out.println ("Sent by  : " +
remote_addr.getHostAddress() );
System.out.println ("Send from: " + packet.getPort());
```

To provide easy access to the contents of the UDP packet, the application uses a ByteArrayInputStream to read from the packet. Reading one character at a time, the program displays the contents of the packet and then finishes. Note that Unicode characters, which are represented by more than just a single byte, cannot be written out in this fashion (readers and writers would be more appropriate if internationalization support is required).

```
// Display packet contents, by reading from byte array
ByteArrayInputStream bin = new ByteArrayInputStream
(packet.getData());

// Display only up to the length of the original UDP packet
for (int i=0; i < packet.getLength(); i++)
{
      int data = bin.read();
      if (data == -1)
            break;
      else
            System.out.print ( (char) data) ;
}
```

### Code for PacketSendDemo

```
import java.net.*;
import java.io.*;

// Chapter 5, Listing 2
public class PacketSendDemo
{
      public static void main (String args[])
      {
            int argc = args.length;

            // Check for valid number of parameters
            if (argc != 1)
            {
                    System.out.println ("Syntax :");
                    System.out.println ("java PacketSendDemo hostname");
                    return;
            }

            String hostname = args[0];

            try
            {
                    System.out.println ("Binding to a local port");

                    // Create a datagram socket, bound to any available
                    // local port
                    DatagramSocket socket = new
                    DatagramSocket();
```

```
                        System.out.println ("Bound to local port "
                        + socket.getLocalPort());
                        // Create a message to send using a UDP packet
                        ByteArrayOutputStream bout = new
                        ByteArrayOutputStream();
                        PrintStream pout = new PrintStream (bout);
                        pout.print ("Greetings!");

                        // Get the contents of our message as an array
                        // of bytes
                        byte[] barray = bout.toByteArray();

                        // Create a datagram packet, containing our byte
                        // array

                        DatagramPacket packet = new
                        DatagramPacket( barray, barray.length );

                        System.out.println ("Looking up hostname "
                        + hostname );

                        // Lookup the specified hostname, and get an
                        // InetAddress
                        InetAddress remote_addr =
                        InetAddress.getByName(hostname);

                        System.out.println ("Hostname resolved as " +
                                    remote_addr.getHostAddress());

                        // Address packet to sender
                        packet.setAddress (remote_addr);

                        // Set port number to 2000
                        packet.setPort      (2000);

                        // Send the packet - remember no guarantee of delivery
                        socket.send(packet);

                        System.out.println ("Packet sent!");
            }
        catch (UnknownHostException uhe)
            {
                        System.err.println ("Can't find host " +
                        hostname);
            }
        catch (IOException ioe)
            {
                        System.err.println ("Error - " + ioe);
            }
        }
    }
}
```

### How PacketSendDemo Works

The second example uses UDP to talk to the first example. This example acts as the sender, dispatching a UDP packet to the receiver, which contains an ASCII text-greeting message. Though it uses some similar classes (Datagram-Socket, DatagramPacket), they are employed in a slightly different way.

The application starts by binding a UDP socket to a local port, which will be used to send the data packet. Unlike the receiver demonstration, it doesn't matter which local port is being used. In fact, any free port is a candidate, and you may find that running the application several times will result in different port numbers. After binding to a port, the port number is displayed to demonstrate this.

```
// Create a datagram socket, bound to any available local port
DatagramSocket socket = new DatagramSocket();
System.out.println ("Bound to local port " +
socket.getLocalPort());
```

Before sending any data, we need to create a DatagramPacket. First, a ByteArrayOutputStream is used to create a sequence of bytes. Once this is complete, the array of bytes is passed to the DatagramPacket constructor.

```
// Create a message to send using a UDP packet
ByteArrayOutputStream bout = new ByteArrayOutputStream();
PrintStream pout = new PrintStream (bout);
pout.print ("Greetings!");

// Get the contents of our message as an array of bytes
byte[] barray = bout.toByteArray();

// Create a datagram packet, containing our byte array
DatagramPacket packet = new DatagramPacket( barray,
barray.length );
```

Now that the packet has some data, it needs to be correctly addressed. As with a postal message, if it lacks correct address information it cannot be delivered. We start by obtaining an InetAddress for the remote machine, and then display its IP address. This InetAddress is passed to the setAddress method of DatagramPacket, ensuring that it will arrive at the correct machine. However, we must go one step further and specify a port number. In this case, port 2000 is matched, as the receiver will be bound to that port.

```
System.out.println ("Looking up hostname " + hostname );

// Lookup the specified hostname, and get an InetAddress
InetAddress remote_addr = InetAddress.getByName(hostname);
```

```
System.out.println ("Hostname resolved as " +
remote_addr.getHostAddress());

// Address packet to sender
packet.setAddress (remote_addr);

// Set port number to 2000
packet.setPort    (2000);
```

The final step, after all this work, is to send the packet. This is the easiest step of all—simply invoke the send method of `DatagramSocket`. Again, remember: there is no guarantee of delivery, so it is possible for a packet to become lost in transit. A more robust application would try to read an acknowledgment and resend the message if it had become lost.

```
// Send the packet - remember no guarantee of delivery
socket.send(packet);
```

### Running the UDP Examples

To run these examples, you'll need to open two console windows. The first application to be run is the receiver, which will wait for a UDP packet.

There are no parameters for the receiver, so to run it use:

```
java PacketReceiveDemo
```

In a second window, you then need to run the sender. This application could be run from any computer on a local network or the Internet (providing there isn't a firewall between the two hosts). If you'd like, you can also run it from the same machine. It takes a single parameter, the hostname of the remote machine:

```
java PacketSendDemo myhostname
```

 **NOTE:** As mentioned in earlier chapters, you can use localhost as the hostname to refer to the local machine.

## 5.7   Building a UDP Client/Server

The previous example illustrates the technical details of how an individual packet may be sent and received. But applications need a series of packets, not just one. The next example shows how to build a UDP server, a long-running system that is capable of serving many requests during its lifetime. The type of service that is provided is an echo service, which echoes back the contents of a packet. The echo service runs on a well-known port, port 7, and if it is known that a system has an echo server installed, the server may be accessed by clients to see if a system is up and running (similar to the ping application). The example below demonstrates how to write an echo client that will send packets to the server as well as read the results back.

**NOTE:** Some systems have an echo service already running in the background, and security restrictions may prevent a service from binding to a well-known port. If this is the case, you will need to change the port number to a different number (and in the case of security restrictions, you should select a number above port 1024) in both the client and the server. The same port number must be used for communication.

### 5.7.1 Building an Echo Service

The following example involves building an echo service, which transmits any packet it receives straight back to the sender. The code uses no new networking classes or methods, but employs a special technique. It loops continuously to serve one client after another. Though only one UDP packet will be processed at a time, the delay between receiving a packet and dispatching it again is negligible, resulting in the illusion of concurrent processing.

```java
import java.net.*;
import java.io.*;

// Chapter 5, Listing 3
public class EchoServer
{
    // UDP port to which service is bound
    public static final int SERVICE_PORT = 7;

    // Max size of packet, large enough for almost any client
    public static final int BUFSIZE = 4096;

    // Socket used for reading and writing UDP packets
    private DatagramSocket socket;

    public EchoServer()
    {
        try
        {
            // Bind to the specified UDP port, to listen
            // for incoming data packets
            socket = new DatagramSocket( SERVICE_PORT );
```

```java
                System.out.println ("Server active on port " +
                socket.getLocalPort() );
        }
        catch (Exception e)
        {
                System.err.println ("Unable to bind port");
        }
    }

    public void serviceClients()
    {
        // Create a buffer large enough for incoming packets
        byte[] buffer = new byte[BUFSIZE];

        for (;;)
        {
                try
                {
                    // Create a DatagramPacket for reading
                    // UDP packets
                    DatagramPacket packet = new DatagramPacket
                        ( buffer, BUFSIZE );

                    // Receive incoming packets
                    socket.receive(packet);

                    System.out.println ("Packet received from " +
                     packet.getAddress() + ":" +
                     packet.getPort() +
                    " of length " + packet.getLength() );

                    // Echo the packet back - address and port
                    // are already set for us !
                    socket.send(packet);
                }
                catch (IOException ioe)
                {
                    System.err.println ("Error : " + ioe);
                }
        }
    }

    public static void main(String args[])
    {
        EchoServer server = new EchoServer();
        server.serviceClients();
    }
}
```

### 5.7.2 Building an Echo Client

The following client can be used with the echo service and can easily be adapted to support other services. Repeated packets are sent to the echo service, and a timeout is caught to prevent the service from stalling if a packet becomes lost, and the client then waits to receive it. Remember that packet loss in an intranet environment is unlikely, but with slow network connections on the Internet it is quite possible.

```java
import java.net.*;
import java.io.*;

// Chapter 5, Listing 4
public class EchoClient
{
    // UDP port to which service is bound
    public static final int SERVICE_PORT = 7;

    // Max size of packet
    public static final int BUFSIZE = 256;

    public static void main(String args[])
    {
        if (args.length != 1)
        {
            System.err.println ("Syntax - java EchoClient hostname");
            return;
        }

        String hostname = args[0];

        // Get an InetAddress for the specified hostname
        InetAddress addr = null;
        try
        {
            // Resolve the hostname to an InetAddr
            addr = InetAddress.getByName(hostname);
        }
        catch (UnknownHostException uhe)
        {
            System.err.println ("Unable to resolve host");
            return;
        }

        try
        {
            // Bind to any free port
            DatagramSocket socket = new DatagramSocket();
```

```java
// Set a timeout value of two seconds
socket.setSoTimeout (2 * 1000);

for (int i = 1 ; i <= 10; i++)
{
    // Copy some data to our packet
    String message = "Packet number " + i ;
    char[] cArray = message.toCharArray();
    byte[] sendbuf = new byte[cArray.length];

    for (int offset = 0; offset <
    cArray.length ; offset++)
    {
        sendbuf[offset] = (byte)
        cArray[offset];
    }

    // Create a packet to send to the UDP
    server
    DatagramPacket sendPacket = new
    DatagramPacket(sendbuf,
        cArray.length, addr, SERVICE_PORT);

    System.out.println ("Sending packet to " +
    hostname);

    // Send the packet
    socket.send (sendPacket);

    System.out.print ("Waiting for packet.... ");

    // Create a small packet for receiving UDP packets
    byte[] recbuf = new byte[BUFSIZE];
    DatagramPacket receivePacket = new
    DatagramPacket(recbuf,
    BUFSIZE);

    // Declare a timeout flag
    boolean timeout = false;

    // Catch any InterruptedIOException that is thrown
    // while waiting to receive a UDP packet

    try
    {
        socket.receive (receivePacket);
    }
    catch (InterruptedIOException ioe)
    {
        timeout = true;
    }
```

```
                        if (!timeout)
                        {
                              System.out.println ("packet received!");
                              System.out.println ("Details : " +
                              receivePacket.getAddress());

                              // Obtain a byte input stream to read the
                              // UDP packet
                              ByteArrayInputStream bin = new
                              ByteArrayInputStream (
                                 receivePacket.getData(), 0,
                                 receivePacket.getLength() );

                              // Connect a reader for easier access
                              BufferedReader reader = new
                              BufferedReader (
                                 new InputStreamReader ( bin ) );

                              // Loop indefinitely
                              for (;;)
                              {
                                    String line = reader.readLine();

                                    // Check for end of data
                                    if (line == null)
                                          break;
                                    else
                                          System.out.println (line);
                              }
                        }
                        else
                        {
                              System.out.println ("packet lost!");
                        }

                        // Sleep for a second, to allow user to see packet
                        try
                        {
                              Thread.sleep(1000);
                        }catch (InterruptedException ie) {}
                  }
            }
            catch (IOException ioe)
            {
                  System.err.println ("Socket error " + ioe);
            }
      }
}
```

### 5.7.3   Running the Echo Client and Server

Before clients can send requests, the echo server must be active. Otherwise, UDP packets will be sent and then ignored, as there is no program running to read them. However, the client will not stall if a response is not sent back; it will send packets again after two seconds of waiting. This is important, as servers may be inactive or packets may become lost in transmission.

To run the echo server, type the following:

```
java EchoServer
```

To run the echo client (either on the same machine as the server or a different one), type the following:

```
java EchoClient hostname
```

where hostname (or localhost, if running locally) is the location of the echo service.

**NOTE:** Remember that on Unix systems, you must have root privileges to bind to a port under 1024. You can change the service port to a higher number, but this must be done in both the client and the server in order to recompile.

## 5.8    Additional Information on UDP

While the UDP is sometimes the best alternative for certain classes of applications, because of its unique properties, it does present some challenges to developers. These challenges can be met, however, by structuring data transmission to overcome the limitations of UDP. Below we examine these limitations and how they may be overcome.

### 5.8.1 Lack of Guaranteed Delivery

Packets sent via UDP may become lost in transit—each additional hop between one router and another introduces more delays and increases the likelihood that a packet may be discarded when its TTL reaches zero. Furthermore, UDP packets can become damaged or lost if the physical network connection they are being routed through goes down. Since Internet packets are being transmitted across a public network, composed of a diverse range of network infrastructures, it is likely that packets will become lost at some point in a connection.

Of course, in some applications the loss of individual packets may not have a noticeable effect. For example, a video stream might lose a few frames of picture, but provided that most of the frames arrive, the loss is bearable. However, if a file is being transferred, then the file contents will become garbled, and the loss of packets becomes unacceptable. If guaranteed delivery is required, the best alternative is to avoid packet-based communication altogether and use a more suitable transport mechanism like the Transmission Control Protocol (TCP), discussed in Chapter 6. Nonetheless, if the use of UDP is called for, one solution is for the party receiving packets to send an acknowledgment packet (also referred to as an ACK) back to the sender. The absence of an ACK indicates that a packet was lost and should be retransmitted.

**NOTE:** Some transport systems send back an ACK for individual packets or for a range of packets. Although it does add additional complexity, acknowledgment of a range of packets makes for a more efficient use of bandwidth. Some systems also use a negative-acknowledgment packet (NAK) to indicate that a specific packet was lost, which triggers immediate retransmission of that packet.

### 5.8.2 *Lack of Guaranteed Packet Sequencing*

Applications that require sequential access to data (and let's face it, that amounts to most software) should include a sequence number in the contents of a datagram packet. If a packet arrives out of order, it can be buffered until the earlier packets have caught up. Sequencing adds a small amount of complexity, but does make a system more reliable—you always know which packet you're dealing with! Duplicate packets must be discarded, and missing packets (due to a lack of guaranteed delivery) requested again.

### 5.8.3 *Lack of Flow Control*

The face of the Internet is changing rapidly, as network connections move from dial-up and wireless modems to broadband communication through cable modems and ISDN lines. Some systems can handle a large amount of data, whereas others still have extremely limited bandwidth. To avoid flooding a system with more data than it can handle, the technique of flow control is used. Flow control places a limit on how much data is sent, and helps to prevent systems from becoming overloaded (and bandwidth from being wasted). Imagine flow control as a water limiter that restricts the amount of liquid flowing through a showerhead.

There are many flow-control techniques, ranging from limiting the number of packets sent per second to limiting the number of packets that have not yet been acknowledged. The settings for the former are hard to determine, as they vary depending on the receiver. The latter is probably the best choice—by limiting the number of unacknowledged packets, control is placed in the hands of the receiver. If the receiver can get and respond to packets quickly, then more packets will be acknowledged and more will be sent. If packets are flooding the network, fewer responses will come back and a throttle is placed on the flow. Some systems may also elect to use a variable flow limit, which can be customized to take into account the length of time for acknowledgments to come back. Since UDP doesn't offer direct control over flow control, for large-scale applications it may be appropriate to limit the number of packets sent to a host (for example, $n$ packets per second, where $n$ is a number suitable for the transmission line and speed of the recipient machine).

## 5.9    Summary

The User Datagram Protocol (UDP) provides a connectionless transport mechanism that allows packets of data to be sent to remote machines. UDP generates less overhead than other transport protocols and is highly desirable for real-time broadcasting of multimedia such as audio, video, and network gaming data. However, due to its lack of guaranteed delivery and sequencing, it creates additional work for developers, and thus the pros and cons of its use must be considered on a case-by-case basis.

Java supports UDP in the form of the `DatagramSocket` and `DatagramPacket` classes. In order to send or receive packets, an application must bind to a local port using `DatagramSocket`. The application creates a `DatagramPacket` with a sufficient buffer to store incoming or outgoing packets, and can then send and receive packets as required.

---

**Chapter Highlights**

In this chapter, you have learned:

- How to bind to a local port using `DatagramSocket`
- How to create a `DatagramPacket`
- How to read from, and write to, a `DatagramPacket` using `ByteArrayInputStream` and `ByteArrayOutputStream`
- How to listen for UDP packets
- How to send UDP packets
- How to create a UDP server and a UDP client

# CHAPTER 6

## *Transmission Control Protocol*

The Transmission Control Protocol (TCP) is a stream-based method of network communication that is far different from any discussed previously. This chapter discusses TCP streams and how they operate under Java.

## 6.1   Overview

TCP provides an interface to network communications that is radically different from the User Datagram Protocol (UDP) discussed in Chapter 5. The properties of TCP make it highly attractive to network programmers, as it simplifies network communication by removing many of the obstacles of UDP, such as ordering of packets and packet loss. While UDP is concerned with the transmission of packets of data, TCP focuses instead on establishing a network connection, through which a stream of bytes may be sent and received.

In Chapter 5 we saw that packets may be sent through a network using various paths and may arrive at different times. This benefits performance and robustness, as the loss of a single packet doesn't necessarily disrupt the transmission of other packets. Nonetheless, such a system creates extra work for programmers who need to guarantee delivery of data. TCP eliminates this extra work by guaranteeing delivery and order, providing for a reliable byte communication stream between client and server that supports two-way communication. It establishes a "virtual connection" between two machines, through which streams of data may be sent (see Figure 6-1).

TCP uses a lower-level communications protocol, the Internet Protocol (IP), to establish the connection between machines. This connection provides an interface that allows streams of bytes to be sent and received, and transparently converts the data into IP datagram packets. A common problem with

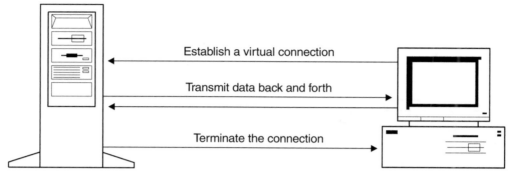

**Figure 6-1**    TCP establishes a virtual connection to transmit data.

datagrams, as we saw in Chapter 5, is that they do not guarantee that packets arrive at their destination. TCP takes care of this problem. It provides guaranteed delivery of bytes of data. Of course, it's always possible that network errors will prevent delivery, but TCP handles the implementation issues such as resending packets, and alerts the programmer only in serious cases such as if there is no route to a network host or if a connection is lost.

The virtual connection between two machines is represented by a socket. Sockets, introduced in Chapter 5, allow data to be sent and received; there are substantial differences between a UDP socket and a TCP socket, however. First, TCP sockets are connected to a single machine, whereas UDP sockets may transmit or receive data from multiple machines. Second, UDP sockets only send and receive packets of data, whereas TCP allows transmission of data through byte streams (represented as an `InputStream` and `OutputStream`). They are converted into datagram packets for transmission over the network, without requiring the programmer to intervene (as shown in Figure 6-2).

## 6.1.1    Advantages of TCP over UDP

The many advantages to using TCP over UDP are briefly summarized below.

### 6.1.1.1 Automatic Error Control

Data transmission over TCP streams is more dependable than transmission of packets of information via UDP. Under TCP, data packets sent through a virtual connection include a checksum to ensure that they have not been corrupted, just like UDP. However, delivery of data is guaranteed by the TCP—data packets lost in transit are retransmitted.

You may be wondering just how this is achieved—after all, IP and UDP do not guarantee delivery; neither do they give any warning when datagram packets are dropped. Whenever a collection of data is sent by TCP using data-

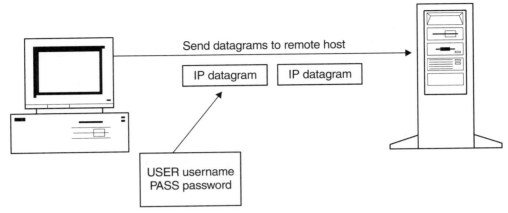

**Figure 6-2** TCP deals with streams of data such as protocol commands, but converts streams into IP datagrams for transport over the network.

grams, a timer is started. Recall our UDP examples from Chapter 5, in which the `DatagramSocket.setSoTimeout` method was used to start a timer for a `receive()` operation. In TCP, if the recipient sends an acknowledgment, the timer is disabled. But if an acknowledgment isn't received before the time runs out, the packet is retransmitted. This means that any data written to a TCP socket will reach the other side without the need for further intervention by programmers (barring some catastrophe that causes an entire network to go down). All of the code for error control is handled by TCP.

### 6.1.1.2 Reliability

Since the data sent between two machines participating in a TCP connection is transmitted by IP datagrams, the datagram packets will frequently arrive out of order. This would throw for a loop any program reading information from a TCP socket, as the order of the byte stream would be disrupted and frequently unreliable. Fortunately, issues such as ordering are handled by TCP— each datagram packet contains a sequence number that is used to order data. Later packets arriving before earlier packets will be held in a queue until an ordered sequence of data is available. The data will then be passed to the application through the interface of the socket.

### 6.1.1.3 Ease of Use

While storing information in datagram packets is certainly not beyond the reach of programmers, it doesn't lead to the most efficient way of communication between computers. There's added complexity, and it can be argued that the task of designing and creating software within a deadline provides complexity enough for programmers. Developers typically welcome anything that can reduce the complexity of software development, and the TCP does just this. TCP allows the programmer to think in a completely different way, one that is much more streamlined. Rather than being packaged into discrete units (datagram packets), the data is instead treated as a continuous stream, like the I/O streams the reader is by now familiar with. TCP sockets continue the tradition of Unix programming, in which communication is treated in the same way as file input and output. The mechanism is the same whether the developer is writing to a network socket, a communications pipe, a data structure, the user console, or a file. This also applies, of course, to reading information. This makes communicating via TCP sockets far simpler than communicating via datagram packets.

## 6.1.2  Communication between Applications Using Ports

It is clear that there are significant differences between TCP and UDP, but there is also an important similarity between these two protocols. Both share the concept of a communications port, which distinguishes one application from another. Many services and clients run on the same port, and it would be impossible to sort out which one was which without distributing them by port number. When a TCP socket establishes a connection to another machine, it requires two very important pieces of information to connect to the remote end—the IP address of the machine and the port number. In addition, a local IP address and port number will be bound to it, so that the remote machine can identify which application established the connection (as illustrated in Figure 6–3). After all, you wouldn't want your e-mail to be accessible by another user running software on the same system.

Ports in TCP are just like ports in UDP—they are represented by a number in the range 1–65535. Ports below 1024 are restricted to use by well-known services such as HTTP, FTP, SMTP, POP3, and telnet. Table 6-1 lists a few of the well-known services and their associated port numbers.

## 6.1.3  Socket Operations

TCP sockets can perform a variety of operations. They can:

- Establish a connection to a remote host
- Send data to a remote host
- Receive data from a remote host
- Close a connection

In addition, there is a special type of socket that provides a service that will bind to a specific port number. This type of socket is normally used only in servers, and can perform the following operations:

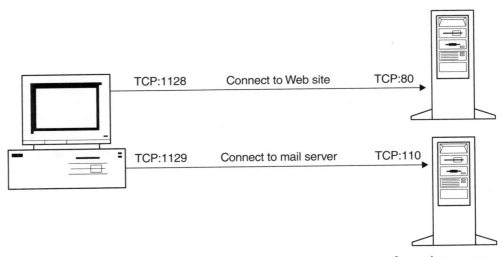

**Figure 6-3** Local ports identify the application establishing a connection from other programs, allowing multiple TCP applications to run on the same machine.

**Table 6-1** Protocols and Their Associated Ports

| Well-Known Services | Service Port |
| --- | --- |
| Telnet | 23 |
| Simple Mail Transfer Protocol | 25 |
| HyperText Transfer Protocol | 80 |
| Post Office Protocol 3 | 110 |

- Bind to a local port
- Accept incoming connections from remote hosts
- Unbind from a local port

These two sockets are grouped into different categories, and are used by either a client or a server (since some clients may also be acting as servers, and some servers as clients). However, it is normal practice for the role of client and server to be separate.

## 6.2 TCP and the Client/Server Paradigm

In network programming (and often in other forms of communication, such as database programming), applications that use sockets are divided into two categories, the client and the server. You are probably familiar with the phrase *client/server programming,* although the exact meaning of the phrase may be unclear to you. This paradigm is the subject of the discussion below.

### 6.2.1  The Client/Server Paradigm

The client/server paradigm divides software into two categories, clients and servers. A client is software that initiates a connection and sends requests, whereas a server is software that listens for connections and processes requests. In the context of UDP programming, no actual connection is established, and UDP applications may both initiate and receive requests on the same socket. In the context of TCP, where connections are established between machines, the client/server paradigm is much more relevant.

When software acts as a client, or as a server, it has a rigidly defined role that fits easily into a familiar mental model. Either the software is initiating requests, or it is processing them. Switching between these roles makes for a more complex system. Even if switching is permitted, at any given time one software program must be the client and one software program must be the server. If they both try to be clients at the same time, no server exists to process the requests!

The client/server paradigm is an important theoretical concept that is widely used in practical applications. There are other communications models as well, such as peer to peer, in which either party may initiate communication. However, the client/server concept is a popular choice due to its simplicity and is used in most network programming.

### 6.2.2  Network Clients

Network clients initiate connections and usually take charge of network transactions. The server is there to fulfill the requests of the client—a client does not fulfill the requests of a server. Although the client is in control, some power still resides in the server, of course. A client can tell a server to delete all files on the local file system, but the server isn't necessarily compelled to carry out that action (thankfully!).

The network client speaks to the server using an agreed-upon standard for communication, the network protocol. For example, an HTTP client uses a set of commands different from a mail client, and has a completely different purpose. Connecting an HTTP client to a mail server, or a mail client to an HTTP server, will result not only in an error message but in an error message that the client will not understand. For this reason, as part of the protocol specification, a port number is used so that the client can locate the server. A Web server typically runs on port 80, and while some servers can run on nonstandard ports, the convention for a URL is not to list a port, as it is assumed that port 80 is used. For more information on ports, see Section 6.1.2.

### 6.2.3 Network Servers

The role of the network server is to bind to a specific port (which is used by the client to locate the server), and to listen for new connections. While the client is temporary, and runs only when the user chooses, the server must run continually (even if no clients are actually connected) in the hope that someone, at some time, will want its services. The server is often referred to as a daemon process, to use Unix parlance. It runs indefinitely, and is normally automatically started when the host computer of the server is started. So the server waits, and waits, and waits, until a client establishes a connection to the server port. Some servers can handle only a single connection at a time, while others can handle many connections concurrently, through the use of threads. Multi-threaded programming is discussed in depth in Chapter 7.

When a connection is being processed, the server is submissive. It waits for the client to send requests, and dutifully processes them (though the server is free to respond with an error message, particularly if the request violates some important precept of the protocol or presents a security risk). Some protocols, like HTTP/1.0, normally allow only one request per connection, whereas others, such as POP3, support a sequence of requests. Servers will answer the client request by sending either a response or an error message—the format of which varies from protocol to protocol. Learning a network protocol (when writing either a client or a server) is a little like learning a new language, as the syntax changes. Typically, though, the number of commands is much smaller, making things a little easier. The behavior of the server is determined in part by the protocol and in part by the developer. (Some commands may be optional, and are not always supported by server implementations.)

## 6.3  TCP Sockets and Java

Java offers good support for TCP sockets, in the form of two socket classes, `java.net.Socket` and `java.net.ServerSocket`. When writing client software that connects to an existing service, the `Socket` class should be used. When writing server software that binds to a local port in order to provide a service, the `ServerSocket` class should be employed. This is different from the way a `DatagramSocket` works with UDP—the function of connecting to servers, and the function of accepting data from clients, is split into a separate class under TCP.

## 6.4    Socket Class

The Socket class represents client sockets, and is a communication channel between two TCP communications ports belonging to one or two machines. A socket may connect to a port on the local system, avoiding the need for a second machine, but most network software will usually involve two machines. TCP sockets can't communicate with more than two machines, however. If this functionality is required, a client application should establish multiple socket connections, one for each machine.

### Constructors

There are several constructors for the java.net.Socket class. Two constructors, which allowed a boolean parameter to specify whether UDP or TCP sockets were to be used, have been deprecated. These constructors should not be used and are not listed here—if UDP functionality is required, use a DatagramSocket (covered in Chapter 5).

The easiest way to create a socket is to specify the hostname of the machine and the port of the service. For example, to connect to a Web server on port 80, the following code might be used:

```
try
{
        // Connect to the specified host and port
        Socket mySocket = new Socket ( "www.awl.com", 80);

        // ......
}
catch (Exception e)
{
        System.err.println ("Err - " + e);
}
```

However, a wide range of constructors is available, for different situations. Unless otherwise specified, all constructors are public.

- protected Socket ()—creates an unconnected socket using the default implementation provided by the current socket factory. Developers should not normally use this method, as it does not allow a hostname or port to be specified.
- Socket (InetAddress address, int port) throws java.io.IOException, java.lang.SecurityException—creates a socket connected to the specified IP address and port. If a connection cannot be established, or if connecting to that host violates a security restriction (such as when an applet tries to connect to a machine other than the machine from which it was loaded), an exception is thrown.

- `Socket (InetAddress address, int port, InetAddress localAddress, int localPort)` throws `java.io.IOException, java.lang.Security-Exception`—creates a socket connected to the specified address and port, and is bound to the specified local address and local port. By default, a free port is used, but this method allows you to specify a specific port number, as well as a specific address, in the case of multi-homed hosts (i.e., a machine where the localhost is known by two or more IP addresses).
- `protected Socket (SocketImpl implementation)`—creates an unconnected socket using the specified socket implementation. Developers should not normally use this method, as it does not allow a hostname or port to be specified.
- `Socket (String host, int port)` throws `java.net.UnknownHost-Exception, java.io.IOException, java.lang.SecurityException`—creates a socket connected to the specified host and port. This method allows a string to be specified, rather than an `InetAddress`. If the hostname could not be resolved, a connection could not be established, or a security restriction is violated, an exception is thrown.
- `Socket (String host, int port, InetAddress localAddress, int localPort)` throws `java.net.UnknownHostException, java.io.IOException, java.lang.SecurityException`—creates a socket connected to the specified host and port, and bound to the specified local port and address. This allows a hostname to be specified as a string, and not an `InetAddress` instance, as well as allowing a specific local address and port to be bound to. These local parameters are useful for multihomed hosts (i.e., a machine where the localhost is known by two or more IP addresses). If the hostname can't be resolved, a connection cannot be established, or a security restriction is violated, an exception is thrown.

### 6.4.1 Creating a Socket

Under normal circumstances, a socket is connected to a machine and port when it is created. Although there is a blank constructor that does not require a hostname or port, it is protected and can't be called from normal applications. Furthermore, there isn't a `connect()` method that allows you to specify these details at a later point in time, so under normal circumstances the socket will be connected when created. If the network is fine, the call to a socket constructor will return as soon as a connection is established, but if the remote machine is not responding, the constructor method may block for an indefinite amount of time. This varies from system to system, depending on a variety of factors such as the operating system being used and the default network timeout (some machines on a local intranet, for example, seem to respond faster than some Internet machines, depending on network settings). You can't ever guarantee how long a socket may block for, but this is abnormal behavior and won't happen frequently. Nonetheless, in mission-critical systems it may be appropriate to place such calls in a second thread, to prevent an application from stalling.

**NOTE:** At a lower level, sockets are produced by a socket factory, which is a special class responsible for creating the appropriate socket implementation. Under normal circumstances, a standard `java.net.Socket` will be produced, but in special situations, such as special networking environments in which custom sockets are used (for example, to break through a firewall by using a special proxy server), socket factories may actually return a socket subclass. The details of socket factories are best left to experienced developers who are familiar with the intricacies of Java networking and have a definite purpose for creating custom sockets and socket factories. For more information on this topic, consult the Java API documentation for the `java.net.SocketFactory` and `java.net.SocketImplFactory` class.

### 6.4.2  Using a Socket

Sockets can perform a variety of tasks, such as reading information, sending data, closing a connection, and setting socket options. In addition, the following methods are provided to obtain information about a socket, such as address and port locations:

### Methods

- `void close()` throws `java.io.IOException`—closes the socket connection. Closing a connect may or may not allow remaining data to be sent, depending on the value of the `SO_LINGER` socket option. Developers are advised to flush any output streams before closing a socket connection.
- `InetAddress getInetAddress()`—returns the address of the remote machine that is connected to the socket.
- `InputStream getInputStream()` throws `java.io.IOException`—returns an input stream, which reads from the application this socket is connected to.
- `OutputStream getOutputStream()` throws `java.io.IOException`—returns an output stream, which writes to the application that this socket is connected to.

- `boolean getKeepAlive()` throws `java.net.SocketException`—returns the state of the `SO_KEEPALIVE` socket option.
- `InetAddress getLocalAddress()`—returns the local address associated with the socket (useful in the case of multihomed machines).
- `int getLocalPort()`—returns the port number that the socket is bound to on the local machine.
- `int getPort()`—returns the port number of the remote service to which the socket is connected.
- `int getReceiveBufferSize()` throws `java.net.SocketException`—returns the receive buffer size used by the socket, determined by the value of the `SO_RCVBUF` socket option.
- `int getSendBufferSize()` throws `java.net.SocketException`—returns the send buffer size used by the socket, determined by the value of the `SO_SNDBUF` socket option.
- `int getSoLinger()` throws `java.net.SocketException`—returns the value of the `SO_LINGER` socket option, which controls how long unsent data will be queued when a connection is terminated.
- `int getSoTimeout()` throws `java.net.SocketException`—returns the value of the `SO_TIMEOUT` socket option, which controls how many milliseconds a read operation will block for. If a value of 0 is returned, the timer is disabled and a thread will block indefinitely (until data is available or the stream is terminated).
- `boolean getTcpNoDelay()` throws `java.net.SocketException`—returns "true" if the `TCP_NODELAY` socket option is set, which controls whether Nagle's algorithm (discussed in Section 6.4.4.5) is enabled.
- `void setKeepAlive(boolean onFlag)` throws `java.net.SocketException`—enables or disables the `SO_KEEPALIVE` socket option.
- `void setReceiveBufferSize(int size)` throws `java.net.SocketException`—modifies the value of the `SO_RCVBUF` socket option, which recommends a buffer size for the operating system's network code to use for receiving incoming data. Not every system will support this functionality or allows absolute control over this feature. If you want to buffer incoming data, you're advised to instead use a `BufferedInputStream` or a `BufferedReader`.
- `void setSendBufferSize(int size)` throws `java.net.SocketException`—modifies the value of the `SO_SNDBUF` socket option, which recommends a buffer size for the operating system's network code to use for sending incoming data. Not every system will support this functionality or allows absolute control over this feature. If you want to buffer incoming data, you're advised to instead use a `BufferedOutputStream` or a `BufferedWriter`.

- `static void setSocketImplFactory (SocketImplFactory factory)` throws `java.net.SocketException, java.io.IOException, java.lang.SecurityException` —assigns a socket implementation factory for the JVM, which may already exist, or may violate security restrictions, either of which causes an exception to be thrown. Only one factory can be specified, and this factory will be used whenever a socket is created.

- `void setSoLinger(boolean onFlag, int duration)` throws `java.net.SocketException, java.lang.IllegalArgumentException`—enables or disables the `SO_LINGER` socket option (according to the value of the `onFlag` boolean parameter), and specifies a duration in seconds. If a negative value is specified, an exception is thrown.

- `void setSoTimeout(int duration)` throws `java.net.Socket-Exception`—modifies the value of the `SO_TIMEOUT` socket option, which controls how long (in milliseconds) a read operation will block. A value of zero disables timeouts, and blocks indefinitely. If a timeout does occur, a `java.io.IOInterruptedException` is thrown whenever a read operation occurs on the socket's input stream. This is distinct from the internal TCP timer, which triggers a resend of unacknowledged datagram packets (see Section 6.1.1.1 on error control).

- `void setTcpNoDelay(boolean onFlag)` throws `java.net.Socket-Exception`—enables or disables the `TCP_NODELAY` socket option, which determines whether Nagle's algorithm is used.

- `void shutdownInput()` throws `java.io.IOException`—closes the input stream associated with this socket and discards any further information that is sent. Further reads to the input stream will encounter the end of the stream marker.

- `void shutdownOutput()` throws `java.io.IOException`—closes the output stream associated with this socket. Any data previously written, but not yet sent, will be flushed, followed by a TCP connection-termination sequence, which notifies the application that no more data will be available (and in the case of a Java application, that the end of the stream has been reached). Further writes to the socket will cause an `IOException` to be thrown.

### 6.4.3 Reading from and Writing to TCP Sockets

Creating client software that uses TCP for communication is extremely easy in Java, no matter what operating system is being used. The Java Networking API provides a consistent, platform-neutral interface that allows client applications to connect to remote services. Once a socket is created, it is connected and ready to read/write by using the socket's input and output streams. These streams don't need to be created; they are provided by the Socket. getInputStream() and Socket.getOutputStream() methods. As was shown in Chapter 4 on I/O streams, filtered streams provide easy I/O access.

A filter can easily be connected to a socket stream, to make for simpler programming. The following code snippet demonstrates a simple TCP client that connects a BufferedReader to the socket input stream, and a PrintStream to the socket output stream.

```
try
{
        // Connect a socket to some host machine and port
        Socket socket = new Socket ( somehost, someport );

        // Connect a buffered reader
        BufferedReader reader = new BufferedReader (
            new InputStreamReader ( socket.getInputStream() ) );

        // Connect a print stream
        PrintStream pstream =
            new PrintStream( socket.getOutputStream() );
}
catch (Exception e)
{
        System.err.println ("Error - " + e);
}
```

### 6.4.4 Socket Options

Socket options are settings that modify how sockets work, and they can affect (both positively and negatively) the performance of applications. Support for socket options was introduced in Java 1.1, and some refinements have been made in later versions (such as support for the SO_KEEPALIVE option in Java 2 v 1.3). Generally, socket options should not be changed unless there is a good reason for doing so, as changes may negatively affect application and network performance (for example, enabling Nagle's algorithm may increase performance of telnet type applications but lower the available bandwidth). The one exception to this caveat is the SO_TIMEOUT option—virtually every TCP application should handle timeouts gracefully rather than stalling if the application the socket is connected to fails to transmit data when required.

#### 6.4.4.1 SO_KEEPALIVE Socket Option

The keepalive socket option is controversial; its use is a topic that some developers feel very strongly about. By default, no data is sent between two connected sockets unless an application has data to send. This means that an idle socket may not have data submitted for minutes, hours, or even days in the case of long-lived processes. Suppose, however, that a client crashes, and the end-of-connection sequence is not sent to a TCP server. Valuable resources (CPU time and memory) might be wasted on a client that will never respond. When the keepalive socket option is enabled, the other end of the socket is probed to verify it is still active. However, the application doesn't have any control over how often keepalive probes are sent. To enable keepalive, the `Socket.setSoKeepAlive(boolean)` method is called with a value of "true" (a value of "false" will disable it). For example, to enable keepalive on a socket, the following code would be used.

```
// Enable SO_KEEPALIVE
someSocket.setSoKeepAlive(true);
```

Although keepalive does have some advantages, many developers advocate controlling timeouts and dead sockets at a higher level, in application code. It should also be kept in mind that keepalive doesn't allow you to specify a value for probing socket endpoints. A better solution than keepalive, and one that developers are advised to use, is to instead modify the timeout socket option.

### 6.4.4.2 SO_RCVBUF Socket Option

The receive buffer socket option controls the buffer used for receiving data. Changes can be made to the size by calling the `Socket.setReceiveBufferSize-(int)` method. For example, to increase the receive buffer size to 4,096 bytes, the following code would be used.

```
// Modify receive buffer size
someSocket.setReceiveBufferSize(4096);
```

Note that a request to modify the size of the receive buffer does not guarantee that it will change. For example, some operating systems may not allow this socket option to be modified, and will ignore any changes to the value. The current buffer size can be determined by invoking the `Socket.getReceiveBufferSize()` method. A better choice for buffering is to use a `BufferedInputStream/BufferedReader`.

### 6.4.4.3 SO_SNDBUF Socket Option

The send buffer socket option controls the size of the buffer used for sending data. By calling the `Socket.setSendBufferSize(int)` method, you can attempt to change the buffer size, but requests to change the size may be rejected by the operating system.

```
// Set the send buffer size to 4096 bytes
someSocket.setSendBufferSize(4096);
```

To determine the size of the current send buffer, you can call the `Socket.getSendBufferSize()` method, which returns an int value.

```
// Get the default size
int size = someSocket.getSendBufferSize();
```

Changing buffer size will be more effective with the `DatagramSocket` class. When buffering writes, the preferable choice is to use a `BufferedOutputStream` or a `BufferedWriter`.

### 6.4.4.4 SO_LINGER Socket Option

When a TCP socket connection is closed, it is possible that data may be queued for delivery and not yet sent (particularly if an IP datagram becomes lost in transit and must be resent). The linger socket option controls the amount of time during which unsent data may be sent, after which it is discarded completely. It is possible to enable/disable the linger option entirely, or to modify the duration of a linger, by using the `Socket.setSoLinger(boolean onFlag, int duration)` method:

```
// Enable linger, for fifty seconds
someSocket.setSoLinger( true, 50 );
```

### 6.4.4.5 TCP_NODELAY Socket Option

This socket option is a flag, the state of which controls whether Nagle's algorithm (RFC 896) is enabled or not. Because TCP data is sent over the network using IP datagrams, a fair bit of overhead exists for each packet, such as IP and TCP header information. If only a few bytes at a time are sent in each packet, the size of the header information will far exceed that of the data. On a local area network, the extra amount of data sent probably won't amount to much, but on the Internet, where hundreds, thousands, or even millions of clients may be sending such packets through individual routers, this adds up to a significant amount of bandwidth consumption.

The solution is Nagle's algorithm, which states that TCP may send only one datagram at a time. When an acknowledgment comes back for each IP datagram, a new packet is sent containing any data that has been queued up. This limits the amount of bandwidth being consumed by packet header information, but at a not insignificant cost—network latency. Since data is being queued, it isn't dispatched immediately, so systems that require quick response times such as X-Windows or telnet are slowed. Disabling Nagle's algorithm may improve performance, but if used by too many clients, network performance is reduced.

Nagle's algorithm is enabled or disabled by invoking the `Socket.setTcp-NoDelay(boolean state)` method. For example, to deactivate the algorithm, the following code would be used:

```
// Disable Nagle's algorithm for faster response times
someSocket.setTcpNoDelay(false);
```

To determine the state of Nagle's algorithm and the `TCP_NODELAY` flag, the `Socket.getTcpNoDelay()` method is used:

```
// Get the state of the TCP_NODELAY flag
boolean state = someSocket.getTcpNoDelay();
```

### 6.4.4.6 SO_TIMEOUT Socket Option

This timeout option is the most useful socket option. By default, I/O operations (be they file- or network-based) are blocking. An attempt to read data from an `InputStream` will wait indefinitely until input arrives. If the input never arrives, the application stalls and in most cases becomes unusable (unless multithreading is used). Users are not fond of unresponsive applications, and find such application behavior annoying, to say the least. A more robust application will anticipate such problems and take corrective action.

**NOTE:** In a local intranet environment during testing, network problems are rare, but on the Internet stalled applications are probable. Server applications are not immune—a server connection to a client uses the Socket class as well, and can just as easily stall. For this reason, all applications (be they client or server) should handle network timeouts gracefully.

When the `SO_TIMEOUT` option is enabled, any read request to the `Input-Stream` of a socket starts a timer. When no data arrives in time and the timer expires, a `java.io.InterruptedIOException` is thrown, which can be caught to check for a timeout. What happens then is up to the application developer—a retry attempt might be made, the user might be notified, or the connection aborted. The duration of the timer is controlled by calling the `Socket.setSoTimeout(int)` method, which accepts as a parameter the number of milliseconds to wait for data. For example, to set a five-second timeout, the following code would be used:

```
// Set a five second timeout
someSocket.setSoTimeout ( 5 * 1000 );
```

Once enabled, any attempt to read could potentially throw an `Inter-ruptedIOException`, which is extended from the `java.io.IOException` class.

Since read attempts can already throw an IOException, no further code is required to handle the exception—however, some applications may want to specifically trap timeout-related exceptions, in which case an additional exception handler may be added.

```
try
{
        Socket s = new Socket (...);
        s.setSoTimeout ( 2000 );

        // do some read operation ....
}
catch (InterruptedIOException iioe)
{
        timeoutFlag = true; // do something special like set a flag
}
catch (IOException ioe)
{
        System.err.println ("IO error " + ioe);
        System.exit(0);
}
```

To determine the length of the TCP timer, the Socket.getSoTimeout() method, which returns an int, can be used. A value of zero indicates that timeouts are disabled, and read operations will block indefinitely.

```
// Check to see if timeout is not zero
if ( someSocket.getSoTimeout() == 0)
someSocket.setSoTimeout (500);
```

## 6.5    Creating a TCP Client

Having discussed the functionality of the Socket class, we will now examine a complete TCP client. The client we'll look at here is a daytime client, which, as its name suggests, connects to a daytime server to read the current day and time. Establishing a socket connection and reading from it is a fairly simple process, requiring very little code. By default, the daytime service runs on port 13. Not every machine has a daytime server running, but a Unix server would be a good system to run the client against. If you do not have access to a Unix server, code for a TCP daytime server is given in Section 6.7—the client can be run against it.

### Code for DaytimeClient

```
import java.net.*
import java.io.*;
```

```java
// Chapter 6, Listing 1
public class DaytimeClient
{
    public static final int SERVICE_PORT = 13;

    public static void main(String args[])
    {
        // Check for hostname parameter
        if (args.length != 1)
        {
            System.out.println ("Syntax - DaytimeClient host");
            return;
        }

        // Get the hostname of server
        String hostname = args[0];

        try
        {
            // Get a socket to the daytime service
            Socket daytime = new Socket (hostname,
            SERVICE_PORT);

            System.out.println ("Connection established");

            // Set the socket option just in case server stalls
            daytime.setSoTimeout ( 2000 );

            // Read from the server
            BufferedReader reader = new BufferedReader (
              new InputStreamReader
              (daytime.getInputStream()
            ));

            System.out.println ("Results : " +
            reader.readLine());

            // Close the connection
            daytime.close();
        }
        catch (IOException ioe)
        {
            System.err.println ("Error " + ioe);
        }
    }
}
```

## How DaytimeClient Works

The daytime application is straightforward, and uses concepts discussed earlier
in the chapter. A socket is created, an input stream is obtained, and timeouts

are enabled in the rare event that a server as simple as daytime fails during a connection. Rather than connecting a filtered stream, a buffered reader is connected to the socket input stream, and the results are displayed to the user. Finally, the client terminates after closing the socket connection. This is about as simple a socket client as you can get—complexity comes from implementing network protocols, not from network-specific coding.

### Running DaytimeClient

Running the application is easy. Simply specify the hostname of a machine running the daytime service as a command-line parameter and run it. If you use a nonstandard port for the daytime server (discussed later), remember to change the port number in the client and recompile.

For example, to run the client against a server running on the local machine, the following command would be used:

```
java DaytimeClient localhost
```

**NOTE:** The daytime server must be running, or the client will be unable to establish a connection. If you're using, for example, a Wintel system, instead of Unix, then you'll need to run the DaytimeServer from later in this chapter.

## 6.6  **ServerSocket Class**

A special type of socket, the server socket, is used to provide TCP services. Client sockets bind to any free port on the local machine, and connect to a specific server port and host. The difference with server sockets is that they bind to a specific port on the local machine, so that remote clients may locate a service. Client socket connections will connect to only one machine, whereas server sockets are capable of fulfilling the requests of multiple clients.

The way it works is simple—clients are aware of a service running on a particular port (usually the port number is well known, and used for particular protocols, but servers may run on nonstandard port numbers as well). They establish a connection, and within the server, the connection is accepted. Multiple connections can be accepted at the same time, or a server may choose to accept only one connection at any given moment. Once accepted, the connection is represented as a normal socket, in the form of a Socket object—once you have mastered the Socket class, it becomes almost as simple to write servers as it does clients. The only difference between a server and a client is that the server binds to a specific port, using a ServerSocket object. This ServerSocket object acts as a factory for client connections—you don't need to create instances of the Socket class yourself. These connections are modeled as a normal socket, so you can connect input and output filter streams (or even a reader and writer) to the connection.

### 6.6.1  *Creating a ServerSocket*

Once a server socket is created, it will be bound to a local port and ready to accept incoming connections. When clients attempt to connect, they are placed into a queue. Once all free space in the queue is exhausted, further clients will be refused.

#### Constructors

The simplest way to create a server socket is to bind to a local address, which is specified as the only parameter, using a constructor. For example, to provide a service on port 80 (usually used for Web servers), the following snippet of code would be used:

```
try
{
        // Bind to port 80, to provide a TCP service (like HTTP)
        ServerSocket myServer = new ServerSocket ( 80 );

        // ......
}
catch (IOException ioe)
{
        System.err.println ("I/O error - " + ioe);
}
```

This is the simplest form of the ServerSocket constructor, but there are several others that allow additional customization. All of these constructors are marked as public.

- ServerSocket(int port) throws java.io.IOException, java.lang.SecurityException—binds the server socket to the specified port number, so that remote clients may locate the TCP service. If a value of zero is passed, any free port will be used—however, clients will be unable to access the service unless notified somehow of the port number. By default, the queue size is set to 50, but an alternate constructor is provided that allows modification of this setting. If the port is already bound, or security restrictions (such as security polices or operating system restrictions on well-known ports) prevent access, an exception is thrown.

- `ServerSocket(int port, int numberOfClients)` throws `java.io.IOException, java.lang.SecurityException`—binds the server socket to the specified port number and allocates sufficient space to the queue to support the specified number of client sockets. This is an overloaded version of the `ServerSocket(int port)` constructor, and if the port is already bound or security restrictions prevent access, an exception is thrown.
- `ServerSocket(int port, int numberOfClients, InetAddress address)` throws `java.io.IOException, java.lang.SecurityException`—binds the server socket to the specified port number, and allocates sufficient space to the queue to support the specified number of client sockets. This is an overloaded version of the `ServerSocket(int port, int numberOfClients)` constructor that allows a server socket to bind to a specific IP address, in the case of a multihomed machine. For example, a machine may have two network cards, or may be configured to represent itself as several machines by using virtual IP addresses. Specifying a null value for the address will cause the server socket to accept requests on all local addresses. If the port is already bound or security restrictions prevent access, an exception is thrown.

### 6.6.2 *Using a ServerSocket*

While the `Socket` class is fairly versatile, and has many methods, the `ServerSocket` class doesn't really do that much, other than accept connections and act as a factory for `Socket` objects that model the connection between client and server. The most important method is the `accept()` method, which accepts client connection requests, but there are several others that developers may find useful.

#### Methods

All methods are public unless otherwise noted.

- `Socket accept()` throws `java.io.IOException, java.lang.SecurityException`—waits for a client to request a connection to the server socket, and accepts it. This is a blocking I/O operation, and will not return until a connection is made (unless the timeout socket option is set). When a connection is established, it will be returned as a `Socket` object. When accepting connections, each client request will be verified by the default security manager, which makes it possible to accept certain IP addresses and block others, causing an exception to be thrown. However, servers do not need to rely on the security manager to block or terminate connections—the identity of a client can be determined by calling the `getInetAddress()` method of the client socket.

- `void close()` throws `java.io.IOException`—closes the server socket, which unbinds the TCP port and allows other services to use it.
- `InetAddress getInetAddress()`—returns the address of the server socket, which may be different from the local address in the case of a multihomed machine (i.e., a machine whose localhost is known by two or more IP addresses).
- `int getLocalPort()`—returns the port number to which the server socket is bound.
- `int getSoTimeout()` throws `java.io.IOException`—returns the value of the timeout socket option, which determines how many milliseconds an `accept()` operation can block for. If a value of zero is returned, the accept operation blocks indefinitely.
- `void implAccept(Socket socket)` throws `java.io.IOException`—this method allows `ServerSocket` subclasses to pass an unconnected socket subclass, and to have that socket object accept an incoming request. Using the `implAccept` method to accept the connection, an overridden `ServerSocket.accept()` method can return a connected socket. Few developers will want to subclass the `ServerSocket`, and using this should be avoided unless required.
- `static void setSocketFactory ( SocketImplFactory factory )` throws `java.io.IOException, java.net.SocketException, java.lang.SecurityException` —assigns a server socket factory for the JVM. This is a static method, and should be called only once during the lifetime of a JVM. If assigning a new socket factory is prohibited, or one has already been assigned, an exception is thrown.
- `void setSoTimeout(int timeout)` throws `java.net.SocketException`— assigns a timeout value (specified in milliseconds) for the blocking `accept()` operation. If a value of zero is specified, timeouts are disabled and the operation will block indefinitely. Providing timeouts are enabled, however, whenever the `accept()` method is called a timer starts. When the timer expires, a `java.io.InterruptedIOException` is thrown, which allows a server to then take further actions.

### 6.6.3 *Accepting and Processing Requests from TCP Clients*

The most important function of a server socket is to accept client sockets. Once a client socket is obtained, the server can perform all the "real work" of server programming, which involves reading from and writing to the socket to implement a network protocol. The exact data that is sent or received is dependent on the details of the protocol. For example, a mail server that provides access to stored messages would listen to commands and send back message contents. A telnet server would listen for keystrokes and pass these to a log-in shell, and send back output to the network client. Protocol-specific actions are less network- and more programming-oriented.

The following snippet shows how client sockets are accepted, and how I/O streams may be connected to the client:

```
// Perform a blocking read operation, to read the next socket
// connection
Socket nextSocket = someServerSocket.accept();

// Connect a filter reader and writer to the stream
BufferedReader reader = new BufferedReader (new
                       InputStreamReader
                       (nextSocket.getInputStream() ) );
PrintWriter writer = new PrintWriter( new
                       OutputStreamWriter
                       (nextSocket.getOutputStream() ) );
```

From then on, the server may conduct the tasks needed to process and respond to client requests, or may choose to leave this task for code executing in another thread. Remember that just like any other form of I/O operation in Java, code will block indefinitely while reading a response from a client—so to service multiple clients concurrently, threads must be used. In simple cases, however, multiple threads of execution may not be necessary, particularly if requests are responded to quickly and take little time to process.

Creating fully-fledged client/server applications that implement popular Internet protocols involves a fair amount of effort, especially for those new to network programming. It also draws on other skills, such as multi-threaded programming, discussed in the next chapter. For now, we'll focus on a simple, bare-bones TCP server that executes as a single-threaded application.

## 6.7    Creating a TCP Server

One of the most enjoyable parts of networking is writing a network server. Clients send requests and respond to data sent back, but the server performs most of the real work. This next example is of a daytime server (which you can test using the client described in Section 6.5).

### Code for DaytimeServer

```
import java.net.*;
import java.io.*;
```

```
// Chapter 6, Listing 2
public class DaytimeServer
{
    public static final int SERVICE_PORT = 13;

    public static void main(String args[])
    {
        try
        {
            // Bind to the service port, to grant clients
            // access to the TCP daytime service
            ServerSocket server = new ServerSocket
            (SERVICE_PORT);

            System.out.println ("Daytime service started");

            // Loop indefinitely, accepting clients
            for (;;)
            {
                // Get the next TCP client
                Socket nextClient = server.accept();

                // Display connection details
                System.out.println ("Received request from " +
                    nextClient.getInetAddress() + ":" +
                    nextClient.getPort() );

                // Don't read, just write the message
                OutputStream out =
                nextClient.getOutputStream();
                PrintStream pout = new PrintStream (out);

                // Write the current date out to the user
                pout.print( new java.util.Date() );

                // Flush unsent bytes
                out.flush();

                // Close stream
                out.close();

                // Close the connection
                nextClient.close();
            }
        }
        catch (BindException be)
        {
            System.err.println ("Service already running on port " + SERVICE_PORT );
        }
        catch (IOException ioe)
        {
```

```
            System.err.println ("I/O error - " + ioe);
        }
    }
}
```

### How DaytimeServer Works

For a server, this is about as simple as it gets. The first step in this server is to create a ServerSocket. If this port is already bound, a BindException will be thrown, as no two servers can share the same port. Otherwise, the server socket is created; the next step is to wait for connections.

Since daytime is a very simple protocol and our first example of a TCP server should be a simple one, we use here a single-threaded server. A for loop that loops indefinitely is commonly used in simple TCP servers, or a while loop whose expression always evaluates to true. Inside this loop, the first line you will find is the server.accept() method, which blocks until a client attempts to connect. This method returns a socket that represents the connection to the client. For logging, the IP address and port of the connection is sent to System.out. You'll see this every time someone logs in and gets the time of day.

Daytime is a response-only protocol, so we don't need to worry about reading any input. We obtain an OutputStream and then wrap it in a PrintStream to make it easier to work with. Determining the date and time using the java. util.Date class, we send it over the TCP stream to the client. Finally, we flush all data in the print stream and close the connection by calling close() on the socket.

### Running DaytimeServer

Running the server is very simple. The server has no command-line parameters. For this server example to run on UNIX, you will need to modify the SERVICE_PORT variable to a number above 1,024, unless you turn off the default daytime process and run this example as root. On Windows or other operating systems, this will not be a problem. To run the server on the local machine, the following command would be used:

```
java DaytimeServer
```

## 6.8   Exception Handling: Socket-Specific Exceptions

As a medium for communication, networks are fraught with problems. With so many machines connected to the global Internet, the prospect of encountering a host whose hostname cannot be resolved, one that is disconnected from the network, or one that locks up during a connection, is very likely in the lifetime of a software application. It is important, therefore, to be aware of the conditions that might cause such problems to arise in an application and to deal with them gracefully. Of course, not every application will require precise control, and in simple applications you'll probably want to handle everything with a generic handler. For those more advanced applications, however, it is important to be aware of the socket-specific exceptions that can be thrown at runtime.

**NOTE:** All socket-specific exceptions extend from `SocketException`, so by simply catching that exception, you catch all of the socket-specific ones and write a single generic handler. In addition, `SocketException` extends from `java.io.IOException` if you want to provide a catchall for any I/O exception.

### 6.8.1   SocketException

The `java.net.SocketException` represents a generic socket error, which can represent a range of specific error conditions. For finer-grained control, applications should catch the subclasses discussed below.

### 6.8.2   BindException

The `java.net.BindException` represents an inability to bind a socket to a local port. The most common reason for this will be that the local port is already in use.

### 6.8.3   ConnectException

The `java.net.ConnectException` occurs when a socket can't connect to a specific remote host and port. There can be several reasons for this, such as that the remote server does not have a service bound to that port, or that it is so swamped by queued connections, it cannot accept any further ones.

### 6.8.4   NoRouteToHostException

The `java.net.NoRouteToHostException` is thrown when, due to a network error, it is impossible to find a route to the remote host. The cause of this may be local (i.e., the network on which the software application is running), may be a temporary gateway or router problem, or may be the fault of the remote network to which the socket is trying to connect. Another common cause of this is that firewalls and routers are blocking the client software, which is usually a permanent condition.

### 6.8.5 InterruptedIOException

The `java.net.InterruptedIOException` occurs when a read operation is blocked for sufficient time to cause a network timeout, as discussed earlier in the chapter. Handling timeouts is a good way to make your code more robust and reliable.

## 6.9 Summary

Communication over TCP with sockets is an important technique to master, as many of the most interesting application protocols in use today occur over TCP. The Java socket API provides a clear and easy mechanism by which developers are able to accept communications as a server or initiate communications as a client. By using the concepts discussed earlier involving input and output streams under Java, the transition to socket-based communication is straightforward. With the level of exception handling built into the `java.net` package, it's also very easy to deal with network errors that occur at runtime.

**Chapter Highlights**

In this chapter, you have learned:

- About the Transmission Control Protocol
- About clients and servers
- About how to write and run a simple TCP socket client, using `java.net.Socket`
- About how to write and run a simple TCP socket server, using `java.net.ServerSocket`
- About exception handling with sockets

# CHAPTER 7

## *Multi-threaded Applications*

## 7.1   Overview

Just as a team of developers collaborating together on a project can split the work into small chunks that can be completed concurrently, software applications employ a similar strategy called multi-threading to split tasks into manageable units. Multi-threaded programming is an important concept in Java networking, as networking clients and servers must often perform several different tasks at a time (for example, listening for incoming requests and responses, processing data, and updating the text or graphical user interface for the user). Before undertaking multi-threaded applications in Java, it is important for the developer to understand the differences between single-threaded programming, multiprocess programming, and multi-threaded programming.

### 7.1.1 Single-Threaded Programming

The concept of multi-threading can initially be difficult to grasp. Many of the oldest programming languages and operating systems did not even support it. Some readers will be new to multi-threading, as they never had a reason to use it in their software development or computer science classes at college.

Traditional software written in procedural languages is compiled into a machine-readable format, which is called machine code. This code is read by a central processing unit (CPU), which executes programming statements one after another, in a sequential manner (see Figure 7-1). The time taken to execute each statement may vary (due to the nature of the operation, such as comparing two bytes for equality or adding two numbers together), but until a

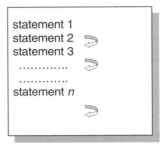

**Figure 7-1**   In single-threaded execution, statements are executed sequentially.

statement is completed, no further statements will run. This is single-threaded execution.

The chief advantage of this type of programming is its simplicity. If a statement has not been completed, the next statement has not been executed. This means that developers can easily predict the state of a machine at any given moment in time. It is guaranteed that a variable being accessed in a single-threaded environment will not be accessed or modified by another copy of the program, as only one copy of the program is running.

## 7.1.2 Multiprocess Programming

Readers familiar with programming for the Unix platform may be acquainted with the concept of multiprocess programming. To support multitasking, Unix uses the concept of processes. Each application runs as a process, with memory allocated for program code and data storage. Multiple processes would run on the same machine (allowing multiple users to connect to their accounts via telnet sessions, for example). The operating system would allocate CPU time to each process, suspending a process when its time was up and allowing another to take its place. Sometimes, a process will become blocked (waiting on I/O), or may voluntarily choose to yield its CPU time. The operating system creates the illusion that these processes are running concurrently, by frequently switching from one process to another and sharing time between them (though not always equally). This type of multitasking is extremely important, as it means that one machine can share its CPU time across many users.

Multiprocess programming has other benefits. Programs themselves could create new processes, having one part of the program performing a task while another part does something else (see Figure 7-2). For example, when checking for e-mail messages on a remote machine, a user interface could display the progress of the operation and allow the user to compose messages or read previously downloaded messages from his or her inbox. At the same time, another

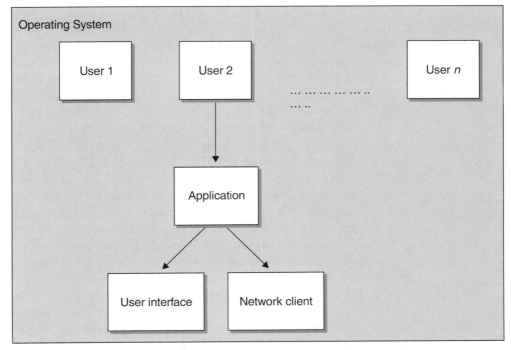

**Figure 7-2** Application processes can fork in two, having one or more subprocesses perform useful work.

process could be acting as a network client, retrieving new messages. This type of programming is useful, as it means that work can be performed even if one part of the program becomes stalled (for example, waiting for input).

Although multiprocess programming works well, there are disadvantages to its use. First, when a process branches into two, there is overlap between the data storage of one process and another. Because two copies of data are being kept, more memory than is needed is consumed. Second, there isn't an easy way for one process to access and modify the data of another. In Unix, Inter-Process Communication (IPC) is used, creating data pipes that allow a process to communicate with another. Nonetheless, it is not as easy to design software that shares data in a multiprocess environment as it is in a multi-threaded one.

### 7.1.3 Multi-threaded Programming

Multi-threaded programming requires a different way of looking at software. Rather than executing a series of steps sequentially, tasks are executed concurrently—that is, many tasks are performed at the same time, rather than one task having to finish before another can start. Multi-threading, also known as multiple threads of execution, allows a program to have multiple instances of itself running, while using the same shared memory space and code (unlike multi-process programming, which uses separate memory address spaces, making communication between processes difficult). An application can be performing many different tasks concurrently, and threads may access shared data variables to work collaboratively.

You've probably seen this type of behavior in software applications, although you might not have recognized it. When programs with a graphical user interface are run, they typically use multi-threading. For example, a GUI application running on a Windows machine may be performing some processing task, such as updating cells in a spreadsheet or spooling a document to the printer. Have you ever wondered why you can move a window around, resize it, or access the file menu, even though the application is performing some other task? The graphical user interface (which often uses GUI components of the underlying operating system) is being continually updated, independent of the actual application, by one or more GUI threads that update screen display and catch GUI events such as mouse clicks and drags.

Most modern operating systems support multitasking. While some applications don't take advantage of multi-threading and are written as single-threaded applications, they are still running in a multi-threaded environment. The operating system can allow other applications and other threads to execute, while the single-threaded application is oblivious. So, how is this achieved?

Unless you have more than one CPU, only a single thread can be running at any given moment in time. The operating system maintains a queue of threads and allocates CPU time to them. However, time must be shared—allocating all the time to a single thread would be unfair, as it would prevent other threads from doing their work (this is known as thread starvation). A preemptive multitasking operating system is one that will suspend a thread (even if it still has work to do) so that other threads can be given CPU time.

Of course, deciding which thread should be allocated CPU time is tricky. The process of determining which thread to run is called scheduling. Not all operating systems allocate thread time fairly, but to give the operating system a guide, threads are allocated a priority level. Some threads operate at a very high level of priority, which means that they are given first shot at CPU time, while other threads operate at a very low level of priority. Low-priority threads don't normally get a fair share of CPU time, and may not run at all if higher-priority threads exhaust all available CPU time. Since the choice of which thread is executed is up to the operating system and not the application, it becomes impossible to predict the order of execution, or how much CPU time will be given.

This has some important implications for application developers. If the order of thread execution cannot be predicted, it is impossible to know which tasks will be completed first or have even been started. Tasks may be preempted before they are completed, which can cause problems if another thread accesses the same memory variable at the same time. Imagine a scenario in which data records are being accessed and modified by multiple threads. Suppose one thread is generating a total of the number of items stored in a warehouse, and is suspended partway through the total to allow another thread to run. This second thread modifies the contents of a record to indicate that an item has been removed. The first thread is resumed, and continues on in its calculations completely unaware that items have been removed and that the records have been modified. At the end of its task, its calculation is inaccurate because it was unable to account for the fact that the record contents had changed.

Such a system may sound anarchical at first. If threads are accessing and modifying data haphazardly, how then can useful work be performed? Careful attention must be paid to concurrent access and modification of data, to prevent data from becoming out of sync. With careful design, however, data can be locked, which will prevent read access while write access occurs. Multi-threaded programming can be difficult to master, but the rewards that it offers are great. Networking clients do not need to lock up the GUI if a network connection stalls, and servers can process multiple clients concurrently. Additionally, threads may use variables independently, and are not forced to share the same data. A thread could, for example, declare its own set of variables that it does not make available to other threads (by marking them as private or protected), thus ensuring that an access conflict does not occur.

## 7.2    Multi-threading in Java

Java, like many modern programming languages, includes support for multi-threaded applications. In Java, threads of execution are represented by the java.lang.Thread class, while code for tasks that are designed to run in a separate thread is represented by the java.lang.Runnable interface. It is very important that developers be aware of both.

### 7.2.1    Creating Multi-threaded Applications with the Thread Class

The java.lang.Thread class provides methods to start, suspend, resume, and stop a thread, as well as to control other aspects such as the priority of a thread or the name associated with it. The simplest way to use the Thread class is to extend it and override the run() method, which is invoked when the thread is

first started. By overriding the run() method, a thread can be made to perform
useful tasks in the background.

**NOTE:** Keep in mind that threads do not start running automatically at creation
time. Instead, the Thread.start() method must be invoked. If it is not, the
thread will not run.

The following example shows how to extend the Thread class and start several
eral instances running, each in a separate thread.

```java
// Chapter 7, Listing 1
public class ExtendThreadDemo extends java.lang.Thread
{
    int threadNumber;

    public ExtendThreadDemo ( int num )
    {
        // Assign to member variable
        threadNumber = num;
    }

    // Run method is executed when thread first started
    public void run()
    {
        System.out.println ("I am thread number " + threadNumber);

        try
        {
            // Sleep for five thousand milliseconds
            // (5 secs), to simulate work being done
            Thread.sleep(5000);
        }
        catch (InterruptedException ie) {}

        System.out.println (threadNumber + " is finished!");
    }

    // Main method to create and start threads
    public static void main(String args[])
    {
        System.out.println ("Creating thread 1");

        // Create first thread instance
        Thread t1 = new ExtendThreadDemo(1);

        System.out.println ("Creating thread 2");
```

```
        // Create second thread instance
        Thread t2 = new ExtendThreadDemo(2);

        // Start both threads
        t1.start(); t2.start();
    }
}
```

When compiled and run, this example shows the threads being created and the output of each. The threads sleep for five seconds, to simulate the occurrence of meaningful work, and then terminate, which has the result of closing the thread. Only once all threads are terminated will the main method exit. Two important things should be noted from this example.

First, the run() method was not invoked when the thread was created, only when the thread was started by invoking the start() method. Though the difference is subtle, it is nonetheless important. You can create threads in advance, and start them only when needed. Remember that the thread object only represents a thread—threads are in fact provided by the operating system itself. When the start() method of a thread is called, it sends a request to launch a separate thread, which will call the run() method.

**NOTE:** The main application does not call the run() method directly. Instead, it calls start() to perform this operation. If your application calls run() directly, it won't be running as a separate thread.

Second, the main method terminates once the two threads are started. There is no pause or sleep command issued in the main thread—yet the application doesn't terminate. It keeps on going (though it has no actual work to do and is idle) until the two threads have finished their work and leave their run() method. When a normal thread (also referred to as a user thread) is created, it is expected that it will complete its work and not shut down prematurely. The Java Virtual Machine (JVM) will not terminate until all user threads have finished, or until a call is made to the System.exit() method, which terminates the JVM abruptly. Sometimes, however, threads are only useful when other threads are running (such as the actual application, which will eventually terminate when the user is finished with it). We call these types of threads daemon threads, as opposed to user threads. If only daemon threads are running, the JVM will automatically terminate.

Next we look at daemon threads in action, modifying the main method as follows (change indicated in bold print) to specify the two threads (t1 and t2) as daemon threads.

```
         // Main method to create and start threads
         public static void main(String args[])
         {
               System.out.println ("Creating thread 1");

               // Create first thread instance
               Thread t1 = new ExtendThreadDemo(1);

               System.out.println ("Creating thread 2");

               // Create second thread instance
               Thread t2 = new ExtendThreadDemo(2);

               // Make both threads daemon threads
               t1.setDaemon(true); t2.setDaemon(true);

               // Start both threads
               t1.start(); t2.start();

               try
               {
                     // Sleep for one second, to allow threads
                     // time to display first message
                     Thread.sleep(1000);
               }
               catch (InterruptedException ie) {}
         }
```

The first change makes both t1 and t2 daemon threads, by calling the Thread.setDaemon(boolean) method. If you need to change the state of a thread to either a daemon or a user thread, this must be done before the thread is started—its state cannot be changed once the thread is running. The second change introduces a slight pause, to allow the daemon threads time to display their first message. When you recompile and run this example, you'll notice that the threads do not complete their work and display their final message. This is because there are no more user threads active once the main method finishes. (The primary thread is always a user thread, never a daemon thread.)

### 7.2.2   Creating Multi-threaded Applications with the Runnable Interface

While extending the Thread class is one way to create a multi-threaded application, it isn't always the best way. Remember, Java supports only single inheritance, unlike languages such as C++, which supports multiple inheritance. This means that if a class extends the java.lang.Thread class, it cannot extend any other class—a feature that is often necessary in the design of Java software. A better way is often to implement the java.lang.Runnable interface.

The `Runnable` interface defines a single method, `run()`, that must be implemented. Classes implement this interface to show that they are capable of being run as a separate thread of execution. The precise signature for the run method is as follows:

```
public void run ()
```

The `Runnable` interface doesn't define any other methods, or provide any thread-specific functionality. Its sole purpose is to identify classes capable of running as threads. When an object implementing the `Runnable` interface is passed to the constructor of a thread, and the thread's `start()` method is invoked, the `run()` method will be called by the newly created thread. When the `run()` method terminates, the thread stops executing.

There are several advantages to using the `Runnable` interface over extending the `Thread` class. The first, as mentioned above, is that an object is free to inherit from a different class. Second, the same `Runnable` object can be passed to more than one thread, so several concurrent threads can be using the same code and acting on the same data. Though this use is not always advised, it can make sense in certain circumstances, providing that due care is taken to prevent conflicts over data access. Third, carefully designed applications can minimize overhead, as creating a new `Thread` instance requires valuable memory and CPU time. A `Runnable` instance, on the other hand, doesn't incur the same burden of a thread, and can still be passed to a thread at a later point in time to be reused and run again if necessary.

Below is an example of a multi-threaded application that uses the `Runnable` interface rather than a subclass of the `Thread` class.

```java
// Chapter 7, Listing 2
public class RunnableThreadDemo implements java.lang.Runnable
{
    // Run method is executed when thread first started
    public void run()
    {
        System.out.println ("I am an instance of the java.lang.Runnable interface");
    }


    // Main method to create and start threads
    public static void main(String args[])
    {
        System.out.println ("Creating runnable object");

        // Create runnable object
        Runnable run = new RunnableThreadDemo();
```

```
        // Create a thread, and pass the runnable object
        System.out.println ("Creating first thread");
        Thread t1 = new Thread (run);


        // Create a second thread, and pass the runnable object
        System.out.println ("Creating second thread");
        Thread t2 = new Thread (run);

        // Start both threads
        System.out.println ("Starting both threads");
        t1.start(); t2.start();
    }
}
```

When the example is compiled and run, two threads can be seen printing a message to the console. What is very different about this program, and the previous one, is that only one Runnable object was created, but two different threads ran it. Although there was no shared data in this example, in more complex systems, threads must share access to resources, to prevent modification while a resource is being accessed. This is achieved by synchronizing access to resources (discussed later in the chapter).

### 7.2.3    Controlling Threads

As shown in the previous two examples, it is relatively easy to start a thread executing. There are other ways, too, of controlling threads.

#### 7.2.3.1 Interrupting a Thread

Observant readers may have noticed that whenever a call to the Thread.sleep(int) method was made in earlier examples, an exception handler was used. This is because the sleep method puts a thread to sleep for a long period of time, during which it is generally unable to rouse itself. However, if a thread must be awakened earlier, interrupting a thread will awaken it; this is achieved by invoking the interrupt() method. Of course, this requires another thread to maintain a reference to the sleeping thread.

The following example demonstrates the interruption of a thread, by using the Thread.interrupt() method:

```
// Chapter 7, Listing 3
public class SleepyHead extends Thread
{
    // Run method is executed when thread first started
    public void run()
    {
```

```
        System.out.println ("I feel sleepy. Wake me in eight hours");

        try
        {
            // Sleep for eight hours
            Thread.sleep( 1000 * 60 * 60 * 8 );

            System.out.println ("That was a nice nap");
        }
        catch (InterruptedException ie)
        {
            System.err.println ("Just five more minutes....");
        }
    }


    // Main method to create and start threads
    public static void main(String args[]) throws java.io.IOException
    {
        // Create a 'sleepy' thread
        Thread sleepy = new SleepyHead();

        // Start thread sleeping
        sleepy.start();

        // Prompt user and wait for input
        System.out.println ("Press enter to interrupt the thread");
        System.in.read();

        // Interrupt the thread
        sleepy.interrupt();
    }
}
```

The sole purpose of the thread in this example is to go to sleep for a very long time. Once the thread is sleeping, it cannot awaken itself. The only course of action is to send an interrupt message from another thread. Run the example, and you'll see that the thread is idle. The primary thread (executing the main method) waits for the user to hit "enter," then sends an interrupt message (which will be caught unless the sleeping thread has awoken of its own accord and terminated). The secondary thread awakens, displays a message, and then terminates, allowing the application to close.

### 7.2.3.2 Stopping a Thread

Sometimes it is necessary to terminate a thread before its task has been completed. For example, if a network client is sending messages to a mail server in a second thread, and the user wants to cancel the operation (perhaps to delete a hastily constructed flame before it is sent), the thread should be stopped immediately. One thread can send a stop message to another thread, by invoking the Thread.stop() method. This requires the controlling thread (issuing the stop message) to maintain a reference to the thread that it wants to shut down. The following example demonstrates the use of the stop() method:

```java
// Chapter 7, Listing 4
public class StopMe extends Thread
{
    // Run method is executed when thread first started
    public void run()
    {
        int count = 1;

        System.out.println ("I can count. Watch me go!");

        for (;;)
        {
            // Print count and increment it
            System.out.print (count++ + " ");

            // Sleep for half a second
            try { Thread.sleep(500); } catch (InterruptedException ie) {}
        }
    }


    // Main method to create and start threads
    public static void main(String args[]) throws java.io.IOException
{
        // Create and start counting thread
        Thread counter = new StopMe();
        counter.start();

        // Prompt user and wait for input
        System.out.println ("Press any enter to stop the thread counting");
        System.in.read();

        // Interrupt the thread
        counter.stop();
    }
}
```

Once started, the thread in this example will display an incrementing count, which will go on indefinitely without terminating. To stop the thread, the Thread.stop() method is used. Sometimes it is absolutely necessary to stop a thread, but this method must be used with caution. It is deprecated in the Java 2 platform, because of a potential problem that can cause data corruption. When a thread is stopped in this way, access monitors that protect two threads from accessing the same resource concurrently are released, but the resource itself might be in an inconsistent state. Although this would rarely happen, it can occur without warning. For this reason, it is advised that threads regularly check whether or not they should continue (for example, by checking the state of a boolean flag), rather than having another thread invoke the `stop()` method.

**NOTE:** An excellent example of this is shown in the Java API documentation for the `java.lang.Thread.stop()` method, which includes sample code for creating a thread that polls to see if it should continue, rather than allowing itself to be "stopped."

### 7.2.3.3 Suspending/Resuming Threads

Prior to Java 2, it was permissible to suspend and resume threads, allowing an application to pause threads without stopping them permanently. This was achieved by using the `Thread.suspend()` and later the `Thread.resume()` methods. However, these methods have been deprecated in the Java 2 platform, as they can sometimes cause a deadlock (a situation whereby one or more threads wait for access to a resource, but the lock on the resource is not released). This can occur if a suspended thread has locked a monitor and cannot release it while suspended. While the methods will still work, it is advised that they are not used.

### 7.2.3.4 Yielding CPU Time

Sometimes a thread might be waiting for an event to occur, or may be entering a section of code where releasing CPU time to another thread will improve either system performance or the user experience (for example, after performing a calculation that should be displayed to the user and before starting another one). It is sometimes advantageous, in these situations, for a thread to yield CPU time to another thread rather than sleeping for a long period of time. For example, while waiting for data to become available from an `InputStream`, a thread might yield CPU time instead of going to sleep. In this situation, the static `yield()` method can be used instead of the `sleep()` method. For example, for the currently running thread to yield CPU time, the following method could be invoked:

```
Thread.yield();
```

As this statement takes only a single line of code, and does not require interaction with another thread, no example is provided. Nonetheless, it is a useful method to be aware of, particularly in complex systems where many threads are fighting for CPU time. Remember, too, that it is a static method that affects the currently running thread only—an application cannot yield the time of a specific thread.

### 7.2.3.5 Waiting Until a Thread Is Dead

Sometimes it is necessary to wait until a thread has finished its task (for example, to retrieve the results of the task by invoking a method, or reading a member variable). To determine if a thread has died (i.e., if the run() method has finished), the isAlive() method, which returns a boolean value, can be invoked. But continually checking the value returned by this method (known as polling), and then sleeping or yielding, is a very inefficient use of CPU time. A much better way is to use the Thread.join() method, which waits for a thread to die. There is also an overloaded version of this method, which takes as a parameter a long value. This version waits for a thread death or the specified number of milliseconds, whichever comes first.

The following example demonstrates the use of the Thread.join() method.

```
// Chapter 7, Listing 5
public class WaitForDeath extends Thread
{
    // Run method is executed when thread first started
    public void run()
    {
        System.out.println ("This thread feels a little ill....");

        // Sleep for five seconds
        try
        {
            Thread.sleep(5000);
        }
        catch (InterruptedException ie) {}
    }


    // Main method to create and start threads
    public static void main(String args[]) throws java.lang.InterruptedException
    {
        // Create and start dying thread
        Thread dying = new WaitForDeath();
        dying.start();

        // Prompt user and wait for input
        System.out.println ("Waiting for thread death");
```

```
// Wait till death
dying.join();

System.out.println ("Thread has died");
    }
}
```

When run, the example, shows that the primary application thread launches a secondary thread and waits for its death. When the secondary thread finishes its work, and its run() method terminates, the primary thread will return from the join() method and notify the user.

## 7.3    Synchronization

An important consideration when designing multi-threaded applications is conflict over access to data. If two threads are fighting for the same resource, and a mechanism to resolve access conflicts is not put into place, the integrity of the application is at stake. Built into the Java language are two mechanisms for preventing concurrent access to resources: method-level synchronization and block-level synchronization.

### 7.3.1    *Method-Level Synchronization*

Method-level synchronization prevents two threads from executing methods on an object at the same time. Methods that must be "thread-safe" are marked as synchronized. When a synchronized method of an object is invoked, a thread takes out an object lock, or monitor. If another thread attempts to execute any synchronized method, it finds that it is locked, and enters a state of suspension until the lock on the object monitor is released. If several threads attempt to execute a method on a locked object, a queue of suspended threads will form. When the thread that instituted the lock returns from the method, only one of the queued threads may access the object—the release of a monitor does not allow more than one object to take out a new monitor. One should note, however, that if a method is not synchronized and is executed while the object is locked, the thread will not block and the method can be run.

Method-level synchronization is a common mechanism for synchronizing access to resources. When designing multi-threaded applications, or classes that need to be thread-safe for use in multi-threaded environments, methods can be synchronized to prevent data loss or corruption. Unless data can be accessed atomically (in one operation, without the possibility of a thread being suspended by the JVM and control given to another), synchronization is needed. Consider the simple example of a counter (such as of how many times an action like a hit on a Web page has occurred) stored in a file. This counter may be

incremented (by reading the current value and writing a new one) or read by
multiple threads. If one thread tries to increment the value of the counter before
another thread completes modifying the counter, its value may be set by one
and overwritten by the other. This means that the counter would read an
invalid value. Worse still, if two attempts to overwrite the value were made,
the file might be corrupted. If the methods to access and modify the value of
the counter were synchronized, however, only one thread could perform a write
operation at any given moment.

The *synchronized* keyword is used to indicate that a method should be
protected by a monitor. Every method that could possibly be affected by concurrent access should be marked as synchronized. This keyword should be
used sparingly, however, as it has a performance drawback. While fine for
multi-threaded applications, in a single-threaded context it results in a waste
of CPU time.

```
public class SomeClass
{
        public synchronized void changeData( … )
        {
                .........
        }

        public synchronized Object getData ( … )
        {
                ............
        }
}
```

Let's look at a practical example of thread conflicts, and how they may be
solved using synchronized methods. Suppose we have a counter that can both
be incremented and display a value. If the method that provides access to
the counter isn't thread-safe, and takes some time to complete, then two or
more threads could access it at the same time and overwrite each increment.
Before the value of the counter can be stored, a second thread could write a new
one, which is in turn overwritten (see Figure 7-3). This gets even more confusing when a read is made. Since one update has been lost, an inaccurate tally is
obtained. If frequent changes are made to the counter, it becomes more and
more inaccurate.

The solution is to make the counter thread-safe, by synchronizing each
method that performs a read or write operation. If a synchronized method is
used, only one thread can update the value at any given moment (see Figure 7-4). The thread that first invokes a synchronized method locks the object's
monitor, which is released only when that method terminates. No other thread
can access any synchronized method of the counter object (though if multiple

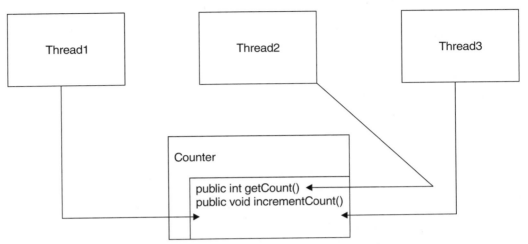

**Figure 7-3**    Concurrent access and modification of data by threads leads to data corruption.

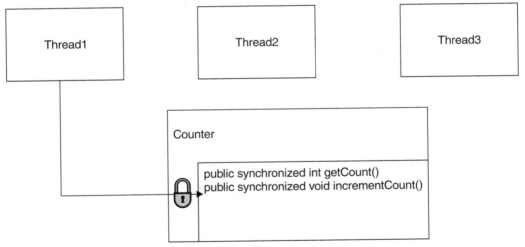

**Figure 7-4**    A thread-safe counter is achieved by synchronizing class methods.

counters are used, this restriction applies only to individual counter instances, and not the Counter class itself). For this reason, synchronized methods should be as brief as possible—threads that go to sleep inside a synchronized method will cause all other threads trying to invoke synchronized methods on that object to be suspended.

Now we will look at method-level synchronization in action. The following class defines a counter with synchronized access and modification methods.

```java
// Chapter 7, Listing 6
public class Counter
{
    private int countValue;

    public Counter()
    {
        countValue = 0;
    }

    public Counter(int start)
    {
        countValue = start;
    }

    // Synchronized method to increase counter
    public synchronized void increaseCount()
    {
        int count = countValue;

        // Simulate slow data processing and modification
        // Removing the synchronized keyword will demonstrate
        // how inaccurate concurrent access can be. Adjusting
        // this value may be necessary on faster machines.
        try
        {
            Thread.sleep(5);
        }
        catch (InterruptedException ie) {}

        count = count + 1;

        countValue = count;
    }

    // Synchronized method to return counter value
    public synchronized int getCount()
    {
        return countValue;
    }
}
```

The next class is an application that uses multiple threads with a single counter. Due to the synchronized keyword, concurrent modification of the counter's value is impossible—but compiling and running the example without the presence of the synchronized keyword reveals some interesting results. As predicted, the count becomes inaccurate. However, as the write operation is so quick, it needs to be slowed down on faster machines to allow other threads time to enter the increaseCount() method. Adjusting the sleep value may be required on very fast machines.

```
// Chapter 7, Listing 7
public class CountingThread implements Runnable
{
    Counter myCounter;
    int     countAmount;

    // Construct a counting thread to use the specified counter
    public CountingThread (Counter counter, int amount)
    {
        myCounter = counter;
        countAmount = amount;
    }

    public void run()
    {
        // Increase the counter the specified number of times
        for (int i = 1; i <= countAmount; i++)
        {
            // Increase the counter
            myCounter.increaseCount();
        }
    }

    public static void main(String args[]) throws Exception
    {
        // Create a new, thread-safe counter
        Counter c = new Counter();

        // Our runnable instance will increase the counter
        // ten times, for each thread that runs it
        Runnable runner = new CountingThread( c, 10 );

        System.out.println ("Starting counting threads");

        Thread t1 = new Thread(runner);
        Thread t2 = new Thread(runner);
        Thread t3 = new Thread(runner);
        t1.start(); t2.start(); t3.start();

        // Wait for all three threads to finish
        t1.join(); t2.join(); t3.join();

        System.out.println ("Counter value is " + c.getCount() );
    }
}
```

Three threads are launched, which increment the counter 10 times each. This means that, when the synchronized keyword is present, a total value of 30 will be returned by the counter's getCount() method. Without the synchronized keyword, each thread overwrites the other and the resulting count is significantly less.

## 7.3.2  Block-Level Synchronization

Method-level synchronization is an effective means of preventing concurrent access to resources. But what if the resource has not been designed as thread-safe, and is a preexisting class that the developer cannot modify (such as a class in the Java API, or a third-party library)? Block-level synchronization, in this case, is the best option.

Block-level synchronization uses the synchronized keyword, but instead of placing a lock around particular methods, a lock is placed around blocks of code. A block of code is synchronized against a particular object, and any thread attempting to enter that block of code is locked out, until the monitor for the specified object is released. The following code snippet shows the syntax for a synchronized block:

```
synchronized (Object o)
{
       ......
}
```

Block-level synchronization locks against a particular object. This means that multiple blocks can protect access to the same object, so block-level synchronization can be applied in thread code wherever an object is accessed or modified. The following example demonstrates block-level synchronization. It is a variation on the previous example, but instead of creating a separate class to represent a counter, an instance variable is used. The access and modification of the variable takes place inside the run() method of a thread, so method-level synchronization cannot be used. Instead, block-level synchronization protects the count, and ensures that when the count is written to a StringBuffer (which is a string that can be appended), it is written in the correct order.

```
// Chapter 7, Listing 8
public class SynchBlock implements Runnable
{
     StringBuffer buffer;
     int counter;

     public SynchBlock()
     {
          buffer = new StringBuffer();
          counter= 1;
     }

     public void run()
     {

          synchronized (buffer)
          {
```

```
            System.out.print ("Starting synchronized block ");
            int tempVariable = counter++;
                int tempVariable = counter++;

            // Create message to add to buffer, including linefeed
            String message = "Count value is : " + tempVariable +
                System.getProperty("line.separator");


            try
            {
                Thread.sleep(100);
            }
            catch (InterruptedException ie) {}

            buffer.append (message);
            System.out.println ("... ending synchronized block");
        }
    }

    public static void main(String args[]) throws Exception
    {
        // Create a new runnable instance SynchBlock block = new SynchBlock();
        SynchBlock block = new SynchBlock();

        Thread t1 = new Thread (block);
        Thread t2 = new Thread (block);
        Thread t3 = new Thread (block);
        Thread t4 = new Thread (block);
        t1.start(); t2.start(); t3.start(); t4.start();

        // Wait for all these threads to finish
        t1.join(); t2.join(); t3.join(); t4.join();

        System.out.println (block.buffer);
    }
}
```

## 7.4    Interthread Communication

While threads can, of course, act in isolation (in fact, a design that requires no communication between threads lends itself to a far simpler implementation), sometimes it is necessary for threads to communicate with each other. Often, the type of communication will be fairly simple, such as reading or modifying a public member variable, or invoking an object method. Other times, more sophisticated communication is called for. Two good options for communication are communication pipes and the wait()/notify() methods, which allow one thread to notify a waiting thread of an event.

### 7.4.1  Communication Pipes between Threads

Like multiprocess communication, which uses pipes to send data from one process to another, threads can also send data directly from one thread to another. This is achieved by using special types of input and output streams, which are linked together. By passing either end of the pipe to another thread, that thread may listen to, or speak to, another thread. In fact, there's no restriction preventing two pipes from being used—a thread could even have two-way communication with another (see Figure 7-5).

Communicating via pipes is not very different from using any other form of input stream or output stream. Other streams may also be connected to a pipe, for easier reading and writing. The following example demonstrates the use of pipes in thread communication.

```java
    import java.io.*;

// Chapter 7, Listing 8
public class PipeDemo extends Thread
{
    PipedOutputStream output;

    // Create an instance of the PipeDemo class
    public PipeDemo(PipedOutputStream out)
    {
        // Copy to local member variable
        output = out;
    }

    public static void main (String args[])
    {
        try
        {
            // Create a pipe for writing
            PipedOutputStream pout = new PipedOutputStream();
```

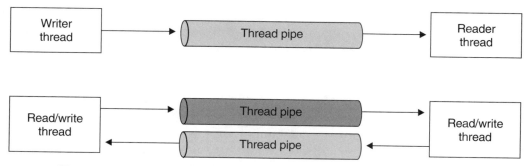

**Figure 7-5**   Piped communication is only one way, but two pipes may be used.

```java
            // Create a pipe for reading, and connect it to
            // output pipe
            PipedInputStream pin = new PipedInputStream(pout);

            // Create a new pipe demo thread, to write to
            // our pipe
            PipeDemo pipedemo = new PipeDemo(pout);

            // Start the thread
            pipedemo.start();

            // Read thread data,
            int input = pin.read();

            // Terminate when end of stream reached
            while (input != -1)
            {
                // Print message
                System.out.print ( (char) input);

                // Read next byte
                input = pin.read();
            }
        }
        catch (Exception e)
        {
            System.err.println ("Pipe error " + e);
        }
    }

    public void run()
    {
        try
        {
            // Create a printstream for convenient writing
            PrintStream p = new PrintStream( output );

            // Print message
            p.println ("Hello from another thread, via pipes!");

            // Close the stream
            p.close();
        }
        catch (Exception e)
        {
            // no code req'd
        }
    }
}
```

Running this example will create a one-way pipe between the primary application thread and a second thread that sends a text message through the pipe. The pipe must be constructed before the thread is started, however, and it must be passed somehow to the thread, so that it has a reference to a pipe object. In this case, the pipe is passed to the thread's constructor—a convenient way of initializing the thread and getting the pipe there.

### 7.4.2   *Notifying a Waiting Thread of an Event*

A common requirement in multi-threaded programming is that one thread cannot proceed until the completion of a task by another thread. Sometimes a thread will be producing information or using resources. Other times, the order of execution is important, and a task cannot take place before another has completed. While it is possible for one thread to wait until another has died (thus indicating that the work was completed) by using the `Thread.join()` method, what if a thread performs an ongoing task and never terminates?

The solution is to notify other threads that a task has been completed. Threads wait until they are notified, and notification can be a repeated process (with several cycles of waiting and notifying). This allows threads to synchronize their actions and communicate that a critical event has occurred, without requiring the extra complexity of pipe-based communication or invoking methods. Sometimes a thread may not even know exactly which threads are waiting for it to complete, so a special type of notification is used.

Every Java object inherits from the `java.lang.Object` class (the superclass of every object) the ability to maintain a queue of threads waiting for an object lock to be released, and to notify one or more waiting threads that the object is freed. This provides a great way to notify a thread that an event has occurred, and for threads to wait indefinitely (or for a limited amount of time) until notification is sent.

To have threads wait for an indefinite amount of time, the `Object.wait()` method is used. An overloaded version of this method also exists, which waits for a limited amount of time (specified in milliseconds). Before the `wait()` method may be invoked, however, the thread must hold a lock on the object's monitor. To gain a lock on an object's monitor, it must be executing a synchronized method or using a synchronized block. When the lock is released, another thread can obtain it—without this, the thread will wait indefinitely.

Once the `wait()` method is executed, the monitor is released and the thread is suspended until a call is made to the `Object.notify()` or `Object.notifyAll()` method. To awaken waiting threads, another thread may call either method. However, the `notify()` method will only notify a single thread, even if multiple threads are waiting. There is no choice over which thread is awakened, either (this is determined by the JVM implementation, so you cannot rely on, for example, a FIFO queue), so it is advised that the notifyAll() method is used if you want to notify a specific thread.

The following example demonstrates the use of the wait/notify methods.

```
// Chapter 7, Listing 9
public class WaitNotify extends Thread
{
    public static void main(String args[]) throws Exception
    {
        Thread notificationThread = new WaitNotify();
        notificationThread.start();

        // Wait for the notification thread to trigger event
        synchronized (notificationThread)
        {
            notificationThread.wait();
        }

        // Notify user that the wait() method has returned
        System.out.println ("The wait is over");
    }

    public void run()
    {
        System.out.println ("Hit enter to stop waiting thread");

        try
        {
            System.in.read();
        }
        catch (java.io.IOException ioe)
        {
            // no code req'd
        }

        // Notify any threads waiting on this thread
        synchronized (this)
        {
            this.notifyAll();
        }
    }
}
```

The example is fairly straightforward. The primary application thread waits until notified by the second thread that an event has occurred. Until the user hits the "enter" key, the second thread will not send the notification message. Though the application terminates once notification is sent and received, a series of wait()/notify() cycles could take place, to indicate irregular, but frequently occurring, events.

## 7.5    Thread Groups

While threads can be created and run individually, sometimes it is easier to work with threads as a group, rather than one at a time. Operations that affect threads, such as suspending and resuming threads, stopping them cold, or interrupting them, can be performed on individual threads, but this requires developers to maintain a list of threads (using a data structure such as a vector or an array). When an operation must be performed, each and every thread in this list must be traversed and then acted upon. This creates extra work for developers by requiring more complex code. An easier alternative is to group threads together and apply an operation on the group rather than on the individual elements of the group.

The Java API provides support for groups of threads in the form of the ThreadGroup class. The purpose of the ThreadGroup class is to represent a collection of threads, and to provide methods that act as shortcuts to invoking methods on individual threads in the collection. It also provides a way of gathering information about commonly related threads, such as the number of threads in a group, and references to the threads stored in a group. If access to individual threads is needed, it can be obtained from the ThreadGroup, rather than having to create some other data structure to act as a container.

When a JVM is first started and a Java application is run, the primary application thread will run the main() method. After that, the application is free to create groups of threads, or individual threads not associated with a specific group. A group may be composed of as many threads as needed, and may be dynamically added to at any point during a program's execution (see Figure 7-6). However, there is no way to unhook a thread (or a thread group) from a group. Note, also, that under controlled environments such as customized security managers, applets running within a browser, or code executing within a servlet engine, restrictions may be placed on creating new thread groups, or on accessing existing ones.

Furthermore, a group of threads may contain additional thread groups, which are counted as subgroups (Figure 7-7). Operations such as stopping or suspending may be performed on the subgroups or the parent group. When an operation is applied to the parent group, it will cause the operation to be propagated to every subgroup, which in turn will pass the operation on to every thread within that subgroup. This means that a single operation can be invoked on several, dozens, or even hundreds of threads. This makes for a much cleaner design—there is no need for endless amounts of loops iterating through a list of threads. The inclusion of subgroups allows for finer-grained control over thread operations, as selected groups can be acted upon while others are left untouched.

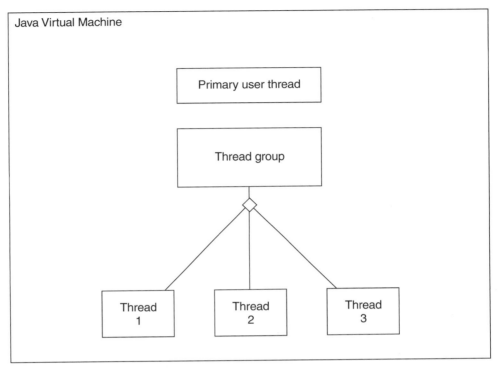

**Figure 7-6**   Thread groups can add additional threads at any time.

## 7.5.1 Creating a Thread Group

### Constructors

There are two constructors for the ThreadGroup class:

- public ThreadGroup(String name) throws java.lang.Security-
  Exception—creates a new thread group, which may be identified by
  the specified String name. The parent group of the ThreadGroup will
  be the parent of the currently running thread.
- public ThreadGroup(ThreadGroup parentGroup, String name)
  throws java.lang.SecurityException—creates a new thread group
  (which may be identified by the specified String name) whose parent
  group will be the specified ThreadGroup. This constructor allows a
  group to be stored as a subgroup, rather than being created as a separate group.

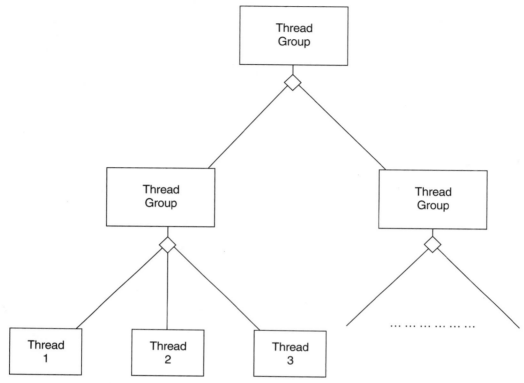

**Figure 7-7**   Thread groups may contain threads and subgroups, which in turn may include more groups and threads.

For example, to create a group and subgroup, the following code could be used:

```
ThreadGroup parent = new ThreadGroup("parent");
ThreadGroup subgroup = new ThreadGroup(parent, "subgroup");
```

### 7.5.2   *Using a Thread Group*

Once created, a thread group can be used in much the same way as a normal thread—it can be suspended, resumed, interrupted, and stopped by calling the appropriate method. However, a further step must be performed before the thread can be used effectively—it must contain threads. After all, an empty thread group isn't of much use.

### Constructors

Threads are associated with a particular group at the time of their creation. Thus, it is not possible to assign a thread to a group at a later date, or move a thread from one group to another. There are three constructors for the `java.lang.Thread` class that accept thread groups as a parameter:

- `Thread (ThreadGroup group, Runnable runnable)`
- `Thread (ThreadGroup group, String name)`
- `Thread (ThreadGroup group, Runnable runnable, String name)`

**NOTE:** When a thread is created and no group is assigned to the constructor, the thread group of the currently running thread will be assigned. Specifying a group gives developers a choice of which group a thread will be located in.

Once threads are associated with the group, group operations can be performed, the number of threads/groups that are active can be checked, and a list of threads can be obtained, simply by invoking the appropriate `ThreadGroup` method.

### Methods

The following methods of the `ThreadGroup` class are public unless otherwise noted.

- `int activeCount()`—returns the number of active threads in this group, and any subgroups of this group.
- `int activeGroupCount()`—returns the number of groups that have active threads in this group, and any subgroups.
- `boolean allowThreadSuspension()`—indicates whether a thread may be suspended under certain conditions. The behavior of this method is not well defined, and it has been deprecated in the Java 2 platform.
- `void checkAccess() throws java.lang.SecurityException`—throws a security exception if the currently installed security manager would prohibit the currently running thread from modifying the thread group.
- `void destroy() throws java.lang.IllegalThreadStateException, java.lang.SecurityException`—destroys this thread group, and every one of its subgroups, providing that they do not contain any active threads (i.e., threads that have yet to stop). If this is not the case, an `IllegalThreadStateException` will be thrown. Before this method is invoked, it is advised that the `ThreadGroup.stop()` method is called.
- `int enumerate(Thread[] threadList) throws java.lang.Security-Exception`—places into the specified array a reference to each and every active thread in this group, and any of its subgroups. If, however, the

size of the array is not large enough to accommodate the number of active threads, no `ArrayOutOfBoundsException` will be thrown—the method will instead leave out the extra threads, and the application may remain unaware of this. For this reason, a sufficiently large array should be used. The number of threads copied into the array is returned by this method, not the number of threads that *should* have been copied. To determine the number of active threads (for the purpose of creating an array), a call should be made to the `ThreadGroup.activeCount()` method. Additional threads may, however, be added to the group, so this call should be made just prior to invoking the `enumerate` method.

- `int enumerate(Thread[] threadList, boolean subgroupFlag)` throws `java.lang.SecurityException`—places into the specified array a reference to all active threads in this group. If the subgroup `boolean` flag is set to "true," threads from subgroups will also be included. A sufficiently large array should be used (to determine the length of this array, see the `enumerate(Thread[] threadList)` method description). However, as the `activeCount()` method returns the number of active threads in this group, and any subgroup, the size of the array may be too large. For this reason, applications should check the return value of this method, which indicates the number of threads stored in the array.

- `int enumerate(ThreadGroup[] groupList)` throws `java.lang.SecurityException`—places a reference to all active groups, and any subgroups, into the specified array. As warned in the `enumerate-(Thread[] threadList)` method description, the array must be allocated to a sufficiently large size to accommodate the number of active thread groups. This can be achieved by calling the `ThreadGroup.activeGroupCount()` method, and allocating this number of elements in the array. The number of groups copied to the array will be returned by this method.

- `int enumerate(ThreadGroup[] groupList, boolean subgroupFlag)` throws `java.lang.SecurityException`—stores a reference to all active groups into the specified array. If the subgroup boolean flag is set to "true," subgroups will also be included, and if set to "false," only groups in the current group will be included (i.e., one level deep). As with all other `ThreadGroup.enumerate(...)` methods, a sufficiently large enough array must be created, or extra thread groups will be excluded. The return value from this method indicates the number of groups stored in the array.

- `int getMaxPriority()`—returns the maximum priority level (discussed earlier in this section) for threads in this group. Threads may not exceed their group's priority level, though an error will not be thrown if an attempt to do so is made.

- `String getName()`—returns the name associated with this thread group.
- `ThreadGroup getParent()` throws `java.lang.SecurityException`— returns the parent group of this thread group. All threads are part of some group, though accessing the parent group could cause an exception to be thrown.
- `void interrupt()` throws `java.lang.SecurityException`—invokes the `Thread.interrupt()` method of every thread in this group, and any subgroups.
- `boolean isDaemon()`—returns "true" if the thread group is a daemon group, and "false" if not. A daemon group may be destroyed when all active threads are terminated.
- `boolean isDestroyed()`—returns "true" if the thread group has been destroyed.
- `void list()`—dumps information about the thread group to `System.out`. This method is useful during testing, to show the threads and groups that are members.
- `boolean parentOf(ThreadGroup otherGroup)`—tests whether the specified thread group is a child group.
- `void resume()`—deprecated method that resumes all suspended threads in the group and any subgroups. The reason for deprecation is because the `Thread.resume()` method has been marked as deprecated in the Java 2 platform.
- `void setDaemon(boolean flag)` throws `java.lang.Security-Exception`—modifies the daemon flag of the thread group. A value of "true" makes the thread group a daemon group, which means that it can be destroyed when all active threads are terminated.
- `void setMaxPriority(int priority)` throws `java.lang.Security-Exception`—assigns a new maximum priority level for this group. This method does not reset the priority of existing threads (i.e., a higher-priority thread that is part of the group will not be reduced in priority, but may not increase its priority further).
- `void stop()` throws `java.lang.SecurityException`—deprecated method that invokes the `Thread.stop()` method for all threads in this group and any subgroups. As the `Thread.stop()` method is deprecated in the Java 2 platform, this method is also deprecated.
- `void suspend()` throws `java.lang.SecurityException`—deprecated method that invokes the `Thread.suspend()` method for all threads in this group and any subgroups. As the `Thread.suspend()` method is deprecated in the Java 2 platform, this method is also deprecated.
- `String toString()`—returns a String version of the thread group.

- void uncaughtException(Thread thread, Throwable error)—called
  whenever a thread fails to catch an exception at runtime. Applications
  that want to trap these types of errors (for example, for logging purposes) must extend the ThreadGroup class and override this method.

### 7.5.2.1 Demonstration of the ThreadGroup Class

The following example shows the construction of thread groups, and the use of
the list() method to display the state of active threads.

```java
// Chapter 7, Listing 11
public class GroupDemo implements Runnable
{
    public static void main(String args[]) throws Exception
    {
        // Create a thread group
        ThreadGroup parent = new ThreadGroup("parent");

        // Create a group that is a child of another thread group
        ThreadGroup subgroup = new ThreadGroup(parent, "subgroup");

        // Create some threads in the parent, and subgroup class
        Thread t1 = new Thread ( parent, new GroupDemo() );
        t1.start();
        Thread t2 = new Thread ( parent, new GroupDemo() );
        t2.start();
        Thread t3 = new Thread ( subgroup, new GroupDemo() );
        t3.start();

        // Dump the contents of the group to System.out
        parent.list();


        // Wait for user, then terminate
        System.out.println ("Press enter to continue");
        System.in.read();
        System.exit(0);
    }

    public void run()
    {
        // Do nothing
        for(;;)
        {
            Thread.yield();
        }
    }
}
```

## 7.6    Thread Priorities

As mentioned at the beginning of the chapter, multi-threading is achieved by rapidly switching between one thread and another to simulate concurrent execution of code. Unless there are multiple CPUs, the operating system will switch between one thread and another based on an arbitrary algorithm over which individual threads have no control. Thus, it is impossible to predict the order in which threads will be executed, or when (if at all) a thread will be scheduled. The best that can be done is to suggest the relative priority of threads, which gives the operating system an indication of which threads are more important (and should be scheduled more frequently, or for a longer duration).

### 7.6.1    Assigning a Thread Priority

In Java, a numerical ranking specifies thread priority, with 10 being the highest priority type and 1 being the lowest. Some thread priorities are defined as static member variables of the `java.lang.Thread` class, a convenient shortcut that eliminates the need for remembering a numerical value. Table 7.1 shows the numerical thread priorities and associated shortcuts.

To set the thread priority, the `Thread.setPriorityMethod (int)` method is used. For example, to set a thread to the minimum priority level, the following code would be used:

```
Thread t = new Thread (runnable);
t.setPriority ( Thread.MIN_PRIORITY ); t.start();
```

**Table 7-1**    Thread Priorities

| | |
|---|---|
| 10 | Thread.MAX_PRIORITY |
| 7 | |
| 8 | |
| 7 | |
| 6 | |
| 5 | Thread.NORM_PRIORITY |
| 4 | |
| 3 | |
| 2 | |
| 1 | Thread.MIN_PRIORITY |

### 7.6.2   Obtaining the Current Thread Priority

A thread that wishes to determine its current thread priority (for example, to see if it is high enough, and take corrective action if it is not), may do so by invoking the `Thread.getPriority()` method. This method returns an int value, which indicates the priority of the thread. For example, to get the priority of the currently running thread, the following code could be used:

```
Thread t = Thread.currentThread();
System.out.println ("Priority : " + t.getPriority());
```

### 7.6.3   Limiting Thread Priority

Sometimes it may be necessary to limit the maximum priority that a thread could request (for example, if executing untrusted code downloaded from over the network). It is possible to install a custom security manager, which would throw a `SecurityException`, but this involves a significant amount of effort. A much easier alternative is to create a `ThreadGroup` (covered in the previous section), and assign a maximum priority level to this group. When creating a thread, the thread group is specified. Any thread that requests a higher priority will not receive it, but nor will an error message be generated. This makes for a clean solution to the problem.

To assign a maximum thread priority for a group, the `ThreadGroup.setMaxPriority(int)` method is used. For example, to set a thread priority of 8, the following code would be used:

```
ThreadGroup group = new ThreadGroup ( "mygroup" );
group.setMaximumPriority(8);
```

## 7.7   Summary

An understanding of multi-threaded programming is important for any type of application or applet programming, but particularly so for software development for networking environments. Networks are slow and unreliable, so networking code will often need to be running in a separate thread from that of the user interface, to prevent a system from locking up or stalling due to changes in network state. Furthermore, most networking software interacts with multiple clients and/or servers, and unless the operations are extremely quick (such as receiving and dispatching a UDP packet), multiple threads will be needed so that interactions can occur concurrently.

Concurrent execution of software, however, introduces complexities. Synchronization of access to data, communication between threads, and thread scheduling are difficult components for the programmer to master, and thus even experienced developers encounter problems when they rely too heavily on predicting the order of thread execution. In many situations, it is important that synchronization of access to resources is used to preserve data integrity and the order of operations. Additionally, communication between threads may be employed to aid threads in collaborating to complete tasks.

**Chapter Highlights**

In this chapter, you have learned:

- How to create multi-threaded applications by extending the `java.lang.Thread` class
- How to create multi-threaded applications by implementing the `java.lang.Runnable` interface
- How to interrupt, stop, and wait for the death of threads
- How to guard against concurrent access to resources, using method-level and block-level synchronization
- How to communicate between threads using pipes
- How to notify waiting threads of an event
- How to group threads together, using the `ThreadGroup` class
- How to access and modify scheduling priorities

# CHAPTER 8

## *Implementing Application Protocols*

This chapter presents an overview of common Internet application protocols, and provides code examples of three protocol implementations under Java. Here we use the techniques covered in Chapter 6 to create client and server software using sockets supporting popular Internet protocols.

## 8.1   Overview

An application protocol facilitates communication between applications, using the services of lower-level Open Systems Interconnection (OSI) model layers (for example, network and physical layers). When you check your e-mail, browse a Web site, play games, or download files over the Internet, the software you run is using an application protocol for communication.

For applications to interoperate, the implementation of application protocols must be precise. You can't have one application speaking one way and another application unable to understand or interpret the message—otherwise the many thousands of software applications running on the many millions of computers in existence couldn't get along. This is not to say that every implementation will support every feature of a protocol, or that they will be implemented in the same way, in the same language, or on the same machine. However, protocol implementations must, at least outwardly, behave in the same way, and when they can't fulfill a request or support a feature, they must communicate that effectively, using a commonly understood process.

The semantics of a protocol are laid out in a protocol specification document. This allows developers to implement the same protocol on a variety of platforms and languages and have them communicate successfully.

## 8.2    Application Protocol Specifications

Early on in the history of the Internet, a system was designed that made it easy to distribute new and updated protocol specifications to protocol implementers. The design of a network protocol tends to be an evolutionary process involving many contributors, with initial drafts being made available to the public and rewrites undertaken. When the protocol nears completion and is ready for applications to implement it, it is published as a Request For Comment (RFC) document.

Most of the popular Internet protocols in use today are published as RFCs. Each RFC details a single protocol or idea about the Internet, and is assigned a number for identification (e.g., RFC 1945 for HTTP/1.0). These documents are extremely detailed and contain all the information required for implementing the protocol. Not every RFC covers a protocol, however—some are general overviews, notes on Internet architecture, or suggestions for revisions to existing protocols.

**NOTE:** There's even the occasional attempt at humor in RFC documents—for those with an interest in all things Java, both the language and the beverage, you might want to take a look at RFC 2324, the Hyper Text Coffee Pot Control Protocol.

### 8.2.1    Finding RFC Documents

RFC documents are freely available and include a text-based version for ease of reading; they can be accessed using a Web browser. Though RFCs are mirrored across many hosts on the Internet, the original and most up-to-date source is the RFC Editor, operated by the Internet Society. It can be found at http://www.rfc-editor.org/rfc.html.

The RFC Editor Web site allows users to search for RFCs by number or by using keywords, authors, or titles. For example, if you wanted to look up RFC 2324, you'd search by number; entering "2324" would return the specification for the coffee pot control protocol mentioned above. If, on the other hand, you knew the name of the protocol but not its number, you'd search by title or keyword. For example, to search for the FTP you could enter the title "File Transfer Protocol." This query returns several RFCs, as some earlier specifications cover modifications to the protocol, or earlier versions of it. The higher the number, the more recent the RFC publication is. By running this query, you can quickly locate RFC 765, which contains the information needed to write compatible FTP clients or servers.

Alternatively, you can access RFCs by using an FTP client and connecting to the site ftp.rfc-editor.org. RFCs can be found under the /in-notes directory. By using a Web search engine, you can also find mirrors of RFC archives, some of which have converted the specifications to HTML format for easy reading.

## 8.3 Application Protocol Implementation

The most enjoyable part of learning network programming is putting the network theory that you've learned into practice, by writing real-life applications that interact with other Internet services or clients. Earlier in this book we covered the theory; now it's time to write some code. In the following sections, we'll examine and code three protocols—SMTP, POP3, and HTTP.

### 8.3.1 SMTP Client Implementation

The Simple Mail Transfer Protocol is used to send messages of various types between users over a TCP/IP network. It should be noted that this protocol assumes that some other method is used to actually read the messages, thus allowing a more stable, flexible, and robust global e-mail system. By separating delivering messages from reading, things are made much simpler.

Together, we'll write a basic SMTP client that allows the user to send a text message to a specific e-mail address. If you require something more elaborate, such as multiple senders or attachments, you could modify the code yourself as a programming exercise, or use the JavaMail API covered in Chapter 13; it provides prewritten support for advanced mail features. The client written here offers a good example of networking, while minimizing such supporting code as that for a user interface. For this reason, simple text-based input is used, and the commands sent to the server are displayed to help the reader understand how the protocol works.

#### Code for SMTPClientDemo

```java
import java.io.*;
import java.net.*;
import java.util.*;

// Chapter 8, Listing 1
public class SMTPClientDemo
{
  protected int port = 25;
  protected String hostname = "localhost";
  protected String from = "";
  protected String to = "";
  protected String subject = "";
  protected String body = "";
```

```java
protected Socket socket;
protected BufferedReader br;
protected PrintWriter pw;

// Constructs a new instance of the SMTP Client
public SMTPClientDemo() throws Exception
{
    try
    {
        getInput();
        sendEmail();
    }
    catch (Exception e)
    {
        System.out.println ("Error sending message - " + e);
    }
}

public static void main(String[] args) throws Exception
{
    // Start the SMTP client, so it can send messages
    SMTPClientDemo client = new SMTPClientDemo();
}

// Check the SMTP response code for an error message
protected int readResponseCode() throws Exception
{
  String line = br.readLine();
  System.out.println("< "+line);
  line = line.substring(0,line.indexOf(" "));
  return Integer.parseInt(line);
}

// Write a protocol message both to the network socket and to
// the screen
protected void writeMsg(String msg) throws Exception
{
  pw.println(msg);
  pw.flush();
  System.out.println("> "+msg);
}

// Close all readers, streams and sockets
protected void closeConnection() throws Exception
{
  pw.flush();
  pw.close();
  br.close();
  socket.close();
}

// Send the QUIT protocol message, and terminate connection
protected void sendQuit() throws Exception
{
```

```
      System.out.println("Sending QUIT");
      writeMsg("QUIT");
      readResponseCode();

      System.out.println("Closing Connection");
      closeConnection();
}

// Send an email message via SMTP, adhering to the protocol
// known as RFC 2821
protected void sendEmail() throws Exception
{
   System.out.println("Sending message now: Debug below");
   System.out.println("-----------------------------------");

   System.out.println("Opening Socket");
   socket = new Socket(this.hostname,this.port);

   System.out.println("Creating Reader & Writer");
   br = new BufferedReader(new
            InputStreamReader(socket.getInputStream()));
   pw = new PrintWriter(new
            OutputStreamWriter(socket.getOutputStream()));

   System.out.println("Reading first line");
   int code = readResponseCode();
   if(code != 220) {
            socket.close();
            throw new Exception("Invalid SMTP Server");
   }

   System.out.println("Sending helo command");
   writeMsg("HELO "+InetAddress.getLocalHost().getHostName());
   code = readResponseCode();
   if(code != 250)
   {
      sendQuit();
      throw new Exception("Invalid SMTP Server");
   }

   System.out.println("Sending mail from command");
   writeMsg("MAIL FROM:<"+this.from+">");
   code = readResponseCode();
   if(code != 250)
   {
      sendQuit();
      throw new Exception("Invalid from address");
   }

   System.out.println("Sending rcpt to command");
   writeMsg("RCPT TO:<"+this.to+">");
   code = readResponseCode();
```

```
      if(code != 250)
      {
        sendQuit();
        throw new Exception("Invalid to address");
      }

      System.out.println("Sending data command");
      writeMsg("DATA");
      code = readResponseCode();
      if(code != 354)
      {
        sendQuit();
        throw new Exception("Data entry not accepted");
      }

      System.out.println("Sending message");
      writeMsg("Subject: "+this.subject);
      writeMsg("To: "+this.to);
      writeMsg("From: "+this.from);
      writeMsg("");
      writeMsg(body);
      code = readResponseCode();
      sendQuit();
      if(code != 250)
        throw new Exception("Message may not have been sent correctly");
      else
        System.out.println("Message sent");
    }

  // Obtain input from the user
  protected void getInput() throws Exception
  {
  // Read input from user console
  String data=null;
  BufferedReader br = new BufferedReader (
              new InputStreamReader(System.in));

      // Request hostname for SMTP server
      System.out.print("Please enter SMTP server hostname: ");
      data = br.readLine();

      if (data == null || data.equals("")) hostname="localhost";
      else
        hostname=data;

      // Request the sender's email address
      System.out.print("Please enter FROM email address: ");
      data = br.readLine();
      from = data;

      // Request the recipient's email address
      System.out.print("Please enter TO email address :");
```

```
          data = br.readLine();
          if(!(data == null || data.equals("")))
            to=data;

          System.out.print("Please enter subject: ");
          data = br.readLine();
          subject=data;

          System.out.println(
                  "Please enter plain-text message ('.' character on
                     a blank line signals end of message):");
          StringBuffer buffer = new StringBuffer();

          // Read until user enters a . on a blank line
          String line = br.readLine();
          while(line != null)
          {
              // Check for a '.', and only a '.', on a line
              if(line.equalsIgnoreCase("."))
              {
                  break;
              }
              buffer.append(line);
              buffer.append("\n");
              line = br.readLine();
          }
          buffer.append(".\n");
          body = buffer.toString();
      }
  }
```

### How SMTPClientDemo Works

As can be seen here, the Simple Mail Transfer Protocol is quite straightforward, consisting of a single connection to a mail server using a TCP socket, followed by a series of short protocol commands that specify the details of the e-mail to be sent, as described in RFC 2821. While many network applications will require multiple threads of execution, as a general rule simple clients such as this one do not. This example merely asks for input from the user and then sends the message.

To simplify understanding of this code, the networking code has been separated from the non-networking code (which consists mainly of code for obtaining input from the user).

The basic skeleton of the application is as follows:

```
public class SMTPClientDemo
{
  public static void main(String[] args) throws Exception
  {
    SMTPClientDemo client = new SMTPClientDemo ();
  }
```

```java
        // Constructs a new instance of the SMTP Client
        public SMTPClientDemo () throws Exception;

        // Send an email message via SMTP, adhering to the protocol
        // known as RFC 2821
        protected void sendEmail() throws Exception;

        // Check the SMTP response code for an error message
        protected int readResponseCode() throws Exception;

        // Write a protocol message both to the network socket and to
        // the screen
        protected void writeMsg(String msg) throws Exception;

        // Close all readers, streams and sockets
        protected void closeConnection() throws Exception;

        // Send the QUIT protocol message, and terminate connection
        protected void sendQuit() throws Exception;

        // Obtain input from the user
        protected void getInput() throws Exception;
    }
```

We'll cover the e-mail-specific code, as the remainder of the application is fairly straightforward Java coding. Our class stores the message and network details inside protected variables (rather than private ones, so readers can create subclasses that access these variables if required). These variables are:

- `String hostname`
- `int port` (set to 25, the default for SMTP)
- `String from`
- `String to`
- `String subject`
- `String body`
- `java.net.Socket socket`
- `BufferedReader br`
- `PrintWriter pw`

The hostname, port, from, to, subject, and body variables are fairly self-explanatory—they are required for locating the mail server to send an SMTP message, and for the e-mail addressing and content details. The socket is used to communicate with the remote TCP server that will relay our mail for us, and the reader/writer objects are used for reading and sending SMTP messages.

When the application is run, the `main()` method is executed by the Java Virtual Machine. This in turn creates an instance of our `SMTPClientDemo` application, which requests input data from the user and attempts to send an e-mail message. The process has been fairly simple, so far. Now let's turn to the application protocol code.

Contained inside the sendEmail() method is the heart of the program. This is where we connect a local TCP socket to a remote SMTP server, and send across protocol requests. While it's certainly possible to group this process into one single method, for convenience and readability, some of the workload has been distributed across several helper methods that decode SMTP responses, send protocol messages, and terminate connections.

The first thing the sendEmail() method does is open a socket connection to the mail server located at port *n*, where *n* is represented by the member variable port. The SMTP normally uses port 25, but if your network/ISP uses a nonstandard port number for this service, you could modify the default value of this to the required port number. If an error occurs, an exception is thrown and caught by our error handler; otherwise a successful connection to the server is established.

Once connected, we obtain input streams and output streams for the socket, and connect these to readers and writers for convenience. According to the SMTP specification, upon connecting, the server will send a response code in greeting, so the application checks for a valid message with the aid of helper method readResponseCode(). This helps identify that we really are talking to an SMTP service, and not some other service using port 25.

The code for determining the response code is wrapped inside a helper method, called readResponseCode(). It takes no parameters, and returns an int representing the code number. It reads a line of text from the buffered reader that communicates with the SMTP server, outputs the result to the screen for illustrative purposes, and then strips off everything after the first space. Finally, it converts the result to an integer and passes it back, giving us the SMTP response code.

```
// Check the SMTP response code for an error message
protected int readResponseCode() throws Exception
{
  String line = br.readLine();
  System.out.println("< "+line);
  line = line.substring(0,line.indexOf(" "));
  return Integer.parseInt(line);
}
```

When we need to send a message back to the SMTP server, we use the helper method writeMsg(String) which displays the message to the screen for illustrative purposes and then sends it (via our PrintWriter) to the server.

```
// Write a protocol message both to the network socket and to
// the screen
```

```
protected void writeMsg(String msg) throws Exception
{
  pw.println(msg);
  pw.flush();
  System.out.println("> "+msg);
}
```

Using these helper methods, the sendEmail() method can send and receive SMTP messages. It checks, upon connecting, that the server has sent an OK message, which is represented by 220.

```
int code = readResponseCode();
if(code != 220) {
          socket.close();
          throw new Exception("Invalid SMTP Server");
}
```

The next step in SMTP is to send an identification message, telling the SMTP server who we really are. We send the hostname identification command, "HELO." The format is "HELO" followed by a space and the local hostname. The correct response is 250, which signals OK.

```
writeMsg("HELO "+InetAddress.getLocalHost().getHostName());
code = readResponseCode();
if(code != 250)
{
  sendQuit();
  throw new Exception("Invalid SMTP Server");
}
```

If the server accepts the identification, the client is free to send a message. Each message has certain key aspects—a "From" address, one or more "To" addresses, a subject line, and a message body (the actual text of the message). The SMTP only requires fields that deal directly with delivery of messages, though other fields can be placed in the message body. For example, it is commonly accepted to put the subject line as the first line, with "Subject:" in front of it. You can include as many other optional fields as you like, but remember that not every mail client will support these fields. Furthermore, you should also repeat the "To" and "From" fields in your message body.

Setting the sender and recipient addressing information under SMTP is fairly straightforward. Two commands are used, the "MAIL FROM:" and "RCPT TO:"

```
writeMsg("MAIL FROM:<"+this.from+">");

// Check response from server
// ………

writeMsg("RCPT TO:<"+this.to+">");
```

```
// Check response from server
// ........
```

In this example, only one recipient is supported, but SMTP can handle multiple recipients. You should note that well-configured servers normally place a limit on the number of possible recipients, to prevent them from being used in spamming campaigns, and that some SMTP servers will reject messages if the sender is not part of their local or dial-up network.

Once the e-mail addresses are set, we can send the data to the server. Our client sends a simple text message, unencumbered by attachments. The first step to send the data is to signal that we are ready to send a message body, by issuing a "DATA" command. The valid response code for this is 354.

```
System.out.println("Sending data command");
writeMsg("DATA");
code = readResponseCode();
if(code != 354)
{
   sendQuit();
   throw new Exception("Data entry not accepted");
}
```

Now the client sends the message body. This must include relevant header fields, such as "To," "From," "Subject," and any other fields you may choose to add. Once the headers are complete, a blank line is sent, indicating that the message text will follow. After outputting the text, the client sends the message, which is then terminated by a period, then a carriage return/line-feed (which the user enters during data input). This tells the server that the message is complete.

```
writeMsg("Subject:"+this.subject);
writeMsg("");
writeMsg(body);
code = readResponseCode();
sendQuit();
if(code != 250)
  throw new Exception("Message may not have been sent correctly");
else
  System.out.println("Message sent");
```

Finally, the "QUIT" command is sent, and the connection is terminated by invoking the sendQuit() method. Our transaction with the SMTP server is complete, and the message is on its way.

```
// Send the QUIT protocol message, and terminate connection
protected void sendQuit() throws Exception
{
   System.out.println("Sending QUIT");
```

```
        writeMsg("QUIT");
        readResponseCode();

        System.out.println("Closing Connection");
        closeConnection();
    }
```

### Running SMTPClientDemo

After compiling, the application can be run by typing:

```
java SMTPClientDemo
```

The application will request the following information:

- The name of a valid SMTP server (such as that used by your e-mail program)
- The "From" address of the sender (e.g., your e-mail address)
- The "To" address of the recipient (e.g., your e-mail address, so you know that it was delivered)
- The "Subject" of the message
- The message contents

## 8.3.2  POP3 Client Implementation

The previous example showed how to write a protocol implementation of SMTP to send a mail message. In order to read mail, you will need the Post Office Protocol version 3, or POP3 as it is commonly referred to. It is also referred to simply as POP, since the earlier Post Office Protocols are not used any more. This term is less confusing for general Internet users, who may wonder what happened to POP1 and POP2, which have been superseded.

When a person reads their e-mail, they are actually retrieving it from a mail server belonging to an Internet service provider or a local network (such as a corporate or private intranet). There are several major types of mail servers, and each type uses a different network protocol to access e-mail. The most common of these is POP, a protocol that provides a contrast with SMTP.

In examining the POP3 client, you'll find that the actual code required for a network implementation is minimal. Much of the actual application involves user input or output. The interface is limited to text I/O; the idea behind this client is to provide a good example of networking while minimizing the need for non-networking code that readers may already be familiar with, such as GUI design. The example will retrieve messages from a mailbox and display their contents, one after another, to the text console screen.

### Code for Pop3ClientDemo

```java
import java.io.*;
import java.net.*;
import java.util.*;


// Chapter 8, Listing 2
public class Pop3ClientDemo
{
   protected int port = 110;
   protected String hostname = "localhost";
   protected String username = "";
   protected String password = "";

   protected Socket socket;
   protected BufferedReader br;
   protected PrintWriter pw;

   // Constructs a new instance of the POP3 client
   public Pop3ClientDemo() throws Exception
   {
     try
     {
         // Get user input
         getInput();

         // Get mail messages
         displayEmails();
     }
     catch(Exception e)
     {
         System.err.println ("Error occured - details follow");
         e.printStackTrace();
         System.out.println(e.getMessage());
     }
   }

   // Returns TRUE if POP response indicates success, FALSE if
   // failure
   protected boolean responseIsOk() throws Exception
   {
         String line = br.readLine();
         System.out.println("< "+line);
         return line.toUpperCase().startsWith("+OK");
   }

   // Reads a line from the POP server, and displays it to
   // screen
   protected String readLine(boolean debug) throws Exception
   {
         String line = br.readLine();
```

```
        // Append a < character to indicate this is a server protocol response
        if (debug)
                System.out.println("< "+line);
        else
                System.out.println(line);
        return line;
}

// Writes a line to the POP server, and displays it to the screen
protected void writeMsg(String msg) throws Exception
{
        pw.println(msg);
        pw.flush();
        System.out.println("> "+msg);
}

// Close all writers, streams and sockets
protected void closeConnection() throws Exception
{
        pw.flush();
        pw.close();
        br.close();
        socket.close();
}

// Send the QUIT command, and close connection
protected void sendQuit() throws Exception
{
        System.out.println("Sending QUIT");
        writeMsg("QUIT");
        readLine(true);

        System.out.println("Closing Connection");
        closeConnection();
}


// Display emails in a message
protected void displayEmails() throws Exception
{
        BufferedReader userinput = new BufferedReader( new
          InputStreamReader (System.in) );

        System.out.println("Displaying mailbox with protocol commands
           " and responses below");
        System.out.println("---------------------------------+
           "-------------------------");

        // Open a connection to POP3 server
        System.out.println("Opening Socket");
        socket = new Socket(this.hostname, this.port);
```

```java
br = new BufferedReader(new
    InputStreamReader(socket.getInputStream()));
pw = new PrintWriter(new
    OutputStreamWriter(socket.getOutputStream()));

// If response from server is not okay
if(! responseIsOk())
{
        socket.close();
        throw new Exception("Invalid POP3 Server");
}

// Login by sending USER and PASS commands
System.out.println("Sending username");
writeMsg("USER "+this.username);
if(!responseIsOk())
{
        sendQuit();
        throw new Exception("Invalid username");
}

System.out.println("Sending password");
writeMsg("PASS "+this.password);
if(!responseIsOk())
{
        sendQuit();
        throw new Exception("Invalid password");
}


// Get mail count from server ....
System.out.println("Checking mail");
writeMsg("STAT" );

// ... and parse for number of messages
String line = readLine(true);
StringTokenizer tokens = new StringTokenizer(line," ");
tokens.nextToken();
int messages = Integer.parseInt(tokens.nextToken());
int maxsize = Integer.parseInt(tokens.nextToken());

if (messages == 0)
{
        System.out.println ("There are no messages.");
        sendQuit();
        return;
}

System.out.println ("There are " + messages + "  messages.");
System.out.println("Press enter to continue.");
userinput.readLine();
```

```java
        for(int i = 1; i <= messages ; i++)
        {
                System.out.println("Retrieving message number "+i);
                writeMsg("RETR "+i);
                System.out.println("--------------------");
                line = readLine(false);
                while(line != null && !line.equals("."))
                {
                        line = readLine(false);
                }
                System.out.println("--------------------");
                System.out.println("Press enter to continue." +
                  "To stop, type Q then enter");
                String response = userinput.readLine();
                if (response.toUpperCase().startsWith("Q"))
                break;
        }
        sendQuit();
}

public static void main(String[] args) throws Exception
{
        Pop3ClientDemo client = new Pop3ClientDemo();
}

// Read user input
protected void getInput() throws Exception
{
        String data=null;
        BufferedReader br = new BufferedReader
                (new InputStreamReader(System.in));
        System.out.print("Please enter POP3 server hostname:");
        data = br.readLine();
        if(data == null || data.equals("")) hostname= "localhost";
        else
                hostname=data;

        System.out.print("Please enter mailbox username:");
        data = br.readLine();
        if(!(data == null || data.equals("")))
                username=data;

        System.out.print("Please enter mailbox password:");
        data = br.readLine();
        if(!(data == null || data.equals("")))
                password=data;
    }
}
```

### How Pop3ClientDemo Works

The application is structured similarly to the SMTP client, in that the `main()` method constructs a new instance of the class, which then performs all of the work. In fact, the chief difference is a call to the `displayEmails` method instead of to the `sendEmail` method. In addition, there are several helper methods that assist in conducting communication via POP3.

Like the SMTP application, several important variables are requested from the user. To retrieve e-mail messages, you need to know the hostname of the mail server, the username of the account, and the password for accessing it. These details are obtained by the `getInput()` method of the application, which uses simple text I/O to request details from the user. These are then stored in member variables for later access. We also store the port number of the server (which is fixed to the default port of 110). If, for example, you needed to support nonstandard POP servers, you could modify this value.

```
public class Pop3ClientDemo
{
  protected int port = 110;
  protected String hostname = "localhost";
  protected String username = "";
  protected String password = "";

  // ......
}
```

The most important part of the application is the Post Office Protocol implementation. This is where we get to write real networking code. To make things clearer and more efficient, some of the protocol code is split into helper methods, which perform tasks such as processing a POP response to see that no error code was issued, and reading/writing protocol commands. The main work is done, however, in the `displayEmails()` method.

We start by creating a network socket to the POP server, using the Socket class. The next step is to obtain readers and writers connected to the socket stream, so that we can communicate with the server.

```
// Open a connection to POP3 server
System.out.println("Opening Socket");
socket = new Socket(this.hostname, this.port);

br = new BufferedReader(new
InputStreamReader(socket.getInputStream()));
pw = new PrintWriter(new
    OutputStreamWriter(socket.getOutputStream()));
```

Upon establishing a connection, the server sends a POP response indicating that the server is ready for commands. If the client does not receive a valid POP response, either the server is malfunctioning or a non-POP server is operating on that port. For this reason, the client must always check the response code after opening a TCP connection. We use the `responseOk()` helper method to determine this, which returns a boolean value. Note the negation of the "if" statement—we close the connection only if the response is not okay (indicated by the "!" operator).

```
// If response from server is not okay
if(!responseIsOk())
{
    socket.close();
    throw new Exception("Invalid POP3 Server");
}
```

Now our application is ready to send POP commands. The first command that is sent is "USER," which identifies the user account that the client is trying to access. We send the command, along with the username, by using the helper method `writeMsg(String)`. This also outputs the command to the text console, so you can see how the protocol is working. We do the same then with the "PASS" command, which is used to authenticate the identity of the user.

```
// Login by sending USER and PASS commands
System.out.println("Sending username");
writeMsg("USER "+this.username);
if(!responseIsOk())
{
   sendQuit();
   throw new Exception("Invalid username");
}

writeMsg("PASS "+this.password);
if(!responseIsOk())
{
   sendQuit();
   throw new Exception("Invalid password");
}
```

At this point, the application will be ready to send commands, unless user authentication failed, in which case the application will have terminated. Now we can request the number of mail messages available from the server. This is achieved by sending the "STAT" command, which returns the number of messages. We parse the response, looking for the message count, and then convert it to an `int` value.

```
writeMsg("STAT");

// ... and parse for number of messages
String line = readLine(true);
StringTokenizer tokens = new StringTokenizer(line," ");
tokens.nextToken();
```

```
int messages = Integer.parseInt(tokens.nextToken());
int maxsize = Integer.parseInt(tokens.nextToken());
```

Armed with this information, we can determine if the mailbox is empty or if there are messages to be retrieved. If so, the application simply loops and displays the message contents. During each loop, the user is presented with the option of quitting in case the message count is too high.

```
System.out.println ("There are " + messages + " messages.");
System.out.println("Press enter to continue.");
userinput.readLine();

for(int i = 1; i <= messages ; i++)
{
  System.out.println("Retrieving message number "+i);
  writeMsg("RETR "+i);
  System.out.println("--------------------");
  line = readLine(false);
  while(line != null && !line.equals("."))
  {
    line = readLine(false);
  }
  System.out.println("--------------------");
  System.out.println("Press enter to continue. To stop, type Q then enter");
   String response = userinput.readLine();
  if (response.toUpperCase().startsWith("Q"))
        break;
}
sendQuit();
```

Finally, we call the sendQuit() method, which shuts down the server connection. The application then quits and the task of reading mail using the Post Office Protocol is complete. As you can see, reading e-mail is a fairly simple task, perhaps even easier than sending it.

### Running Pop3ClientDemo

Running the application, too, is quite manageable. After compiling, simply type:

```
java Pop3ClientDemo
```

You will be prompted for the hostname of your mail server (which, if you're not sure of, can be obtained by looking at your e-mail client's settings), the username, and then the password. For example, a user might type the following:

```
java PopClientDemo
Please enter POP3 server hostname: myserver.myisp.com
Please enter mailbox username: johndoe
Please enter mailbox password: javaduke
```

### 8.3.3 HTTP/1.0 Server Implementation

The HyperText Transfer Protocol (HTTP) originated as a means of sharing documents across the Internet. Since many documents are interrelated, the need to provide a link from one to the other was identified, but given the fact that many researchers from around the world were working independently, a single centralized document server was not the ideal method. By placing a hyperlink over a word (such as a scientific term) or a phrase, users would be able to jump instantly from one document to another, even though the documents could reside on servers located in other countries. Not only that, but hyperlinks could be made within the same document, such as to a glossary of terms. Published as RFC 1945, HTTP became one of the most quickly adopted protocols, and led to what we now know as the World Wide Web. Pioneered by Tim Berners-Lee and his colleagues at the CERN scientific laboratories as a way to share scientific information, it quickly spread to other parts of the academic world, and then to commercial and consumer markets.

The first, and most widely supported version, of HTTP is known as HTTP/1.0. This protocol supports a simple set of commands for retrieving resources from a Web server, such as HTML pages, images, documents, and other file types, as well as commands for posting information to the Web server so as to allow for the interactivity and customization of Web pages. This capability is particularly important for Web sites that support advanced features, such as user customization or shopping carts.

The latest version of the protocol is known as HTTP/1.1. It offers many improvements over the previous version, with a wider set of commands to support new features of use both to browser developers and to those who write server-side Web applications. However, older browsers and servers will not support all of these features, and indeed some are not yet in common use at all.

This next example demonstrates how to write a multi-threaded HTTP server that responds to requests from a Web browser, fetches files or Web pages, and sends them back to the user. For the purposes of this example, we will use version 1.0 of the HTTP protocol and support only the GET method, which is used for file retrieval. Other methods, such as POST, are useful when designing interactive server-side applications. However, for such uses it is advised that the reader consider using a fully-fledged commercial server, and Java servlets (discussed in later chapters).

#### Code for WebServerDemo

```
import java.io.*;
import java.net.*;
import java.util.*;
```

```
                    // Chapter 8, Listing 3
public class WebServerDemo
{
  // Directory of HTML pages and other files
  protected String docroot;
  // Port number of web server
  protected int port;
  // Socket for the web server
  protected ServerSocket ss;

  // Handler for a HTTP request
  class Handler extends Thread
  {
    protected Socket socket;
    protected PrintWriter pw;
    protected BufferedOutputStream bos;
    protected BufferedReader br;
    protected File docroot;

    public Handler(Socket _socket, String _docroot) throws Exception
    {
      socket=_socket;
      // Get the absolute directory of the filepath
      docroot=new File(_docroot).getCanonicalFile();
    }

    public void run()
    {
      try
      {
        // Prepare our readers and writers
        br = new BufferedReader(new
        InputStreamReader(socket.getInputStream()));
        bos = new
        BufferedOutputStream(socket.getOutputStream());
        pw = new PrintWriter(new OutputStreamWriter(bos));

        // Read HTTP request from user (hopefully GET /file...... )
        String line = br.readLine();

        // Shutdown any further input
        socket.shutdownInput();

        if(line == null)
        {
          socket.close();
          return;
        }
        if(line.toUpperCase().startsWith("GET"))
        {
```

```java
    // Eliminate any trailing ? data, such as for a CGI
    // GET request
    StringTokenizer tokens = new StringTokenizer(line," ?");
    tokens.nextToken();
    String req = tokens.nextToken();

    // If a path character / or \ is not present, add it
    // to the document root
    // and then add the file request, to form a full
    // filename
    String name;
    if(req.startsWith("/") || req.startsWith("\\"))
      name = this.docroot+req;
    else
      name = this.docroot+File.separator+req;

    // Get absolute file path
    File file = new File(name).getCanonicalFile();

    // Check to see if request doesn't start with our
    // document root ....
    if(!file.getAbsolutePath().startsWith(this.docroot.getAbsolutePath()))
    {
      pw.println("HTTP/1.0 403 Forbidden");
      pw.println();
    }
    // ... if it's missing .....
    else if(!file.exists())
    {
      pw.println("HTTP/1.0 404 File Not Found");
      pw.println();
    }
    // ... if it can't be read for security reasons ....
    else if(!file.canRead())
    {
      pw.println("HTTP/1.0 403 Forbidden");
      pw.println();
    }
    // ... if its actually a directory, and not a file ....
    else if(file.isDirectory())
    {
      sendDir(bos,pw,file,req);
    }
    // ... or if it's really a file
    else
    {
      sendFile(bos, pw, file.getAbsolutePath());
    }
  }
}
```

```
      // If not a GET request, the server will not support it
      else
      {
        pw.println("HTTP/1.0 501 Not Implemented");
        pw.println();
      }

      pw.flush();
      bos.flush();
    }
    catch(Exception e)
    {
      e.printStackTrace();
    }
    try
    {
      socket.close();
    }
    catch(Exception e)
    {
      e.printStackTrace();
    }
}

protected void sendFile(BufferedOutputStream bos,
        PrintWriter pw, String filename) throws Exception
{
  try
  {
    java.io.BufferedInputStream bis = new
      java.io.BufferedInputStream(new FileInputStream(filename));
    byte[] data = new byte[10*1024];
    int read = bis.read(data);

    pw.println("HTTP/1.0 200 Okay");
    pw.println();
    pw.flush();
    bos.flush();

    while(read != -1)
    {
      bos.write(data,0,read);
      read = bis.read(data);
    }
    bos.flush();
  }
  catch(Exception e)
  {
    pw.flush();
    bos.flush();
  }
}
```

```java
    protected void sendDir(BufferedOutputStream bos,
            PrintWriter pw, File dir, String req) throws Exception
{
    try
    {
        pw.println("HTTP/1.0 200 Okay");
        pw.println();
        pw.flush();

        pw.print("<html><head><title>Directory of ");
        pw.print(req);
        pw.print("</title></head><body><h1>Directory of ");
        pw.print(req);
        pw.println("</h1><table border=\"0\">");

        File[] contents=dir.listFiles();

        for(int i=0;i<contents.length;i++)
        {
            pw.print("<tr>");
            pw.print("<td><a href=\"");
            pw.print(req);
            pw.print(contents[i].getName());
            if(contents[i].isDirectory())
                pw.print("/");
            pw.print("\">");
            if(contents[i].isDirectory())
                pw.print("Dir -> ");
            pw.print(contents[i].getName());
            pw.print("</a></td>");
            pw.println("</tr>");
        }
        pw.println("</table></body></html>");
        pw.flush();
    }
    catch(Exception e)
    {
        pw.flush();
        bos.flush();
    }
}
}

// Check that a filepath has been specified and a port number
protected void parseParams(String[] args) throws Exception
{
    switch(args.length)
    {
        case 1:
        case 0:
            System.err.println ("Syntax: <jvm> "+
                this.getClass().getName()+"
                docroot port");
            System.exit(0);
```

```
            default:
                this.docroot = args[0];
                this.port = Integer.parseInt(args[1]);
            break;
        }
    }

    public WebServerDemo(String[] args) throws Exception
    {
        System.out.println ("Checking for paramaters");

        // Check for command line parameters
        parseParams(args);

        System.out.print ("Starting web server...... ");

        // Create a new server socket
        this.ss = new ServerSocket(this.port);

        System.out.println ("OK");

        for (;;)
        {
            // Accept a new socket connection from our server socket
            Socket accept = ss.accept();

            // Start a new handler instance to process the request
            new Handler(accept, docroot).start();
        }
    }

    // Start an instance of the web server running
    public static void main(String[] args) throws Exception
    {
        WebServerDemo webServerDemo = new WebServerDemo(args);
    }
}
```

### How WebServerDemo Works

The typical Web server must respond to requests from a number of browsers, and will usually handle more than one request for each browser (for example, the parallel downloading of a number of images in an HTML document). This means that such servers need to handle requests for files concurrently, and the simplest method of doing this is to use multiple threads of execution. Those readers who have not yet covered the topic of threads in Java are advised to consult the previous chapter, which examines multi-threading in detail.

This example Web server is designed to be extremely compact and rather plain. It supports the bare minimum of features needed to function as a Web server, namely the HTTP/1.0 GET request. No support for dynamic server-side content, such as CGI scripts or Java servlets, is offered—this is a bare-bones

Web server example that illustrates how to write a basic server implementation of an RFC, and is intended primarily as a teaching aid. However, it could be used as the scaffolding for a more ambitious project.

For ease of implementation, the server combines all of its code into a single Java source file. This involves the use of an inner class (`Handler`) that deals with the processing of each incoming HTTP request. Most of this server's work is done inside this handler. The reason for this is to give high performance and to handle blocking I/O correctly so that if one client stalls, no others will be affected (since each request handler operates independently).

The outline of the server looks like this:

```
import java.io.*;
import java.net.*;
import java.util.*;

public class WebServerDemo
{
    class Handler extends Thread
    {
    }
}
```

Within the `WebServerDemo` class are stored several variables that are crucial to the server's operation. These are:

- String docroot
- int port
- ServerSocket ss

The docroot variable points to a location on a hard drive or network drive where the HTML pages and associated files (such as images) are stored for the Web server to read. The port number is used to track which port the server is operating on. Remember that while port 80 is standard for HTTP, it is common to run on nonstandard ports as well, particularly when an existing server is already running. A popular secondary standard is port 8080. Finally, the `ServerSocket` represents a socket that is bound to a specific port and is listening for incoming client requests. It is from this that we will accept browser requests.

When executed, the `main(String[])` method of the server creates a new server instance. Inside the constructor, the server checks for the presence of the necessary command-line parameters (a filepath for the HTML pages and a port number). This code is handled by the `parseParams(String[])` method, which involves only simple error-checking and string processing. As for the networking code, an attempt is made to bind a server socket to that port, and then the server loops indefinitely while it waits for socket connections.

```
public WebServerDemo(String[] args) throws Exception
{
    System.out.println ("Checking for paramters");

    // Check for command line parameters
    parseParams(args);

    System.out.print ("Starting web server...... ");

    // Create a new server socket
    this.ss = new ServerSocket(this.port);

    System.out.println ("OK");

      for (;;)
      {
          // Accept a new socket connection from our server@@@
          // socket
            Socket accept = ss.accept();

          // Start a new handler instance to process the
          // request
            new Handler(accept, docroot).start();
      }
    }
```

As you can see, the code for accepting a connection and launching a new handler thread to process it is fairly simple. One thing that is readily apparent is that writing a server for one particular protocol is not very different from writing one for another (though, as with everything else in life, there are always exceptions to the rule). The main HTTP-specific work lies in the actual `Handler` class.

Let's examine the `Handler` class in more detail. The handler's constructor is very simple—just enough to store the incoming parameters. We also convert the Web server directory to an absolute location. (Since some operating systems allow directory/drive mappings, it is important to know the actual location, as later we must check for browser attempts to access other, forbidden locations.)

```
public Handler(Socket _socket, String _docroot) throws Exception
{
socket=_socket;
  // Get the absolute directory of the filepath
  docroot=new File(_docroot).getCanonicalFile();
}
```

When the Handler thread is started, the `run()` method will be executed. This is a lengthy method, so we'll break it down into manageable chunks.

As is usual with any networking code, we must wrap it in an exception handler to deal with network errors at runtime. Fortunately, we don't need to do anything about the errors—simply terminating the connection is sufficient. The first step in writing our protocol handler will be to obtain I/O streams and wrap them in a reader/writer.

```
// Prepare our readers and writers
br = new BufferedReader(new  InputStreamReader(socket.getInputStream()));
bos = new BufferedOutputStream(socket.getOutputStream());
pw = new PrintWriter(new OutputStreamWriter(bos));
```

The next step is to read a line of text sent by the browser, which (it is hoped) will contain a valid HTTP command. Of course, under HTTP/1.0, it is possible for commands such as "POST" to be composed of multiple lines, but these commands are not supported by this example. Therefore, we will use the socket's shutdownInput() method, which allows for a graceful shutdown of the input reader and instructs the socket to send back acknowledgment of any data coming in and then to silently discard it.

```
// Read HTTP request from user (hopefully GET /file...... )
String line = br.readLine();

// Shutdown any further input
socket.shutdownInput();
```

The next step is to process the HTTP request and work out if the operation is a valid one. We determine first if the line is null and disconnect if it is. As we accept GET requests, we check for a "GET" command, and process the request. If not, the request method sent by the browser is not supported, and we can send back an "HTTP 501 Not Implemented" response. Finally, the output writer and stream are flushed to make sure that the client receives a response.

```
if(line == null)
{
   socket.close();
   return;
}
if(line.toUpperCase().startsWith("GET"))
{
// Process GET request ......................
}
else
{
   pw.println("HTTP/1.0 501 Not Implemented");
   pw.println();
}
pw.flush(); bos.flush();
```

The task of processing the GET request is somewhat more complex, and involves some fancy string processing. While some Java programmers will be comfortable with processing text strings (indeed, Java is an excellent language for this purpose), others may not have come across this before, and may be unaware of the java.util.StringTokenizer class. It allows a string to be easily broken into separate pieces, and we use it in this instance to strip off any data (if it exists) after a "?" character. Remember that additional data can be passed to CGI scripts, or to embedded JavaScript, and we must remove it to determine the actual filename that is being requested. Finally, we add the requested filename to our document root, as well as an OS-specific file separator if needed (such as "/" on Wintel systems or "\" on Unix systems).

```
// Eliminate any trailing ? data, such as for a CGI
// GET request
StringTokenizer tokens = new StringTokenizer (line," ?");
tokens.nextToken();
String req = tokens.nextToken();

// If a path character / or \ is not present, add it
// to the document root
// and then add the file request, to form a full filename
String name;
if(req.startsWith("/") || req.startsWith("\\"))
  name = this.docroot+req;
else
  name = this.docroot+File.separator+req;
```

We then convert this requested file to an absolute filename, and verify that it isn't out of bounds (for example, that it doesn't use a directory mapping on the server to access another drive, or that it doesn't use path operators such as ".." to look at parent directories). This is one part of a sequence of conditions that must be tested for, such as the existence of a file, if it can be accessed and if it is a directory request instead of a file request. Two methods, sendDir and sendFile, are used if it is a successful request—otherwise, the appropriate HTTP error status codes are sent to the browser.

```
// Get absolute file path
File file = new File(name).getCanonicalFile();

// Check to see if request doesn't start with our
// document root ....
if(!file.getAbsolutePath().startsWith(this.docroot.getAbsolutePath()))
{
  pw.println("HTTP/1.0 403 Forbidden");
  pw.println();
}
```

```
else if(!file.exists())
{
  pw.println("HTTP/1.0 404 File Not Found");
  pw.println();
}
else if(!file.canRead())
{
  pw.println("HTTP/1.0 403 Forbidden");
  pw.println();
}
else if(file.isDirectory())
{
  sendDir(bos,pw,file,req);
}
else // assume this is a file
{
  sendFile(bos, pw, file.getAbsolutePath());
}
```

Breaking the code into two methods (sendDir and sendFile) simplifies things somewhat, as it leads to easier-to-read code. Since sending a file is pretty much the whole point of HTTP, we'll cover this important method first.

Reading from a file involves the use of a FileInputStream. We could, if we positively knew that only text data would be encountered, use a FileReader— but often, binary data such as data files and images are sent over HTTP, so we must read and write at the byte level. Starting by sending a valid HTTP 200 response code, we proceed to read the contents of the file and forward it on to the browser. We use the byte array method of reading and writing data for improved efficiency.

```
java.io.BufferedInputStream bis = new
        java.io.BufferedInputStream(new FileInputStream(filename));
byte[] data = new byte[10*1024];
int read = bis.read(data);

pw.println("HTTP/1.0 200 Okay");
pw.println();
pw.flush();
bos.flush();

while(read != -1)
{
  bos.write(data,0,read);
  read = bis.read(data);
}
bos.flush();
```

The final major method of our HTTP handler that must be discussed is sendDir. The task of sending a directory listing, with hyperlinks to files and underlying subdirectories, involves the use of the File class, to obtain a list of file entries within a directory. For this method, we will be using a bit of simple HTML, using tables, to create a simple yet readable output.

Now, we start with the HTML. If you're not familiar with raw HTML, don't panic—the code is very brief, and easily understood when examined piece by piece. We start by adding a title to the Web page, which is the directory location that is being requested. Next we create a simple table, which is used to format our data. The directory location is displayed in a large heading (using the <H1>...</H1> tags).

```
pw.print("<html><head><title>Directory of ");
pw.print(req);
pw.print("</title></head><body><h1>Directory of ");
pw.print(req);
pw.println("</h1><table border=\"0\">");
```

To obtain a list of files, we use the `File.listFiles()` method, which returns an array of File objects. This gives us not only whatever files are stored in our directory, but also the names of any subdirectories. Once obtained, it is a simple process of looping through each element of the array and displaying the output. If the File object is actually representing a directory, we also add a / to the URL and Dir -> to the displayed name of the entry.

```
File[] contents=dir.listFiles();
for(int i=0;i<contents.length;i++)
{
  pw.print("<tr>");
  pw.print("<td><a href=\"");
  pw.print(req);
  pw.print(contents[i].getName());
  if(contents[i].isDirectory())
    pw.print("/");
  pw.print("\">");
  if(contents[i].isDirectory())
    pw.print("Dir -> ");
  pw.print(contents[i].getName());
  pw.print("</a></td>");
  pw.println("</tr>");
}
pw.println("</table></body></html>");
pw.flush();
```

### Running WebServerDemo

Unlike other examples, running the server involves a little more complexity. Under some operating systems, such as Unix, many ports are restricted by security settings, or your machine may already have a Web server running. For this reason, you may need to run the server on a nonstandard port (e.g., 8080 rather than 80), although if you're running a plain Wintel system, port 80 should work fine. You must also specify the location of your HTML pages, although for testing you can point it to a directory on your hard drive where you have some images or text documents.

After compiling the Web server, you can run it by typing:

```
java WebServerDemo port docroot
```

where `port` is a TCP port such as 80 or 8080, and `docroot` is a directory.

Next, using your browser, enter the URL http://hostname:port/, where "hostname" is the name or IP address of your machine, and "port" is the port you specified when running the server. If you're not connected to a network, you can use "localhost" as the hostname. You should see a directory listing and a series of hyperlinks to files and directories. Click on an image or a Web page, and you'll be able to view them just like a real Web server!

## 8.4   Summary

The ultimate end of learning networking is for the programmer to write network applications. Theory, while interesting intellectually, cannot replace the experience of actually working with and writing network code. Whether you're writing your own network protocol to suit a special task, or implementing an existing network protocol described by others (such as an RFC), the basics remain the same. Network communication in Java, at its lowest level, takes place over sockets and involves clients and servers.

You're now armed with the knowledge and skill to write your own network applications.

**Chapter Highlights**

In this chapter, you have learned:

- Where to find specifications of common application protocols (RFCs)
- How to write and run a simple SMTP e-mail client
- How to write and run a simple POP3 e-mail client
- How to write and run a simple HTTP/1.0 server

# CHAPTER 9

## HyperText Transfer Protocol

## 9.1 Overview

The HyperText Transfer Protocol (HTTP) is perhaps the most prolific network application protocol in the short history of the Internet. With the possible exception of e-mail, HTTP has changed the face of the Internet more profoundly than any other protocol. Without HTTP, there would be no World Wide Web, no electronic commerce as we know it today, nor the rapid, phenomenal growth of Internet usage.

In previous chapters, we examined HTTP as an application protocol and constructed a simple Web server that serves up Web pages. In this chapter, we'll look at the protocol in greater detail, and how it can be used in Java.

### 9.1.1 What Is HTTP?

HTTP is an application-level protocol that uses the Transmission Control Protocol (TCP) as a transport mechanism. HTTP provides access to documents and files stored on a Web server. Web browsers use HTTP to request files or dynamically generated content produced by CGI scripts, and other server-side applications. Hypertext documents contain hyperlinks, which are links to other hypertext documents and files. The World Wide Web is a collection of hypertext documents, stored on a wide variety of Web servers and accessed by an even larger number of Web browsers and HTTP clients.

### 9.1.2 How Does HTTP Work?

When an HTTP client, such as a Web browser or a search engine, needs to access a file, it establishes a TCP connection to the Web server (which, by default, uses

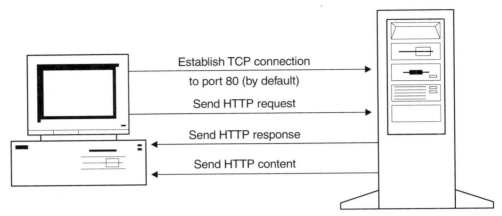

**Figure 9-1**   HyperText Transfer Protocol request/response cycle

**Table 9-1**   HTTP Transaction between Client and Server

| GET /index.html HTTP/1.0 | Client HTTP GET Request |
|---|---|
| HTTP/1.0 200 OK | ← Status line |
| Last-Modified: Monday, 27-Dec-99 22:14 | ← Header (composed of several fields) GMT |
| Content-Type: text/html | |
| Content-Length: 1639 | |
| <HTML> | ← Entity body |
| <HEAD> | |
|    <TITLE> Our homepage </TITLE> | |
|  </HEAD> | |
| | |
| <BODY> | |
| …..    // BODY GOES HERE | |
| </BODY> | |
| </HTML> | |

TCP port 80 for communication). The client sends a request for a particular file, and receives an HTTP response, which will often include the contents of the file, as shown in Figure 9.1. The response includes a status code (indicating the success or failure of a request), some HTTP header information such as the length of the content and its type, and, if appropriate, the file contents. Each request is for a single file; if subsequent files are needed, additional connections must be made.

To understand what type of communication takes place between an HTTP client and a Web server, let's look at a sample transaction in which a browser fetches a Web page (see Table 9-1). Highlighted in bold font is the client request; the server sends the remainder of the transaction.

To fetch the file index.html in the root directory of a Web server, an HTTP client establishes a TCP connection to port 80 and makes an HTTP request. The server processes the request and outputs an HTTP response. Don't be concerned if the meaning of each part of the request and response is not clear to you at this point. The client request and server response are described later in the chapter; for now it is simply important to be aware of what a simple HTTP request/response looks like.

### 9.1.3 Web Clients

A Web client, connecting to the Web server via a TCP socket, will send an HTTP request and then read back a server response. Earlier versions of HTTP used a simple request format, which would only fetch a resource from the server. Under HTTP/1.0, which most, if not all, servers and clients now support, there are three types of requests that a client application can issue to a Web server:

1. GET
2. HEAD
3. POST

The most common HTTP request is a GET request, which fetches a resource from the Web server. More sophisticated requests are possible with HEAD and POST. Each request can also include header fields, which give the server more information about the client.

#### 9.1.3.1 GET Request Method

When a client needs to retrieve a resource from a Web server, it uses the GET request. The GET request takes two parameters: the pathname of the resource and the version of HTTP being used. For example:

```
GET /index.html HTTP/1.0
GET /images/banner.gif HTTP/1.0
GET /links.html HTTP/1.0
```

**NOTE:** CGI parameters can also be passed using the GET method. While often only files are requested, it is possible to invoke a CGI script or server-side application.

There are two major variations on the GET request, depending on which protocol version of HTTP is in use. The most commonly used version by clients is HTTP/1.0, but servers must maintain backward compatibility with the earlier HTTP/0.9. To issue the older-style request, no HTTP version is specified.

```
GET /index.html
GET /images/adserver.cgi
```

When this style of request is made, no header fields will be returned in the HTTP response. This type of request is rare, and clients should use the HTTP/1.0 version if at all possible.

### 9.1.3.2 HEAD Request Method

Sometimes a client will be interested in information about a resource but not the resource itself. For example, if a large file is already cached, the client may want to know if it has been modified recently. If so, a new copy would be downloaded, and if not, the cached version would be used. Some clients may be unable to process certain types of content, so they may want to know the MIME content type of the resource. In these situations, a HEAD request can be made. The HEAD request takes the same parameters as a GET request, and will return a normal HTTP response with information about the resource stored in header fields. However, no actual content will be returned, conserving network bandwidth. An example of a HEAD request is as follows:

```
HEAD /files/averybigfile.zip HTTP/1.0
```

### 9.1.3.3 POST Request Method

One of the great advantages of the Web is that Web sites can be interactive. The earliest form of interactivity came in the form of CGI scripts, written in languages such as Perl. CGI is an acronym for the Common Gateway Interface, which defines a standard mechanism for communicating data from browser to server. CGI scripts, and later, server-side applications such as Java servlets (discussed in Chapter 10) and Active Server Pages (a proprietary Microsoft technology), make it possible for users to interact with server-side applications. However, there must be a way for the browser to pass information from the user to the Web server.

This is where the Common Gateway Interface comes in. CGI parameters are used for this purpose. While it is possible to use the GET request to encode such parameters, limitations on the length of a URL are restrictive. A better way is to use the POST method, which allows clients to send much more information (including large files) to server-side scripts and applications.

The POST request method has a format similar to a GET request. After header fields have been sent, however, the client sends an entity body, which contains CGI parameters and other information. When the entity body is complete, the server will process the information and output an HTTP response. Table 9-2 gives a sample transaction, in which a browser submits information from an HTML form using the POST request method.

### 9.1.3.4 Client Request Header Fields

Attached to any request may be header information and a number of optional fields. Header fields are sent after the request line, and are terminated with a carriage return/linefeed. If no headers are specified, the carriage return/linefeed must still be sent.

The HTTP specification defines several header fields that can be used, and clients are free to add their own. However, not every server will honor such

**Table 9-2** POST Request Sending Data to a Server

| | |
|---|---|
| `POST /cgi-bin/information.pl HTTP/1.0` | ❑ Client HTTP POST request |
| `Content-type: application/x-www-form-urlencoded` | ❑ Header (composed of several fields) |
| `Content-length: 21` | |
| `User-Agent: SomeBrowser/1.0` | |
| `Name=David%20Reilly&answer=yes` | ❑ Entity body |
| `HTTP/1.0 200 OK` | ← HTTP Server Response |
| `Last-Modified: Monday, 27-Dec-99 22:14 GMT` | |
| `Content-Type: text/html` | |
| `Content-Length: 4855` | |
| `<HTML>` | ← Entity body |
| `<HEAD>` | |
| `   <TITLE> Thanks for your feedback </TITLE>` | |
| `</HEAD>` | |
| | |
| `<BODY>` | |
| `.....    // BODY GOES HERE` | |
| `</BODY>` | |
| `</HTML>` | |

fields. If a field is not supported, it will be ignored—no error condition should be generated. The major fields a client is likely to use are covered below.

### "Cookie" Field

Persistent client-side objects (cookies) are small pieces of data sent by a Web server and echoed back on every subsequent request. Cookies are used for tracking client requests and customizing server output for individual users. Not every client supports cookies, and cookie support can be disabled for privacy and security in most clients. An example of this field is:

```
Cookie: secret_id=553235996
```

### "From" Field

The "From" field specifies the e-mail address of the user in control of the client. Most Web browsers do not divulge this information (much to the dismay of direct-mail marketers); however, specialized or experimental HTTP clients may. For example, a search engine that sends out requests to remote Web sites may include a contact e-mail address, to help establish contact if the search engine runs wild and requests too many pages in a given period. An example of this field is:

```
From: myemail@mydomain.com
```

### "If-Modified-Since" Field

A client that has already requested a resource can use this header field to check whether the resource has been updated. For example, a Web browser that caches pages may send the "If-Modified-Since" field, specifying the date when the resource was last requested. If the resource has been updated, the server will output a normal response and a normal entity body. If, however, it has not been updated, the server will issue a response with a status code of 304 and no entity body. The client then knows to use the cached version. An example of this field is:

```
If-Modified-Since: Tue, 27 Oct 1998, 09:00:00 GMT
```

### "Referer" Field

This is an extremely important field for the server, and is often stored for statistical purposes. The "Referer" field specifies the URL that linked to the request URL. If an HTTP client follows a link to a new page, the "Referer" field will specify the page that linked to it. This information is useful for Web masters, as it shows which pages are linking to a site and which search engine queries delivered specific users. Most Web browsers send this field automatically, without the ability to disable it. An example is:

```
Referer: http://www.davidreilly.com/links.html
```

### "User-Agent" Field

The "User-Agent" field identifies the type of HTTP client that is making the request. This information can be collected for statistical purposes or used to customize the response issued by the server. For example, an opportunistic Web master might output many random keywords to search engines in an effort to boost the traffic on his or her site. "Real" users would see the original page, since the server would read a browser identification string and not a search engine identification string. Such behavior on the part of a Web master is frowned upon, however, and would eventually result in penalization, or blacklisting of the site.

Developers of HTTP clients should always include this field, to identify the software that is making the request (by default, Java sends a field that identifies HTTP requests as being made by a Java application). Some sites, strange as it may seem, use this information to blacklist certain HTTP clients such as search engines, so it is important that a legitimate "User-Agent" field is sent. By convention, browser applications begin their identification string with the keyword *Mozilla,* which was the identification string of the Netscape browser. An example of this field is:

```
User-Agent: Mozilla (MyNewBrowser/1.0)
```

## 9.1.4  Web Servers

When a client connects to a Web server, it will send an HTTP request that the server will read and process. The server returns a response. That response is made up of the following components:

- A status line, with a numerical status code and human-readable text message
- A response header, with one or more header fields followed by a blank line
- An entity body (optional), which contains the contents of a file or server-side output

Servers should also support the older HTTP/0.9 simple request, for the purpose of backward compatibility. In response to a simple request, a server should return only the entity body and no header information.

### 9.1.4.1 Status Line

The status line indicates whether or not a request could be performed successfully. If a request could not be completed, it also gives an indication of the reason. It does so by using a three-digit numerical code. The first digit corresponds to an error group, with the two remaining digits indicating a precise error condition.

Each group represents a generic error state (see Table 9-3). Clients can respond to the first digit (knowing only that an error occurred or that a request was accepted), or they can act based on the type of error that occurred.

### Informational (1xx)

The informational set of status codes is rarely used. The HTTP specification states that this code indicates a partial response (such as header information), but with no entity body. These status codes are not a valid response for any HTTP/1.0 request and so should be used only in experimental systems, not for production systems.

### Successful (2xx)

This is, under ideal circumstances, the most common set of status codes returned. This indicates that a request was processed and completed without any errors. Although there are several status codes in this group, the most common will be the 200 status code.

### Redirection (3xx)

When a resource moves to a new location or a new server, redirection is occasionally used. When a status code from the redirection group is issued, the client should look for a "Location" header field giving the new location of the resource. The entity body of the response may also include a hyperlink to the new resource, in the event that the HTTP client is unable to automatically follow redirect requests.

**Table 9-3**    Status Codes Used in HTTP

| Status Group | Error Group Name |
| --- | --- |
| 1xx | Informational |
| 2xx | Successful |
| 3xx | Redirection |
| 4xx | Client Error |
| 5xx | Server Error |

There is also one circumstance in which a redirection status code will be sent, but where no redirection location is specified. If a client issues a conditional request, by specifying an "If-Modified-Since" field in the request header, a 304 status code will be returned, indicating that the resource has not been modified and that the previous cached version should be used. No entity body is returned in this situation.

### Client Error (4xx)

When an HTTP client sends an incorrect request, a status code from the client error group will be sent. Reasons for the error can vary, from a bad request, to an invalid URL, to a URL that is forbidden for that client's IP address. The most common of all client error status codes is 404, indicating that the resource was not found. Though this is classed as a client error, sometimes a resource is deleted from the server, making invalid a URL that clients have previously accessed.

### Server Error (5xx)

Servers themselves are not impervious to error conditions. When a server is overloaded, for example, it can issue a 503 status code. A server-side CGI script or servlet could malfunction, causing a 501 status code to be issued. Generally, however, servers are reasonably stable—there are more likely to be client errors than server errors.

### 9.1.4.2 Server Response Header Fields

The response header is composed of two groups of header fields (either a "Response-Header" field, or an "Entity-Header" field). In actual practice, the header group names are irrelevant, as the headers are sent together and only the field name is of interest to a client. Each header field is optional and will not be present in every request. However, some fields will be present in almost all situations, such as the "Content-Type" and "Last-Modified" fields. Covering every possible field would be impossible, as servers can add custom fields. However, the most frequently encountered fields described in the HTTP specification are worth being aware of when writing HTTP clients.

### "Location" Field

The location field specifies a URL to a resource. In the case where a redirection status code is specified, the client should fetch the content specified in this header field. For example, in response to a URL request to http://davidreilly. com/, a redirection to http://www.davidreilly.com/ is made using

```
Location: http://www.davidreilly.com/
```

### "Server" Field

The "Server" field gives information about the server vendor and server version number. This information often isn't that useful to the client and, as the HTTP specification warns, could represent a security risk. If a server returns this field, and a known security flaw in that vendor/version combination exists, it may open the server to hostile attack. An example of this field is:

```
Server: MyServer v1.05
```

### "Content-Length" Field

This field indicates the number of bytes of the entity body. Although not strictly necessary, since the client will stop reading when the entity body terminates, this information can be useful when dealing with large file downloads. At the beginning of the transaction, the client can give the user an estimate of how much content needs to be downloaded, and the time remaining. If a connection terminates prematurely, the client can detect that the file was not completely downloaded, and attempt the request again. An example of this field is:

```
Content-Length: 5934
```

### "Content-Type" Field

This field specifies the MIME content type of the entity body. The MIME content type is divided into two sections, separated by a "/" character. The first section indicates the general type of the content (e.g., text, image, application file); the second section indicates the specific type. For example, the content type of a Web page is text/html, whereas a plain text document is text/plain. An image in GIF format is of type "image/gif," whereas a JPEG is of type "image/jpeg." The Internet Assigned Number Authority defines MIME content types, and it is best not to assign arbitrary types in production systems. An example is:

```
Content-Type: image/png
```

### "Expires" Field

When a server wishes to prevent caching of a resource for too long a period, it can specify a "use-by" date for a resource. For example, the front page of a news site could specify one hour into the future, to prevent proxy servers (servers that forward HTTP requests on behalf of other machines, such as those trapped within a firewall) and HTTP clients from caching the content longer than an hour. Some content may also be marked as not cacheable, using the

"Pragma" header field (see below). However, the "Expires" field allows caching for a specified period of time. An example of this field is:

```
Expires: Thu, 12-Jan-2001 10:00:00 GMT
```

### "Last-Modified" Field

The "Last-Modified" field indicates when a resource was last changed or last updated. This information may be useful to proxy servers and clients, to prevent the downloading of large files that are already cached and have not changed since the last request. An example of this field is:

```
Last-Modified: Fri, 22-Feb-1998 15:23:11 GMT
```

### "Pragma" Field

Sometimes a server may wish to prevent caching of a resource entirely. For example, a page that changes every few minutes (such as a stock-price information page) or that contains sensitive information that would best not be cached by an intermediary proxy server may be marked with the "Pragma" field. The "Pragma" field can also be used to indicate other restrictions and information on the behavior of clients, though clients are not guaranteed to support such restrictions. An example is:

```
Pragma: nocache
```

### "Set-Cookie" Field

Although not defined in the original HTTP specification, cookies have been quickly adopted by Web browser manufacturers and the Web developer community. When a server-side application wants to send a cookie to the browser, it adds a "Set-Cookie" field to the HTTP response. Subsequent requests by that browser will include the cookie, so that the client can be tracked. Not all browsers have cookies enabled, and server-side applications should be aware that there is no error message sent if a browser does not accept cookies. An example of this field is:

```
Set-Cookie: secret_id=553235996; domain=mysite.com; path=/
```

## 9.1.4.3 Entity Body

The entity body is the stream of bytes that form the actual content of the requested resource. This content may be static (a file whose content changes infrequently or not at all) or dynamic (a custom server-side response to the client request). Meta-information about the entity body is contained in entity header fields such as "Content-Type" and "Content-Length."

## 9.2    HTTP and Java

Java provides extremely good support for the HyperText Transfer Protocol. While developers are free to write their own HTTP implementations using TCP sockets, the java.net package provides several classes that offer HTTP functionality:

- `java.net.URL`
- `java.net.URLConnection`
- `java.net.HttpURLConnection`

### 9.2.1   URL Class

The URL class represents one of the most frequently used address types of the Internet, the Uniform Resource Locator (URL). URLs can point to files, Web sites, ftp sites, newsgroups, e-mail addresses, and other resources. Some fictitious examples of non-Web URLs are:

- ftp://records.area51.mil/roswell/subjects/autopsy/
- telnet://localhost:8000/
- mailto:president@whitehouse.gov?subject=My%20Opinion

In the context of HTTP and this chapter, we'll be dealing with URLs that point to a Web site, but it is important to remember that other network protocols also use URLs.

The URL is composed of several components (shown in Figure 9-2), each of which can be parsed by the URL class and returned separately. Some components (namely the port and the reference fields) are optional, and will not be present in many URLs. As mentioned earlier, CGI parameters can also be included as part of the path field.

#### 9.2.1.1  Creating a URL

The URL class can be used to parse URLs, or as an identifier of a remote resource that can be employed (in conjunction with the other Java HTTP classes) to retrieve that resource.

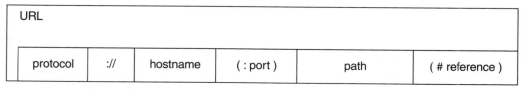

**Figure 9-2**   Format of the Universal Resource Locator

## Constructors

There are six constructors for the URL class; the choice of which to use depends largely on how much control you require over the URL. For most situations, the following constructor will be used:

- URL ( String url_str ) throws java.net.MalformedURLException—creates a URL object based on the string parameter. If the URL cannot be correctly parsed, a MalformedURLException will be thrown.

However, not every application will have a String representation of a URL. For convenience, a wide range of constructors is offered, which some developers may find easier to use.

- URL ( String protocol, String host, String file ) throws java.net. MalformedURLException—creates a URL object with the specified protocol, host, and file path.
- URL ( String protocol, String host, int port, String file ) throws java.net.MalformedURLException—creates a URL object with the specified protocol, host, port, and file path.
- URL ( String protocol, String host, int port, String file, URL StreamHandler handler ) throws java.net.MalformedURLException—creates a URL object with the specified protocol, host, port, file path, and stream handler.
- URL ( URL context, String relative ) throws java.net.Malformed-URLException—creates a URL object using the context of an existing URL and a relative URL. For example, if we had an existing URL of http://somewebsite.com/, and a relative URL of /images/icon.gif, the new URL would be http://somewebsite.com/images/icon.gif.
- URL ( URL context, String relative, URLStreamHandler handler ) throws java.net.MalformedURLException—creates a URL object using the context of an existing URL and a relative URL. Any stream handler specified will override the default stream handler of the context URL.

### 9.2.1.2 Using a URL

The URL class provides the following methods to parse a URL and extract individual components (such as the protocol or the hostname of the URL), as well as to open an HTTP connection to the resource that it specifies.

## Methods

- boolean equals( Object object )—compares two URLs for equality. If the object is not an instance of the URL class, or if the object does not point to an identical resource, a value of "false" is returned.

- `Object getContent()` throws `java.io.IOException`—retrieves the contents of the resource located at the URL. The type of object returned will vary, depending on the MIME content type of the remote resource and the available content handlers (classes responsible for processing and retrieving objects from a `URLConnection`). This method is shorthand for calling the `openConnection()` method, which returns a `URLConnection`, and then invoking the `getContent()` method upon the `URLConnection` that was returned. As a network connection will be established, an `IOException` may be thrown.
- `String getProtocol()`—returns the protocol component of a URL.
- `String getHost()`—returns the hostname component of a URL.
- `String getPort()`—returns the port component of a URL. This is an optional component, and if not present a value of –1 will be returned.
- `String getFile()`—returns the pathname component of a URL.
- `String getRef()`—returns the reference component of a URL. This is an optional component, and a reference may not be present. A null value will be returned if no reference was specified.
- `public int hashCode()`—returns an identifier for a URL object, for the purpose of hash table indexing.
- `URLConnection openConnection()`—returns a `URLConnection` object, which can be used to establish a connection to the remote resource. The name of this method can be deceiving, though, as no connection will be established until further methods of the `URLConnection` object are invoked.
- `InputStream openStream()` throws `java.io.IOException`—establishes a connection to the remote server where the resource is located, and provides an `InputStream` that can be used to read the resource's contents. This method provides a quick and easy way to retrieve the contents of a URL, without the added complexity of dealing with a `URLConnection` object.
- `boolean sameFile (URL url)`—compares two URLs for equality, similar to that of the `equals(Object)` method. However, only the protocol, hostname, port, and pathname fields are compared—the reference field of the URL is excluded. While the `equals(Object)` method checks that a URL points to the same place in the same file, the `sameFile(URL)` method does not test where in the file the URL points to.
- `String toString()`—returns a `String` representation of a URL. There is no difference between this method and the `toExternalForm()` method.
- `String toExternalForm()`—returns a `String` representation of a URL. There is no difference between this method and the `toString()` method.

### 9.2.2 Parsing with the URL Class

To demonstrate how the URL class is used, and how it can extract the individual components out of a URL, we'll examine a small application that creates an instance of the URL class from the command-line parameter passed to it.

*Code for URLParser*

```java
import java.net.*;

// Chapter 9, Listing 1
public class URLParser
{
    public static void main(String args[])
    {
        int argc = args.length;

        // Check for valid number of parameters
        if (argc != 1)
        {
            System.out.println ("Syntax :");
            System.out.println ("java URLParser url");
            return;
        }

        // Catch any thrown exceptions
        try
        {
            // Create an instance of java.net.URL
            java.net.URL myURL = new URL ( args[0] );

            System.out.println ("Protocol : " +
                myURL.getProtocol() );
            System.out.println ("Hostname : " +
                myURL.getHost() );
            System.out.println ("Port      : " +
                myURL.getPort() );
            System.out.println ("Filename : " +
                myURL.getFile() );
            System.out.println ("Reference: " +
                myURL.getRef() );
        }
        // MalformedURLException indicates parsing error
        catch (MalformedURLException mue)
        {
            System.err.println ("Unable to parse URL!");
            return;
        }
    }
}
```

## How URLParser Works

The example starts by checking that a command-line parameter was passed to the application. A null value for the command-line parameter would cause a runtime exception to be thrown. Next, the application begins a try/catch block, which is required since the URL constructor can throw an instance of `java.net.MalformedURLException`. If an exception is thrown, it will be caught, and a warning sent to the user before terminating.

```
// Catch any thrown exceptions
try
{
    // Create an instance of java.net.URL
    java.net.URL myURL = new URL ( args[0] );

    // Code to process the URL goes here
    ...........
}
// MalformedURLException indicates parsing error
catch (MalformedURLException mue)
{
    System.err.println ("Unable to parse URL!");
    return;
}
```

The code to create a URL instance is relatively easy. Once you have a URL, you can look at the various components of which it is comprised. The application prints out the protocol, host, port, pathname, and reference of the URL. Note that the port and reference fields may be blank, so a –1 and null value, respectively, would be displayed in this case.

```
System.out.println ("Protocol : " + myURL.getProtocol() );
System.out.println ("Hostname : " + myURL.getHost() );
System.out.println ("Port     : " + myURL.getPort() );
System.out.println ("Filename : " + myURL.getFile() );
System.out.println ("Reference: " + myURL.getRef() );
```

## Running URLParser

The `URLParser` application takes a valid URL as its only parameter. A valid URL must contain a protocol, hostname, and pathname components, but it does not necessarily need to point to a valid resource. Thus, the following URLs would be accepted without throwing a `MalformedURLException`:

- http://thisisnotarealmachine/noristhisarealpath
- http://www.davidreilly.com:80/#top
- ftp://ftp.davidreilly.com/pub/

However, these URLs could not be parsed:

- abcdef://abcdef.com/alphabetsoup/
- ttp://www.davidreilly.com:80/#top

To run the URLParser, specify the URL as the only parameter, as follows:

```
java URLParser url
```

Try running some of the sample URLs, and examine the output for URLs with and without port and reference fields.

### 9.2.3 Retrieving a Resource with the URL Class

The URL class can be used for more than just parsing, however. There are two URL methods that can assist in retrieving the contents of a remote resource:

1. InputStream URL.openStream()

2. URLConnection URL.openConnection();

For greater control over how the request is made, a URLConnection object created by invoking the URL.openConnection() method would be used. In many situations, however, a simpler way to retrieve the contents of a resource is called for. The openStream() method returns an InputStream, which makes reading a resource simple. Examine the following application, which will fetch a URL passed as a command-line parameter.

#### Code for FetchURL

```
import java.net.*;
import java.io.*;

// Chapter 9, Listing 2
public class FetchURL
{
    public static void main(String args[]) throws Exception
    {
        int argc = args.length;

        // Check for valid number of parameters
        if (argc != 1)
        {
            System.out.println ("Syntax :");
            System.out.println ("java FetchURLConnection  url");
            return;
        }

        // Catch any thrown exceptions
        try
        {
```

```java
        // Create an instance of java.net.URL
        java.net.URL myURL = new URL ( args[0] );

        // Fetch the content, and read from an
        // InputStream
        InputStream in = myURL.openStream();

        // Buffer the stream, for better performance
        BufferedInputStream bufIn = new
            BufferedInputStream(in);

        // Repeat until end of file
        for (;;)
        {
            int data = bufIn.read();

            // Check for EOF
            if (data == -1)
                break;
            else
                System.out.print ( (char) data);
        }

        // Pause for user
        System.out.println ();
        System.out.println ("Hit enter to continue");
        System.in.read();

    }
    // MalformedURLException indicates parsing error
    catch (MalformedURLException mue)
    {
        System.err.println ("Unable to parse URL!");
        return;
    }
    // IOException indicates network or I/O error
    catch (IOException ioe)
    {
        System.err.println ("I/O Error : " + ioe);
        return;
    }
  }
}
```

## How FetchURL Works

You may notice some similarity between this example and the previous one. Since we're working with the same URL class, the code to check for a valid parameter, to construct the URL, and catch a possible MalformedURLException remains the same. Observant readers may notice an extra catch statement, which handles any network or I/O errors. This is necessary in case the host machine could not be contacted or is invalid. Remember that a MalformedURLException will not be thrown if the hostname is invalid, only if the URL syntax was not followed.

```
// IOException indicates network or I/O error
catch (IOException ioe)
{
    System.err.println ("I/O Error : " + ioe);
    return;
}
```

Inside the try/catch block, the application creates a new URL object and calls the openStream() method. This establishes a connection to the remote machine (or, if a connection could not be opened, throws an IOException). The method returns an InputStream, which can then be used for reading from the remote resource.

```
// Create an instance of java.net.URL
java.net.URL myURL = new URL ( args[0] );

// Fetch the content, and read from an InputStream
InputStream in = myURL.openStream();
```

While we could read directly from the input stream, one byte at a time, a more efficient alternative is to connect another stream, one which is better suited to the task at hand. In this case, we use a BufferedInputStream and read a byte at a time. However, a DataInputStream or a Reader object could just as easily have been used.

```
// Buffer the stream, for better performance
BufferedInputStream bufIn = new BufferedInputStream(in);

// Repeat until end of file
for (;;)
{
    int data = bufIn.read();

    // Check for EOF
    if (data == -1)
        break;
    else
        System.out.print ( (char) data);
}

// Pause for user
System.out.println ();
System.out.println ("Hit enter to continue");
System.in.read();
```

While this example is quite simple, it provides only limited control over the connection. For example, what is the MIME content type of the resource? By reading from an InputStream, we lose some of the details. The URLConnection class, as we'll see in Section 9.2.4, offers greater control over requests and responses.

### Running FetchURL

Running the application is straightforward. Simply specify a valid URL as the only command-line parameter, either of a local machine on your network or a Web site, if you are connected to the Internet.

```
java FetchURL url
```

## 9.2.4   URLConnection Class

The URLConnection class is used to send HTTP requests and read HTTP responses. URLConnection has methods that allow you to connect to a Web server, to set request header fields, to read response header fields, and of course, to read the contents of the resource.

### 9.2.4.1  Creating a URLConnection

There are no public constructors for the URLConnection class. The single constructor for URLConnection is marked as a protected method, meaning that only a class in the java.net package can create one. Instead, you should call the URL.openConnection() method, which will return a URLConnection instance.

```
URL url = new URL ( some_url );
URLConnection connection = url.openConnection();
```

### 9.2.4.2 Using a URLConnection

The URLConnection provides many methods, the most important of which are listed below. Some are shortcuts to other methods (such as response header fields). For completeness, even advanced methods are included, although for normal programming you would likely use a small subset of these.

### Methods

- void connect() throws java.io.IOException—establishes a connection between the application (the client) and the resource (stored on the server). The act of creating a URLConnection object does not establish this connection, and until this method is executed, the remote host will not be contacted. Before invoking this method, the client application should specify any request headers, as these will be sent when the connection is made. Some URLConnection methods will call the connect() method in order to complete their task.

- `boolean getAllowUserInteraction()`—returns the state of the "allow-UserInteraction" field, which indicates whether the URL is being used in a way that supports user interaction, such as providing authentication details.
- `Object getContent()` throws `java.io.IOException`—attempts to process the contents of a resource and return it as an `Object`. The method checks the MIME content type of the resource and attempts to find a suitable content handler.
- `String getContentEncoding()`—returns the value of the "Content-encoding" header field, if such a field exists. Returns null if no content-encoding field was specified.
- `int getContentLength()`—returns the value of the "Content-length" header field, if such a field exists. Returns −1 if no content-length field was specified.
- `String getContentType()`—returns the value of the "Content-type" header field, if such a field exists. Returns null if no content-type field was specified. If no type of information is available, the `guessContentTypeFromStream(InputStream)` method may be used as an indication.
- `long getDate()`—returns the value of the "Date" header field, expressed as the number of seconds since January 1, 1970 GMT. If no such header field was specified, a value of zero will be returned.
- `static boolean getDefaultAllowUserInteractionField()`—returns the default value for the "allowUserInteraction" field. The state of this default value determines the "allowUserInteraction" value of all future `URLConnection` objects that are created.
- `static String getDefaultRequestProperty(String key)`—returns the value of the specified default property, applied to all `URLConnection` objects. Returns null if no such property exists.
- `boolean getDefaultUseCaches()`—returns the default value of the cache flag. The state of this default value determines the cache flag value of all future `URLConnection` objects that are created.
- `boolean getDoInput()`—returns a flag, indicating whether the connection should be used for input. By default, this value will be "true," unless modified by the `setDoInput(boolean)` method.
- `boolean getDoOutput()`—returns a flag indicating whether the connection should be used for output. By default, this value will be "false," unless modified by the `setDoOutput(boolean)` method.
- `long getExpiration()`—returns the value of the "Expires" header field, expressed as the number of seconds since January 1, 1970 GMT. If no such header field was specified, a value of zero will be returned.
- `static FileNameMap getFileNameMap()`—returns an object that implements the `FileNameMap` interface, which is used to map MIME content

types to filenames. The content type for a resource may also be determined by calling the getContentType() method.

- String getHeaderField(int n)—returns the value of the *n*th response header field, or null if this exceeds the number of response header fields available. Unlike an array, which is zero-indexed, the first element of the set of header fields will have an index value of one.

- String getHeaderField(String field)—returns the value of the specified header field name, or null if no such field exists.

- long getHeaderFieldDate (String field, long default_value)—attempts to parse the specified header field name as a date, expressed as the number of seconds since January 1, 1970 GMT. If a parsing error occurs (such as an invalid date or a missing header field), the default_value will be returned.

- int getHeaderFieldInt (String field, int default_value)—attempts to parse the specified header field as a number. If a parsing error occurs (such as an invalid number), the default_value will be returned.

- String getHeaderFieldKey(int n)—returns the name of the *n*th response header field, or null if this exceeds the number of response header fields available. Unlike an array, which is zero-indexed, the first element of the set of header fields will have an index value of one.

- long getIfModifiedSince()—returns the date of the "If-Modified-Since" request header field. This field is modified by calling the setIfModifiedSince(long) method.

- InputStream getInputStream() throws java.io.IOException, java.net.UnknownServiceException—returns an InputStream object that reads the contents of the resource pointed to by the URLConnection. If a connection cannot be established, an IOException is thrown. In addition, if the connection does not support reading, an UnknownServiceException is thrown.

- long getLastModified()—returns the date of the "Last-Modified header field, expressed as the number of seconds since January 1, 1970 GMT. If no such header field was specified, a value of zero will be returned.

- OutputStream getOutputStream() throws java.io.IOException, java.net.UnknownServiceException—returns an OutputStream object that writes to the remote connection. If a connection cannot be established, an IOException is thrown. In addition, if the connection does not support writing, an UnknownServiceException is thrown.

- Permission getPermission() throws java.io.IOException—returns a Permission object, representing the security permissions required to access a resource. If a specialized subclass of URLConnection is written, this method should be overridden. Developers won't normally need to use this method, unless special security policies are specified for an application.

- String getRequestProperty(String key)—returns the value of the specified property, and null if no such property exists.
- URL getURL()—returns a URL object representing the location of the resource pointed to by the URLConnection.
- boolean getUseCaches()—returns a flag indicating whether or not resources will be cached. If "true," caching will be used wherever possible, and if "false," a new request will be sent each time.
- protected static String guessContentTypeFromStream(String file)—returns an estimate of the MIME content type, based on the extension of the specified file.
- static String guessContentTypeFromStream(InputStream stream)—returns an estimate of the MIME content type, based on the bytes at the beginning of an InputStream. The method does a nondestructive read, in an attempt to determine the content type if header information does not specify it.
- void setAllowUserInteraction(boolean flag)—modifies the state of the "allowUserInteraction" field, which indicates whether the URL is being used in a way that supports user interaction, such as providing authentication details.
- static void setContentHandlerFactory (ContentHandlerFactory factory) throws java.lang.SecurityException, java.lang.Error—assigns a content handler factory to all URLConnections. A content handler factory is responsible for creating the appropriate Content-Handler based on the MIME content type of the resource. If a content handler already exists, or if the current security manager prohibits the operation, an error will occur.
- static void setDefaultAllowUserInteraction(boolean flag)—modifies the default value of the state of the "allowUserInteraction" field, which will be assigned to all future URLConnection objects.
- static void setDefaultRequestProperty(String key)—modifies the value of the specified default property applied to all URLConnection objects.
- void setDefaultUseCaches(boolean flag)—modifies the default value of the cache flag. The state of this default value determines the cache flag value of all future URLConnection objects that are created.
- void setDoInput()—modifies the input flag, indicating whether the connection should be used for reading.

- void setDoOutput()—modifies the output flag, indicating whether the connection should be used for writing.
- void setIfModifiedSince(long date)—sets the "If-Modified-Since" request header, indicating that a resource should only be fetched if modified after a certain date. This method must be invoked prior to the connect() method if the setting is to take effect.
- void setRequestProperty(String key, String value)—assigns the specified value to the specified request header field. This method must be invoked prior to the connect() method if the setting is to take effect.
- void setUseCaches(boolean flag)—modifies the flag indicating whether caching of requests should be allowed. If "true," caching will be used wherever possible, and if "false," a new request will be sent each time.

### 9.2.5   *Retrieving a Resource with the URLConnection Class*

While the URL class does allow you to retrieve a resource by using the URL. openStream() method, information about the resource is lost, as is the ability to prevent caching of requests and to specify additional header fields, since only a stream object is returned. The example below shows how to use the URL-Connection class to retrieve a resource and to determine its MIME content type and the length of the resource. Since we still use the URL class, some of the code is similar to previous examples.

#### Code for FetchURLConnection

```java
import java.net.*;
import java.io.*;

// Chapter 9, Listing 3
public class FetchURLConnection
{
    public static void main(String args[]) throws Exception
    {
        int argc = args.length;

        // Check for valid number of parameters
        if (argc != 1)
        {
            System.out.println ("Syntax :");
            System.out.println ("java FetchURLConnection url");
            return;
        }

        // Catch any thrown exceptions
        try
        {
```

```
// Create an instance of java.net.URL
java.net.URL myURL = new URL ( args[0] );

// Create a URLConnection object, for this URL
// NOTE : no connection has yet been
// established
URLConnection connection =  myURL.openConnection();

// Now open a connection
connection.connect();

// Display the MIME content-type of the
// resource (e.g. text/html)
String MIME = connection.getContentType();
System.out.println ("Content-type: " + MIME);

// Display, if available, the content length
int contentLength =  connection.getContentLength();
if (contentLength != -1)
{
      System.out.println ("Content-length: " +  contentLength);
}

// Pause for user
System.out.println ("Hit enter to continue");
System.in.read();

// Read the contents of the resource from the
// connection
InputStream in = connection.getInputStream();

// Buffer the stream, for better performance
BufferedInputStream bufIn = new  BufferedInputStream(in);

// Repeat until end of file
for (;;)
{
      int data = bufIn.read();

      // Check for EOF
      if (data == -1)
          break;
      else
          System.out.print ( (char) data);
}
}
// MalformedURLException indicates parsing error
catch (MalformedURLException mue)
{
```

```
        System.err.println ("Unable to parse URL!");
        return;
}
// IOException indicates network or I/O error
catch (IOException ioe)
{
        System.err.println ("I/O Error : " + ioe);
        return;
}
    }
}
```

### How FetchURLConnection Works

We start by checking for a valid parameter, and create a URL instance, as in previous examples. Rather than calling URL.openStream() once we have a URL object, however, the openConnection() method is called instead, returning a URLConnection instance.

```
// Create an instance of java.net.URL
java.net.URL myURL = new URL ( args[0] );

// Create a URLConnection object, for this URL
// NOTE : no connection has yet been established
URLConnection connection = myURL.openConnection();
```

The name of the openConnection() method is somewhat misleading. Although it creates an instance of the URLConnection object, it does not establish an HTTP session with the Web server. This can be advantageous, as it allows us to set any request header fields we need. For a simple example like this, however, this functionality is not needed, so we can connect to the Web server immediately, which sends a request for the URL associated with this connection.

```
// Now open a connection
connection.connect();
```

Once the connection is established and the request sent, a response will be issued by the Web server. This response will include a variety of header fields, as discussed earlier in the chapter. The most important field of all is the "Content-Type," which tells an application whether the resource is text, an image, a data file, or some other resource. The application could read this data by calling the URLConnection.getHeaderField(String) method and passing a value of "Content-Type." However, a shortcut method exists that makes for more readable source code.

```
// Display the MIME content-type of the resource (e.g. text/html)
String MIME = connection.getContentType();
System.out.println ("Content-type: " + MIME);
```

Another important piece of information is the length of the resource. Large files can take minutes or even hours to download, and the user benefits from knowing the length of the resource at the beginning of the transaction. This information is provided in the "Content-Length" header field, and a shortcut method exists for this data that converts it to an int value. After displaying the length, the application pauses, to allow the user time to read it before displaying the requested resource.

```
// Display, if available, the content length
int contentLength = connection.getContentLength();
if (contentLength != -1)
{
    System.out.println ("Content-length: " + contentLength);
}

// Pause for user
System.out.println ("Hit enter to continue");
System.in.read();
```

The next step is to get an `InputStream` to the contents of the resource. Just like a URL object, `URLConnection` provides a method to create an `InputStream` for reading a resource. For this purpose, the `URLConnection.getInputStream()` method is used.

```
// Read the contents of the resource from the connection
InputStream in = connection.getInputStream();
```

Once an `InputStream` has been obtained, the resource is read in the same way as the previous example. The chief difference between `FetchURL` and `FetchURLConnection` is that more information about the resource was provided. The `URLConnection` class can be used for more than just content type and length information, however. In the next examples, we'll unleash the power of the `URLConnection` class.

### Running FetchURLConnection

This application takes the same command-line parameter as the previous example. Specify a valid URL as the only command-line parameter, either of a local machine on your network, or a Web site, if you are connected to the Internet.

```
java FetchURLConnection url
```

The application will issue an HTTP request, the display the MIME content type and length of the resource and then the resource itself.

### 9.2.6 Modifying and Examining Header Fields with URLConnection

In the previous example, you learned how to use the URLConnection to fetch HTTP resources, and how to determine the length and MIME content type of a resource. However, there are many more HTTP response header fields to examine, and you can also modify HTTP request header fields to make it possible for server-side applications (such as CGI scripts, Active Server Pages, or Java servlets) to customize their output. In this next example, you'll learn how to modify request properties, and how to get response header fields.

#### Code for HTTPHeaders

```java
import java.net.*;
import java.io.*;

// Chapter 9, Listing 4
public class HTTPHeaders
{
    public static void main(String args[]) throws Exception
    {
        int argc = args.length;

        // Check for valid number of parameters
        if (argc != 1)
        {
            System.out.println ("Syntax :");
            System.out.println ("java HTTPHeaders url");
            return;
        }

        // Catch any thrown exceptions
        try
        {
            // Create an instance of java.net.URL
            java.net.URL myURL = new URL ( args[0] );

            // Create a URLConnection object, for this URL
            // NOTE : no connection has yet been established
            URLConnection connection =  myURL.openConnection();

            // Set some basic request fields

            // Set user agent, to identify the application
            // as Netscape compatible
            connection.setRequestProperty ("User-Agent",
              "Mozilla/4.0 (compatible; JavaApp)");
```

```
// Set our referer field - set to any URL you'd
// like
connection.setRequestProperty ("Referer",
 "http://www.davidreilly.com/");

// Set use-caches field, to prevent caching
connection.setUseCaches(false);

// Now open a connection
connection.connect();

// Examine request properties, to verify their
// settings
 System.out.println ("Request properties...."); System.out.println();
System.out.println ("User-Agent: " +
    connection.getRequestProperty("User-Agent"));
System.out.println ("Referer: " +
    connection.getRequestProperty("Referer"));
System.out.println (); System.out.println ();

// Examine response properties, to see their
// settings
System.out.println ("Response properties....");
System.out.println();

int i = 1;

// Search through each header field, until no
// more exist
while ( connection.getHeaderField ( i ) != null )
{
     // Get the name of this header field
     String headerName =  connection.getHeaderFieldKey(i);

     // Get the value of this header field
     String headerValue =  connection.getHeaderField(i);

     // Output header field key, and header
     //field value
     System.out.println ( headerName + ": " +  headerValue);

     // Goto the next element in the set of
     // header fields
     i++;
}

// Pause for user
System.out.println ("Hit enter to continue");
System.in.read();
}
```

```
        // MalformedURLException indicates parsing error
        catch (MalformedURLException mue)
        {
            System.err.println ("Unable to parse URL!");
            return;
        }
        // IOException indicates network or I/O error
        catch (IOException ioe)
        {
            System.err.println ("I/O Error : " + ioe);
            return;
        }
    }
}
```

### How HTTPHeaders Works

Like previous examples, this example uses an instance of the URLConnection class to issue HTTP requests. The chief difference here is that, before any request is sent, custom HTTP request fields are added. These header fields provide additional information to server-side applications, which can then be used to customize the HTTP response. When a Web browser sends a request, it identifies itself by sending a "User-Agent" field in the request. Well-behaved HTTP clients do the same, and it is often advantageous to pose as a Web browser by including the *Mozilla* keyword in the identification string and then appending a legitimate-sounding application name, since CGI scripts and servlets sometimes offer different output depending on whether it's an HTTP agent like a search engine or an actual browser. Other request fields can also be set, such as the referring URL and the cache flag, which determines whether or not a unique request will be sent each time to the server.

```
// Create a URLConnection object, for this URL
// NOTE : no connection has yet been established
URLConnection connection = myURL.openConnection();

// Set some basic request fields

// Set user agent, to identify the application as Netscape compatible
connection.setRequestProperty ("User-Agent",
  "Mozilla/4.0 (compatible; JavaApp)");

// Set our referer field
connection.setRequestProperty ("Referer", "http://www.davidreilly.com/");

// Set use-caches field, to prevent caching
connection.setUseCaches(false);
```

Once the request settings are made, the URLConnection object can send the request. If a call to the connect() method is made before assigning request properties, then the server will not receive them and they will not take effect. After connecting and sending the request, the application displays the request fields to the user.

```
// Now open a connection
connection.connect();

// Examine request properties, to verify their settings
System.out.println ("Request properties....");
System.out.println();
System.out.println ("User-Agent: " +
connection.getRequestProperty("User-Agent"));
System.out.println ("Referer: " +
connection.getRequestProperty("Referer"));
System.out.println (); System.out.println ();
```

The next set of header fields displayed by the application is from the server response. In the previous section, the names of the request fields were known. It would be impossible, however, to know the name of every field that might be sent back by a server. Not all servers support the same fields, and some server-side applications may send back custom fields that a client has never before encountered. The URLConnection offers several methods that provide access to request fields, two of which support a numerical index value rather than a key name. This allows us to read the *n*th key, and to iterate through every element in the set of header fields. The program prints out both the name of the field and its contents.

```
// Examine response properties, to see their settings
System.out.println ("Response properties....");
System.out.println();

int i = 1;

// Search through each header field, until no more exist
while ( connection.getHeaderField ( i ) != null )
{
    // Get the name of this header field
    String headerName = connection.getHeaderFieldKey(i);

    // Get the name of this header field
    String headerValue = connection.getHeaderField(i);

    // Output header field key, and header field value
    System.out.println ( headerName + ": " + headerValue);

    // Goto the next element in the set of header fields
    i++;
}
```

Finally, the application pauses to allow the user to read the header fields, and then terminates. The actual contents of the resource are not displayed, although code for this exists in the previous example.

### Running HTTPHeaders

This application takes the same command-line parameter as previous examples. You should pass a valid URL as the only command-line parameter, either of a local machine on your network, or a Web site, if you are connected to the Internet. Try URLs pointing to different Web servers, to see a variation in the type of headers returned.

```
java HTTPHeaders url
```

The application will issue an HTTP request, display all request and response headers, and then terminate.

## 9.2.7   HttpURLConnection Class

One of the problems of reading resources using URL.openStream() or the URL Connection class is that access to HTTP-specific functionality is not available. Any protocol for which a registered protocol handler exists can be fetched in this manner, including the File Transfer Protocol (FTP). But there is no notion of a request method, or a response status code, in these other protocols. How does an application know whether a resource was found, or a 404 "Not Found" error message was sent?

Indeed, many servers output custom pages, designed more for end users than for HTTP client applications. However, there is no uniform error message placed in the message body that is standard across all Web servers. The solution is to read the response status code (discussed earlier in this chapter), as it is the only appropriate way to determine the success or failure of requests.

Though support for HTTP-specific functionality did not exist in earlier versions of Java, as of JDK1.1 there is a solution in the form of the HttpURL Connection class. This class extends the URLConnection class, and provides additional methods and fields that encapsulate HTTP functionality.

### 9.2.7.1   Creating a HttpURLConnection

There are no public constructors for the HttpURLConnection class, just as in the case of URLConnection. The single constructor for HttpURLConnection is marked as a protected method, meaning that only a class in the java.net package can create one. Instead, you should call the URL.openConnection() method, which will return a URLConnection instance. The URLConnection class is the superclass of HttpURLConnection, and if the protocol field of the URL is set to HTTP, this method will actually return an HttpURLConnection instance. To gain access to HTTP-specific functionality, you should test to see whether or not the object is an instance of HttpURLConnection; if so, the object must be cast as such.

```
URL url = new URL ( some_url );
URLConnection connection = url.openConnection();

if (connection instanceof java.net.HttpURLConnection)
{
    HttpURLConnection httpConnection = (HttpURLConnection) connection;

    //  do something with httpConnection
}
```

**NOTE:** Even if an HttpURLConnection object is expected, it is good programming practice to test the class type using the *instanceof* keyword. If an unexpected class is returned by the URL.openConnection() method (for example, if a different protocol to HTTP was specified by the URL), a runtime error will occur and the application may not handle it gracefully.

### 9.2.7.2 Using an HttpURLConnection

The HttpURLConnection class inherits all of the functionality (including fields and methods) of its parent class, URLConnection. It also adds additional functionality, in the form of methods that allow greater access to HTTP features, and static fields that represent common HTTP states.

#### Fields

The HttpURLConnection class defines many static fields, which represent HTTP status codes. While an application can refer to a status code by a numerical value, these fields may make for more readable code. The following fields are all public static final int fields. (To conserve space, the public static final access identifiers have been omitted.)

- int HTTP_OK—HTTP status code (200) indicating that the request was successful.
- int HTTP_CREATED—HTTP status code (201) indicating that a resource was created.
- int HTTP_ACCEPTED—HTTP status code (202) indicating that the request was accepted but has not yet been acted upon.

- int HTTP_NOT_AUTHORITATIVE—HTTP status code (203) indicating that the set of header fields is not from the original source. This may indicate that it has been cached locally or read from a third-party copy, and may represent a subset or superset of fields.
- int HTTP_NO_CONTENT—HTTP status code (204) indicating that an entity body was not available. For example, if data was sent to a server-side application but no entity body was needed, this code might be returned.
- int HTTP_RESET—HTTP status code (205) indicating that the browser should reset the view of the document, but that no new document is available. For example, an HTML form should be cleared, to allow new data to be input by the user.
- int HTTP_PARTIAL—HTTP status code (206) indicating that the Web server was able to fulfill a partial GET request for a resource. Partial requests occur when an HTTP client has part, but not all, of a resource, and wishes to request only the missing data. If a resource is modified, the new resource will be sent and this status code will not be issued.
- int HTTP_MULT_CHOICE—HTTP status code (300) indicating that the resource can be found at multiple locations, from which the client can choose. When a resource is located elsewhere, a "Location" entity field will be sent, along with a 3xx redirection status code, but in the case of multiple choices of location, this status code will be issued.
- int HTTP_MOVED_PERM—HTTP status code (301) indicating that the location of a resource has moved permanently and the client should look for a "Location" field in the HTTP response. The new location of the resource should be used in future.
- int HTTP_MOVED_TEMP—HTTP status code (302) indicating that a temporary change has been made to the location of the resource, indicated by a "Location" field in the HTTP response.
- int HTTP_SEE_OTHER—HTTP status code (303) indicating that a GET request should be used to fetch the resource, at a location specified by the "Location" field. This is often issued in response to a POST request, which processes the information and redirects to a standard page.
- int HTTP_NOT_MODIFIED—HTTP status code (304) used to inform the client that a resource has not been modified and that no entity body was sent. This is used in conjunction with the "If-Modified-Since" request field, which performs a conditional GET request.
- int HTTP_USE_PROXY—HTTP status code (305) that informs the client that a proxy server (a server that makes requests on behalf of clients,

usually ones trapped within a firewall) must be used to access this resource. The "Location" field indicates the location of the proxy server, which should be used to reissue the request.

- int HTTP_BAD_REQUEST—HTTP status code (400) that is issued in response to an invalid HTTP request, which fails to follow the correct syntax.
- int HTTP_UNAUTHORIZED—HTTP status code (401) indicating that access to the resource requires user authentication.
- int HTTP_PAYMENT_REQUIRED—HTTP status code (402) used to indicate that payment is required for access to this resource. This status code is reserved for the future, and is not in common use.
- int HTTP_FORBIDDEN—HTTP status code (403) indicating that access to a resource is strictly forbidden.
- int HTTP_NOT_FOUND—HTTP status code (404) used to notify a client that the resource could not be found or has been permanently removed.
- int HTTP_BAD_METHOD—HTTP status code (405) that tells the client that the request method is not supported by the server. A list of allowed methods will be specified in the "Allow" response header field.
- int HTTP_NOT_ACCEPTABLE—HTTP status code (406) that notifies the client that the response contains content with attributes violating those prescribed in the request.
- int HTTP_PROXY_AUTH—HTTP status code (407) indicating that the client must authenticate itself to the proxy. This is a slight, but important, difference between that of status code 401.
- int HTTP_CLIENT_TIMEOUT—HTTP status code (408) that occurs when a client fails to send a request within the required timeframe set by the server.
- int HTTP_CONFLICT—HTTP status code (409) that notifies the client that access to a resource is temporarily unavailable but may be available at a later date. For example, an access conflict might occur if a resource is being modified, and a request to read that resource occurs.
- int HTTP_GONE—HTTP status code (410) that indicates that a resource has been permanently removed. This is similar to the 404 status code, but indicates that the resource is gone forever.
- int HTTP_LENGTH_REQUIRED—HTTP status code (411) issued when a client fails to specify a required "Content-Length" field.
- int HTTP_PRECON_FAILED—HTTP status code (412) indicating that a precondition placed on the request evaluated to false, and the request could not proceed.
- int HTTP_ENTITY_TOO_LARGE—HTTP status code (413) indicating that the request entity was too large to process.

- `int HTTP_REQ_TOO_LONG`—HTTP status code (414) indicating that the request path was too long to process.
- `int HTTP_UNSUPPORTED_TYPE`—HTTP status code (415) notifying the client that the format of the request entity was unsupported.
- `int HTTP_SERVER_ERROR`—HTTP status code (500) indicating that a server error occurred and the request could not be processed.
- `int HTTP_INTERNAL_ERROR`—HTTP status code (501) indicating that a server did not know how to perform the request.
- `int HTTP_BAD_GATEWAY`—HTTP status code (502) indicating that an error occurred while acting as a gateway or proxy server.
- `int HTTP_UNAVAILABLE`—HTTP status code (503) indicating that the server could not process the request due to a temporary condition such a server overload.
- `int HTTP_GATEWAY_TIMEOUT`—HTTP status code (504) indicating that the server, while acting as a gateway or proxy, did not receive a response in time from another server.
- `int HTTP_VERSION`—HTTP status code (505) indicating that the server did not support that HTTP version of the request.

## Methods

New methods added by `HttpURLConnection` are listed below. To conserve space, we have not listed here methods inherited from the `URLConnection` class.

- `void disconnect()`—if a connection to the Web server is still active, the connection is closed.
- `InputStream getErrorStream()`—returns an `InputStream` instance that can be used to read error messages sent by the server. If a connection has not yet been established, or no errors have yet occurred, this method returns null.
- `static boolean getFollowRedirects()`—indicates whether HTTP redirects will be automatically followed. Returns "true" if redirection will occur automatically, and "false" if not.
- `String getRequestMethod()`—returns the request method (e.g., GET) being used.
- `int getResponseCode()`—returns the response status code. Applications can hardwire the numerical value of codes, or use the `HttpURL Connection` fields that define state conditions.
- `String getResponseMessage()`—returns the message from the response status line, such as "OK," or "Not Found."
- `static void setFollowRedirects(boolean flag)` throws `java.lang. SecurityException`—determines whether the resource specified in a

redirection response will be automatically followed. This must be invoked prior to the `connect()` method for the setting to take effect. If this violates the settings of the security manager, a `SecurityException` will be thrown.

- `void setRequestMethod(String method) throws java.net.Protocol Exception`—sets the request method for this connection. This must be invoked prior to the `connect()` method for the setting to take effect. If the method is not supported, a `ProtocolException` will be thrown. The method name must be capitalized, as the protocol names are case sensitive.

- `boolean usingProxy()`—shows whether a proxy server is being used for this connection. Returns "true" if using a proxy server, "false" if not.

### 9.2.8 Accessing HTTP-Specific Functionality Using HttpURLConnection

This next example shows how to read the status code and message of a response. Most URLs will generate a "normal" response, with a 200 status code and a normal entity body. However, in some situations (for example, if a resource has moved or if the request method is not supported) this will not be the case.

#### Code for UsingHttpURLConnection

```
import java.net.*;
import java.io.*;

// Chapter 9, Listing 5
public class UsingHttpURLConnection
{
    public static void main(String args[]) throws Exception
    {
        int argc = args.length;

        // Check for valid number of parameters
        if (argc != 1)
        {
            System.out.println ("Syntax :");
            System.out.println ("java UsingHttpURLConnection url");
            return;
        }

        // Catch any thrown exceptions
        try
        {
```

```java
// Create an instance of java.net.URL
java.net.URL myURL = new URL ( args[0] );

// Create a URLConnection object, for this URL
// NOTE : no connection has yet been established
URLConnection connection = myURL.openConnection();

// Check to see if connection is a HttpURLConnection instance
if (connection instanceof java.net.HttpURLConnection)
{
    // Yes... cast to a HttpURLConnection instance
    HttpURLConnection hConnection =
            (HttpURLConnection) connection;

    // Disable automatic redirection, to see the status header
    hConnection.setFollowRedirects(false);

    // Connect to server
    hConnection.connect();

    // Check to see if a proxy server is being used
    if (hConnection.usingProxy())
    {
        System.out.println
          ("Proxy server used to access resource");
    }
    else
    {
        System.out.println
          ("No proxy server used to access resource");
    }


    // Get the status code
    int    code = hConnection.getResponseCode();

    // Get the status message
    String msg = hConnection.getResponseMessage();

    // If a 'normal' response
    if ( code == HttpURLConnection.HTTP_OK )
    {
        // Notify user
        System.out.println ("Normal response returned : " +
          code + " " + msg );
    }
    else
        {
        // Output status code and message
        System.out.println ("Abnormal response returned : "
          + code + " " + msg );
    }
```

```
                    // Pause for user
                    System.out.println ("Hit enter to continue");
                    System.in.read();
            }
            else
            {
                    System.err.println ("Invalid transport protocol - not http!");
                    return;
            }
    }
    // MalformedURLException indicates parsing error
    catch (MalformedURLException mue)
    {
            System.err.println ("Unable to parse URL!");
            return;
    }
    // IOException indicates network or I/O error
    catch (IOException ioe)
    {
            System.err.println ("I/O Error : " + ioe);
            return;
    }
  }
}
```

### How UsingHttpURLConnection Works

The program starts by creating a URL object, and from this, a URLConnection object. If the protocol being used to request the resource is HTTP, then the URLConnection will also be an instance of the HttpURLConnection class. It is not advisable to presume that this will always be the case, however. A guard statement checks to see if it is an HttpURLConnection object and performs a casting operation. If not, an error message is displayed and the program terminates.

```
// Create a URLConnection object, for this URL
// NOTE : no connection has yet been established
URLConnection connection = myURL.openConnection();

// Check to see if connection is a HttpURLConnection instance
if (connection instanceof java.net.HttpURLConnection)
{
     // Yes... cast to a HttpURLConnection instance
     HttpURLConnection hConnection = (HttpURLConnection) connection;

// Do something with hConnection
     ...
}
else
{
```

```
System.err.println ("Invalid transport protocol - not http!");
return;
}
```

If all proceeds according to plan, the application now has an HttpURL
Connection, and the extra HTTP-specific functionality it gives. Before a connection is established, it is possible to modify the properties of the request.
For example, a different request method could be used, or the "follow redirection" flag could be modified. So that users can see the redirection status
code, automatic redirection is disabled by the application, and then the connection is established.

```
// Disable automatic redirection, to see the status header
hConnection.setFollowRedirects(false);

// Connect to server
hConnection.connect();
```

Once a connection has been established, all sorts of useful information
becomes available, such as the status code and message and whether or not a
proxy server is being used. The application checks for the presence of a proxy
server, and displays it to the user, by using the boolean HttpURLConnection.
usingProxy() method.

```
// Check to see if a proxy server is being used
if (hConnection.usingProxy())
{
    System.out.println ("Proxy server used to access resource");
}
else
{
    System.out.println ("No proxy server used to access resource");
}
```

Next, the status code and message are retrieved. This is the most useful
information of all, as it tells a client whether or not a request was successful
and, if it was not successful, gives an indication of why. The human-readable
shortcut for the 200 status code (HttpURLConnection.HTTP_OK) is used to
check whether the request was successful. If not, the status code and message
are displayed to the user, and an application could take further steps, such as
resending a request or following a redirection notice.

```
// Get the status code
int    code = hConnection.getResponseCode();

// Get the status message
String msg = hConnection.getResponseMessage();

// If a 'normal' response
if ( code == HttpURLConnection.HTTP_OK )
{
    // Notify user
    System.out.println ("Normal response returned : " + code + " " + msg );
}
else
{
    // Output status code and message
    System.out.println ("Abnormal response returned : " + code + " " + msg );
}
```

### Running UsingHttpURLConnection

The `UsingHttpURLConnection` application accepts as a single parameter the URL of the resource you want to investigate. The syntax is as follows:

```
java UsingHttpURLConnection url
```

## 9.3    Common Gateway Interface (CGI)

The Common Gateway Interface (CGI) is an interface that allows HTTP clients, such as Web browsers and other user agents, to pass information back to a server for processing. CGI took the Web from static pages written by a Web master to interactive sites generated on the fly, in response to interactions with a user. When you use a search engine, buy a book at an online store, or read a customized newspaper tailored to your interests, your browser is using CGI to communicate with a server-side application.

Earlier, we briefly discussed the POST method, which is used by HTTP clients to send information. The GET method may also be used to transmit information, although there are limitations on the length of data that may be passed. Let's look further at how GET and POST are used to send CGI requests to a server-side application.

### 9.3.1    Sending Data with the GET Method

The GET method is used to request documents, images, and other files, and may also be used to call up server-side applications. Normally, when called, data will be passed to the CGI application using a query string.

A query string is a string that is appended to the end of a URL in order to pass additional information such as the results of an HTTP form. Let's look at an example query string, to better understand their syntax.

```
http://www.someserver.org/cgi-bin/form_submit?name=First%20Last&answer=no
```

Because we know the format of a URL, we see nothing unexpected in the example before the "?" character in the middle. But what does the question mark signify, and what comes after it? That's the query string.

Everything that follows the question mark is a CGI parameter. These parameters are separated by an ampersand ("&") character. You'll notice too that instead of the expected space between one's first and last names, there is a percentage sign and a number. This has been encoded, as Web browsers and CGI scripts don't easily handle certain ASCII characters (such as spaces, punctuation, and line separators). URL encoding substitutes problematic characters when sent through a query string. At the other end in the CGI script, URL decoding restores the characters to their original state.

Since query strings are passed as a URL, they may be viewed by looking at the URL location string within a browser. In addition, the length of query strings is limited; long forms should be passed using the POST method.

### 9.3.2  Sending Data with the POST Method

Sending data with the POST method removes the length limitations of GET and allows more complex data to be sent. While a query string may still be sent, data such as entire files and serialized objects may also be included. Query strings should still be URL encoded, and are sent by writing to the output stream of a URLConnection object. The format of a POST request was covered earlier, in Section 9.1.3, and the syntax of a query string is discussed above.

### 9.3.3  Sending a GET Request in Java

Sending a GET request in Java is simple, almost as easy as reading the contents of a static resource such as a Web page. The only difference is in the construction of the URL. To do this, all the parameters must be put together and their values encoded and then appended as a query string to a URL.

The following example shows how this is done.

### Code for SendGET

```java
import java.net.*;
import java.io.*;

// Chapter 9, Listing 6
public class SendGET
{
    public static void main(String args[]) throws IOException
    {
        // Check command line parameters
        if (args.length < 1)
        {
            System.out.println
              ("Syntax-  SendGET baseurl");
            System.in.read();
            return;
        }

        // Get the base URL of the cgi-script/servlet
        String baseURL = args[0];

        // Start with a ? for the query string
        String arguments = "?";

        // Create a buffered reader, for reading CGI
        // parameters from the user
        BufferedReader reader = new BufferedReader (
            new InputStreamReader ( System.in )
          );

        // Loop until no parameters left
        for (;;)
        {
            System.out.println ("Enter field ( . terminates )");

            String field = reader.readLine();

            // If a . char entered, terminate loop
            if (field.equals ("."))
                break;

            System.out.println ("Enter value");

            String value = reader.readLine();

            // Encode the URL value
            arguments += URLEncoder.encode(field)
                    + "=" + URLEncoder.encode(value) + "&";
        }

        // Construct the full GET request
        String finalURL = baseURL + arguments;
```

```java
System.out.println ("Sending GET request - " + finalURL);

// Send the GET request, and display output
try
{
    // Construct the url object
    URL url = new URL(finalURL);

    // Open a connection
    InputStream input = url.openStream();

    // Buffer the stream, for better performance
    BufferedInputStream bufIn = new BufferedInputStream(input);

    // Repeat until end of file
    for (;;)
    {
        int data = bufIn.read();

        // Check for EOF
        if (data == -1)
            break;
        else
            System.out.print ( (char) data);
    }

    // Pause for user
    System.out.println ();
    System.out.println ("Hit enter to continue");
    System.in.read();

}
catch (MalformedURLException mue)
{
    System.err.println ("Bad URL - " + finalURL);
}
catch (IOException ioe)
{
    System.err.println ("I/O error " + ioe);
}
}
}
```

### How SendGET works

The main work of the application takes place during the construction of the GET request. First, a base URL is read from the command line, and the argument string (representing a query string) is assigned a question mark value.

```java
// Get the base URL of the cgi-script/servlet
String baseURL = args[0];
```

```
// Start with a ? for the query string
String arguments = "?";
```

The next step is to read command-line parameters from the user, which is fairly self-explanatory. When a full-stop character is encountered, no more parameters are read and the request is sent. A URL object is constructed representing the GET request, and then the results are displayed to the user by reading from the stream returned by the URL.openStream() method.

### Running SendGET

To run the application, you must specify the URL of a CGI script or Java servlet (discussed in Chapter 10), and then enter one or more CGI parameters when prompted. To finish entering parameters, simply enter a "." character as the field name.

**NOTE:** If you don't have a CGI script you can use, a good start would be the AltaVista search engine (or your preferred search engine if you want to try something different). At the time of writing, a query could be sent by invoking the http://www.altavista.com/cgi-bin/query cgi-script, with a parameter "q" that represents the search query. For example, to search for "java networking" you might type the following command line and responses to questions:

```
java SendGET http://www.altavista.com/cgi-bin/query

Enter field ( . terminates )
q
Enter value
"java networking"
Enter field ( . terminates )
```

## 9.3.4 Sending a POST Request in Java

A POST request is a bit more complex than a simple GET request. With a GET request, parameters are appended to a URL, but a POST request requires you to write parameters to the output stream of an HTTP connection. This means you can't use the URL.openStream() method, and must instead use a URLConnection object.

Here is the code for a simple example that sends a POST request.

### Code for SendPOST

```
import java.net.*;
import java.io.*;
```

```java
// Chapter 9, Listing 7
public class SendPOST
{
    public static void main(String args[]) throws IOException
    {
        // Check command line parameters
        if (args.length < 1)
        {
            System.out.println ("Syntax-  SendPOST baseurl");
            System.in.read();
            return;
        }

        // Get the base URL of the cgi-script/servlet
        String baseURL = args[0];

        // No query string question mark required, so use
        // a blank string
        String arguments = "";

        // Create a buffered reader, for reading CGI
        // parameters from the user
        BufferedReader reader = new BufferedReader (
            new InputStreamReader ( System.in )
          );


        boolean firstParameter = true;

        // Loop until no parameters left
        for (;;)
        {
            System.out.println ("Enter field ( . terminates )");

            String field = reader.readLine();

            // If a . char entered, terminate loop
            if (field.equals ("."))
                break;

            System.out.println ("Enter value");

            String value = reader.readLine();

            if (!firstParameter)
                arguments += "&";
            else
                firstParameter = false;
```

```java
    // Encode the URL value
    arguments += URLEncoder.encode(field)
                + "=" + URLEncoder.encode(value);
}

String query = arguments;

System.out.println ("Sending POST request - " + query);

// Send the POST request, and display output
try
{
    // Construct the url object representing cgi
    // script
    URL url = new URL( baseURL );

    // Get a URLConnection object, to write to POST
    // method
    URLConnection connect = url.openConnection();

    // Specify connection settings
    connect.setDoInput(true);
    connect.setDoOutput(true);

    // Get an output stream for writing
    OutputStream output = connect.getOutputStream();

    // Create a print stream, for easy writing
    PrintStream pout = new PrintStream (output);

    pout.print ( query );
    pout.close();

    // Open a connection
    InputStream input = connect.getInputStream();

    // Buffer the stream, for better performance
    BufferedInputStream bufIn = new  BufferedInputStream(input);

    // Repeat until end of file
    for (;;)
    {
        int data = bufIn.read();

        // Check for EOF
        if (data == -1)
            break;
        else
            System.out.print ( (char) data);
    }
```

```
                    // Pause for user
                    System.out.println ();
                    System.out.println ("Hit enter to continue");
                    System.in.read();

            }
            catch (MalformedURLException mue)
            {
                    System.err.println ("Bad URL - " + baseURL);
            }
            catch (IOException ioe)
            {
                    System.err.println ("I/O error " + ioe);
            }
        }
    }
```

### How SendPOST Works

Writing to the POST method of a CGI script or servlet is accomplished by using a URLConnection object. Before the connection can be established, however, some initialization work needs to be done. By default, a URLConnection allows read access but no write access. You can override these defaults, by calling the setDoInput(boolean) and setDoOutput(boolean) methods, to allow data to be written as part of the POST HTTP request.

```
// Construct the url object representing cgi script
URL url = new URL( baseURL );

// Get a URLConnection object, to write to POST method
URLConnection connect = url.openConnection();

// Specify connection settings
connect.setDoInput(true);
connect.setDoOutput(true);
```

Now, the POST data must be sent to the CGI application by obtaining an OutputStream instance connected to the remote service. You can then connect any output stream or writer to it, so that the CGI parameters may be sent.

```
// Get an output stream for writing
OutputStream output = connect.getOutputStream();

// Create a print stream, for easy writing
PrintStream pout = new PrintStream (output);
pout.print ( query );
pout.close();
```

Once sending the data for the request is complete, the results may be displayed by obtaining an `InputStream` to the `URLConnection`. The request is sent, and the results returned just as if a `GET` request had been made.

### Running SendPOST

To run the application, you must specify the URL of a CGI script or Java servlet that supports the `POST` method. Not every script will, so you may need to search on your local intranet, or the Internet, for a suitable script. Once one is selected and passed as a command-line parameter, the application will prompt you for one or more CGI parameters. To finish entering parameters, simply enter a ".." character as the field name.

One good example for demonstrating this is Sun's "Backwards" CGI script, at http://java.sun.com/cgi-bin/backwards. This script reverses output. For example, to see what "Java Duke" looks like spelled backward, try

```
java SendPOST http://java.sun.com/cgi-bin/backwards

Enter field ( . terminates )
string
Enter value
Java Duke
Enter field ( . terminates )
```

Another good example is the Altavista search engine, which allows you to execute queries. You can perform searches on your own, by passing a query string to the search engine. For example, to search for "Java networking" as a term, you could pass the following data to Altavista:

```
java SendPOST http://www.altavista.com/sites/search/web

Enter field ( . terminates )
q
Enter value
java networking
Enter field ( . terminates )
```

**NOTE:** This would also be a good starting point for an application of your own that searched the Web by harnessing existing search engines. These types of applications are called *metacrawlers*, and are a useful way of aggregating results from many search engine databases.

## 9.4    Summary

The HyperText Transfer Protocol (HTTP) is one of the most frequently used application protocols, and can be employed to access both static content (such as pages and files) and interactive content powered by scripts or servlets that use the Common Gateway Interface (CGI) for communication. Although the performance of simple tasks such as accessing the content of resources is relatively easy, HTTP is capable of complex and rich behavior. For example, additional functionality can be added to HTTP through the use of request and response fields, and more information can be obtained about a connection by examining status codes.

Java provides excellent support for HTTP in the form of the `java.net.URL`, `java.net.URLConnection`, and `java.net.HttpURLConnection` classes. These make it possible to write HTTP clients capable of a wide range of behavior, such as interacting with CGI applications. However, they are only useful for client-side HTTP programming; for server-side HTTP applications, a different technology is used, that of Java servlets (discussed in Chapter 10).

### Chapter Highlights

In this chapter, you have learned:

- About the general theory of HTTP clients and servers
- How to parse URLs and create a `URL` object
- How to retrieve the content of a static URL document or file
- How to modify and examine header fields by using the `URLConnection` class
- How to examine HTTP-specific details, such as the request method or status code, by using the `HttpURLConnection`
- How to connect to a CGI application and pass data by using the GET request method
- How to connect to a CGI application and pass data by using the POST request method

# CHAPTER 10

## *Java Servlets*

This chapter provides an introduction to server-side programming in Java. Thus far, we've dealt with stand-alone applications, and many readers may already be familiar with applets for client-side programming. One of Java's strengths as a programming platform lies in server-side programming, as a substitute for CGI scripts that interact with browsers and users to provide a custom experience. Here, as in applications, Java software is less restricted in its activities, having access to local resources and fewer security restrictions than the traditional applet.

**NOTE:** Java servlets form part of a broad complement of technologies known as the Java 2 Enterprise Edition (J2EE). These technologies are suited to medium- to large-scale application development, and include topics such as Enterprise Java Beans (EJBs), Java Server Pages (JSPs), and much more. Such technologies merit book-length coverage in their own right, and are beyond the scope of an introductory network programming book such as this.

## 10.1   Overview

While the dynamic and interactive nature of Java applets makes them an attractive choice for Web masters, applets are severely limited by security policies. Such policies, aimed at protecting users, can be restrictive for developers who want to create full-fledged applications that run inside a browser. When combined with slow loading times and lack of universal Java 2 support across all browsers, the advantages of server-side content often outweigh those of Java applets.

Previously, developers would need to master one or more scripting languages, such as Perl or VBScript for Active Server Pages, to create server-side applications. Such approaches often tied developers into a particular Web server framework or operating system. This was frustrating for developers, as they no longer had access to the rich Java API they were familiar with, nor the freedom of portable application development. Fortunately, Sun Microsystems perceived the need for server-side Java, and servlets were born. While Sun currently provides only a baseline and HTTP implementation of servlets, it is possible to use servlets with other request-response protocols.

Java servlets are server-side applications that execute similar to CGI scripts, but without a separate process for each request (which consumes both CPU and memory resources). Servlets are multi-threaded, and thus can share resources across servlet instances. The performance increase that comes with using a compiled language over a scripting interpreter also makes servlets a good choice for developers. Of course, the most obvious benefit for servlet developers is that servlets are written in Java. All of the features of the Java language, such as object orientation, portability, the extensive API including networking support, and ease of use, are provided, without the security restrictions that applets are subject to.

## 10.2   How Servlets Work

When a client sends a request to a servlet-enabled server that invokes a servlet, the server first checks to see if the servlet is loaded. If it is not, the servlet class is loaded and a new instance is created. The servlet is then initialized by a call to its `init()` method, which can contain startup code similar to the `init()` method of an applet. Once the servlet is ready, a call to its `service()` method is made. This lifecycle is relatively simple, as shown in Figure 10-1. Figure 10-2 shows the process by which a servlet is loaded, initialized, and made ready to service client requests in a servlet-enabled Web server.

As already mentioned, different servers may use servlets over different protocols, such as HTTP or even FTP, since the specification was written to be

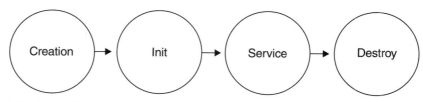

**Figure 10-1**   Servlet life cycle

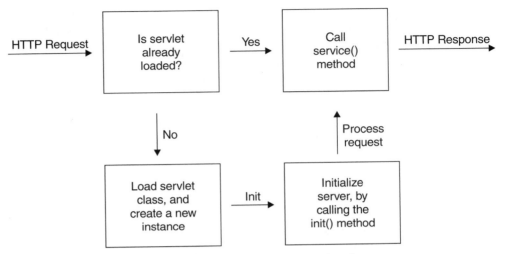

**Figure 10-2**   Servlet instantiation, initialization, and processing of a request

generic. By default, Sun provides an HTTP implementation only for servlets, and in this chapter we will use that implementation. However, the information can apply to other servlet implementations as well, and readers may find them of use in developing their own custom protocol servers.

## 10.3   Using Servlets

Servlets rely on classes defined in the `javax.servlet` and `javax.servlet.http` packages. These packages are a standard extension to the Java API, and ship with the Java Servlet Development Kit (JSDK) as well as many servlet-compatible Web servers.

The starting point for a servlet is the servlet interface. This interface provides the basic structure methods for servlets, such as the initializing, service, and destruction methods. It also provides structure methods for accessing the servlet's context and configuration, as shown later in this chapter. By default, servlets that implement this interface use a shared threading model that drastically improves the performance of servlets to handle large numbers of requests. An alternative single-threading model, discussed in Section 10.6, is also available. As we shall see, this can be a flawed model and should not be used under normal circumstances.

In the shared threading model, the servlet engine creates a single instance of each servlet that is shared by all requests. The engine then creates a thread for each request that comes in and passes the servlet's service method to the threads. What this means is that class and instance variables cannot be presumed to be thread-safe variables. Constants, of course, are immutable and are not of any concern.

Using method variables and passing those variables around in method calls does not require much more work and only necessitates that class and instance variables be avoided. The example below shows the proper use of badVariable and goodVariable.

```
public int badVariable;
public void doGet(HttpServletRequest req,
    HttpServletResponse res) throws IOException
{
    public int goodVariable;
}
```

For the actual creation of a servlet, Sun provides the GenericServlet and HTTPServlet classes. These classes function very much like applets, in that they can be extended to provide additional functionality.

The GenericServlet provides a generic protocol-independent starting point with simple implementations of init() and destroy(), so that the developer needs only to extend service. However, if the goal is to write an HTTP servlet that is used for the Web, the HTTPServlet class should be extended; it extends from GenericServlet and provides the starting point for Web servlets.

Unless the functionality is changed, the service() method of HttpServlet will check the type of HTTP request sent by the browser and pass it off to special handler functions. While it is possible to write a custom service() method, in most cases it is easier to use the default service method. For each of the major HTTP request types, there is a corresponding handler function that can be overridden by developers. Table 10-1 shows the mapping between HTTP requests and servlet methods.

**Table 10-1**   Mapping of HTTP Request Types to Servlet Methods

| HTTP Request | Servlet Handler Function |
| --- | --- |
| GET | doGet (HttpServletRequest, HttpServletResponse) |
| POST | doPost (HttpServletRequest, HttpServletResponse) |
| PUT | doPut (HttpServletRequest, HttpServletResponse) |
| DELETE | doDelete (HttpServletRequest, HttpServletResponse) |
| TRACE | doTrace (HttpServletRequest, HttpServletResponse) |
| OPTIONS | doOptions (HttpServletRequest, HttpServletResponse) |

Developers are free to override one, several, or all of these handler functions. However, if a handler function is not overridden, it will return an HTTP_BAD_ REQUEST error response. For example, suppose a form servlet supported only the POST request. Here is a sample of what such a transaction might look like.

```
Browser: GET /servlet/form_handler?email=me@me.com HTTP/1.0
Server: 400 Bad request from browser
```

**NOTE:** Since all of the handler functions take the same parameters (an instance of HttpServletRequest and HttpServletReponse), it is easy to write a handler for either GET or POST that passes control off to the other. This means that if you accidentally specify the wrong HTTP method in your HTML forms, the servlet will handle it gracefully. For example, to pass GET requests off to a POST method, you could add the following lines:

```
public void doGet (HttpServletRequest  req,
                   HttpServletResponse res)
                   throws IOException
{
    doPost(req,res);
}
```

Once a servlet handler function is called, it can respond to the request and its parameters, perform some processing, and then output a response. However, developers should be mindful of the fact that each servlet is capable of servicing multiple requests simultaneously, so normal thread safety issues apply.

Finally, when the Web server shuts down or terminates a servlet due to inactivity after a specified period of time, the destroy() method will be invoked. This is the servlet's last opportunity to close open files, remove temporary or unnecessary data files, commit changes to disk, or close open network/database connections. As with applets, servlets have a definite lifecycle from creation to destruction. First the init() method is called, followed by one or more service() requests, and finally a destroy() call is made.

## 10.3.1 GET and POST

The GET and POST HTTP request types are used to retrieve data from a Web server, and both have the ability to encode parameters into the request. The only major difference between them is that GET has a limit of 255 characters for its parameters, while POST has no limit.

A GET request involves using a question mark in the URL to signify that the rest of the URL includes encoded parameters. An example of a simple GET request that encodes parameters is:

```
GET  /servlet/Query?name=tom&age=28 HTTP/1.0
```

A POST request, on the other hand, does not modify the URL that is requested. Instead, the POST request is followed by the actual parameters that are sent to the server-side script or servlet. An example of a simple POST request, which performs the same job as the previous GET request, is the following:

```
POST  /servlet/Query HTTP/1.0
name=tom
age=28
```

According to the Java Servlet API, these two types of requests are treated completely differently. However, these differences are transparent to the developer, as the API provides generic methods that abstract the differences between them. In many cases, it is easier to write a single handler than to divide the work between a GET and a POST handler. Assuming that you would like your servlet to be easily manageable, you can refer both GET and POST requests to a single handler, as shown in this example:

```
public void doGet(HttpServletRequest req,
  HttpServletResponse res) throws IOException
{
  doGetPost(req,res);
}

public void doPost(HttpServletRequest req,
  HttpServletResponse res) throws IOException
{
  doGetPost(req,res);
}

public void doGetPost(HttpServletRequest req,
  HttpServletResponse res) throws IOException
{
  // Implementation goes here
}
```

### 10.3.2 PUT and DELETE

PUT and DELETE were originally used for adding and removing files from the Web server's storage space. For example, you could use PUT to send a new file across, and DELETE to remove one. Of course, their usefulness in most applications is limited—the thought of someone overwriting your page, uploading a rogue servlet, or deleting your Web site is fairly frightening. Nonetheless, some readers might want to co-opt the methods for other uses, or may want to create a controlled upload system for their Web site.

### 10.3.3 TRACE

According to the HTTP/1.1 specification in relation to the TRACE result, "The TRACE method is used to invoke a remote, application-layer loop-back of the request message." It is used as a diagnostic test of the servlet request, and it is not necessary to override this method to provide an implementation. If an override is necessary for debugging purposes, however, Sun has included this capability.

### 10.3.4 OPTIONS

The OPTIONS request type in HTTP is used to probe the server in general or a single servlet about what types of HTTP request types are valid.

For instance, when you extend the `HTTPServlet` and implement only the `doGet` method, you receive the following output from an OPTION request:

```
Allow: GET, HEAD, TRACE, OPTIONS
```

Unless you plan on adding extra methods that are beyond HTTP/1.1, you do not need to implement this method.

## 10.4 Running Servlets

To run a servlet, you need either a Web server with servlet support or a servlet engine that will augment an existing server.

A popular choice of Web server for Java developers is the iPlanet Web Server. This Web server was originally developed as the Netscape Enterprise Server and the Java Web Server. However, Sun and Netscape created an alliance, and the iPlanet Web Server took the best of both these servers. It includes built-in support for servlets and other dynamic server-side features.

Another common choice is the free open-source Apache, which runs on a variety of Unix platforms as well as Windows. Apache can be easily modified to support servlets with the Apache JServ add-on. If you're using other servlets, products like JRun and ServletExec can add support to existing servers, such as Netscape servers, O'Reilly's Website, and Microsoft's Internet Information Server (IIS). If you're planning on doing a lot of servlet development, it might be wise to evaluate several options.

- Apache (http://www.apache.org/)
- Apache JServ (http://java.apache.org/jserv/)

- Apache's Jakarta-Tomcat (http://jakarta.apache.org/)
- JRun (http://www.allaire.com/products/jrun/)
- ServletExec (http://www.newatlanta.com/)
- BEA Weblogic (http://www.beasys.com/)
- Borland Enterprise Application Server (http://www.inprise.com/bes/appserver/) integrated with JBuilder

**NOTE:** Originally, the choice for many developers was the standard promoted by Sun, the Java Web Server (http://www.sun.com/software/jwebserver/index.html). However, it has been discontinued, and instead Sun recommends the use of the iPlanet Server (either Enterprise or FastTrack Edition). For more information see http://www.iplanet.com/products/platform_layer/web_application_2_1d.html

Of course, during development, you don't need a high-powered (and possibly expensive) Web server. Sun includes a basic Web server with servlet support as part of the free Java Servlet Development Kit (JSDK), which can be downloaded from the Sun Microsystems Web site. Downloading this tool will be essential for using the examples throughout this chapter; however, you can use other servlet engines if you wish.

**NOTE:** Earlier editions of the Java Servlet Development Kit used a tool called `servletrunner` to start a simple Web server with a servlet engine. Later editions use a slightly different method of running the tool, using the `startserver` and `stopserver` batch scripts. Readers are free to use these, or any other servlet engines that they choose. Where the command `servletrunner` is used, the command `startserver` can be used interchangeably with later editions.

### 10.4.1 Downloading the Java Servlet Development Kit

A servlet engine ships as part of the Java Servlet Development Kit (JSDK), which is available from the Sun Microsystems Web site at http://java.sun.com/products/servlet/archive.html. You may use either edition of the JSDK, 2.0 or 2.1—both will run equally well with respect to the examples in this chapter. You will need to download either to use the examples here.

### 10.4.2 Installing a Servlet Engine

The `servletrunner` application is located in the /bin/directory of your Java Servlet Development Kit installation, whereas the startserver script will be located in the installation's root directory. Before running it, however, you will need to install your servlet (in this case, HelloWorld).

### Step One

Verify that your classpath is set correctly and that JSDK is correctly configured. If you have difficulty, consult the JSDK instructions (setup may vary slightly across different versions).

For example, with the JSDK2.0 and a Wintel platform, you would add to your autoexec.bat file the following statement:

```
set classpath=%classpath%;c:\java\jsdk2.0\lib\jsdk.jar
```

With the JSDK2.1 installation and a Wintel platform, you would add to your autoexec.bat file this statement:

```
set classpath=%classpath%;c:\java\jsdk2.1\servlet.jar
```

Refer to your preferred servlet engine's installation guide for precise instructions, as they vary from version to version and platform to platform. You will need to rerun your autoexec.bat file to make sure that the classpath is set.

### Step Two

Compile the HelloWorld servlet using the javac application.

```
javac HelloWorld.java
```

### Step Three

Copy the compiled HelloWorld.class into the appropriate directory of your JSDK installation. For example, under JSDK2.0 you would copy servlets into the /examples/ directory, in order for servletrunner to find them. Under JSDK2.1, however, you would place your servlets under the /examples/ WEB-INF/servlets directory.

### Step Four

If you're using servletrunner and not startserver, you will need to open the servlets.properties file, located in the /examples/ directory of your JSDK installation. You can use any text editor you want, such as notepad, edit, pico, or vi. Add the following entry to your servlets.properties file, so that your servlet has a name associated with it.

```
servlet.hello.code = HelloWorld
```

Note, for the future, that the pattern is

```
servlet.servlet-name.code = servlet-class-file
```

### Step Five

Start the servletrunner application by running it. Under JSDK 2.0, the process for running servletrunner is straightforward—simply run the servletrunner executable. Under JSDK2.1 you need to run the startserver script to get the server running, and stopserver to shut it down again. By default, servletrunner will bind to port 8080 of the local machine.

### Step Six

Run the servlet from the next section (`HelloWorld`), or come back to this section once you've looked at your first servlet's code. Load a Web browser (any browser will do), and enter the following URL:

> http://localhost:8080/servlet/Hello

Or (under JSDK2.1):

> http://localhost:8080/examples/servlet/HelloWorld

**NOTE:** Remember that if you customize the port number, you will need to change the URL.

You should see a window similar to that shown in Figure 10-3. If not, recheck each step. Installing your first servlet can be a little tricky, but after doing it once, the process becomes simple.

**Figure 10-3**    HelloWorld servlet from a servlet in action (Netscape 4.7)

## 10.5   Writing a Simple Servlet

Servlets are extremely easy to write. Let's take a look at a simple servlet, which outputs the proverbial "Hello World" message. We start by importing the servlet and I/O packages, and extending `javax.servlet.http.HttpServlet`, which provides our servlet with a basic framework. Since `HttpServlet` offers a default service method, all we need to do is write a handler function to output our message.

```java
import java.io.*;
import javax.servlet.*;
import javax.servlet.http.*;
public class HelloWorld extends HttpServlet
{
    public void doGet(HttpServletRequest req,
      HttpServletResponse res)
      throws IOException
    {
       // Code for response goes here
    }
}
```

The first thing that our servlet must do is to specify the MIME content type of the response. In this case, HTML output will be returned, but there is no reason why different text formats, images, or binary files can't be returned by a servlet. Next, we request an output stream and series of writers that will be used to send HTML data. Since JDK 1.1.x and higher versions are commonly available, this code will use the Writer classes, which provide efficient character-based communication. A simple buffer will be put in the middle, using a `BufferedWriter`. Finally, we write our message and close the output streams and writers.

```java
// Set the content type of the response
res.setContentType("text/html");

// Get output stream and writers
OutputStream out  = res.getOutputStream();
PrintWriter pw = new PrintWriter ( new
    BufferedWriter (new OutputStreamWriter ( out ) ) );

// Print HTML page header
pw.println("<HTML>");
pw.println("<HEAD> <TITLE> Hello World! </TILE> </HEAD>");
pw.println ("<BODY>");

// Print "Hello World" message
pw.println ("<CENTER><H3> Hello World </H3></CENTER>");

// Print HTML page footer
```

```
pw.println ("</BODY>");
pw.println ("</HTML>");

pw.flush();
pw.close();
```

The listing below shows the source code for the HelloWorld servlet example. As you can see, it's relatively straightforward. The next step is to install the servlet on a Web server and run it.

### Code for HelloWorld

```
import java.io.*;
import javax.servlet.*;
import javax.servlet.http.*;

// Chapter 10, Listing 1
public class HelloWorld extends javax.servlet.http.HttpServlet
{
    public void doGet(HttpServletRequest req,
      HttpServletResponse res)
      throws IOException
    {
        // Set the content type of the response
        res.setContentType("text/html");

        // Get output stream and writers
        OutputStream out  = res.getOutputStream();
        PrintWriter pw = new PrintWriter (
                                        new BufferedWriter (
                                        new OutputStreamWriter ( out ) )
);
        // Print HTML page header
        pw.println("<HTML>");
        pw.println("<HEAD> <TITLE> Hello World! </TILE> </HEAD>");
        pw.println ("<BODY>");


        // Print "Hello World" message
        pw.println ("<CENTER><H3> Hello World </H3> </CENTER>");

        // Print HTML page footer
        pw.println ("</BODY>");
        pw.println ("</HTML>");

        pw.flush();
        pw.close();
    }
}
```

### Running HelloWorld

The steps and procedures for running a normal servlet were outlined previously (to install the appropriate servlet engine, compile and copy class files to the appropriate path, modify the appropriate properties file, and finally to start the servlet engine). Running this example should produce the "Hello World" message rendered in HTML.

## 10.6   SingleThreadModel

Earlier in this chapter you learned that servlets can be shared between a potentially large number of client requests that come in through the Web server. For this reason, great care should be used to provide thread-safe code in the servlet. The reasoning behind this is to alleviate the amount of memory needed and reduce unnecessary CPU usage.

In some instances, a servlet developer may find that providing thread-safe code is neither possible nor desirable. In this case, there is the option of implementing the SingleThreadModel interface. This interface is without any explicit operations, and is used only as a marker for the Web server. However, the servlet developer should note that this interface wipes out one of the major benefits of servlets over ASP, CGI, and Fast-CGI implementations, and also that the various implementations of servlets may handle this interface slightly differently or ignore it totally.

An example of how to do this is shown here.

```
public class STMExample extends javax.servlet.http.HttpServlet
implements javax.servlet.SingleThreadModel
{
 public void doGet(HttpServletRequest req,
     HttpServletResponse res) throws IOException
   {
     // implementation here
   }
}
```

Instead of sharing one global instance of the servlet, the single-threaded model requires a fresh servlet instance to be created for each request. The servlet instance will be destroyed like any other class instance once the request is finished, or may be pooled by the servlet container in some implementations. Therefore, a servlet should probably clear its instance variables to the defaults after the request has been handled. This allows for the use of instance variables in the servlet. However, class variables will still not be safe to use, as they may be accessed by other servlet instances running on the same JVM.

Since the servlet will most likely be destroyed after a request, there will be no way to access the instance variables afterward, and hence a clever servlet developer will quickly realize that the SingleThreadModel is only a crutch for servlet developers and should seldom be used.

## 10.7   ServletRequest and HttpServletRequest

The ServletRequest and HttpServletRequest classes hold all of the accessible information about the client and the server. HttpServletRequest is a subclass of ServletRequest, and is passed to each servlet handler method (such as doGet(..), doPut(..), etc.) This request may be in the form of parameters, a text or binary body, or a combination of both.

In addition, most of the standard CGI environment variables have corresponding methods that allow easy access, such as CONTENT_LENGTH and the getContentLength(). Others require an explicit request via the getHeader() method, such as HTTP_USER_AGENT and REMOTE_ADDR. Commonly used variables are shown in Table 10-2.

**Table 10-2**   CGI Variables that a Servlet Can Access

| CGI Variable | Corresponding Method |
| --- | --- |
| CONTENT_LENGTH | getContentLength() |
| CONTENT_TYPE | getContentType() |
| SERVER_PROTOCOL | getProtocol() |
| SERVER_NAME | getServerName() |
| SERVER_PORT | getServerPort() |
| REMOTE_ADDR | getRemoteAddr() |
| REMOTE_HOST | getRemoteHost() |
| REQUEST_METHOD | getMethod() |
| SCRIPT_NAME | getServletPath() |
| PATH_INFO | getPathInfo() |
| PATH_TRANSLATED | getPathTranslated() |
| QUERY_STRING | getQueryString() |
| REMOTE_USER | getRemoteUser() |
| AUTH_TYPE | getAuthType() |
| HTTP_USER_AGENT | getHeader("UserAgent") |
| HTTP_REFERRER | getHeader("Referrer") |

Apart from the CGI variables, these classes provide methods to obtain the data that form the request. In an HTTP request, these could be the decoded form of the query string in a GET request or the key-value pairs of a POST request. Another possibility is for the data to be binary or character data in a form request, such as an uploaded file.

Other methods also exist that give other details about the request, such as the cookies sent in the request and HTTP headers. Table 10-3 lists the various methods and their uses.

One important note is that parameter names can map to multiple values, so unless you are sure that a parameter will have only one entry, you should use

**Table 10-3**  ServletRequest Parameter and Miscellaneous Methods

| Method | Function |
|---|---|
| GetScheme | Returns the schema of URL, such as http |
| GetInputStream | Returns an input stream pointing to the body |
| GetParameter | Returns a single parameter value |
| GetParameterValues | Returns an array of parameter values |
| GetParameterNames | Returns an array of parameter names |
| GetReader | Returns a reader pointing to the body |
| GetCharacterEncoding | Returns the encoding for the body |
| GetContentType | Returns the MIME type of the body |
| GetCookies | Returns the cookie objects |
| GetRequestURI | Returns the part of the URL that points to a file or a script |
| GetHeaderNames | Returns HTTP header names |
| GetHeader | Returns an HTTP header |
| getIntHeader, getDateHeader | Helper methods for headers |
| GetSession | Returns the session object (explained in Section 10.13) |
| GetRequestedSessionId | Returns the session ID (explained in Section 10.13) |
| IsRequestedSessionIdValid | Returns if the session ID is valid (explained in Section 10.13) |
| isRequestedSessionIdFromCookie | Returns if the session ID is from a cookie (explained in Section 10.13) |
| IsRequestedSessionIdFromUrl | Returns if the session ID is from an encoded URL (explained in Section 10.13) |

getParameterValues. An example of how to display a few of these to the
servlet engine's System.out for diagnostic purposes is shown below.

### Code for RequestDisplay

```
import java.io.*;
import javax.servlet.*;
import javax.servlet.http.*;

// Chapter 10, Listing 2
public class RequestDisplay extends HttpServlet
{
    public void doGet(HttpServletRequest req,
      HttpServletResponse res) throws IOException
    {
        PrintWriter pw = new PrintWriter ( new BufferedWriter (
                         new OutputStreamWriter
                            ( res.getOutputStream() ) ) );

        pw.println("req.getScheme()="+req.getScheme());
        pw.println("req.getRequestURI()="+req.getRequestURI());
        pw.println("req.getProtocol()="+req.getProtocol());
        pw.println("req.getHeader(\"User-Agent\")="
            +req.getHeader("User-Agent"));
        pw.close();
    }
}
```

### Running RequestDisplay

After compiling and installing RequestDisplay in the preferred servlet engine
or servletrunner, for testing purposes, you'll notice that whenever a request for
this servlet is made, diagnostic information about the request will be displayed,
such as the type of browser. If you view it in another browser, you will notice
a different version number.

## 10.8   ServletResponse and HttpResponse

For servlets, the ServletResponse and its subclass HttpResponse are two of the
most vital classes. These classes perform the function of sending the MIME-
encoded data back to the client. Without this, there would be no servlets at all.
This class supports both writers (for communicating text-based characters) and
output streams (for sending back binary data), as well as enabling the setting of
content length and type parameters.

The HttpResponse class adds extra functionality in that it allows the
developer to set the HTTP status codes, add cookies and headers, and encode
session IDs into URLs. For the moment, we'll leave these advanced topics

for Section 10.12, but it is important to be aware of the versatility of the HttpResponse class.

One important fact to note is that once data is flushed or written the first time, many of the options of a servlet become locked; this is especially so with respect to the HttpResponse class. The reason for this is that most servlet engines first automatically write out the HTTP header information for you, and changing horses in midstream is impossible. Since your data has been partially written out and the HTTP protocol does not have any way to alter this, any newly changed values are ignored. One way to make sure this doesn't happen is to use an internal buffer in the servlet that you write to and only write that buffer out at the very end. A second is to specify the settings of an Http Response before actually writing out any data.

Another point is that you should not close the output stream or writer, as this may close the socket connection from the client before data is written. Some servlet engines may do their own internal buffering, and problems could arise with performance of the close operation. Table 10-4 gives an overview of important ServletResponse methods.

In addition to methods, the HttpResponse class defines integer static constants for each of the HTTP/1.1 status codes. Table 10-5 lists these status codes and their values.

**Table 10-4**   Response Methods

| Method | Function |
| --- | --- |
| GetOutputStream | Returns an output stream pointing to the client |
| GetWriter | Returns a writer pointing to the client |
| GetCharacterEncoding | Returns the encoding that the writer uses |
| SetContentLength | Returns a value to use as the length of the output |
| SetContentType | Returns the MIME type to use for the output |
| AddCookie | Adds a cookie object |
| ContainsHeader | Checks to see if a header has been set yet |
| SendError | Sends an error response and message back to client |
| SendRedirect | Sends a redirect response and URL back to client |
| SetHeader | Sets a response header |
| setIntHeader, setDateHeader | Helper methods for headers |
| SetStatus | Sets the HTTP status code |
| encodeURL, encodeRedirectURL | Encodes session ID into URLs |

**Table 10-5**   HTTP Status Codes

| Code | Value | Code | Value |
|------|-------|------|-------|
| SC_CONTINUE | 100 | SC_CONTINUE | 101 |
| SC_OK | 200 | SC_CREATED | 201 |
| SC_ACCEPTED | 202 | SC_NON_AUTHORITATIVE_<br>INFORMATION | 203 |
| SC_NO_CONTENT | 204 | SC_RESET_CONTENT | 205 |
| SC_PARTIAL_CONTENT | 206 | SC_MULTIPLE_CHOICES | 300 |
| SC_MOVED_PERMANENTLY | 301 | SC_MOVED_TEMPORARILY | 302 |
| SC_SEE_OTHER | 303 | SC_NOT_MODIFIED | 304 |
| SC_USE_PROXY | 305 | SC_BAD_REQUEST | 400 |
| SC_UNAUTHORIZED | 401 | SC_PAYMENT_REQUIRED | 402 |
| SC_FORBIDDEN | 403 | SC_NOT_FOUND | 404 |
| SC_METHOD_NOT_ALLOWED | 405 | SC_NOT_ACCEPTABLE | 406 |
| SC_PROXY_AUTHENTICATION_REQUIRED | 407 | SC_REQUEST_TIMEOUT | 408 |
| SC_CONFLICT | 409 | SC_GONE | 410 |
| SC_LENGTH_REQUIRED | 411 | SC_PRECONDITION_FAILED | 412 |
| SC_REQUEST_ENTITY_TOO_LARGE | 413 | SC_REQUEST_URI_TOO_LONG | 414 |
| SC_UNSUPPORTED_MEDIA_TYPE | 415 | SC_INTERNAL_SERVER_ERROR | 500 |
| SC_NOT_IMPLEMENTED | 501 | SC_BAD_GATEWAY | 502 |
| SC_SERVICE_UNAVAILABLE | 503 | SC_GATEWAY_TIMEOUT | 504 |
| SC_HTTP_VERSION_NOT_SUPPORTED | 505 | | |

An example of a servlet that modifies response settings is offered below.

### Code for ResponseExample

```
import java.io.*;
import javax.servlet.*;
import javax.servlet.http.*;

// Chapter 10, Listing 3
public class ResponseExample extends HttpServlet
{
    public void doGet(HttpServletRequest req,
      HttpServletResponse res) throws IOException
    {
    PrintWriter pw = new PrintWriter ( new BufferedWriter (
        new OutputStreamWriter ( res.getOutputStream() ) ) );

    StringBuffer buf=new StringBuffer();
```

```
        buf.append("Output from servlet:\n");
        buf.append("200 A-OK\n");

        // Set status code to 200 OK
        res.setStatus(HttpServletResponse.SC_OK);

        res.setContentType("text/plain");
        res.setContentLength(buf.length());

        pw.print(buf.toString());
        pw.flush();
    }
}
```

### Running ResponseExample

After compiling and installing `RequestDisplay` in your preferred servlet engine, or servletrunner for testing purposes, you'll see that output of this servlet is actually rendered as text by your browser instead of HTML. This is because the MIME content type was modified to accommodate text/plain, instead of text/html output. We could just as easily have modified the response code from 200 to something more exotic, such as the more advanced HTTP/1.1 codes available; however, few browsers support the entire range of status codes.

## 10.9  ServletConfig

As a servlet developer, you can take advantage of the ability to specify configuration parameters. This makes your software more flexible and eliminates the need to hardwire specific parameters into your code. An example of this could be the username and password for a database connection, or the filepath to a local directory where data is stored.

To allow access to these parameters, you need to obtain a reference to the `ServletConfig` instance that is associated with your servlet. This can be done by using the following code:

```
ServletConfig sconf = this.getServletConfig();
```

Once this reference is obtained, you have access to the parameters by calling the `getInitParameter` method and specifying a parameter name. In cases in which you do not know the names of the parameters, you can call `getInitParameterNames( )`, which returns an enumeration of available parameters. The following code prints the names of parameters out to a servlet's output stream:

```
public void doGet(HttpServletRequest req,
    HttpServletResponse res) throws IOException
{
    ServletConfig sconf = this.getServletConfig();
```

```
        OutputStream out  = res.getOutputStream();
                    PrintWriter pw = new PrintWriter (
                        new BufferedWriter (
                        new OutputStreamWriter ( out ) ) );

    pw.println ("<html><body><pre>");

    for(Enumeration enum = sconf.getInitParameterNames();
        enum.hasMoreElements();)
    {
      pw.println(enum.nextElement());
    }

    pw.println ("</pre></body></html>");

    pw.flush();
    pw.close();

}
```

## 10.10 ServletContext

Another important class is the `ServletContext`. This class allows access to servlets that can pose a potential security risk but at times may be necessary, and offers other useful functions. Sun provides a convenient way to access this context, through the `getServletContext()`, as shown below:

```
ServletContext scont = this.getServletContext();
```

The `ServletContext` provides a variety of information that is useful for debugging (such as logging an error condition to a server log), as well as for diagnostic purposes. These methods are shown in Table 10-6.

The logging methods allow entries to be made in the server-wide servlet log file. You can provide a simple message, or a message with an exception, such as this:

```
public void doGet(HttpServletRequest req,
  HttpServletResponse res) throws IOException
{
  ServletContext scont = this.getServletContext();
  scont.log("This servlet only does logging");
  scont.log("This is a throwable IOException",new
      IOException("dummy"));
}
```

The `getMajorVersion` and `getMinorVersion` methods are used to obtain the servlet version number, such as 1.2. The `getMimeType` method is used to obtain

**Table 10-6**  Method of Functions in ServletContext

| Method name | Function |
|---|---|
| `log( String )`, `log( String, Throwable )` | Logs an error message |
| `int getMajorVersion( )`, `int getMinorVersion( )` | Obtains the version number of the Servlet API supported by the server |
| `String getMimeType( String )` | Obtains MIME type of a file using server's internal mapping from file extension to MIME type |
| `String getRealPath( String )` | Converts from virtual paths to file system paths |
| `URL getResource( String )`, `InputStream getResourceAsStream (String)` | Obtains a resource either as a URL or as an open `InputStream` to the resource |

the MIME type of a file. This can be used to determine what should be sent to the client as the MIME type in a documentation check-in/check-out system.

The `getRealPath` method is used to provide access to convert from a "virtual" path (such as /categories/index.html) into a "real" local URL. This is determined by looking at the location where the Web server stores its files (e.g., c:\www\files\), and combining both to form the appropriate location (i.e., c:\www\files\categories\index.html). The following code snippet illustrates this in action, by resolving the real path of a file.

```
public void doGet(HttpServletRequest req,
  HttpServletResponse res) throws IOException
{
  ServletContext scont = this.getServletContext();
  String realPath = scont.getRealPath("/data/file.html");
  URL url = scont.getResource("/data/file.html");
  InputStream is = scont.getResourceAsStream("/data/file.html");
}
```

**NOTE:** Converting virtual paths to real paths can, if the operation is not carefully controlled, pose a grave security risk by allowing access to local files, particularly if a symbolic link or path operator such as ".." is used. This should not deter one from using such a design, but developers should be aware of the potential misuse of such operators.

## 10.11 Servlet Exceptions

When writing servlets that are anything more than the most basic of handlers, the developer will find that exceptions and errors can occur during runtime. For example, the servlet may be temporarily unavailable due to administrative action or failure to obtain certain resources such as memory or access to an external server. As with any Java application, a good knowledge of exception handling is required to create for the user a stable and robust system.

The general exception that servlets throw is the `ServletException`. This can be used to cover problems in most cases, and is normally handled correctly by the servlet engine, allowing other servlets to continue running.

The next exception is the `UnavailableException`, which is a subclass of `ServletException`. This exception states that the servlet cannot handle a particular request. It has two forms: one for permanent and the other for temporary unavailability. The permanent exception has a simple reference to the servlet and a message to log, while the temporary one adds an integer-holding estimation for how long it is expected to be out of action. A nonpositive result should be given when there is no estimation, such as due to an external resource.

## 10.12 Cookies

In 1992 Netscape Communications Corporation publicly released the specifications of a revolutionary concept that would forever shape and improve the quality of Web applications. This concept was called the cookie.

The original HTTP protocol developed at CERN in 1989 was not designed for the purposes for which it is used today, such as the shopping cart model employed in many electronic commerce systems. As a protocol, it was designed using a stateless model to allow CERN's scientists to access static and linked hypertext documents, mostly research papers. Today, a lot of the WWW's content is dynamic, such as customized news reports, Web portals, and shopping in online bookstores such as Amazon.com.

The basic idea of cookies is to get around HTTP's stateless nature. The cookie concept does this by allowing an application to store small amounts of state data in the user's client. This could be used to store small amounts of preferences in the browser or a unique session identifier that allows the servlet to look up state information stored on the server side for the user.

Each cookie is a name-value key pair with optional attributes. Cookies are stored per hostname with an expectation of user-agents storing a maximum of 20 per host and no more than 4KB per cookie. The use of large numbers of cookies should be discouraged—large state data should be stored server-side and accessed via a unique identifier.

In the Java Servlet API, Sun designed a special class that represents a cookie that is (surprise!) named Cookie. Servlet developers should note that cookies affect caching, and currently this class does not support the HTTP/1.1 caching controls.

One important note for servlet developers is the common bane of all cookie-based applications. During initial development, Netscape reasoned that forcing users to accept cookies would raise privacy issues that could destroy the widespread adoption of cookies. In recognition of these concerns, the ability to ignore cookies was included in their popular Web browsers. Since then, most if not all HTTP clients provide the ability to ignore cookies as well. What this means to servlets is that when a cookie is set, the user may accept it unconditionally, accept it on a per-cookie basis, or reject all cookies completely. When this happens, you will need to use alternative methods of storing state, such as URL rewriting. Servlets provide the ability to let you know if cookies will not be accepted.

A cookie consists of the following variables with the appropriate GET and SET methods for each:

- A comment that is displayed when the browser presents the cookie for acceptance
- A domain name pattern for the browser to determine who to send the cookie back to
- A maximum age for the cookie to be stored
- A host-unique identifying name for the cookie
- A path to be stored with the cookie so that it will only be sent to certain pages
- A value for the cookie
- The version of the cookie specification that should be used
- A flag to determine if it should only be sent over HTTP

Certain variables listed above exist only in version 1 of the cookie specification, such as displayed comments.

The following example shows how cookies can be used by servlets to store state data.

### Code for CookieTest

```
import java.io.*;
import javax.servlet.*;
import javax.servlet.http.*;
import java.util.*;

// Chapter 10, Listing 4
public class CookieTest extends javax.servlet.http.HttpServlet
{
```

```java
public void doGet(HttpServletRequest req,
  HttpServletResponse res) throws IOException
{
    OutputStream out  = res.getOutputStream();
    PrintWriter pw = new PrintWriter (
      new BufferedWriter (
      new OutputStreamWriter ( out ) ) );

    Cookie[] cookies = req.getCookies();
    Cookie current = null;

    // Check to see if no cookies exist
    if(cookies != null)
    {
        // For each and every cookie, display name and
        // value
        for(int i=0;i<cookies.length;i++)
        {
         pw.println("name="+cookies[i].getName());
         pw.println("value="+cookies[i].getValue());
         pw.println("version="+cookies[i].getVersion());
         if(cookies[i].getName().equals("cookie"))
         {
             current=cookies[i];
         }
         pw.println();
        }


    }

    int count=0;
    if(current != null)
    {
      count = Integer.parseInt(current.getValue());

      // Add new cookie, so we have more than one cookie
      // stored in browser
      res.addCookie(new Cookie("previouscookie",new
         Integer(count).toString()));

    }

    // Increment count
    pw.println("Count of value stored in cookie =  "+count);
    count++;

    // Add cookie to save state data for next invocation
    res.addCookie(new Cookie("cookie",new
        Integer(count).toString()));

    pw.flush();
    pw.close();
}
}
```

### How CookieTest Works

The code for the cookie servlet is fairly straightforward. At the beginning, we retrieve an array containing every cookie accessible by the servlet. None, one, or many cookies may be accessible, so we must first check to see if the array is empty before attempting to access any of its elements.

```
Cookie[] cookies = req.getCookies();
Cookie current = null;

// Check to see if no cookies exist
if(cookies != null)
{
    // . . . . . .
}
```

Next, for demonstration purposes we echo to the browser any cookies that have been detected by the servlet. In this example, we'll be using two cookies (one for the current value of the counter and one for the previous value), but your applications may use more, subject to the size limits imposed by browsers.

```
// For each and every cookie, display name and
// value
for(int i=0;i<cookies.length;i++)
{
    pw.println("name="+cookies[i].getName());
    pw.println("value="+cookies[i].getValue());
    pw.println("version="+cookies[i].
        getVersion());

    if(cookies[i].getName().equals("cookie"))
    {
        current=cookies[i];
    }
    pw.println();
}
```

### Running CookieTest

After compiling and installing CookieTest in your preferred servlet engine, or servletrunner for testing purposes, you'll notice that a cookie will be added to your browser. If you have security settings on your browser to reject cookies, or to manually accept/deny cookies, this will be easier to observe. Cookie data will be retained on subsequent executions. Please note that to see the cookie change, you'll need to "refresh" your browser so that a new HTTP request is sent to the servlet.

## 10.13 HTTP Session Management in Servlets

As mentioned in Section 10.12, the HTTP protocol uses a stateless model. Since useful HTTP-based applications will most likely require a stateful model, this presents an interesting challenge.

During development of servlets, Sun wisely decided to provide a helper system to allow the base HTTP servlet and the servlet engine behind it to handle the issues of keeping track of state over multiple HTTP requests. The HTTPSession class provides this session management. This class, by default, determines whether cookies or URL rewriting should be used. In the case of URL rewriting, a unique session identifier can be sent as a parameter between the server and client in each request-response for the servlet. HTTPSession also provides other helper methods to keep track of data that should be held across sessions. Sessions have automatic timeouts and can be created or cancelled at will by the servlet.

To obtain an HTTPSession, the getSession method of the HTTPServlet-Request class is called. The getSession(boolean createNewSession) method is used to obtain the current servlet session, and if the createNewSession flag is set to "true," one is created if none already exists. This method returns a reference to a session, which can then be used to obtain information about it, and get, set, or remove values associated with it. The ability to obtain the session ID from this class also exists.

These values are stored on the server side in the servlet engine with a unique identifier being sent across only to the client. Therefore, you should feel safe in storing confidential or secure information in the session without worrying about it being detected by packet sniffing between server and client. However, the potential for abuse still exists, if the session identifier and IP address of the client are forged. Thus, no system is absolutely secured.

### Code for SessionServlet

```
import java.io.*;
import javax.servlet.*;
import javax.servlet.http.*;

// Chapter 10, Listing 5
public class SessionServlet extends HttpServlet
{
    public void doGet(HttpServletRequest req,
      HttpServletResponse res) throws IOException
    {
      // Set the content type of the response
      res.setContentType("text/html");
```

```
// Get output stream and writers
OutputStream out  = res.getOutputStream();
PrintWriter pw = new PrintWriter (
                    new OutputStreamWriter ( out ) );

// Determine whether an existing session exists
HttpSession session = req.getSession(false);

// If no existing session, add a visit value of one
// to a new session
if(session == null)
{
    session=req.getSession(true);
    session.putValue ("VisitCount", "1");
}

pw.println("<html><body><pre>");

pw.println("session.isNew()="+session.isNew());
pw.println("session.getCreationTime()="+
    new java.util.Date( session.getCreationTime()));
pw.println("session.getID()="+session.getId());
pw.println("session.getLastAccessedTime()=" +
    new java.util.Date(session.getLastAccessedTime()));

// Modify a session variable, so state
// information is changed from one invocation to
// another of this servlet
String strCount = (String) session.getValue("VisitCount");
pw.println("No. of times visited = " + strCount);

// Increment counter
int count = Integer.parseInt(strCount);  count++;

// Place new session data back for next servlet invocation
session.putValue("VisitCount", Integer.toString(count));

pw.println ("</pre></body></html>");
pw.flush();
    }
}
```

### Running SessionServlet

After compiling and installing `SessionServlet` in your preferred servlet engine, or the JSDK for testing purposes, you'll notice that on the first time through, a brand-new session is created. Subsequent executions, however, will contain previous state data, with a counter being incremented along with the last accessed time. Please note that to see the output change, you will need to "refresh" your browser so that a new HTTP request is sent to the servlet.

## 10.14 Summary

Java servlets provides a comprehensive and well-thought-out API that offers a powerful and flexible alternative to the CGI API. This technology gives far superior performance and built-in support for cookies and session management. The ability to extend servlets to other transport mechanisms is another plus for this API.

---

**Chapter Highlights**

In this chapter, you have learned:

- How to install and set up the Java Servlet Development Kit (JSDK)
- How to run the JSDK reference servlet engine
- How to write a simple servlet
- How to use the `HTTPServletRequest` and `HTTPServletResponse` objects to retrieve and send data
- How to use cookies to store simple data
- How to create a new session, and to add data to it, for more advanced servlets

# CHAPTER 11

## Remote Method Invocation (RMI)

## 11.1 Overview

Remote Method Invocation (RMI) is a distributed systems technology that allows one Java Virtual Machine (JVM) to invoke object methods that will be run on another JVM located elsewhere on a network. This technology is extremely important for the development of large-scale systems, as it makes it possible to distribute resources and processing load across more than one machine.

### 11.1.1 What Is Remote Method Invocation?

RMI is a Java technology that allows one JVM to communicate with another JVM and have it execute an object method. Objects can invoke methods on other objects located remotely as easily as if they were on the local host machine (once a few initialization tasks have been performed). Figure 11-1 provides an example of this process, whereby an object running on one JVM invokes a method of an object hosted by another. Communication like this does not have to be a one-way process, either—a remote object method can return data as well as accept it as a parameter.

Each RMI service is defined by an interface, which describes object methods that can be executed remotely. This interface must be shared by all developers who will write software for that service—it acts as a blueprint for applications that will use and provide implementations of the service. More than one implementation of the interface can be created, and developers do not need to be aware of which implementation is being used or where it is located.

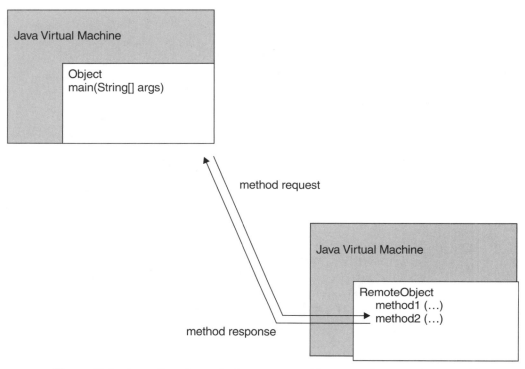

**Figure 11-1**    Invocation of a method on a remote object, executing on a remote machine

## 11.1.2  *Comparison of Remote Method Invocation with Remote Procedure Calls*

Object method invocation is not a new concept. Even before object-oriented programming, technologies existed that allowed software to call functions and procedures remotely. Systems such as remote procedure calls (RPCs) have been in use for years and continue to be used today. A popular implementation of RPC was developed by Sun Microsystems and published as RFC 1057 (making obsolete an earlier version, published as RFC 1050). Remote procedure calls were designed as a platform-neutral way of communicating between applications, regardless of any operating system or language differences.

The difference between RPC and Java RMI is subtle. Java is, after all, a platform-neutral language, and conceivably would allow Java applications to communicate with Java applications running on any hardware and operating system environment that supported a JVM. The principal difference between the two goals is that RPC supports multiple languages, whereas RMI only supports applications written in Java.

**NOTE:** With the introduction of the Java 2 Platform, Enterprise Edition, a new technology known as RMI over IIOP helps bridge the gap between RMI and CORBA systems. This technology allows for translation between RMI services and CORBA services, via the Internet Inter-ORB Protocol (more detailed information on IIOP is provided in Chapter 12). In general practice, however, RMI is used primarily with Java-only systems.

Beyond the language that either system supports, there are some fundamental differences in the way that RPC and RMI work. Remote method invocation deals with objects, and allows methods to accept and return Java objects as well as primitive datatypes. Remote procedure calls, on the other hand, do not support the notion of objects. RPC services offer procedures, which are not associated with a particular object. Messages to an RPC service are represented by the External Data Representation (XDR) language, which abstracts the differences between byte ordering and structure of datatypes. Only datatypes that are definable by XDR can be passed, and while this amounts to a large variety of primitive datatypes and structures composed of primitive datatypes, it does not allow objects to be passed.

Neither system is perfect. Many RPC services already exist, and RMI is not compatible with these legacy applications. However, it is easier for Java developers to use RMI, rather than using a library that implements RPC, as services can exchange entire objects, rather than just individual data fields. By writing distributed systems in RMI, however, the ability to develop systems in other languages is lost. There are, however, distributed systems technologies that do support other languages. The most popular choice for this is the Common Object Request Broker Architecture (CORBA), which the Java 2 platform supports. CORBA has many advantages, as well as some limitations, and is discussed further in Chapter 12.

## 11.2 How Does Remote Method Invocation Work?

Systems that use RMI for communication typically are divided into two categories: clients and servers. A server provides an RMI service, and a client invokes object methods of this service.

RMI servers must register with a lookup service, to allow clients to find them, or they can make available a reference to the service in some other fashion. Included as part of the Java platform is an application called *rmiregistry,* which runs as a separate process and allows applications to register RMI services or obtain a reference to a named service. Once a server has registered, it will then wait for incoming RMI requests from clients. Figure 11-2 illustrates services registering with a single RMI registry. Associated with each service registration is a name (represented as a string), to allow clients to select the appropriate service. If a service moves from one server to another, the client need only look up the registry again to find the new location. This makes for a more fault-tolerant system—if the service is unavailable because a machine is down, a system administrator could launch a new instance of the service on another system and have it register with the RMI registry. Providing the registry remains active, you can have your servers go online and offline or move from host to host. The registry doesn't care which host a service is offered from, and clients get the service location directly from the registry.

RMI clients will send RMI messages to invoke an object method remotely. Before any remote method invocation can occur, however, the client must have a remote object reference. This is normally obtained by looking up a service in the RMI registry. The client application requests a particular service name, and receives a URL to the remote resource. Remember, URLs are not just for HTTP—most protocols can be represented using URL syntax. The following format is used by RMI for representing a remote object reference:

```
rmi://hostname:port/servicename
```

where `hostname` represents the name of a server (or IP address), `port` the location of the service on that machine, and `servicename` a string description of the service.

Once an object reference is obtained (either through the rmiregistry, a custom lookup service, or by reading an object reference URL from a file), the client can then interact with the remote service. The networking details of requests are completely transparent to the application developer—working

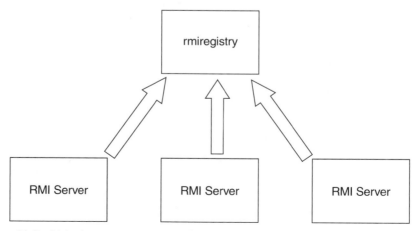

**Figure 11-2**　Multiple services can register with the same registry.

with remote objects becomes as simple as working with local ones. This is achieved through a clever division of the RMI system into two components, the stub and the skeleton.

The stub object acts as a proxy object, conveying object requests to the remote RMI server. Remember that every RMI service is defined as an interface, not as an implementation. The stub object implements a particular RMI interface, which the client application can use just like any other object implementation. Rather than performing the work itself, however, the stub passes a message to a remote RMI service, waits for a response, and returns this response to the calling method. The application developer doesn't need to be concerned about where the RMI resource is located, on which platform it is running, or how it will fulfill the request. The RMI client simply invokes a method of the proxy object, which handles all the implementation details. Figure 11-3 illustrates how this is achieved; shown is an RMI client invoking an object method on the stub proxy, which conveys this request to the remote server.

At the RMI server end, the skeleton object is responsible for listening for incoming RMI requests and passing these on to the RMI service. The skeleton object does not provide an implementation of an RMI service, however. It only acts as a receiver for requests, and passes these requests on further. After a developer creates an RMI interface, he or she must still provide a concrete implementation of the interface. This implementation object will be called by the skeleton object, which invokes the appropriate method and passes the results back to the stub object in the RMI client. This model makes for much simpler programming, as the skeleton is separated from the actual implementation of the service. All the developer of the server needs to be concerned about is some brief initialization code (to register a service and accept requests), and providing an implementation of the RMI service interface.

With respect to the question of how messages are sent, the answer is fairly straightforward. Communication occurs between stub and skeleton using TCP sockets. The skeleton, once it is created, listens for incoming socket requests

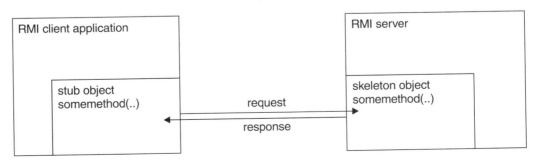

**Figure 11-3** The RMI client stub calls the RMI server skeleton.

issued by stubs. Parameters in an RMI system are not limited to primitive datatypes—any object that is serializable can be passed as a parameter or returned from a remote method. When a stub passes a request to a remote skeleton, it must package the parameters (either primitive datatypes, objects, or both) for transmission, which is known as data marshalling. At the skeleton end the parameters are reconstituted to form primitive datatypes and objects, which is known as unmarshalling. For this task, specialized subclasses of the `ObjectOutputStream` and `ObjectInputStream` classes are used, to read and write the contents of objects. Parameters are normally passed by value in this case, unless the parameter is itself a reference to a remote object.

## 11.3  Defining an RMI Service Interface

Any system that uses RMI will use a service interface. The service interface defines the object methods that can be invoked remotely, and specifies parameters, return types, and exceptions that may be thrown. Stub and skeleton objects, as well as the RMI service, will implement this interface. For this reason, developers are urged to define all methods in advance, and to freeze changes to the interface once development begins.

**NOTE:** It is possible to make changes to an interface, but all clients and servers must have a new copy of the service interface, and code for the stubs and skeletons must be rebuilt.

All RMI service interfaces extend the `java.rmi.Remote` interface, which assists in identifying methods that may be executed remotely. To define a new interface for an RMI system, you must declare a new interface extending the `Remote` interface. Only methods defined in a `java.rmi.Remote` interface (or its subclasses) may be executed remotely—other methods of an object are hidden from RMI clients.

For example, to define an interface for a remote lightbulb system (a high-tech version of the traditional on-off switch for a networked world), we could define an interface such as the following:

```
//Chapter 11, Listing 1
public interface RMILightBulb extends java.rmi.Remote
{
      public void on () throws java.rmi.RemoteException;
      public void off() throws java.rmi.RemoteException;
      public boolean isOn() throws java.rmi.RemoteException;
}
```

The interface is identified as remotely accessible, by extending from the Remote interface. Each method is marked as public, and may throw a java. rmi.RemoteException. This is important, as network errors might occur that will prevent the request from being issued or responded to. In an RMI client, a stub object that implements this interface will act as a proxy to the remote system—if the system is down, the stub will throw a RemoteException error that must be caught. If a method is defined as part of an RMI interface, it must be marked as able to throw a RemoteException—if it is not, stub and skeleton classes cannot be generated by the "rmic" tool (a tool that ships with the Java SDK which automates the generation of these classes).

Methods are not limited to throwing only a RemoteException, however. They may throw additional exceptions that are already defined as part of the Java API (such as an IllegalArgumentException to indicate bad method parameters), or custom exceptions created for a system. For example, the on() method could be modified to throw a BrokenBulb exception, if it could not be successfully activated.

## 11.4  Implementing an RMI Service Interface

Once a service interface is defined, the next step is to implement it. This implementation will provide the functionality for each of the methods, and may also define additional methods. However, only those methods defined by the RMI service interface will be accessible remotely, even if they are marked public in scope or as being able to throw a RemoteException.

For our lightbulb system, the following implementation could be created.

### Code for RMILightBulbImpl

```
// Chapter 11, Listing 2
public class RMILightBulbImpl
        // Extends for remote object functionality
        extends java.rmi.server.UnicastRemoteObject
        // Implements a light bulb RMI interface
        implements RMILightBulb
{

        // A constructor must be provided for the remote object
        public RMILightBulbImpl() throws java.rmi.RemoteException
        {
            // Default value of off
            setBulb(false);
        }

        // Boolean flag to maintain light bulb state information
        private boolean lightOn;
```

```
// Remotely accessible "on" method - turns on the light
public void on() throws java.rmi.RemoteException
{
    // Turn bulb on
    setBulb (true);
}

// Remotely accessible "off" method - turns off the light
public void off() throws java.rmi.RemoteException
{
    // Turn bulb off
    setBulb (false);
}

// Remotely accessible "isOn" method, returns state of bulb
public boolean isOn() throws java.rmi.RemoteException
{
    return getBulb();
}

// Locally accessible "setBulb" method, changes state of
// bulb
public void setBulb (boolean value)
{
    lightOn = value;
}

// Locally accessible "getBulb" method, returns state of
// bulb
public boolean getBulb ()
{
    return lightOn;
}
    }
```

## How RMILightBulbImpl Works

An object that can be accessed remotely must—at a minimum—extend the java.server.RemoteObject class. However, a support class exists that provides all the necessary functionality for exporting an object remotely. When implementing an interface, the class should extend the java.server.UnicastRemoteObject class—this saves significant time and effort and provides for simpler code.

Extending from UnicastRemoteObject is the only RMI-specific code that needs to be written for a service implementation. As can be seen from the code, there is very little work that needs to be done to create RMI service implementations. Methods defined in the service interface must be implemented (or the class would fail to compile until implemented or marked abstract), but beyond that there is no actual networking code required. This means that even developers not experienced with networking could contribute to RMI systems, although writing code for a server and client requires somewhat more effort.

## 11.5 Creating Stub and Skeleton Classes

The `stub` and `skeleton` classes are responsible for dispatching and processing RMI requests. Developers should not write these classes, however. Once a service implementation exists, the rmic tool, which ships with the JDK, should be used to create them.

The implementation and interface should be compiled, and then the following typed at the command line:

```
rmic implementation
```

where `implementation` is the name of the service implementation class.

For example, if the class files for the `RMILightBulb` system are in the current directory, the following would be typed to produce stub and skeleton classes:

```
rmic RMILightBulbImpl
```

Two files would then be produced in this case:

- `RMILightBulbImpl_Stub.class`
- `RMILightBulbImpl_Skeleton.class`

RMI clients, and the RMI registry, will require these classes as well as the service interface class. They can be copied to a local file system, or distributed remotely via a Web server using dynamic class loading (discussed in Section 11.10.1).

## 11.6 Creating an RMI Server

The RMI server is responsible for creating an instance of a service implementation and then registering it with the remote method invocation registry (rmiregistry). This actually amounts to only a few lines of code, and is extremely easy to do. In small systems, the server could even be combined with the service implementation by adding a `main()` method for this purpose, though a separation of classes is a cleaner design.

### Code for LightBulbServer

```
import java.rmi.*;
import java.rmi.server.*;

// Chapter 11, Listing 3
public class LightBulbServer
{
```

```java
public static void main(String args[])
{
System.out.println ("Loading RMI service");

try
{
    // Load the service
    RMILightBulbImpl bulbService = new RMILightBulbImpl();

    // Examine the service, to see where it is stored
    RemoteRef location = bulbService.getRef();
    System.out.println (location.remoteToString());


    // Check to see if a registry was specified
    String registry = "localhost";
    if (args.length >=1)
    {
        registry = args[0];
    }

    // Registration format //registry_hostname :port /service
    // Note the :port field is optional
    String registration = "rmi://" + registry + "/RMILightBulb";

    // Register with service so that clients can find us
    Naming.rebind( registration, bulbService );

}
catch (RemoteException re)
{
    System.err.println ("Remote Error - " + re);
}
catch (Exception e)
{
    System.err.println ("Error - " + e);
}
}
}
```

### How LightBulbServer Works

The lightbulb server defines a single method, main, which allows it to be run as
an application. The application encloses almost all of the code in a try { .. }
catch block, since networking errors that occur at runtime must be caught. The
most likely error to occur is for a RemoteException to be thrown, if the service
could not be started or if the server is unable to register with the rmiregistry.

```java
public static void main(String args[])
{
    System.out.println ("Loading RMI service");
```

```
        try
        {
            ….
        }
        catch (RemoteException re)
        {
            System.err.println ("Remote Error - " + re);
        }
        catch (Exception e)
        {
            System.err.println ("Error - " + e);
        }
}
```

The next step is to create an instance of the RMI lightbulb service defined by the `RMILightBulbImpl` class. The constructor for this class takes no parameters and is simple to invoke. Once the service has been created, the application obtains a remote reference to the newly created lightbulb service and displays its contents so that it is possible to see exactly where the service is located. Each service binds to a local TCP port through which it is located, and the reference is composed of the hostname and port of the service.

```
// Load the service
RMILightBulbImpl bulbService = new RMILightBulbImpl();

// Examine the service, to see where it is stored
RemoteRef location = bulbService.getRef();
System.out.println (location.remoteToString());
```

The final step is to register the service with the rmiregistry, so that other clients can access it. This registry could be located on any computer on the local network, or on the Internet, or it could be found on the current host. By default, the server will attempt a registration on the local machine, but if the hostname of a registry is specified on the command line, this setting will be overridden.

```
// Check to see if a registry was specified
String registry = "localhost";
if (args.length >=1)
{
    registry = args[0];
}

// Registration format //registry_hostname:port /service
// Note the :port field is optional
String registration = "rmi://" + registry + "/RMILightBulb";

// Register with service so that clients can find us
Naming.rebind( registration, bulbService );
```

The registration details include the location of the registry, followed by an optional port and then the name of the service. Using static methods of the class java.rmi.Naming, which is responsible for retrieving and placing remote object references in the registry, we register the service so that clients can access it. The details, represented by our registration string, are passed to the Naming. rebind(..) method, which accepts as a parameter a registration name and an instance of the java.rmi.Remote interface. We pass the service created earlier, and the service becomes bound to the registry. The binding process creates an entry in the registry for clients to locate a particular service, so that if the service is shut down, it should of course unbind itself. If no errors occur, the service is then available for remote method invocation.

## 11.7   Creating an RMI Client

Writing a client that uses an RMI service is easy compared with writing the service itself. The client needs only to obtain an object reference to the remote interface, and doesn't need to be concerned with how messages are sent or received or the location of the service. To find the service initially, a lookup in the RMI registry is made, and after that, the client can invoke methods of the service interface just as if it were a local object. The next example demonstrates how to turn a remote lightbulb on and off.

### Code for LightBulbClient

```
import java.rmi.*;

// Chapter 11, Listing 4
public class LightBulbClient
{
    public static void main(String args[])
    {
        System.out.println ("Looking for light bulb service");

        try
        {
            // Check to see if a registry was specified
            String registry = "localhost";
            if (args.length >=1)
            {
                registry = args[0];
            }

            // Registration format //registry_hostname (optional):port /service
            String registration = "rmi://" + registry + "/RMILightBulb";
```

```
        // Lookup the service in the registry, and obtain
        // a remote service
        Remote remoteService = Naming.lookup ( registration );

        // Cast to a RMILightBulb interface
        RMILightBulb bulbService = (RMILightBulb) remoteService;

        // Turn it on
        System.out.println ("Invoking bulbservice.on()");
        bulbService.on();

        // See if bulb has changed
        System.out.println ("Bulb state : " + bulbService.isOn()  );

        // Conserve power
        System.out.println ("Invoking bulbservice.off()");
        bulbService.off();

        // See if bulb has changed
        System.out.println ("Bulb state : " + bulbService.isOn() );
    }
    catch (NotBoundException nbe)
    {
        System.out.println (
            "No light bulb service available in registry!");
    }
    catch (RemoteException re)
    {
        System.out.println ("RMI Error - " + re);
    }
    catch (Exception e)
    {
        System.out.println ("Error - " + e);
    }
  }
}
```

### How LightBulbClient Works

As in the lightbulb server, the client application must be careful to catch any exceptions thrown at runtime, if the server or rmiregistry is unavailable. It also needs to create a URL to the registry and service name, which by default will point to the local machine, but can be overridden by a command-line parameter. The code for this is similar to that in the server, and for this reason is not repeated here. Once a URL to the registry entry has been created, the application attempts to look up the location of the service and obtain an object reference to it, by using the Naming.lookup(String) method. An explicit cast is made to the RMILightBulb interface; if no such interface is found, a NotBoundException will be thrown and caught.

```
// Lookup the service in the registry, and obtain a remote
// service
Remote remoteService = Naming.lookup ( registration );

// Cast to a RMILightBulb interface
RMILightBulb bulbService = (RMILightBulb) remoteService;
```

Here the networking code ends and the service code begins. Three methods were defined in the service interface:

- public void RMILightBulb.on()
- public void RMILightBulb.off()
- public boolean RMILightBulb.isOn()

Each of the three methods is tested, and the changes in bulb state displayed to the user. Once this is done, the application will terminate, its task complete.

## 11.8   Running the RMI System

Running any RMI system takes a little care, as there is a precise order to the running of applications. Before the client can invoke methods, the registry must be running. Nor can the service be started before the registry, as an exception will be thrown when registration fails. Furthermore, the client, server, and registry need access to the interface, stub, and skeleton classes, which means they must be available in the class path, unless dynamic loading is used (discussed in Section 11.10). This means compiling these classes, and copying them to a directory on the local file system of both client and server (as well as the registry, if it is located elsewhere), before running them.

**NOTE:** Remember to run the rmic tool over the RMILightBulbImpl class, to generate stub and skeleton classes before copying the class files.

The following steps show how to run the lightbulb system, but apply to other RMI systems as well.

1. Copy all necessary files to a directory on the local file system of all clients and the server.

2. Check that the current directory is included in the classpath, or an alternate directory where the classes are located.

3. Change to the directory where the files are located, and run the rmiregistry application (no parameters are required), by invoking the following command: rmiregistry

4. In a separate console window, run the server (specifying if necessary the hostname of the machine where the rmiregistry application was run): java `LightBulbServer` hostname.

5. In a separate console window, and preferably a different machine, run the client (specifying the hostname of the machine where the rmiregistry application was run): java `LightBulbClient` hostname.

You will then see a message indicating that the bulb was activated and then switched off using RMI.

## 11.9 Remote Method Invocation Packages and Classes

Now that you're familiar with the basics of RMI and how to write an RMI service, server, and client, let's look at the packages and classes that comprise the RMI subset of the Java API.

### 11.9.1 Packages Relating to Remote Method Invocation

Five packages deal with RMI. The two most commonly used are `java.rmi` and `java.rmi.server`, but it's important to be aware of the functionality provided by the remaining three.

1. `java.rmi`—defines the Remote interface, classes used in RMI, and a number of exceptions that can occur at runtime.

2. `java.rmi.activation`—introduced in the Java 2 platform, this package supports "activation" of remote services. Activation allows a service to be started on demand, rather than running continually and consuming system resources.

3. `java.rmi.dgc`—provides an interface and two classes to support distributed garbage collection. Just as objects can be garbage-collected by the JVM, distributed objects may be collected when clients no longer maintain a reference to them.

4. `java.rmi.registry`—provides an interface to represent an RMI registry and a class to locate an existing registry or launch a new one.

5. `java.rmi.server`—provides interfaces and classes related to RMI servers, as well as a number of server-specific exceptions that may be thrown at runtime.

### 11.9.1.1    Package java.rmi

There are one interface, three classes, and a large number of exception classes defined by this package. Each is discussed separately.

### Remote Interface

The `java.rmi.Remote` interface is unusual, in that it does not define any methods for implementing classes. It is, instead, used as a means of identifying a remote service. Every RMI service interface will extend the Remote interface. Being an interface, it cannot be instantiated (only a class that implements an interface may be instantiated). However, an implementing class may be cast to a Remote instance at runtime.

When creating a service that extends the `java.rmi.Remote` interface, you should be aware that methods must declare a throws clause, listing at least `java.rmi.RemoteException`, and (optionally) any application-specific exceptions. This is not declared in the API documentation for the Remote interface, but is a condition imposed by the rmic tool. Failure to adhere to this condition will cause an error when stub and skeleton classes are generated. This condition is needed, as a client that invokes a remote method may not be able to connect to the RMI service (due to firewall/network issues, or if the server is inactive). By declaring a throws clause, clients that use the service are forced to catch and deal with the `RemoteException`, rather than having it surprise users at runtime.

### MarshalledObject

This class represents a serialized object, using the same mechanism for serialization as used in marshalling and unmarshalling parameters and return values. Objects serialized in this way have the codebase of their class definition files annotated, so that they can be dynamically loaded by RMI clients or servers.

### Naming Class

The `Naming` class offers static methods to assign or retrieve object references of the RMI object registry (rmiregistry). Each method takes as a parameter a Java string, representing a URL to a registry entry. The format of these entries is as follows:

```
rmi://registry_hostname:registry_port/servicename
```

where `registry_hostname` is the hostname or IP address of a rmiregistry, `registry_port` is an optional port field for nonstandard registry locations, and `servicename` is the name of an RMI service. The default port for an rmiregistry is 1099.

### Methods

All methods provided by the `Naming` class have public access modifiers. The `Naming` class defines the following methods:

- `static void bind ( String url, Remote obj)` throws `java.rmi.AlreadyBoundException, java.rmi.AccessRestriction, java.net.MalformedURLException, java.rmi.RemoteException`—inserts a registry entry (specified by the URL string) for the remote service into the registry, and "binds" the entry to that object. If the remote service is already bound, the operation is not permitted, an invalid URL is specified, or the registry is not available, an exception will be thrown.

- `static String[] list( String url )` throws `java.net.MalformedURLException, java.rmi.RemoteException`—returns a list of services available from the specified rmiregistry (denoted by the URL string). If an invalid URL is specified, or the registry was not contactable, then an exception will be thrown.

- `static Remote lookup( String url )` throws `java.rmi.AccessException, java.rmi.NotBoundException, java.net.MalformedURLException, java.rmi.RemoteException`—returns a reference for the remote object represented by the specified registry entry (denoted by the URL string). This reference may then be cast to a particular RMI service interface (for example, an `RMILightBulb`, as used earlier in the chapter). If the operation is not permitted, the registry entry does not exist, or the registry is not contactable, then an exception will be thrown.

- `static void rebind( String url, Remote obj)` throws `java.rmi.AccessException, java.net.MalformedURLException, java.rmi.RemoteException`—modifies an existing registry entry, or creates a new registry entry if one does not exist, for the specified remote object. If the operation is not permitted, an invalid URL is specified, or the registry is not available, an exception will be thrown.

- `static void unbind( String url)` throws `java.rmi.AccessException, java.rmi.NotBoundException, java.net.MalformedURLException, java.rmi.RemoteException`—removes a registry entry (specified by the URL string) for a remote service and "unbinds" the remote service associated with that entry. If removal of the entry is not permitted, an entry for that service does not exist, an invalid URL is specified, or the registry is not available, an exception will be thrown.

## RMISecurityManager Class

All RMI servers and clients that support dynamic class loading (discussed in Section 11.10) will require a security manager to be registered with the JVM. For convenience, an RMI-specific manager is provided that protects rogue code from initiating network connections, masquerading as servers, or gaining file access. This is a more restrictive form of security than that imposed on applets, but may be modified to grant additional privileges by using a security policy file.

The RMISecurityManager class extends the java.lang.SecurityManager class. The default action of each method is to throw a SecurityException, unless additional privileges have been granted by a security policy. The number of methods of any security manager is extremely large and not particularly relevant to a networking text. However, more information about these methods may be found in the Java API documentation.

## AccessException Class

An AccessException may be thrown by the Naming class to indicate that a bind, rebind, lookup, or unbind operation cannot be performed. This class extends the java.rmi.RemoteException class.

## AlreadyBoundException Class

If a remote object is already bound to a registry entry, or if another object has already bound that service name, then AlreadyBoundException class is used to indicate that the bind operation could not proceed. The RMI service could unbind and attempt the bind operation again, or it could use the rebind method of the Naming class. This class extends the generic java.lang.Exception class.

## ConnectException Class

This exception class represents an inability to connect to a remote service, such as a registry. This class extends the java.rmi.RemoteException class.

## ConnectIOException Class

Similar to the ConnectException class, this represents an inability to connect to a service to execute a remote method call. This class extends the java.rmi.RemoteException class.

## MarshalException Class

This class represents an error that has occurred during the marshalling of parameters for a remote method call, or when sending a return value. For example, if the server connection is disconnected while writing arguments, this may be thrown. If it occurs at the client end, it is impossible to tell whether the method was invoked by the remote system—a subsequent method invocation may actually cause the method to be invoked twice. While not always significant, it is something that developers should be mindful of, if the method causes state information to change. This class extends the `java.rmi.RemoteException` class.

### NoSuchObjectException Class

If an attempt to invoke a remote method is made, and the object to which the reference points no longer exists, a `NoSuchObjectException` may be thrown. This indicates that the method call never reached the object, and may be transmitted at a later date (or to another machine), without a duplicate of the method call being sent. This class extends the `java.rmi.RemoteException` class.

### NotBoundException Class

When attempts are made to look up or unbind a registry entry that does not exist, the `NotBoundException` class is thrown by the `Naming` class. This class extends the generic `java.lang.Exception` class.

### RemoteException Class

The `RemoteException` class represents an error that occurs performing a RMI operation. It is the superclass of many exceptions defined in the `java.rmi` and `java.rmi.server` packages. It extends the `java.io.IOException` class.

### ServerError Class

Representing an error that occurs in an RMI server, this class indicates that the method invocation caused a `java.lang.Error` to be thrown. This error extends the `java.rmi.RemoteException` class.

### ServerException Class

When a method call to an RMI server causes a `RemoteException` to be thrown by the object implementing the service interface, a `ServerException` is thrown.

### StubNotFoundException Class

If a stub for an RMI service interface cannot be located on the local file system (or externally, if dynamic class loading is enabled), this exception is used to indicate failure to locate the necessary class definition. For a remote object to be passed as a reference and unmarshalled, or a remote object method to be invoked, stub class definitions are required. This class extends the `java.rmi.RemoteException` class.

### UnexpectedException Class

The `UnexpectedException` class is used by clients to represent an exception thrown by a remote method that was not declared in the throws clause of the RMI interface. This class extends the `java.rmi.RemoteException` class.

### UnknownHostException Class

If a client making a remote method request can't resolve a hostname, the `java.rmi.UnknownHostException` will be thrown. This should not be confused with the similarly named `java.net.UnknownHostException`, which is not RMI specific. This class extends the `java.rmi.RemoteException` class.

### UnmarshalException Class

The `UnmarshalException` class represents an error during the unmarshalling process, either of arguments or of return values. If, for example, the class definition for a remote interface could not be located due to a `java.lang.ClassNotFoundException` being thrown, it would be represented by an `UnmarshalException`. This class extends the `java.rmi.RemoteException` class.

### 11.9.1.2    Package java.rmi.activation

The `java.rmi.activation` package supports remote object activation, an advanced topic discussed later in the chapter (see Section 11.12). As the reader is unlikely to use every class and interface from this package, only the most important classes and exceptions are covered. Readers are advised that activation is an advanced topic of RMI, and is not essential for the development of RMI systems. Nonetheless, some readers may be interested in learning more about the `java.rmi.activation` package, or may wish to come back to it at a later time. Furthermore, only the most important of classes, interfaces, and methods used to create activation RMI systems are discussed. For further coverage of this package, see the Java API documentation for `java.rmi.activation`.

### Activatable Class

This class provides a base from which remote objects that support activation can be built. Just as the `UnicastRemoteObject` class provides all of the necessary code to create remote objects, so too does the `Activatable` class. Developers creating activatable services must extend the `Activatable` class, implement a remote service interface, and provide their own implementing methods for that service interface. All of the constructors for the `Activatable` class are marked protected, and not used by developers, but there are several useful methods that the reader may want to be aware of.

#### Methods

Unless noted otherwise, all methods of the `Activatable` class are public.

- `static Remote exportObject ( Remote obj, ActivationID id, int port ) throws java.rmi.RemoteException`—makes the specified remote service available at the specific port. `Activatable` objects should not invoke this static method; only nonactivatable objects use this method.

- `static Remote exportObject ( Remote obj, ActivationID id, int port, RMIClientSocketFactory csf, RMIServerSocketFactory ssf)` throws `java.rmi.RemoteException`—makes the specified remote service available at the specific port, using the specified client and server socket factories for obtaining sockets. `Activatable` objects should not invoke this static method; only nonactivatable objects use this method.

- `static ActivationID exportObject ( Remote obj, String location, MarshalledObject data, boolean restart, int port)` throws `java.rmi.RemoteException`—used to register an `Activatable` object's activation descriptor, which provides essential information to the activation daemon process. An `ActivationID` object is returned, which uniquely identifies the remote object and contains a reference to the object's activator. Again, this should only be used by objects that do not extend the `Activatable` class.

- `static ActivationID exportObject ( Remote obj, String location, MarshalledObject data, boolean restart, int port, RMIClient SocketFactory csf, RMIServerSocketFactory ssf)` throws `java.rmi.RemoteException`—this method is used to register an `Activatable` object's activation descriptor, which provides essential information to the activation daemon process. An `ActivationID` object is returned, which uniquely identifies the remote object and contains a reference to the object's activator. Connections to and from the remote object will use the specified socket factories for communication. Again, this should only be used by objects that do not extend the `Activatable` class.

- `protected ActivationID getID()`—returns the object's `ActivationID`, which serves to uniquely identify the object and contains a reference to the object's activator. As a protected field, only subclasses of the `Activatable` class may access this method, which means that any remote object that extends the `Activatable` class may access its ID but other objects may not.

- `static boolean inactive(ActivationID id)` throws `java.rmi.activation.UnknownObjectException, java.rmi.activation.ActivationException, java.rmi.RemoteException`— notifies the activation system that a previously active object, associated with the specified `ActivationID`, is no longer active. If a client issues an RMI request at a later date, the object may be reactivated again. If the specified activation ID, or the activation group associated with that ID, is already inactive, an exception may be thrown. If the operation was successful, a value of "true" is returned; otherwise a value of "false" is returned.

- `static Remote register(ActivationDesc descriptor)` throws `java.rmi.activation.UnknownGroupException java.rmi.activation.ActivationException, java.rmi.remoteException`—registers an activation descriptor object with the activation system, and returns a stub for the activatable object. If the activation group associated with the specified descriptor is not known to the activation system, or if the activation system is not running, an exception will be thrown.
- `static boolean unexportObject(Remote obj, boolean force)` throws `java.rmi.NoSuchObjectException`—deactivates the specified remote object so that it will no longer respond to object requests. This method takes a single `boolean` flag as a parameter. If the value of the flag is "true," the object is terminated even if it is still responding to client requests. If "false" and there are pending requests from clients, the object will not be deactivated. A `boolean` flag is also returned by this method—if the operation was successful, a value of "true" is returned, otherwise a value of "false" is returned.
- `static void unregister(ActivationID id )` throws `java.rmi.activation.UnknownObjectException java.rmi.activation.ActivationException, java.rmi.remoteException`—removes registration of the object associated with the specified `ActivationID` from the RMI activation daemon.

## ActivationDesc Class

An activation descriptor contains information that identifies an activatable object, such as the `codebase` of the object, class name, and the activation group associated with the object. Descriptors are registered with an activation system, which uses this information to activate the object in response to a remote method call from a client.

### Constructors

Constructors of the `ActivationDesc` class are as follows.

- `public ActivationDesc( ActivationGroupID group, String classname, String codebase, MarshalledObject data)` throws `java.lang.IllegalArgumentException`—creates an activation descriptor associated with the specified activation group. The `classname` parameter specifies the name of the class, and the `codebase` parameter specifies a URL to the resource (though this can also be a local file:// URL). If the activation group is null, an `IllegalArgumentException` will be thrown.
- `public ActivationDesc( ActivationGroupID group, String class name, String codebase, MarshalledObject data, boolean restart Flag)` throws `java.lang.IllegalArgumentException`—creates an

activation descriptor associated with the specified activation group. The `classname` parameter specifies the name of the class, and the `code base` parameter specifies a URL to the resource (though this can also be a local file:// URL). The `restartFlag` parameter specifies whether the object will be restarted when the activator is restarted—if set to a value of "false," it will be started on demand. If the activation group is null, an `IllegalArgumentException` will be thrown.

- `public ActivationDesc( String classname, String codebase, MarshalledObject data) throws java.rmi.activation.Activation-Exception`—creates an activation descriptor associated with the default activation group for the JVM. The `classname` parameter specifies the name of the class, and the `codebase` parameter specifies a URL to the resource (though this can also be a local file:// URL).

- `public ActivationDesc( String classname, String codebase, MarshalledObject data, boolean restart ) throws java.rmi.activation.ActivationException`—creates an activation descriptor associated with the default activation group for the JVM. The `class name` parameter specifies the name of the class, and the `codebase` parameter specifies a URL to the resource (though this can also be a local file:// URL). The `restartFlag` parameter specifies whether the object will be restarted when the activator is restarted. If set to a value of "false," it will be started on demand.

## Methods

Methods of the `ActivationDesc` class are listed below; all are public.

- `boolean equals(Object obj)`—tests two objects for equality. If the specified object is an activation descriptor, and holds identical contents, this method returns "true."
- `String getClassName()`—returns the name of the class represented by this activation descriptor.
- `MarshalledObject getData()`—returns a marshalled object containing initialization data for the remote object.
- `ActivationGroupID getGroupID()`—returns the activation group ID for this descriptor.
- `String getLocation()`—returns the codebase of the class represented by this activation descriptor.
- `boolean getRestartMode()`—returns a `boolean` flag, indicating whether the object represented by the activation descriptor should be restarted when the activation daemon restarts, or whether it should only be activated on demand.
- `int hashCode()`—returns an `int` value, representing a hashcode of the activation descriptor.

### ActivationGroup Class

The `ActivationGroup` class is responsible for creating new instances of activatable objects, and notifying the activation system when objects (and the group itself) becomes active or inactive. The only constructor for the `Activation Group` class is protected and thus inaccessible—to create an activation group the `createGroup(..)` method is instead used, which returns an `ActivationGroup` instance. Several methods are provided by this class, but are unlikely to be used by developers. Instead, the group will be registered with an activation system, which will return an `ActivationGroupID`. This will be passed to activation descriptor constructors.

### ActivationGroupDesc Class

Just as the activator needs a descriptor, so too do groups require some form of descriptor. The `ActivationGroupDesc` class contains information about the group's classname and location. The developer, however, does not normally control these—the RMI library provides a default implementation. The `ActivationGroupDesc` class also makes it possible to specify command-line arguments and system properties for activation groups. In normal practice, this will not be required, and only experienced activation developers are advised to modify the default settings.

### ActivationGroupID Class

This class serves as a unique identifier for an activation group, and provides a reference to the group's activation system.

#### Constructors

The class's single constructor takes as a parameter an `ActivationSystem` instance with which the group will be associated.

- `public ActivationGroupID ( ActivationSystem )`—creates a unique activation group ID.

#### Methods

Methods of the `ActivationGroupID` class include:

- `boolean equals(Object o)`—compares two activation group IDs for equality.
- `ActivationSystem getSystem()`—returns the activation system associated with this group ID.
- `int hashCode()`—returns an int, representing a hashcode for this activation group ID.

### ActivationID Class

To uniquely identify activatable remote objects, an `ActivationID` class is used. Each remote object has a single `ActivationID`, which contains a reference to the remote object's activator and a unique ID code. To create an `ActivationID`, an object must be registered with an activation system; applications should not create new instances of the ID themselves.

### ActivationSystem

The `ActivationSystem` interface is used to register activation groups, as well as activatable objects. The `ActivationSystem` is used to handle tasks related to both the `ActivationID` and `ActivationGroupID` objects. Further usage of this class is described in the section on activatable objects later in Section 11.12.4.

### Activation Exceptions

The exceptions defined by this package are as follows:

- `ActivationException`—a generic exception used by the classes of the activation package. It is the superclass of several activation-specific exceptions.
- `ActivateFailedException`—represents the error condition that activation of a remote object has failed. This class extends the `java.rmi.RemoteException` class.
- `UnknownGroupException`—thrown when an activation group ID is unknown to the activation system, and therefore invalid. For example, an invalid or expired activation group ID might be stored in an `ActivationDesc`, and then found to be invalid by the activation system. This class extends the `java.rmi.activation.ActivationException` class.
- `UnknownObjectException`—similar to the `UnknownGroupException` class, this is thrown when an activation ID is not recognized by the activation system. For an activation ID to be valid, the object associated with that ID must be registered with the activation system; otherwise an `UnknownObjectException` could be thrown when it is used.

### 11.9.1.3    Package java.rmi.dgc

This package provides support classes for distributed garbage collection.

### VMID Class

The Virtual Machine Identifier (VMID) is used to uniquely identify a client JVM. As there can be more than one JVM interacting with an RMI service, it is necessary to distinguish between one JVM and another. An IP address alone isn't always sufficient, either, as one machine can host multiple clients. Instead, the VMID should be used, which guarantees to offer a unique identifier on the proviso that an IP address for the client machine is available.

### Constructors

There is only one constructor for the VMID class, which accepts no parameters.

- `public VMID()`—creates a unique virtual machine identifier for the host machine.

### Methods

The following methods (all of which are public) are defined by the VMID class.

- `boolean equals (Object o )`—compares two virtual machine identifiers for equality.
- `int hashCode()`—creates a hash code for the virtual machine identifier.
- `static boolean isUnique()`—returns a `boolean` value, indicating whether a virtual machine identifier can be generated that is truly unique. A VMID is guaranteed unique, if and only if an IP address can be determined for the host machine on which it was generated; if not, there is the slight possibility of an overlap between one VMID and another.
- `String toString()`—returns a string representation of the virtual machine identifier.

## Lease Class

When an RMI server creates an object for use by a client, it offers it for a short duration of time (called a lease). If the client makes further calls, the lease is renewed, but if the lease expires, the object is safe to garbage collect to conserve memory. The Lease class represents a lease between a server and a client JVM, and stores the lease duration and the virtual machine identifier of the client.

### Constructors

There is only one constructor for the Lease class.

- `public Lease (VMID vmid, long duration)`—creates a lease, storing the duration of the lease and the virtual machine identifier of the client machine to which the lease is offered.

### Methods

Methods of this class are public.

- `long getDuration()`—returns the duration of a lease between an RMI server and an RMI client.
- `VMID getVMID()`—returns the virtual machine identifier for this lease.

### 11.9.1.4    Package java.rmi.registry

The registry package defines an interface (Registry) for accessing a registry service, and the `LocateRegistry` class, which can create a new RMI registry (if the rmiregistry application has not been run), as well as locating an existing registry.

### Registry Interface

This interface defines methods for accessing, creating, or modifying registry entries of an RMI object registry. Similar method signatures are used for the `java.rmi.Naming` class, but there are some small changes. The `java.rmi.Naming` class is designed to support registry entries on any remote registry, whereas the `Registry` interface deals with a specific registry. This means that some methods don't require as many parameters, and others don't require a hostname and port to be specified in the URL for the registry entry.

### Methods

All methods provided by the `Registry` class have public access modifiers.

- `static void bind ( String name, Remote obj)` throws `java.rmi.AlreadyBoundException`, `java.rmi.AccessRestriction`, `java.net.MalformedURLException`, `java.rmi.RemoteException`—adds a registry entry matching the specified name. Note that a service name should be specified, not the URL as used in the `Naming` class. For example, to insert the remote lightbulb service created earlier in the chapter, the name parameter would be `RMILightBulb`. If the service is already bound, the operation is not permitted, an invalid URL is specified, or the registry is not available, then an exception will be thrown.
- `static String[] list()` throws `java.net.MalformedURLException`, `java.rmi.RemoteException`—returns a list of services available from the registry. If the registry is not contactable, an exception will be thrown.
- `static Remote lookup( String name )` throws `java.rmi.AccessException`, `java.rmi.NotBoundException`, `java.net.MalformedURLException`, `java.rmi.RemoteException`—returns a reference for the remote object bound to the specified name, if one is available. This reference may then be cast to a particular RMI service interface (for example, an `RMILightBulb` as used earlier in the chapter). If the

operation is not permitted, the registry entry does not exist, or the registry is not contactable, an exception will be thrown.

- `static void rebind( String name, Remote obj)` throws `java.rmi.AccessException, java.net.MalformedURLException, java.rmi.RemoteException`—replaces an existing registry entry, or creates a new one, and "binds" the specified remote object to the registry entry. If the operation is not permitted, an invalid URL is specified, or the registry is not available, an exception will be thrown.
- `static void unbind( String name)` throws `java.rmi.Access Exception, java.rmi.NotBoundException, java.net.Malformed URLException, java.rmi.RemoteException`—removes a registry entry for a remote service, and "unbinds" the remote service associated with that entry. If removal of the entry is not permitted, an entry for that service does not exist, an invalid URL is specified, or the registry is not available, an exception will be thrown.

### LocateRegistry Class

This class can be used to locate a remote object registry or to create a new one. Sometimes it is more convenient for a registry to be launched by a server, rather than separately in a new window.

### Methods

The `LocateRegistry` class defines several public methods, all of which return a Registry instance.

- `static Registry createRegistry(int port)` throws `java.rmi.Remote Exception`—attempts to install a registry at the specified port location, on the local machine.
- `static Registry createRegistry(int port, RMIClientSocket Factory csf, RMIServerSocketFactory ssf)` throws `java.rmi.Remote Exception`—attempts to install a registry at the specified port location, and to use the specified client and server socket factories for making and receiving registry connections.
- `static Registry getRegistry()` throws `java.rmi.RemoteException`—returns a reference to the registry located at the default port of 1099 on the local machine. An exception will not be thrown if no such registry exists—this is only an object reference, and the application will only encounter an error if and when the Registry instance is used.
- `static Registry getRegistry(int port)` throws `java.rmi.Remote Exception`—returns a reference to the registry located at the specified TCP port on the local machine. An exception will not be thrown if no

such registry exists; this is only an object reference, and the application will encounter an error if and only if it uses the Registry instance.

- `static Registry getRegistry(String host) throws java.rmi.Remote Exception`—returns a reference to the registry located at the default port of 1099, on the specified host. Even if the hostname is invalid, or there exists no registry at that location, no exception will be thrown, as this is only an object reference.
- `static Registry getRegistry(String host, int port) throws java. rmi.RemoteException`—returns a reference to the registry located at the specified TCP port, on the specified host. Even if the hostname/port is invalid, or there exists no registry at that location, no exception will be thrown, as this is only an object reference.
- `static Registry getRegistry(String host, int port, RMIClient SocketFactory csf) throws java.rmi.RemoteException`—returns a reference to the registry located at the specified TCP port, on the specified host, and using the specified client socket factory to create network connections. Even if the hostname is invalid, or there exists no registry at that location, no exception will be thrown, as this is only an object reference.

### 11.9.1.5 Package java.rmi.server

The `java.rmi.server` package defines a number of interfaces, objects, and exceptions relating to RMI servers and remote objects. While a number of useful classes are defined, developers do not normally use most of the classes in this package in the production of RMI services. For this reason, only the most important classes are discussed herein.

### RemoteRef Interface

The remote reference interface is a handle to the remote object. Stubs can use a remote reference to issue method requests and to compare two remote objects for equality.

### RMIClientSocketFactory Interface

Classes that provide alternate types of socket communication for sending RMI requests should implement this interface, which acts as a factory for producing client sockets. For example, in a special network environment where TCP communication is restricted by a firewall, or where for security reasons encrypted sockets must be used, a custom socket factory could be produced, so that normal TCP sockets are replaced. Under normal circumstances, developers will not create custom sockets and socket factories.

## Methods

The RMIClientSocketFactory defines a single method:

- public Socket createSocket ( String host, int port ) throws java. io.IOException—returns a Socket instance, connected to the specified host and port. If a connection can't be established, an IOException will be thrown.

### RMIServerSocketFactory Interface

Classes that provide alternate types of socket communication for listening for RMI requests should implement this interface, which acts as a factory for producing server sockets. For example, in a high-security network system, or a system that uses an insecure network connection such as a public communications network, encryption of sockets may be required. A custom server socket might automatically decrypt communications transparently to the developer, to allow encrypted RMI requests to be sent.

## Methods

The RMIClientSocketFactory defines a single method:

- public Socket createServerSocket ( int port ) throws java.io. IOException—returns a custom ServerSocket instance, bound to the specified port. If the service can't bind to that port, an IOException will be thrown.

### RemoteObject Class

The RemoteObject class implements the java.rmi.Remote interface, and provides a base template for all remote object implementations. It overrides several important methods defined in the java.lang.Object class, making them "remote" aware.

## Methods

The RemoteObject class provides implementations for the equals, hashCode(), and toString() methods, as well as the following new methods (both of which are public):

- RemoteRef getRef()—returns a remote reference for this object.
- static Remote toStub( Remote obj ) throws java.rmi.NoSuchObject Exception—returns a stub for the specified remote object. If invoked before the object has been exported, a NoSuchObjectException will be thrown.

## RemoteServer

The `RemoteServer` class extends the `RemoteObject` class, and adds additional functionality. It is also the superclass of the abstract `Activatable` class, and the `UnicastRemoteObject` class from which most RMI servers will be extended.

### Methods

The `RemoteServer` class provides several methods of use during development (all of which are public):

- `static String getClientHost()` throws `java.rmi.server.Server NotActiveException`—returns the location of the RMI client. If not called from a thread handling a RMI client, a `ServerNotActive Exception` will be thrown. This method assists in adding some degree of security to RMI calls, as servers can handle requests differently, based on the IP address of the client. However, due to IP spoofing, this may not guarantee the authenticity of a client. Nonetheless, it may be useful in less secure systems, as well as in logging the origin of RMI requests.
- `static PrintStream getLog()`—returns the RMI logging stream, which can be used to store information for debugging purposes, or to maintain a history of requests. This logging stream is extremely useful—anything written to it includes the time and date automatically, making logging easier on developers.
- `static void setLog(OutputStream out)`—logs RMI calls, as well as additional information written to a `PrintStream` instance returned by `RemoteServer.getLog()`, to the specified output stream. Additional information such as time, date, hostname/IP address, and the method being called is also sent to this stream.

## RMISocketFactory

The `RMISocketFactory` class implements both the `RMIClientSocketFactory` interface and the `RMIServerSocketFactory` interface (both of which are part of the `java.rmi.server` package). This class creates the socket used in remote method invocation. By extending the `RMISocketFactory` class, and overriding the factory methods defined in the `RMIClientSocketFactory` and `RMIServer SocketFactory` interfaces, customized sockets can be used for RMI communication. For example, encrypted sockets, or sockets that use an alternate transport mechanism for communication (such as piggybacking requests on another network protocol), can be used as an alternative to TCP sockets by registering a new `RMISocketFactory`. By default, three mechanisms are used for communication. In the event that the first method fails, the second method is attempted, followed if necessary by the third. These mechanisms are:

1. A direct TCP socket used to create client sockets
2. An HTTP connection to the server, using the port number of the service (e.g., http://server:1095/)
3. A modified HTTP connection to the server, using the default HTTP port number and invoking a CGI script that is sometimes used for accepting requests over HTTP (e.g., http://server:80/cgi-bin/java-rmi.cgi)

When a firewall restricts direct TCP access, HTTP is often used. If an HTTP server is specified as a Java system property, this will sometimes allow a client to break through the firewall. However, this is not guaranteed to work in all circumstances, and will result in a slower response time.

### Constructors

With respect to constructors, as two methods of this class are abstract (requiring a subclass to implement them), it is impossible to instantiate the RMISocketFactory class. Instead, a subclass should be implemented and instantiated, then registered as the default RMISocketFactory, by invoking the setSocketFactory(RMISocketFactory) method.

### Methods

It is advised that only experienced developers create customized sockets and a custom RMISocketFactory. This class defines the following methods (all of which are public):

- Socket createSocket ( String host, int port ) throws java.io. IOException—returns a Socket instance connected to the specified host and port. If a connection cannot be established, an IOException will be thrown.
- Socket createServerSocket ( int port ) throws java.io.IOException—returns a custom ServerSocket instance bound to the specified port. If the service cannot bind to that port, an IOException will be thrown.
- static RMISocketFactory getDefaultSocketFactory()—returns the default socket factory used for creating client and server sockets for RMI.
- static RMIFailureHandler getFailureHandler()—returns a handler object, which is called when an attempt to create a ServerSocket fails.
- static RMISocketFactory getSocketFactory()—returns the socket factory that has been assigned by the setSocketFactory(RMISocket Factory) method. If no such handler has been assigned, this method returns null.

- `static void setFailureHandler (RMIFailureHandler failure Handler)`—assigns an `RMIFailureHandler` to the socket factory. This failure handler will be invoked whenever an attempt to create a `ServerSocket` is made but fails. The failure handler controls whether a subsequent attempt to create a `ServerSocket` should be made.
- `static void setSocketFactory (RMISocketFactory factory)`—assigns a new socket factory, which will be used by the RMI library whenever a client or server socket needs to be constructed. By registering a custom socket factory, it is possible to create custom sockets (such as encrypted sockets, compressed sockets, or sockets that use an alternate transport mechanism).

## UnicastRemoteObject Class

The `UnicastRemoteObject` provides a base from which remote services can be constructed. It provides methods to "export" a remote object and make it available for receiving incoming method requests, as well as to "unexport" a remote object and remove it from service. Generally, the easiest way to develop a remote service is to extend the `UnicastRemoteObject` class, and to implement the interface associated with the remote service. All of the required functionality to export objects is provided by the `UnicastRemoteObject`, which saves considerable time and effort.

### Constructors

The `UnicastRemoteObject` class provides the following constructors (which may also be called from the constructors of subclasses):

- `protected UnicastRemoteObject()` throws `java.rmi.Remote Exception`—creates and exports a remote object, using any available server port. If the object could not be exported, a `RemoteException` will be thrown.
- `protected UnicastRemoteObject(int port)` throws `java.rmi.Remote Exception`—creates and exports a remote object using the specified server port. If the object could not be exported (for example, if the port is already taken by another service), a `RemoteException` will be thrown.
- `protected UnicastRemoteObject(int port, RMIClientSocket Factory csf, RMIServerSocketFactory ssf)` throws `java.rmi.Remote Exception`—creates and exports a remote object using the specified server port and the specified client/server socket factories. This allows custom sockets to be used for receiving RMI requests and issuing requests to clients.

Methods

The `UnicastRemoteObject` class provides the following methods (all of which are public):

- `Object clone()` throws `java.lang.CloneNotSupportedException`—creates a "clone" of the remote object. Not every remote object will support cloning—subclasses may choose to override this method and throw a `CloneNotSupportedException`.
- `static RemoteStub exportObject(Remote obj)` throws `java.rmi.RemoteException`—exports the remote object using any available server port. If the object could not be exported, a `RemoteException` will be thrown.
- `static Remote exportObject(Remote obj, int port)` throws `java.rmi.RemoteException`—exports the remote object using the specified server port. If the object could not be exported (for example, if the port was already taken by another service), a `RemoteException` will be thrown.
- `static Remote exportObject(Remote obj, int port, RMIClientSocket Factory csf, RMIServerSocketFactory ssf)` throws `java.rmi.Remote Exception`—exports the remote object using the specified server port and the specified client/server socket factory. If the object could not be exported (for example, if the port was already taken by another service), a `RemoteException` will be thrown.
- `static boolean unexportObject(Remote obj, boolean force)` throws `java.rmi.NoSuchObjectException`—attempts to "unexport" the specified remote object and remove it from active duty. The second parameter, a `boolean` flag, indicates whether or not the object should be forcefully removed. If set to a value of "true," the object will be deactivated even if there are pending client requests. If set to a value of "false," the object will only be deactivated if there are no requests pending. The success or failure of the operation will be returned as a boolean value.

## Exceptions

Several server-specific exceptions are also defined by the `java.rmi.server` package.

- `ExportException Class`—represents a failure to export an object. Objects are exported via the constructors of the `UnicastRemoteObject` and `Activatable` classes, as well as their `exportObject(..)` methods. This class is a subclass of the `java.rmi.RemoteException` class.
- `ServerCloneException Class`—thrown when an attempt to clone a `UnicastRemoteObject` (or one of its subclasses) fails. It extends the `java.lang.CloneNotSupportedException` class.

- `ServerNotActiveException` Class—thrown when the `RemoteServer`.
  `getClientHost()` method is invoked by a thread not associated with
  fulfilling an RMI client request. This class extends the `java.lang`.
  `ExceptionException` class.
- `SkeletonMistmatchException` Class—occurs when a call is made to a
  skeleton but the method signatures have changed (for example, if an
  out-of-date `skeleton` class generated by the rmic tool is being used).
  This class extends the `java.rmi.RemoteException` class.
- `SkeletonNotFoundException` Class—represents the error condition
  that a skeleton for a remote object could not be located. Though skeletons are no longer used in the Java 2 platform, they are still required
  for backward compatibility in JDK1.1. This class extends the `java.
  rmi.RemoteException` class.
- `SocketSecurityException` Class—thrown in cases in which an
  object is unable to be exported due to security restrictions (for example, if a port lower than 1024 on a Unix system was chosen, or if an
  `RMISecurityManager` is installed but no security policy file was specified). This is a subclass of the `ExportException` class.

## 11.10  Remote Method Invocation Deployment Issues

Remote method invocation, during development and testing, runs very
smoothly and with very few problems (other than perhaps out-of-date stub files
if a service interface or implementation is changed). However, when it comes to
deploying RMI services and clients on a network, some additional complexities
may be encountered. Class definitions for services and clients must be distributed, and there are issues with different JVM implementations (such as a
Microsoft JVM versus one from Sun Microsystems) and even between JDK versions. Finally, applet communication with RMI services is an issue that must be
considered during deployment.

### 11.10.1  Dynamic Class Loading

The effort required to distribute stub and skeleton classes to every client may
be trivial in some situations (such as in a small organization in which only a few
clients are going to be using a service). However, what if a large number of
clients are going to be using the service? If a central RMI registry is to be used
for all services, and a new service is introduced to the system, stub files for the
service must be copied to the classpath of the registry before the server can
register. Is this the most efficient way of organizing services? Or in a more complex system, where object parameters or return values are marshalled and
unmarshalled using serialization, what happens if an object subclass is passed

that a client or server hasn't encountered before? For example, a remote thread execution system might accept as a parameter tasks that implement the Runnable interface—but the exact class being passed at runtime may not be known. Clients might submit new tasks, and the remote JVM needs to be able to load the classes. Restricting a system to defined types only limits its usefulness. This problem is overcome by employing a technique known as dynamic class loading.

When objects are serialized by stub and skeleton objects, only the contents of the object are sent, not the actual bytecode representing all of the object's methods and member variables. To do otherwise would slow down the speed of each request and cause unnecessary waste of bandwidth. A specialized version of the object serialization classes (ObjectOutputStream, and ObjectInput Stream) is used by stub and skeleton objects. In the case of the ObjectOutput Stream subclass, the annotateClass(...) method is overridden to include the location from which the class definition can be located. A corresponding method (resolveClass) exists for ObjectInputStream that will read the class location. This means that class definitions can be kept at different locations, and an RMI system isn't limited to storing files in a central location.

During the unmarshalling process, an attempt is made to locate the appropriate class definition locally (see Figure 11-4). If not available, then an attempt

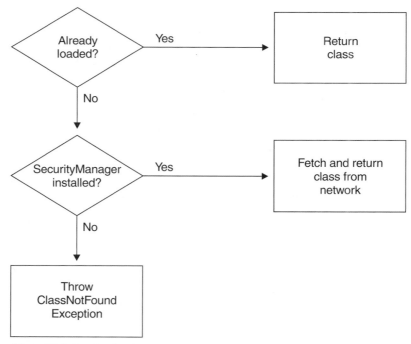

**Figure 11-4**  RMI class loader decision process

is made to fetch the class definition from the specified location by the RMI ClassLoader object. This allows new behavior to be introduced into a system, but at a penalty. As a security safeguard, the RMIClassLoader will not fetch class definitions unless a security manager has been registered with the JVM.

Without the presence of a security manager, new class definitions might be sent that could damage the host system or the data contained within it, such as deleting essential files or accessing/modifying sensitive information. Imagine the damage that could be caused by the introduction of a rogue subclass that overrides methods to introduce dangerous functionality. Whether it be reading password data from /etc/passwd on a Unix system or executing the "format c:" command on a Wintel host, such effects could be devastating. For this reason, a security manager must be installed for an RMI system to use dynamic class loading. The most common security manager used in an RMI system is the java.rmi.RMISecurityManager. This creates some additional deployment issues with the Java 2 platform that were not present in previous JVMs, however. For additional information about changes to RMI security under Java 2, see Section 11.10.2.3.

Before fetching a class definition, however, the location must be identified. The way that this location is specified to a client, or the server, is by setting the system property java.rmi.server.codebase. This should be set to a URL, which points to a codebase directory (just like the codebase of an applet). From there, the RMIClassLoader may download classes used in the RMI system.

The easiest way to set the codebase would be to use a JVM command-line parameter specifying the property. For example, to assign a remote codebase to a service called RMIServer, the following syntax would be used:

```
java –Djava.rmi.server.codebase=http://hostname:port/path
RMIServer
```

where hostname is an IP address or hostname of a machine, port is an optional number specifying the port of the HTTP service, and path is the directory of the codebase.

**NOTE:** If the rmiregistry can find class definitions locally, it will override the codebase setting and confuse clients. If the client is not on the same file system, it will then be unable to locate the classes, and a ClassNotFoundException will be thrown at runtime. Unsetting the classpath, and running the rmiregistry from a location different from the directory where the server is located will guarantee that this does not occur. If dynamic class loading is not being utilized, however, the rmiregistry *must* be able to find the class definitions in the classpath.

While servers can specify a codebase, so too can a client. If a client sends an object as a parameter that the server is not aware of, the server will be instructed to retrieve the class definition from the client's codebase, which may or may not be the same location as that specified to the server. For example, to assign a remote codebase to a client called RMIClient, the following syntax would be used:

```
java –Djava.rmi.server.codebase=http://hostname:port/path
RMIClient
```

## 11.10.2 Differences between Java Virtual Machines

There are many differences in the support of RMI between the various editions of the Java platform. These deployment issues can affect clients that use the software, as well as RMI servers that may be located across a wide variety of JVMs running on machines throughout a network.

### 11.10.2.1    Lack of Remote Method Invocation Support in Microsoft JVMs

Despite the fact that the RMI packages are part of the "core" Java API, RMI is not generally supported by Microsoft JVMs. This means that RMI clients or servers cannot be easily run on these JVMs, making the use of RMI in applets difficult, as Microsoft Internet Explorer is widely used by a large number of Internet users. An additional download is available from Microsoft to patch the Microsoft JVM to support RMI; however, it is used infrequently and thus installation on client machines can't be guaranteed.

### 11.10.2.2    Changes in Remote Method Invocation from JDK1.02 to JDK1.1

Under JDK1.02, implementations of an RMI service would extend the `java.rmi.server.UnicastRemoteServer` class. This class is not available under JDK1.1, and should be replaced with `java.rmi.server.UnicastRemoteObject`. Support for RMI in JDK1.02 was an interim release only, and should be avoided in production systems. The availability of JDK1.1 or higher JVMs on most operating system platforms makes it a better choice for RMI.

### 11.10.2.3    Changes in RMI from JDK1.1 to Java 2

Applications that use dynamic class loading, and thus install as their default security manager the `RMISecurityManager`, will not run without a few changes under the Java 2 platform. Security precautions have been increased, and the security manager will restrict network access entirely, unless modified by a security policy file. This means that RMI clients can't connect to RMI servers, and that RMI servers can't bind to a TCP port to accept incoming requests or to register with the rmiregistry.

There are several options available to developers under the Java 2 platform:

- Remove the RMISecurityManager entirely, and disable dynamic class loading
- Replace the RMISecurityManager with a custom security manager, which requires extra code to write such a manager.
- Specify a security policy file, which allows network access and (optionally) file access for systems that need it.

Of the three options, the first is the simplest, but requires classpath access to class definitions. In small systems, this might be fine, but the advantages of dynamic class loading in more complex systems make it an attractive feature to keep. The second option requires much more work, and demands that you override the appropriate security manager methods to allow access to the network, file system, and other resources. The best choice, if dynamic class loading is required, is to specify a security policy file when running a client or server.

Security policy files are simple text files that specify what access to resources is permitted. Once a security manager such as RMISecurityManager is loaded, access to most resources is disabled. To add a security manager, the following code can be added to the application (but must take place before any actions that could cause dynamic class loading to occur).

```
System.setSecurityManager ( new RMISecurityManager() );
```

Basically, it excludes access to resources unless specific permission is given to grant access. By specifying a security policy, you can override these settings and assign new permissions for networking security. The idea of a policy file makes sense—it gives fine-grained control over security settings and forces system administrators and users to consider carefully what types of access are being given (as opposed to granting universal access and then excluding or restricting certain types of access). It's easy to forget to exclude some feature, and forcing a system to specify only the permissions it needs will help to prevent a backdoor to the system being left open.

The format of the security policy file is specified in the Java 2 security documents, but for most RMI applications, a policy file like the following will suffice. It grants permission to bind to a TCP port above 1024, but leaves privileged ports for well-known protocols (such as HTTP/FTP) unavailable, to prevent rogue code from masquerading as a legitimate server. It also grants limited file read access to the c:\rmi directory, and grants write access to the c:\rmi\data directory. By convention, double slash characters ("\") are used as a path separator on Windows systems. For other operating systems such as Unix, an alternate file separator will be used, such as "/."

### Code for rmi.policy

```
Grant
{
    permission java.net.SocketPermission "*:1024-65535",
        "accept, connect, listen, resolve";
    permission java.net.SocketPermission "*:1-1023", "connect, resolve";
    permission java.io.FilePermission "c:\\rmi\\", "read";
    permission java.io.FilePermission "c:\\rmi\\data\\", "write";
}
```

> **NOTE:** Further information on the format of policy files can be found in the Java 2 Security Guide, http://java.sun.com/products/jdk/1.2/docs/guide/security/index.html.

To specify a security policy when running RMI software, the system policy `java.security.policy` is set; this points to the file location of the policy. For example, to specify the `rmi.policy` file discussed earlier for an RMI client, the following command would be used:

```
java –Djava.security.policy=c:\rmi\rmi.policy RMIClient
```

## 11.10.3 Remote Method Invocation and Applets

RMI presents some unique difficulties for applets. Aside from issues of RMI support in Internet Explorer (discussed earlier), there is also the problem of applet network restrictions. These restrictions can be very serious, and prevent RMI-based applets from communicating with RMI services.

### 11.10.3.1   Inability to Bind to TCP Ports

Since an applet can't bind to a TCP port, it cannot be an RMI server. While not every applet will need this functionality, it does mean that RMI services cannot be run from inside a Web browser. This means that callbacks cannot be easily implemented using RMI—a client applet can invoke methods on a server, but cannot export a remote object and have it invoked during the callback by another service.

### 11.10.3.2   Restrictions on Network Connections

An applet can only connect to the host machine from which its codebase was loaded. When an applet is loaded from a machine, such as www.davidreilly. com, for example, it can only make TCP and UDP connections to that server (see Figure 11.5). This is a restriction placed on applets by browsers; while the restriction is in the best interest of users, it limits developers.

This means that applets don't make good RMI clients, unless of course the same machine is used for the rmiregistry, every service that the applet may need to use, and the Web server. Digitally signed applets can lift this restriction, but this adds an extra level of complexity.

### 11.10.3.3   Firewall Restrictions

A considerable number of Web users are protected by a firewall, which usually prohibits direct socket connections. Many companies, organizations, and other institutions use firewalls to protect themselves against security breaches from outside and to restrict the types of applications being run from the inside. This means that some users will be able to use an applet that used RMI, and others will not. Even a digitally signed applet won't get through, unless RMI requests are tunneled through the firewall using a trusted protocol such as HTTP. Tunneling allows one protocol to be piggybacked on top of another more innocuous protocol, to overcome the limitations of firewalls and network security.

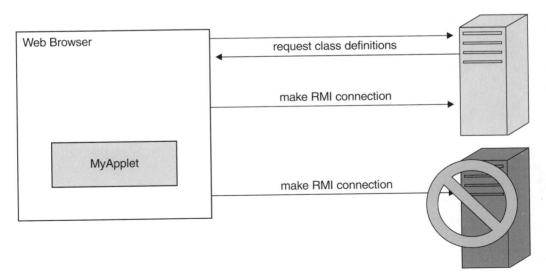

**Figure 11-5**   Applets are restricted in their ability to make network connections.

**NOTE:** The RMI specification does support firewall tunneling using HTTP, and an example CGI script that supports this is available from the Sun Microsystems Java RMI page, http://java.sun.com/products/jdk/rmi/. However, the specification states that such tunneling is at least one order of magnitude slower than direct socket requests. While RMI is an excellent technology for distributed computing, it is not normally feasible for Java applets.

## 11.11 Using Remote Method Invocation to Implement Callbacks

A common technique used in event-driven programming is the callback. The simplest way of understanding a callback is to think of a phone call. Suppose you want to know if a stock price hits a certain level, and you ask your broker to call back when it does. When the broker (the source of the event) notices that the stock price reflects your parameters, he or she calls you back, to notify you of the new price. That's a callback.

### 11.11.1 Object-Oriented Callbacks

Of course, in an object-oriented system, we're talking about software components or entire systems, not people. When one object needs to be notified of events as they occur (as opposed to continually polling to see if an event has happened), a callback is used. This is often a more efficient way of implementing a system, as the object doesn't need to periodically check the state of another object—it is instead notified if an event is triggered. Multiple listeners can register with the same event source, as shown in Figure 11-6.

When an event is triggered (either as a result of an interaction with external objects or systems, or an internal process such as completing a work unit or interacting with a user), the event source will notify each and every registered listener (see Figure 11-7). This means that the event source must maintain a list of active listeners, and then pass a message back to them that an event has occurred, and optionally give some details.

The next issue to understand about callbacks is how the notification is achieved. Some systems are designed to send and receive messages, but how can one object pass information to another (and hence inform the object that an event has occurred)?

While you may not realize it, objects do this all the time, by invoking methods. In object-oriented systems, callbacks are achieved by passing an object reference (the listener) to the object that is the event source. The event source, at the appropriate time, will then invoke one of the listener's methods to notify it

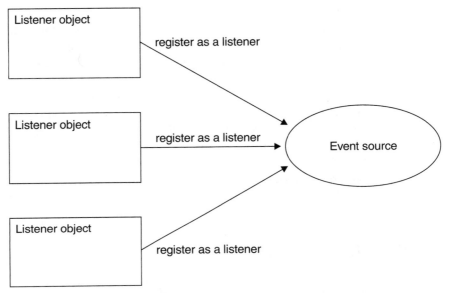

**Figure 11-6** Multiple listeners can register with one or more event sources.

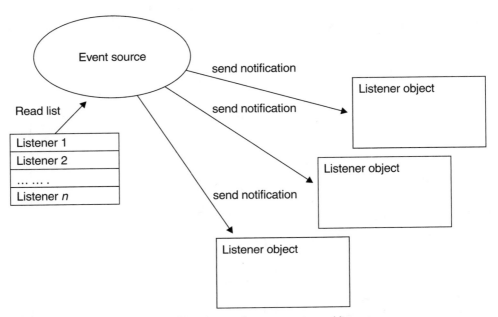

**Figure 11-7** Callback notification of event, for every registered listener

of an action and allow it to respond, as illustrated in Figure 11-8. A listener interface is defined for each major event type, and interested objects then register implementations of that interface with the listener.

This type of system is widely used in object-oriented programming, and in the context of Java, the Abstract Windowing Toolkit. The AWT event-handling model requires application developers to implement a listener interface and have that listener register with each component that needs to be monitored. Multiple listeners can register with the same component, and listeners can also register with multiple components (although due care must be taken to check which component was the source in this case). When building a system, you can create your own listener interfaces, and add for each type of event relevant methods to register and deregister listeners. While implementing callbacks in local objects is one thing, what about callbacks using RMI?

### 11.11.2 RMI Callbacks

Callbacks can be easily implemented using RMI. The chief difference between a local callback and a remote callback is that some extra initialization must occur, and that both the listener interface and the event source must be implemented as an RMI service. For the listener to register itself with the remote event source, it must invoke a remote method and pass an object reference to the remote listener interface it defines. This sounds complex in theory, but is reasonably straightforward in practice, requiring only a small amount of additional code.

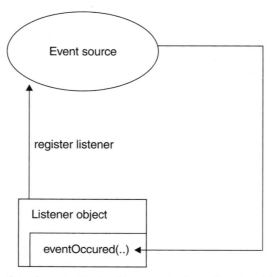

**Figure 11-8**   Callback implemented by invoking a method on a listening object

This next example works through implementing a callback using RMI, and shows how a listener can be a client and a server. For the purpose of this example, the server supplies information about changes in temperature, which can be accessed remotely. However, it would be inefficient to check the monitor continually, polling for changes, as the time at which a change will occur is not known. A temperature monitor registers with a temperature sensor service, and passes a reference to a remote temperature listener object. When the temperature does change, a callback is made, notifying registered listeners.

### 11.11.2.1  Defining the Listener Interface

The listener interface defines a remote object with a single method. This method should be invoked by an event source whenever an event occurs, so as to act as notification that the event occurred. The method signifies a change in temperature, and allows the new temperature to be passed as a parameter.

```
Chapter 11, Listing 5
interface TemperatureListener extends java.rmi.Remote
{
    public void temperatureChanged(double temperature)
        throws java.rmi.RemoteException;
}
```

### 11.11.2.2  Defining the Event Source Interface

The event source must allow a listener to be registered and unregistered, and may optionally provide additional methods. In this case, a method to request the temperature on demand is offered.

```
Chapter 11, Listing 6
interface TemperatureSensor extends java.rmi.Remote
{
    public double getTemperature() throws
        java.rmi.RemoteException;
    public void  addTemperatureListener
        (TemperatureListener listener )
        throws java.rmi.RemoteException;
    public void removeTemperatureListener
        (TemperatureListener listener )
        throws java.rmi.RemoteException;
}
```

### 11.11.2.3  Implementing the Event Source Interface

Once interfaces have been defined, the next step is to implement them. A `TemperatureSensorServer` class is defined, which acts as an RMI server. This server will also notify registered listeners as a client. The server must extend `UnicastRemoteObject`, to offer a service, and implement the `Temperature`

Sensor interface defined earlier. After creating an instance of the service and registering it with the rmiregistry, the server launches a new thread, responsible for updating the value of the temperature, based on randomly generated numbers. Both the amount (plus or minus 0.5 degrees) and the time delay between changes are generated randomly. As each change occurs, registered listeners are notified, by reading from a list of listeners stored in a java.util.Vector object. This list is modified by the remote addTemperature Listener(TemperatureListener) and removeTemperatureListener(Tempera tureListener) methods. Additionally, if a remote exception occurs while notifying a listener (indicating the temperature client is inaccessible or has terminated), it will be dropped.

```java
import java.util.*;
import java.rmi.*;
import java.rmi.server.*;

// Chapter 11, Listing 7
public class TemperatureSensorServer extends UnicastRemoteObject
implements TemperatureSensor, Runnable
{
    private volatile double  temp;
    private Vector list = new Vector();

    public TemperatureSensorServer() throws java.rmi.RemoteException
    {
        // Assign a default setting for the temperature
        temp = 98.0;
    }

    public double getTemperature() throws java.rmi.RemoteException
    {
        return temp;
    }

    public void  addTemperatureListener ( TemperatureListener listener )
        throws java.rmi.RemoteException
    {
        System.out.println ("adding listener -" + listener);
        list.add (listener);
    }

    public void  removeTemperatureListener ( TemperatureListener listener )
        throws java.rmi.RemoteException
    {
        System.out.println ("removing listener -" + listener);
        list.remove (listener);
    }
```

```
public void run()
{
     Random r = new Random();

     for (;;)
     {
          try
          {
               // Sleep for a random amount of time
               int duration = r.nextInt() % 10000 + 2000;

               // Check to see if negative, if so, reverse
               if (duration < 0) duration = duration * -1;

               Thread.sleep(duration);
          }
          catch (InterruptedException ie) { }

          // Get a number, to see if temp goes up or down
          int num = r.nextInt();

          if (num < 0)
          {
               temp += 0.5;
          }
          else
          {
               temp -= 0.5;
          }

          // Notify registered listeners
          notifyListeners();
     }
}

private void notifyListeners()
{
     // Notify every listener in the registered list
     for (Enumeration e = list.elements(); e.hasMoreElements(); )
     {
          TemperatureListener listener = (TemperatureListener) e.nextElement();

          // Notify, if possible a listener
          try
          {
               listener.temperatureChanged (temp);
          }
          catch (RemoteException re)
          {
               System.out.println ("removing listener -" + listener);
```

```java
                        // Remove the listener
                        list.remove( listener );
                }
        }
}

public static void main(String args[])
{
        System.out.println ("Loading temperature service");
         // Only required for dynamic class loading
        //System.setSecurityManager ( new RMISecurityManager() );

        try
        {
                // Load the service
                TemperatureSensorServer sensor = new TemperatureSensorServer();

                // Check to see if a registry was specified
                String registry = "localhost";
                if (args.length >=1)
                {
                        registry = args[0];
                }

                // Registration format //registry_hostname:port /service
                // Note the :port field is optional
                String registration = "rmi://" + registry +  "/TemperatureSensor";

                // Register with service so that clients can
                // find us
                Naming.rebind( registration, sensor );

                // Create a thread, and pass the sensor server.
                // This will activate the run() method, and
                // trigger regular temperature changes.
                Thread thread = new Thread (sensor);
                thread.start();

        }
        catch (RemoteException re)
        {
                System.err.println ("Remote Error - " + re);
        }
        catch (Exception e)
        {
                System.err.println ("Error - " + e);
        }
    }
}
```

### 11.11.2.4  Implementing the Listener Interface

The temperature monitor client must implement the `TemperatureListener` interface, and register itself with the remote temperature sensor service, by invoking the `TemperatureSensor.addTemperatureListener` (`Temperature Listener`) method. By registering as a listener, the monitor client will be notified of changes as they occur, using a remote callback. The client waits patiently for any changes, and though it does not ever remove itself as a listener, functionality to achieve this is supplied by the `TemperatureSensor.removeTemper atureListener(TemperatureListener)` method.

```java
import java.rmi.*;
import java.rmi.server.*;

// Chapter 11, Listing 5
public class TemperatureMonitor extends UnicastRemoteObject
    implements TemperatureListener
{
    // Default constructor throws a RemoteException
    public TemperatureMonitor() throws RemoteException
    {
        // no code req'd
    }

    public static void main(String args[])
    {
        System.out.println ("Looking for temperature sensor");

        // Only required for dynamic class loading
        //System.setSecurityManager(new RMISecurityManager());

        try
        {
            // Check to see if a registry was specified
            String registry = "localhost";
            if (args.length >=1)
            {
                registry = args[0];
            }

            // Registration format //registry_hostname :port/service
            // Note the :port field is optional
            String registration = "rmi://" + registry +  "/TemperatureSensor";

            // Lookup the service in the registry, and obtain
            // a remote service
            Remote remoteService = Naming.lookup ( registration );
```

```java
            // Cast to a TemperatureSensor interface
            TemperatureSensor sensor = (TemperatureSensor) remoteService;

            // Get and display current temperature
            double reading = sensor.getTemperature();
            System.out.println ("Original temp : " + reading);

            // Create a new monitor and register it as a
            // listener with remote sensor
            TemperatureMonitor monitor = new TemperatureMonitor();
            sensor.addTemperatureListener(monitor);
        }
        catch (NotBoundException nbe)
        {
            System.out.println ("No sensors available");
        }
        catch (RemoteException re)
        {
            System.out.println ("RMI Error - " + re);
        }
        catch (Exception e)
        {
            System.out.println ("Error - " + e);
        }
    }

    public void temperatureChanged(double temperature)
        throws java.rmi.RemoteException
    {
        System.out.println ("Temperature change event : " +
            temperature);
    }
}
```

### 11.11.2.5    Running the Callback Example

When developing an RMI callback system, both parties (listener and event source) will act as servers and as clients. This means that both parties need to have a copy of the class definitions, or access to a Web server if dynamic class loading is needed.

 **NOTE:** To use dynamic class loading, class files must be copied to a Web server, which must be specified as a command-line parameter (see Section 11.10.1), and a security manager must be installed by uncommenting the line //System.setSecurityManager ( new RMISecurityManager() );.

The following steps should be performed, in order, to run the example.

1. Compile the applications and generate stub/skeleton files for both `TemperatureSensorServer` and `TemperatureSensorMonitor`.

2. Run the rmiregistry application.

3. Run the `TemperatureSensorServer`.

4. Run the `TemperatureSensorMonitor`.

When first connected, the monitor will display the current temperature. It registers itself with the server and is notified of changes by a callback. Terminating the client will cause it to be unregistered in the `TemperatureSensorServer`, when the sensor is unable to notify the client. In addition, the callback will be unregistered if the server is unable to notify the client due to a network error.

## 11.12 Remote Object Activation

One of the chief disadvantages of using RMI for large and complex systems is the amount of overhead generated by RMI server software. Suppose you are constructing a massive system, with many different RMI service interfaces and server implementations. In such a system, each server would have to be running continually, even if it was seldom used by client software. Servers must create and export remote objects that implement RMI service interfaces, which consumes memory and CPU time. If each implementation is created as a separate server, this means that there will be as many JVM instances as there are services (unless all servers are combined into one, which is a messy solution and still wastes memory, as an instance of each service must still be created even if not used). So a system with a dozen separate RMI servers would need at least a dozen JVMs, and possibly one more if the rmiregistry application is being used. Of course, this is only a moderately sized distributed system—imagine large ones that run indefinitely but are infrequently used. This translates into wasted CPU cycles and more memory than is needed (particularly if each service allocates memory for state information and loads many objects into memory).

Prior to JDK1.2 and the Java 2 platform, there was no way to solve this problem (other than to distribute RMI services across the network and not on a single server). As this is a serious issue for medium-to-large-scale software development projects that employ RMI, Sun Microsystems took it seriously, and introduced a solution in the Java 2 platform release—remote object activation.

Readers may find both the concept and the implementation of remote object activation to be quite complex. Designing and implementing an activatable RMI service will not be appropriate in every circumstance—for example, if you have only a few services and they are running almost constantly, the performance gains from an activatable version may be small in comparison with the headaches involved. Nonetheless, for large-scale systems, this is an important technology to be aware of, and extremely useful.

### 11.12.1 What Is Remote Object Activation?

Remote object activation is a technique that solves the problem of running a large number of idle RMI services. It allows services to be registered with the rmiregistry, but not instantiated. Instead, they remain inactive, until called upon by a client, when they will awaken and perform their operation. A special daemon process called the *remote method invocation activation system daemon* (rmid) listens for these requests and instantiates RMI services on demand. Using some special trickery behind the scenes, a request is forwarded onto the activation daemon process, which creates the service. Requests are then forwarded onto the newly created service, transparently to the client, just as if it were a normal RMI service that had been running indefinitely. This means that services will lie dormant until invoked, and activated just in time (JIT) for use by a RMI client.

### 11.12.2 How Does Remote Object Activation Work?

Remote object activation works a little differently from normal RMI servers. To be locatable, a service must be available through an RMI registry, but to do that normally requires an object to be instantiated. Since the whole point is to avoid instantiating RMI servers and instead to activate them as required, a faulting remote reference is registered in its place. A faulting remote reference is a remote reference that acts as a proxy between the remote client and the as-yet-unactivated server. Unlike a UnicastRemoteObject server, which runs indefinitely, a server installation program runs for a short duration. Its purpose is to notify the activation system of an activatable remote object, and to register the faulting remote reference with the rmiregistry (see Figure 11-9). Once the registration is complete, the server installation program can terminate; creating the remote object is now the responsibility of the faulting reference and the remote method activation system daemon.

At some point in time in the future, an RMI client will look up the rmiregistry and select the service provided by the faulting remote reference. When the faulting reference is activated, it checks to see if it already has a ref-

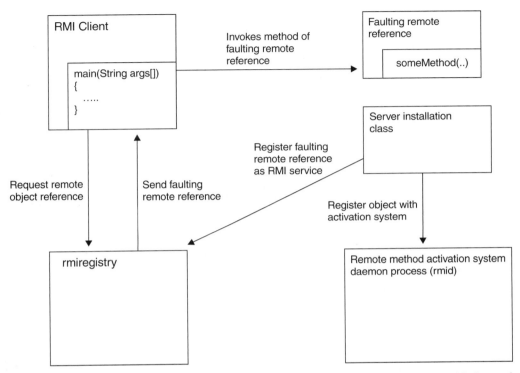

**Figure 11-9**  Server installation program registers activatable object with rmid, and faulting reference with rmiregistry.

erence to the server. The first time the faulting reference receives a call, the reference will be null, indicating that the server must be activated before being used. It enlists the aid of the rmid application, to create a new instance of the server, and then passes the call to the newly activated object (see Figure 11-10). Method requests to the faulting reference are forwarded onward to the activated object, and then returned back to the client. Though there is a slight delay on wakeup, this is not repeated for subsequent requests, as the service is ready for action.

The elegance of this solution resides in the fact that the client is, at all times, completely unaware of the details of server implementation. Although there may be some slight delay in creating the remote object initially, subsequent calls are faster, and the client does not know whether the server has always been running or was only recently activated. This means no extra code to compile, and no extra work for client developers.

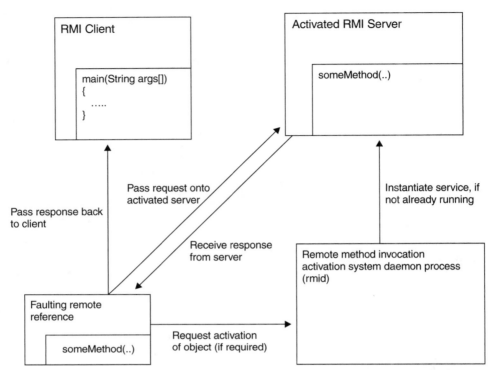

**Figure 11-10**  Faulting reference, with the aid of activation system, passes information from activated object back to client.

### 11.12.3 Creating an Activatable Remote Object

Creation of an activatable remote object is a little different from that of a UnicastRemoteObject, but the code is fairly similar. Let's start with an extremely simple remote interface, and see how it would be implemented as an activatable remote object.

```
public interface MyRemoteInterface extends java.rmi.Remote
{
     public void doSomething () throws java.rmi.RemoteException;
}
```

The RMI service interface contains a single method, doSomething(), which takes no parameters and may throw a RemoteException. There's no difference between a normal remote interface and one that will be implemented by an activatable remote object. In fact, an interface can be implemented by both an activatable object and a UnicastRemoteObject.

The next step is to create an implementation that extends the `java.rmi.activation.Activatable` class. It must implement our RMI interface and provide both a constructor and a doSomething() method. Unlike classes that extend the `UnicastRemoteObject` class, a different constructor signature is used. This constructor calls the parent constructor and exports the object on any available port. The service is then available for use by clients.

```java
public class MyRemoteInterfaceImpl extends
        java.rmi.activation.Activatable
        implements MyRemoteInterface
{
    public MyRemoteInterfaceImpl (
    java.rmi.activation.ActivationID activationID,
        java.rmi.MarshalledObject data) throws
        java.rmi.RemoteException
    {
        // call the Activatable(ActivationID activationID,
        // int port) parent constructor
        super (activationID, 0);
    }

    public void doSomething()
    {
        System.out.println ("Doing something....");
    }
}
```

Comparing this class to one extended from the `UnicastRemoteObject` class reveals relatively few differences. However, there's a little more work to do, as the object must still be registered with the activation system and the rmiregistry.

### 11.12.4 Registering an Activatable Remote Object

Registering an activatable object with the RMI activation daemon is a more complex task than just creating one, and requires a fair bit of extra code. This code can be included in a separate application class, or added in a main(..) method of the activatable remote object. To demonstrate how this is achieved, we'll create an activatable version of the `RMILightBulb` service discussed earlier in the chapter, and create a main(..) method to register the object with the rmid and rmiregistry applications.

#### Code for ActivatableLightBulbServer

```java
import java.rmi.*;
import java.rmi.server.*;
import java.rmi.activation.*;
import java.net.URLEncoder;
import java.util.Properties;
```

```java
// Chapter 11, Listing 9
public class ActivatableLightBulbServer
    // Extends the Activatable class
    extends Activatable
    // Implements a light bulb RMI interface
    implements RMILightBulb
{
    public ActivatableLightBulbServer(ActivationID
        activationID, MarshalledObject data)
        throws RemoteException
    {
        // Call the constructor of the parent class (Activatable)
        // to export the object on any available port
        super( activationID, 0);

        // Default to value of off
        setBulb(false);
    }

/*
    // Normally defined for UnicastRemoteObject subclasses...
    // not for an Activatable class
    public ActivatableLightBulbServer()
        throws RemoteException
    {
        // no code req'd
    }
*/
    public static void main(String args[])
    {
        System.out.println ("Loading Activatable RMI service");
        System.out.println ();

        // Set a RMI security manager
        System.setSecurityManager(new RMISecurityManager());

        try
        {
            // Step one : create an ActivationGroupDesc
            // instance
            ActivationGroupDesc groupDescriptor = new
                ActivationGroupDesc (new Properties(), null);

            // Step two : register that activation group descriptor
            //            with the activation system, and get
            //            groupID
            ActivationSystem system = ActivationGroup.getSystem();

            // Register the group descriptor -
            // without registering the group, no execution
            ActivationGroupID groupID =
                system.registerGroup(groupDescriptor);
```

```
// Output the group ID to screen
System.out.println ("Group ID : " + groupID);

// Step three: create an activation group,
// passing the group ID and
// descriptor as parameters
ActivationGroup.createGroup(groupID,
    groupDescriptor, 0);


// Specify a location for the codebase of
// the activated object. By default, the current
// directory will be used.
// However, if dynamic class loading is used,
// a HTTP URL may be specified instead
java.io.File location = new java.io.File (".");

// Encode URL, for Win32 systems. This may
// be required on other operating systems that don't
// support spaces and punctuation in filenames
String strLoc = "file://" +
    URLEncoder.encode(location.getAbsolutePath());
System.out.println ("Activation codebase : " + strLoc);

// Step four : Create an activation descriptor,
//             whose constructor requires the class
//             name, codebase, and an optional
//             marshalled object
ActivationDesc desc = new ActivationDesc
    ("ActivatableLightBulbServer", strLoc, null);

// Step five : Register the object with the
//             activation system
//             Returns a stub, which may be registered
//             with rmiregistry
Remote stub = Activatable.register(desc);

// Check to see if a registry was specified
String registry = "localhost";
if (args.length >=1)
{
    registry = args[0];
}

// Registration format
// registry_hostname ( optional):port /service
String registration = "rmi://" + registry +
    "/RMILightBulb";


// Step six :  Register the stub with the rmiregistry
Naming.rebind(registration, stub);
```

```
                System.out.println(
                "Service registered with rmid.Now terminating...");
                System.exit(0);
        }
        catch (RemoteException re)
        {
                System.err.println ("Remote Error - " + re);
        }
        catch (Exception e)
        {
                System.err.println ("Error - " + e);
        }
    }

    /*
        Remainder of code implements RMILightBulb interface,
        and is not RMI specific
     */
    // Boolean flag to maintain light bulb state information
    private boolean lightOn;

    // Remotely accessible "on" method - turns on the light
    public void on() throws java.rmi.RemoteException
    {
        // Turn bulb on
        setBulb (true);
    }

    // Remotely accessible "off" method - turns off the light
    public void off() throws java.rmi.RemoteException
    {
        // Turn bulb off
        setBulb (false);
    }

    // Remotely accessible "isOn" method, returns state of bulb
    public boolean isOn() throws java.rmi.RemoteException
    {
        return getBulb();
    }

    // Locally accessible "setBulb" method, changes state of bulb
    public void setBulb (boolean value)
    {
        lightOn = value;
    }

    // Locally accessible "getBulb" method, returns state of bulb
    public boolean getBulb ()
    {
        return lightOn;
    }
}
```

### How *ActivatableLightBulbServer* Works

Other than the main method, there really isn't a great deal of difference between the `ActivatableLightBulbServer` and the `LightBulbServer` class used earlier in the chapter. The real source of complexity is in the registration of the object with the activation daemon in the `main(..)` method, as there is a fair amount of initialization that must take place before an object may be activated.

The first thing you should notice is that a security manager is installed by the application. Activation requires some form of security manager to be installed, so this means that a security policy must be specified as a command-line parameter when running the server. Also, registration code is wrapped in an exception handler, as errors could occur when contacting the rmid or rmiregistry applications.

```
// Set a RMI security manager
System.setSecurityManager(new RMISecurityManager());

try
{
    // registration code goes here …..
}
catch (RemoteException re)
{
    System.err.println ("Remote Error - " + re);
}
```

The procedure for registering an activatable remote object can be broken down into a series of steps. Each of these steps is difficult to understand initially, but varies very little from service to service. When developing activatable services of your own, you can use these steps as guidelines for registering other classes.

### Step One

The first step is to create an activation group descriptor. This descriptor is associated with an activation group, and allows you to specify system properties. In this example, no system properties are required and a new instance of the Properties class is created.

```
// Step one : create an ActivationGroupDesc instance
ActivationGroupDesc groupDescriptor = new ActivationGroupDesc
(new Properties(), null);
```

### Step Two

The second step is to register the activation group descriptor with the RMI activation daemon process. This process is represented by the `Activation System` interface. Applications do not create or extend this interface. Instead, a

reference to the activation daemon process is obtained by invoking the static
`ActivationGroup.getSystem()` method.

```
// Step two : register that activation group descriptor
//            with the activation system, and get groupID
ActivationSystem system  = ActivationGroup.getSystem();
```

Once a reference to the `ActivationSystem` class is obtained, the group
descriptor is registered using the `ActivationSystem.registerGroup` method,
which returns an `ActivationGroupID` instance.

```
// Register the group descriptor - without registering the
// group, no execution
ActivationGroupID groupID =
system.registerGroup(groupDescriptor);
```

### Step Three

Once a group descriptor has been registered with the activation system and
a valid `ActivationGroupID` obtained, the next step is to actually create the
activation group. The act of registering it is not sufficient—one must be created,
by calling the static `ActivationGroup.createGroup(ActivationGroupID id,
ActivationGroupDesc descriptor)` method. This creates and assigns an activation
group for the JVM, and notifies the activation system that the group is
active.

```
// Step three: create an activation group, passing the
//             group ID and descriptor as parameters
ActivationGroup.createGroup(groupID, groupDescriptor, 0);
```

### Step Four

The fourth step is to create an activation descriptor, which describes an
activatable remote object. It stores three key pieces of information: the class
name of the remote object, the URL location of the remote object, and
(optionally) a `MarshalledObject` that contains a serialized version of the
remote object.

Determining the codebase location of a remote object can be a little tricky.
If class definitions are stored on a Web server for the purpose of dynamic class
loading, this is made simple—but what if the class files are stored locally? In
this example, the current directory is used as the codebase and converted to a
file:// URL. However, if dynamic class loading is to be used by client and server,
it may be more convenient to copy class files to a Web server and specify an
HTTP URL instead. Once a location has been determined, it is then passed to
the `ActivationDesc` constructor.

```
java.io.File location = new java.io.File (".");

// Encode URL, for Win32 systems. This may not be required
// on other operating systems that don't support spaces and
// punctuation in filenames
String strLoc = "file://" +
URLEncoder.encode(location.getAbsolutePath());
System.out.println ("Activation codebase : " + strLoc);

// Step four : Create an activation descriptor, whose
//             constructor requires the class name,
//             codebase, and an optional marshalled object
ActivationDesc desc = new ActivationDesc
("ActivatableLightBulbServer", strLoc, null);
```

## Step Five

The fifth step is to register the activation descriptor with the activation system. This instructs the activation system of the class name and the location of the class definition file. A remote stub will be returned, which can then be registered as an RMI service.

```
// Step five : Register the object with the activation system
//             Returns a stub, which may be registered with
//             rmiregistry
Remote stub = Activatable.register(desc);
```

## Step Six

The sixth and final step is to add a registry entry for the RMI service, so that clients may locate the service. The code for this is similar to that of the previous RMI lightbulb server, except that a remote stub is registered, not an instance of a remote object.

```
// Check to see if a registry was specified
String registry = "localhost";
if (args.length >=1)
{
    registry = args[0];
}

// Registration format //registry_hostname:port/service
// Note the :port field is optional
String registration = "rmi://" + registry + "/RMILightBulb";

// Step six :  Register the stub with the rmiregistry
Naming.rebind(registration, stub);

System.out.println("Service registered with rmid. Now terminating...");
System.exit(0);
```

### Running ActivatableLightBulbServer

Before running the `ActivatableLightBulbServer`, you will need to compile it and produce stub/skeleton files. Launch the rmiregistry and rmid applications (either in the same directory as the server, if classes are being loaded locally, or in a different directory if dynamic class loading is being used).

Now you can run the `ActivatableLightBulbServer`. However, a security policy file must be specified for the server. The security policy file must grant many additional privileges, beyond the standard socket and file permissions. Since no actual objects are being passed (and hence no dynamic code is being loaded from the client), it is safe to grant access to all permissions; on a more complex and secure system, individual permissions could be assigned.

The format for the security policy is as follows (the policy should be saved as `active.policy`):

```
grant
{
 permission java.security.AllPermission;
};
```

To specify the security policy file when running the server, use the following syntax:

```
java -Djava.security.policy=active.policy
ActivatableLightBulbServer
```

Now, run the client application from earlier in the chapter against the server. No code needs to be changed in the client—it will treat the activatable lightbulb server just as if it were a normal RMI server.

```
java LightBulbClient localhost
```

## 11.13   Summary

Remote method invocation (RMI) is a distributed systems technology that allows object methods located in remote Java Virtual Machines (JVMs) to be invoked remotely. This is often a simpler way of communicating between one application and another than direct TCP socket communication, which requires both parties to adhere to a network protocol. Instead of writing protocol implementations, developers interact with object methods defined by an RMI service interface. Once a reference to a remote object has been obtained, it can be treated just like a local object, which is a more intuitive way of developing network applications.

**Chapter Highlights**

In this chapter, you have learned:

- How to define a remote method invocation service
- How to create a server implementation of an RMI service
- How to create a client that locates and uses an RMI service implementation
- How to create an activatable RMI server

# CHAPTER 12

## *Java IDL and CORBA*

This chapter introduces readers to the Common Object Request Broker Architecture and to writing CORBA clients and services in Java. At the conclusion of this chapter, readers should be able to design and implement systems in Java that make use of CORBA for communication.

## 12.1 Overview

Remote Method Invocation (RMI) was covered in Chapter 11, and as with many things in life, there is more than one way to achieve the same goal. CORBA is a standard for making object method invocation requests over a network. The Object Management Group (OMG), a large consortium of companies devoted to improving remote object method invocation, developed the CORBA specification.

**NOTE:** Information on the work of the Object Management Group can be found at http://www.omg.org/.

CORBA has been designed from the ground up to support a wide range of network, operating system, and language configurations. This makes it, for some purposes, a more attractive solution than RMI, which is limited primarily to the Java platform. While not hardware or operating system specific, it is still fairly language specific unless you use a bridge from Java to another language, which requires considerable effort.

CORBA, on the other hand, is not limited to invoking objects running within a JVM. It is not a language per se, but a specification for how objects will interact. Thus, it is not limited to a single language—CORBA services and clients can be written in a variety of languages.

Suppose you wanted to write a business object that would fulfill requests for a range of machine types, and that would integrate with almost any major programming language such as C++ and Java. CORBA would be an ideal solution, as it does not lock the developer into a single language for development and use of the business object. That's the purpose behind the CORBA vision—to make objects accessible from any language and platform. Older legacy systems can be integrated with Java software and revitalized (for example, adding on a Web interface to an old inventory management system). The ability to interconnect with existing legacy systems isn't the only factor in CORBA's favor though. CORBA makes a good choice for Java developers, not just now but also in the future. Languages of the future that supercede Java will still be able to communicate with "legacy" systems that we are now writing and will write in the future. Consider it a way to make your systems "future-proof."

While CORBA itself is not a language, it introduces a new language. CORBA services are described by a schema, which is a template for the methods an object makes available. Such schemas are expressed using the Interface Definition Language (IDL). Languages like Java that support CORBA can implement an IDL schema, thus allowing other software to invoke methods. IDL is language neutral, so any programming language for which an IDL mapping has been written can use it.

Currently, the following specifications for IDL language mappings are available from the OMG:

- C
- C++
- Smalltalk
- COBOL
- Ada
- Java

While this discussion covers CORBA only from a Java perspective, it is important for the reader to be aware that CORBA can be used from other languages. This makes it more interoperable than Java's RMI, and ideal as a middle layer between Java and legacy systems.

Let's examine the Common Object Request Broker Architecture in detail.

## 12.2   Architectural View of CORBA

CORBA is made up of a collection of objects and software applications that work together cooperatively. A schema specification, written in IDL, describes the objects that are exported for remote usage. An object request broker (ORB) implements the interface between remote object and software client. The ORB handles requests for an object's services, as well as sending a response. Figure 12-1 provides an overview of how clients and servants (the end implementation of the service) interact using an ORB.

Even though objects are treated as local objects, and you can invoke methods on them as if they were normal objects, there's an extra step involved. Acting as an intermediary between client and servant is the ORB. Communication between client and servant occurs over the network via the Internet Inter-ORB Protocol (IIOP), shown in Figure 12-2.

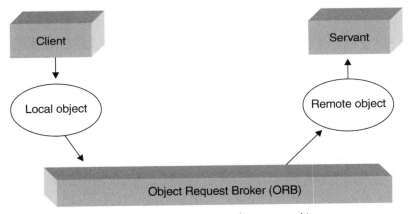

**Figure 12-1**    Objects accessed locally act as a proxy for remote objects.

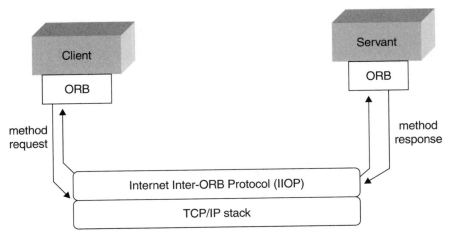

**Figure 12-2**    Communication takes places using IIOP.

IIOP is not something that you, as a developer, would write software for. Nonetheless, it's important to be aware of, as communication takes place over sockets. Therefore, you should remember that software using IIOP as a transport mechanism will have all the strengths and weaknesses of TCP/IP. Your CORBA software will be limited by network restrictions on applets, as well as firewalls. Generally, however, CORBA services are used within an intranet, as the extra overhead of transmission over the Internet is slower, and users may have a firewall in between.

In addition to object method invocation, the CORBA standard defines a host of other features, such as transaction handling, messaging, and object persistence. Such topics, however, are beyond the scope of this book, and are worthy of book-length discussions in their own right.

### 12.2.1 CORBA Services

Within the CORBA architecture, software services are described by a schema and implemented by a servant. The servant is a special piece of software that registers itself with a lookup service, so that other CORBA software can locate and access its services. Typically a CORBA server will create a CORBA servant, and is then responsible for creating an ORB for the servant and registering the service for access by other clients. Figure 12-3 shows this process in action.

### 12.2.2 CORBA Clients

Clients, on the other hand, don't need to register with a name service. They do, however, want to use the name service to look up services (as shown in Figure 12-4). Such services might always be located on the same machine, but in the event that they move, the name server helps locate them. CORBA has been designed for robustness, so the movement of a service to a new machine won't confuse clients that rely on a name server—the next time they look up

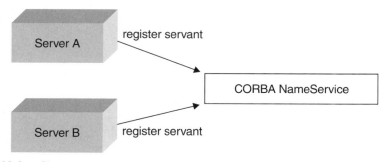

**Figure 12-3.**  Clients register with a name service.

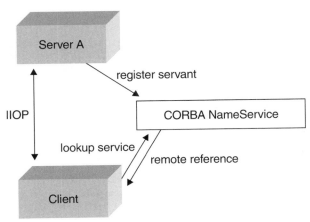

**Figure 12-4** Client uses name server to locate CORBA servant.

the location of a particular service they will be referred to the new machine. This is, in fact, very similar to what occurs with RMI. Such a system is much more fault tolerant and versatile than relying on hard-coded locations in your source code or configuration files, and allows network administrators to distribute services across the network for the purposes of load balancing.

## 12.3 Interface Definition Language (IDL)

The Interface Definition Language (IDL) is a crucial language to learn and attain, as all CORBA services are described by it. It is not, however, a complex language to learn. If you've managed to acquire a reasonably difficult language like Java, then picking up IDL will be a breeze.

### 12.3.1 Overview of the Language

The IDL defines many language constructs, allowing a rich schema of objects to be described. We'll cover each of the basic ones, but readers are advised to read the "Java Language Mapping to OMG IDL Specification," published by the Object Management Group.

**NOTE:** The IDL documentation is available from the OMG Web site, at http:// www.omg.org/technology/documents/formal/java_language_mapping_to_omg_idl. htm. If the page has moved from this location, you can access it from the main OMG site at http://www.omg.org/, by searching for "Java Language Mapping to OMG IDL."

## 12.3.2 IDL Datatypes

IDL defines a set of primitive datatypes, such as numbers and text, as well as the ability to create more powerful constructs like arrays, sequences, and data structures. Readers interested in the more complex constructs are advised to consult the "Java Language Mapping to OMG IDL Specification" document, on which Table 12-1, showing the basic IDL datatypes, is based.

## 12.3.3 IDL Interfaces

Interface definitions describe a remote object, the methods that the object exposes, as well as member variables, such as constants. The *interface* keyword is used to describe an interface. The following is an example of an interface:

```
interface UserAccount
{
    float getBalance();
    void setBalance(in float amount);
};
```

## 12.3.4 IDL Modules

Modules are a convenient way of grouping logically related interfaces together for convenience. Consider modules similar to a package in Java; related classes are grouped together into categories.

**Table 12-1**   Java Datatypes and Their Mapping to IDL Datatypes

| Java Datatype | IDL Datatype |
| --- | --- |
| Void | void |
| Boolean | boolean |
| Char | wchar |
| Byte | octet |
| Short | short |
| Int | long |
| Long | long long |
| Float | float |
| Double | double |
| java.lang.String | string / wstring |

```
module AccountTypes
{
    interface UserAccount
    {
        // code for account would go here
    };

      interface UserID
    {
        // code for userid would go here
    };

      interface Subscriptions
    {
        // code for subscriptions would go here
    }
}
```

### 12.3.5 IDL Attributes

Interfaces can have variables, as well as providing member variables. While you can write accessor functions to obtain the value of a variable and/or modify it, an easier alternative is to define an attribute. Attributes may be mutable or immutable to the remote client through the *readonly* keyword. Remember, however, that if you make an attribute mutable instead of hiding it through a set of accessor functions, you lose control over how modifications are made.

The following is an example of an attribute, in contrast to our first interface example, which defined accessor functions:

```
interface UserAccount
{
        // balance is not protected, and can be easily changed
    attribute float balance;
        // account id may be read but not remotely modified
    readonly attribute long long accountid;
};
```

### 12.3.6 IDL Operations

While attributes have their uses, the most important part of an IDL schema will be the operations that are defined. These operations may be invoked remotely, and can perform both simple and complex tasks, limited only by the imagination.

Operations are functions that can return a value upon completion and can accept parameters. There are three types of parameters that may be specified for an IDL operation:

1. in—parameter used for input only, and is immutable
2. out—parameter whose contents may be modified, and is not immutable

3. inout—parameter that combines the properties of in and out. Such parameters may be used as input and may also be modified.

A cleaner implementation will result when you use input parameters only, and a single return value. However, sometimes it may be necessary to use the other modifiers; readers are advised to use discretion.

The following interface shows three simple operations, two of which accept an input parameter. Each operation also specified a return value (in this case, of type float).

```
interface UserBalance
{
        float getBalance();
        float addBalance(in float amount);
        float subtractBalance(in float amount);
};
```

Note that if a method does not have a return value, just as in Java you should specify this by using the *void* keyword.

### 12.3.7 IDL Exception Handling

Exception handling in CORBA is a good way to indicate abnormal situations. Rather than returning a simple error code as a return value, you can throw an exception. Exception handling in CORBA varies slightly from that of Java, in that exceptions may not be subclasses. This is in contrast to Java, where generic exceptions are commonly identified as being throwable, but more concrete implementations are thrown. For example, java.net.Socket Exception may be thrown when using the Socket class, but actually a subclass is being thrown (such as java.net.ConnectException or java.net.NoRouteTo HostException).

You can, however, define several exceptions within an IDL schema, and have an operation throw more than one type of exception. This is an easy workaround to the subclass limitation.

The following is an example of two IDL exceptions thrown by an operation. The *raises* keyword is used to identify a method that throws an exception.

```
module BankingSystem
{
    // Account inactive exception
    exception AccountInactive
    {
            string reason;
    };
```

```
                    // Account overdrawn exception
                    exception AccountOverdrawn
                    {
                        string reason;
                    };

                    interface BankAccount
                    {
                        double withdrawMoney(in double amount) raises
                    (AccountInactive, AccountOverdrawn);

                        // Further bank account methods might go here ...
                    };
                };
```

## 12.4  From IDL to Java

So far, we've covered the basic syntax of the Interface Definition Language. The next step is to write a CORBA service described by an IDL schema and implemented in Java. We'll also need to write a CORBA client that will access our service. So you can compare between CORBA and RMI, we'll carry on the example of a distributed lightbulb service, first introduced in Chapter 11.

For efficiency's sake, we will use the CORBA reference implementation that is included in the Java 2 platform. While this is not a full production implementation, it is perfectly adequate for the purposes of learning CORBA, and it comes free as part of Java.

### 12.4.1  A Sample Schema

The following schema describes our distributed lightbulb service, which will be saved as a text file called LightBulb.idl.

```
exception BulbBrokenException
{
};

interface LightBulb
{
        void on () raises (BulbBrokenException);
        void off();
        boolean isOn() raises (BulbBrokenException);
};
```

The next step involves mapping this IDL schema to Java.

### 12.4.2 *Mapping an IDL Schema to Java*

Rather than manually converting an IDL schema to Java source code, we'll use a simple tool to automate the process. This tool, idlj.exe, ships as standard with the Java 2 SDK v1.3 or higher for Windows. Previous versions of the Java 2 SDK did not include the tool, and required you to download a program called idl2java.exe. The reader is advised, if this hasn't been done already, to install the latest version of the Java 2 SDK for Windows—further instructions presume that readers are able to run the idlj.exe program.

If you've already saved the lightbulb schema as LightBulb.idl (preferably in a directory of its own), the next step is to generate the Java mapping, using idlj.exe. Type the following command:

```
idlj -fall LightBulb.idl
```

You'll notice that we specify an extra parameter, -fall. You can specify that you want to generate only the client mapping by using -fclient, and only the server mapping by using -fserver. For convenience, you'll usually do all mappings at once.

If you do a directory listing, you'll notice that there are quite a few new files. These are stub and skeleton files, created automatically as part of the mapping process. You should not modify these files directly; if you run the idlj program in the future your changes will be overwritten. Instead, we'll use these classes as the scaffolding for a CORBA servant and a CORBA client.

### 12.4.3 *Writing the Servant Code*

Writing code to implement a CORBA service is fairly straightforward. Most of the hard work has already been done, remember, by the IDL mapping tool. When you define an interface, you'll get a variety of files. The two most important ones for writing a servant are the following:

- InterfaceOperations.java
- _InterfaceImplBase.java

So, when we compiled the LightBulb schema, it produced (among other files), LightBulbOperations.java and _LightBulbImplBase.java.

The Operations source file provides the Java mapping of operations a CORBA servant must implement. You can copy and paste these method signatures into your servant, and then provide an implementation. The second file, ImplBase, should be extended using class inheritance by your servant, and should then implement the methods of the Operations file. The following example shows an implementation of a CORBA servant, for our distributed lightbulb service.

### Code for LightBulbServant

```java
import java.util.Random;
import org.omg.CORBA.*;
import org.omg.CosNaming.*;
import org.omg.CosNaming.NamingContextPackage.*;

// Chapter 12, Listing 1
public class LightBulbServant extends _LightBulbImplBase
{
    // Boolean flag representing light bulb state
    private boolean bulbOn;

    // Boolean flag representing light bulb working
    private boolean bulbOk = true;

    public LightBulbServant()
    {
        // Off by default
        bulbOn = false;
    }

    // Implementing operations defined by the LightBulb
    // interface
    // Remember, the Operations class of any interface contains
    // the Java method signatures you must implement.

    // Turn on the bulb
    public void on () throws BulbBrokenException
    {
        // Check to see if bulb already on
        if (bulbOn)
            return;

        // Check to see if bulb broken
        if (!bulbOk)
            throw new BulbBrokenException();

        // Check to see if bulb will break
        Random r = new Random();

        // Make it a one in four chance, since it is an
        // old bulb and we want to test the throwing of
        // an exception
        int chance = r.nextInt() % 4;

        if ( chance == 0 )
        {
            bulbOk = false;
            bulbOn = false;
            throw new BulbBrokenException();
        }
```

```java
        else
        {
            bulbOn = true;
        }
    }

    // Turn off the bulb
    public void off ()
    {
        bulbOn = false;
    }

    // Is the bulb on and working?
    public boolean isOn () throws BulbBrokenException
    {
        // Check to see if broken
        if ( !bulbOk )
            throw new BulbBrokenException();

        // Return bulb state
        return bulbOn;
    }

    public static void main(String args[])
    {
        System.out.println ("Loading ORB");

        try
        {

            // Create the ORB
            ORB orb = ORB.init(args, null);

            // Create a new light bulb servant...
            LightBulbServant servant = new
            LightBulbServant();

            // ... and connect it to our orb
            orb.connect(servant);

            // Object Request Broker ready
            System.out.println ("Light bulb service loaded");

            // Next step : export the orb to our name service

            // Get a name service reference
            org.omg.CORBA.Object object =
            orb.resolve_initial_references("NameService");

            // Narrow to a NamingContext object
            NamingContext namingContext =
                NamingContextHelper.narrow(object);
```

```
                              // Creating a naming component for our servant
                              NameComponent component =
                                  new NameComponent ("LightBulb", "");

                              // NamingContext requires an array, not a single
                              // NameComponent
                              NameComponent componentList[] = { component };

                              // Now notify naming service of our new interface
                              namingContext.rebind(componentList, servant);

                              System.out.println ("Servant registered");

                              // Wait indefinitely for clients to use the
                              // servant
                              for (;;)
                              {
                                  Thread.sleep(1000);
                              }
                      }
                      catch (Exception e)
                      {
                              System.err.println ("Error - " + e);
                      }


              }
      }
```

### How LightBulbServant Works

As you can see from the source code, we've implemented the on(), off(), and isOn() methods of the remote interface. The code for these is fairly simple, and consists of modifying boolean flags that control whether the light is on, off, or broken. As such, they are not networking or CORBA specific.

What is important to understand from this example is how to export a CORBA servant and list it in the CORBA naming service. You could, if you wanted a clean separation between application and network code, create a separate class to handle the CORBA-specific code. However, it is often easier to combine the two, by adding a main(String[]) method to your servant, to allow it to be run as a stand-alone application.

The first step is to obtain a reference to the object request broker and register the servant with it. You don't create an ORB, as there is only one ORB per JVM instance. Instead, you obtain a reference to it by calling the ORB.init(..) method. Then, we connect the servant to the ORB.

```
// Create the ORB
ORB orb = ORB.init(args, null);

// Create a new light bulb servant ...
LightBulbServant servant = new LightBulbServant();
```

```
// ... and connect it to our orb
orb.connect(servant);
```

The second step for writing a servant is to register it with a name service. The name service allows the servant to be located by clients. This part gets a little tricky, and involves a few extra lines of code. The first part of the procedure is to obtain a reference to the name service. We do this by asking our ORB to locate the `NameService`, and we then narrow the service from a generic CORBA object to a `NamingContext` object, which represents the `NameService`. This is, effectively, a cast from a generic type to a more specific one.

```
// Get a name service reference
org.omg.CORBA.Object object =
    orb.resolve_initial_references("NameService");

// Narrow to a NamingContext object
NamingContext namingContext = NamingContextHelper.narrow(object);
```

The next step is to create a descriptor for our servant, using the `Name Component` class. This descriptor will then be passed to the `NamingContext` object. It accepts an array of descriptors, not individual ones, so we'll wrap it in a single element array. Finally, we notify the naming service by calling the `rebind(..)` method of `NamingContext`.

```
// Creating a naming component for our servant
NameComponent component = new NameComponent ("LightBulb", "");

// NamingContext requires an array, not a single
// NameComponent
NameComponent componentList[] = { component };

// Now notify naming service of our new interface
namingContext.rebind(componentList, servant);
```

Now our server will wait patiently for incoming client requests. The next step, of course, is to write the client!

## 12.4.4  Writing the Client Code

The code required for a CORBA client differs only slightly from that of a server, in that instead of locating and registering a servant with a name service, the client instead looks up a servant. Both client and server still need to initialize an object request broker and locate the name service, so much of the code is identical. Let's look at the source code of the CORBA lightbulb client.

### Code for LightBulbClient

```java
import org.omg.CORBA.*;
import org.omg.CosNaming.*;

// Chapter 12, Listing 2
public class LightBulbClient
{
    public static void main(String args[])
    {
        try
        {
            // First step : initialize our client ORB

            // Create the ORB
            ORB orb = ORB.init(args, null);

            // Second step: lookup the light bulb using name
            // service
            // We use the same code from our servant to create
            // the nameservice reference and namecomponent.

            System.out.println ("Looking for lightbulb");

            // Get a name service reference
            org.omg.CORBA.Object object =
            orb.resolve_initial_references("NameService");

            // Narrow to a NamingContext object
            NamingContext namingContext =
                NamingContextHelper.narrow(object);

            // Creating a naming component for our light bulb
            // servant
            NameComponent component =
                new NameComponent ("LightBulb", "");

            // NamingContext requires an array, not a single
            // NameComponent
            NameComponent componentList[] = { component };

            // Now, here the client differs. We want to
            // resolve (look up) the name component
            //  representing the light bulb.
            org.omg.CORBA.Object remoteRef =
                namingContext.resolve(componentList);

            // Next, we narrow it to get an address book
            LightBulb lb = LightBulbHelper.narrow remoteRef);
```

```
// Finally, we have a remote reference to our
// light bulb.
System.out.println ("Found light bulb");

// Turn bulb on and off till it fails,
// demonstrating exceptions
for (;;)
{
    try
    {
        lb.on();
        System.out.print ("Light on.... ");
        lb.off();
        System.out.print ("Light off.... ");
    }F
    catch (BulbBrokenException bbe)
    {
        System.err.println ();
        System.err.println ("Bulb broken exception encountered");
        break;
    }
}

}
catch (Exception e)
{
    System.err.println ("Error - " + e);
}

}

}
```

### How LightBulbClient Works

To conserve space and avoid repetition, we'll use the same code as in Light
BulbServant to initialize the object request broker, and to locate the name
service that will provide a remote reference to the CORBA servant. The code
required for a CORBA client to perform this operation is no different from that
of a CORBA servant.

Once the client has obtained a reference to the NameService, it will ask for
a servant matching a specified NamingComponent. The code, to prepare the component, is identical to that of the servant and should match, otherwise the servant will not be locatable. Where the client differs from the servant is that
it obtains a remote reference, by asking the name service to locate a matching
service.

```
// Creating a naming component for our light bulb servant
NameComponent component = new NameComponent ("LightBulb", "");

// NamingContext requires an array, not a single
// NameComponent
NameComponent componentList[] = { component };

// Now, here the client differs. We want to resolve (look up)
// the name component representing the light bulb.
org.omg.CORBA.Object remoteRef =
namingContext.resolve(componentList);
```

The service, if able to find a match, will return a reference, which is initially a generic CORBA object and not a more specific object instance. It must therefore be narrowed to a specific LightBulb instance through the use of a "helper" class, created by the idlj compiler. We as programmers do not need to concern ourselves with how the helper class works—it is instead created automatically by the idlj tool. The helper class is custom written by the compiler to create a mapping from each element of the IDL schema to the appropriate Java code and therefore must not be tampered with by the developer.

```
// Next, we narrow it to get an address book
LightBulb lb = LightBulbHelper.narrow (remoteRef);
```

Once you have an instance of the servant, it will act just like a local object. It is, in fact, acting as a proxy, carrying the remote request to the servant and returning the response. In this way, a CORBA service differs little from that of one written using remote method invocation—both are just as easy to use once a reference is obtained.

The remainder of the client code deals with the matter of turning on and off the lightbulb. To demonstrate exception handling, our bulb will expire after a random number of switches on and off, so a repeated call to turn it on and off will eventually generate a BulbBrokenException, as defined in our CORBA schema. The client loops indefinitely, waiting for the bulb to break, and then catches the thrown exception. It should be noted, too, that other exceptions may be thrown at runtime, such as if a CORBA nameservice or a remote Light Bulb servant cannot be located.

### 12.4.5 Putting It All Together

With the servant and client complete, the final process is to run both software applications to demonstrate remote communication between objects using CORBA. Follow the steps as delineated below.

### Step One

Compile the client and the server code, as well as any other associated files generated by the idjl.exe application. By placing all of your source files in the same directory, you can use a single command to perform this operation:

```
javac *.java
```

### Step Two

Start the CORBA name service. Included as part of the Java 2 Standard Edition, the application tnameserv.exe will be used as our name service. It can be found in either the \bin\ or \jre\bin of your Java 2 installation. You'll want to run this in a separate console window, as the program runs continually.

### Step Three

Run the CORBA servant. In a separate console window, type:

```
java LightBulbServant
```

If you get an exception reading `org.omg.CORBA.COMM_FAILURE`, it means CORBA couldn't find the name server. You should double-check that tnameserv is still running.

### Step Four

Run the CORBA client. In a separate console window, type:

```
java LightBulbClient
```

Your client will attempt to look up the appropriate lightbulb service from the CORBA name service application. Your console should display the message "Looking for lightbulb" followed by "Found lightbulb," unless either the name service or server is not yet running. Now your client will enter a loop turning the bulb on and off until it breaks, thus demonstrating exception handling under CORBA.

Congratulations, you have now run your first CORBA client-server application!

## 12.5   Summary

CORBA provides a language-independent means of invoking object methods remotely to create a distributed system. While many developers prefer the technique of remote method invocation (RMI) covered in the previous chapter, CORBA does have its advantages as well. Chiefly, it is supported by a wide range of languages, and supports additional features such as transaction handling, messaging, and persistence. However, such topics are of less importance to most Java developers, and most will be concerned about language independence and the long-term interoperability of their Java software with legacy and future systems. The pros and cons of CORBA over RMI have been outlined in this chapter, and only you as a developer can decide which technology is the most appropriate, on a case-by-case (or project-by-project) basis.

**Chapter Highlights**

In this chapter, you have learned:

- The differences between remote method invocation and CORBA
- How to understand, and to write your own, IDL schemas
- How to compile an IDL schema using the Java 2 platform
- About running a name service under Java 2, so that clients can locate servants
- How to write, compile, and run both a CORBA client and servant
- About exception handling under CORBA and Java

# CHAPTER 13

## *JavaMail*

The ability to send messages electronically across the Internet has changed the face of communication. E-mail, and to a lesser extent other forms of messaging such as newsgroups, have become an essential part of modern life. Recognizing the need to support such communication within Java, Sun Microsystems released the JavaMail API.

The JavaMail API provides a common framework for managing electronic mail, by defining a set of abstract classes that represent the components of a mail system. The JavaMail API provides access to electronic mail systems, as well as the ability to create and transmit new mail messages. It has been designed to make it easy for developers to incorporate mail functionality into software, and to be interoperable with current and future mail/messaging services.

Rather than prescribing a particular set of protocols and supplying an implementation for these, the JavaMail API leaves the choice of implementation open to service providers. Though the API ships with minimal implementations for SMTP, IMAP, and POP as of JavaMail 1.2, these alone are not sufficient for every program or situation, due to the wide variety of mail and messaging protocols used today on the Internet. The API allows third-party developers to plug in their own providers and support other protocols. For example, implementations are already available for the popular POP3 and NNTP message stores. This makes JavaMail far more powerful than just an implementation of a few mail protocols—JavaMail is a flexible framework providing a common interface to mail systems, regardless of the details of their implementation.

## 13.1   Overview

The JavaMail API is targeted toward several types of audiences, as identified in the JavaMail API specification:

- Developers writing mail applications (such as an e-mail client or a newsreader)
- Developers whose applications must be "mail-aware" or able to use mail as a transport mechanism
- Third-party mail implementation providers developing an implementation of a mail store or mail-delivery mechanism

The first two audiences rely on implementations supplied by messaging service providers. Figure 13-1 shows an architectural overview of JavaMail. The API designers have chosen a layered approach, separating the implementation details from the API interface.

When an application must access a mail service or send a message to a mail service, it uses the JavaMail API to request an implementation. The API returns an instance of that implementation (if one is available), and the application can then use it to retrieve or send mail. The actual details of the implementation are transparent to the application developer. While the application can request an

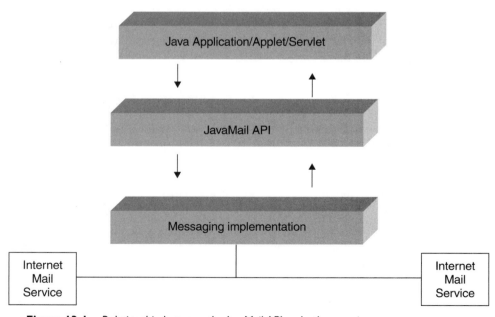

**Figure 13-1.**   Relationship between the JavaMail API and other services

implementation of a particular protocol, the interface to a mail service remains the same.

**NOTE:** Few protocol implementations ship with the JavaMail API. Many third-party implementations of protocols are available, however. A list of these can be found at the JavaMail API Web site, at http://java.sun.com/products/javamail/.

## 13.2   Installing the JavaMail API

The JavaMail API is not part of the standard Java API, and must be installed before it can be used. The JavaMail API is a Java extension; it is approved by Sun Microsystems but not part of the core Java API provided by Java Virtual Machine implementers. Before you can use JavaMail, you must install it, along with the JavaBeans Activation Framework (JAF), which is a package required by JavaMail to determine the datatype of mail messages (for example, to determine the MIME type of a message body or attachment). When applications are deployed to third parties, the latter will also require installation of JavaMail and JAF.

**NOTE:** The code and instructions in this chapter apply to JavaMail 1.1.3. Readers who prefer to use later versions of JavaMail should consult the installation instructions for any changes, and should be mindful that any additions to the API may not be backward compatible with older JavaMail installations.

Installing the JavaMail API is a relatively straightforward process. First you'll need to download the API from Sun Microsystems, along with the JavaBeans Activation Framework. Then you'll need to unzip the archives in which they are stored and add JavaMail and JAF to your classpath. The following steps should be taken:

1. Download the most recent JavaMail API implementation from http://java.sun.com/products/javamail.

2. Download the JavaBeans Activation Framework (JAF) from http://java.sun.com/beans/glasgow/jaf.html.

3. Extract the files from both archives into separate directories underneath your JDK installation directory; for example, c:\jdk1.2\javamail and c:\jdk1.2\jaf.

4. Add the JavaMail API to your classpath environmental variable. On a Windows machine, add the following to your autoexec.bat file (substituting for your installation directory):

```
set CLASSPATH=%CLASSPATH%;c:\jdk1.2\javamail\mail.jar
```

5. Add the JavaBeans Activation Framework to your classpath environmental variable. On a Windows machine, add the following to your autoexec.bat file:

```
set CLASSPATH=%CLASSPATH%;c:\jdk1.2\jaf\activation.jar.
```

This will install the basic JavaMail implementation, but if you'd like to support Post Office Protocol (POP3) e-mail accounts under JavaMail 1.1.3, you need to do one more thing (JavaMail 1.2 already includes a POP3 provider, so no additional steps are necessary). Sun provides a POP3 implementation that can be downloaded from the JavaMail Web site at http://java.sun.com/products/javamail/pop3.html. You'll then need to add the POP3.jar file from this implementation to your classpath, to support POP3 accounts (e.g., set CLASSPATH=%CLASSPATH%;c:\jdk1.2\javamail\POP3.jar).

Once this is complete, JavaMail has been installed, and you're ready to start writing applications or to run existing ones. The JavaMail API ships with some demonstration applications. If you're eager to see its capabilities, check out the demonstration applications in the javamail\demo directory, or read on.

## 13.3   Testing the JavaMail Installation

JavaMail ships with a small number of protocol providers (code plug-ins for the JavaMail API that implement specific Internet protocols). Currently, the Simple Mail Transfer Protocol (SMTP) and the Internet Message Applications Protocol (IMAP) are included. Third-party implementations are also available, and a separate download from Sun Microsystems is offered for POP3 support. Our first example lists the available mail protocol implementations and their properties.

**NOTE:** Again, developers using JavaMail 1.2 will not require the additional download of a POP3 provider.

*Code for ProviderList*

```
import javax.mail.*;
import javax.mail.internet.*;
```

```java
// Chapter 13, Listing 1
public class ProviderList
{
    public static void main (String args[]) throws Exception
    {
        // Get a session, with default system properties
        Session mySession = Session.getDefaultInstance
            (System.getProperties(), null);

        // Get a list of available providers
        Provider[] providerList = mySession.getProviders();

        // Look at each provider
        for (int i = 0; i< providerList.length; i++)
        {
            // Print out protocol name
            System.out.println ("Protocol : " +
                providerList[i].getProtocol());

            // Print type (store or transport)
            if (providerList[i].getType() ==
                Provider.Type.STORE)
                System.out.println ("Provider type : STORE");
            else
                System.out.println (
                    "Provider type : TRANSPORT");

            // Print out vendor name
            System.out.println ("Vendor : " +
                providerList[i].getVendor());
            System.out.println ("--");
        }
    }
}
```

### Running ProviderList

The ProviderList application requires no parameters, and is simple to run:

```
java ProviderList
```

When run, it will display the name of each protocol, the type of protocol, and the vendor name. As protocols are added, the output will change. If you've installed JavaMail and the POP3 provider, you should see output similar to the following:

Protocol : pop3
Provider type : STORE
Vendor : Sun Microsystems, Inc
...

Protocol : imap
Provider type : STORE
Vendor : Sun Microsystems, Inc

--

Protocol : smtp
Provider type : TRANSPORT
Vendor : Sun Microsystems, Inc

--

As shown in this sample output, the Post Office Protocol version 3, the Internet Message Application Protocol, and the Simple Mail Transfer Protocol are supported by this machine.

## 13.4   Working with the JavaMail API

JavaMail provides a set of interfaces to mail protocol implementations. Once you've mastered the basic concepts and interfaces, you'll be able to write applications that work with any protocol for which an implementation is available.

Below are some of the important classes that form the core of the JavaMail API, as well as the methods offered by these classes. The JavaMail API is extensive, and a first review of it can be overwhelming. Readers should not be concerned with the details of every method; a preliminary examination will provide a sufficient idea of how they work. The methods can be referred back to as necessary.

### 13.4.1 Address Class

The Address class represents an Internet messaging address, as distinct from another type of Internet address such as the Uniform Resource Locator (java.net.URL). This is an abstract class; it may not be instantiated. Instead, developers create a subclass of this class, or use one of two subclasses provided with the JavaMail API: the InternetAddress and NewsAddress classes.

### 13.4.2 Message Class

The Message class is an abstract class that represents a mail message. It is responsible for storing the contents of a mail message and any associated properties (such as the subject, date, and "To" and "From" addresses). Messages may be sent using a message transport object, or retrieved from a mail folder. This is also an abstract class; it may not be instantiated.

## Methods

The following methods of the `Message` class are public unless otherwise noted.

- `void addFrom(Address[] addressArray) throws javax.mail.Illegal WriteException, java.lang.IllegalStateException, javax.mail. MessagingException`—adds the specified mail addresses to the "From" field of the message. If the message is read only, or does not allow modification, an exception will be thrown.

- `void addRecipient (Message.RecipientType type, Address address) throws javax.mail.IllegalWriteException, javax.mail.Messaging Exception`—adds the address to the message as a recipient. There are three types of recipients (to, carbon copy, and blind carbon copy) that may be specified, either as `Message.RecipientType.TO`, `Message.RecipientType.CC`, or `Message.RecipientType.BCC`.

- `void addRecipients (Message.RecipientType type, Address[] address) throws javax.mail.IllegalWriteException, javax.mail. MessagingException`—modified form of the `addRecipient` method that allows multiple addresses to be added by specifying an array of `Address` objects.

- `Flags getFlags() throws javax.mail.MessagingException`—returns flag settings for the message, such as whether it has been sent or seen.

- `Folder getFolder()`—returns the folder of the message. If a message has been created, and not retrieved from a folder, a null value will be returned.

- `Address[] getFrom() throws javax.mail.MessagingException`—returns the senders of a message, as identified by the "From" field. A null value may be returned if no sender could be identified.

- `int getMessageNumber()`—returns the number of the message within a folder. This number is usually greater than or equal to one (a value of zero indicates a message that was created and not retrieved from a folder).

- `Date getReceivedDate throws javax.mail.MessagingException`—returns the date when the message was retrieved, if available.

- `Address[] getAllRecipients() throws javax.mail.MessagingExcep ,tion`—returns all recipients of the message.

- `Address[] getRecipients(Message.RecipientType) throws javax. mail.MessagingException throws javax.mail.MessagingException`—returns message recipients of the specified type (to, cc, bcc). To access all recipients, use the `Message.getAllRecipients()` method.

- `Address[] getReplyTo() throws javax.mail.MessagingException`—returns addresses specified by the "Reply To" field. This field indicates that messages should be directed to a different address than the sender.

- `Date getSentDate()`—returns the date when a message was sent, if available.
- `String getSubject()`—returns the message subject, as identified by the "Subject" field.
- `boolean isExpunged()`—returns a boolean value, indicating whether a message has been deleted.
- `boolean isSet ( Flags.Flag flag_type ) throws javax.mail.MessagingException`— checks to see whether a particular flag is set for this message. Returns a boolean value, to indicate flag state.
- `boolean match (SearchTerm term) throws javax.mail.Messaging Exception`— checks to see if a message matches a specific search condition.
- `Message reply (boolean all) throws javax.mail.MessagingException`—returns a new message, with the appropriate header fields set to deliver the message to the sender of the message. If the specified boolean flag is set to "true," all recipients of the message will be sent the reply.
- `void saveChanges() throws javax.mail.IllegalWriteException, java.lang.IllegalStateException, javax.mail.MessagingException`—saves any changes made to the message to the folder from which it was accessed. For example, if a flag was modified, this method would update the message's flag settings.
- `protected void setExpunged(boolean flag)`—modifies the expunged field, which controls the return value of the `Message.getExpunged()` method.
- `void setFlag(Flags.flag, boolean value) throws java.lang.IllegalStateException, javax.mail.IllegalWriteException, javax.mail.MessagingException`—modifies the specified flag to the specified state, for the message.
- `void setFlags(Flags, boolean value) throws java.lang.IllegalStateException, javax.mail.IllegalWriteException, javax.mail.MessagingException`—modifies the specified flags to the specified state.
- `void setFrom() throws javax.mail.IllegalWriteException, java.lang.IllegalStateException, javax.mail.MessagingException`—sets the value of the "From" field to that defined by the system property mail.user, or if it does not exist, user.name.
- `void setFrom(Address sender) throws javax.mail.IllegalWriteException, java.lang.IllegalStateException, javax.mail.MessagingException`—sets the value of the "From" field to the specified address.

- `protected void setMessageNumber(int num)`—specifies a message number for the message.
- `void setRecipient(Message.RecipientType type, Address recipient)` throws `javax.mail.IllegalWriteException`,`java.lang.Illegal StateException`, `javax.mail.MessagingException`—sets a recipient of the specified type for the message, overwriting all previous values for that type.
- `void setRecipients(Message.RecipientType type, Address[] recipients)` throws `javax.mail.IllegalWriteException`, `java.lang. IllegalStateException`, `javax.mail.MessagingException`—sets multiple recipients of the specified type for the message, overwriting all previous values for that type.
- `void setSentDate(Date date)`—specifies a date at which the message was sent.
- `void setSubject(String subject)`—specifies a subject for the message.

In addition, the `Message` class implements the `javax.mail.Part` interface, which provides a set of methods for modifying the contents of a message. You'll learn how to specify the contents of a mail message in an example later in the chapter.

### 13.4.3 Service Class

The `Service` class is an abstract class, representing a messaging-related networking service. It may not be instantiated by application developers, and usually is not extended directly, as there are already subclasses to represent mail stores and transports.

#### Methods

The following methods of the `Service` class are public unless otherwise noted.

- `void addConnectionListener(ConnectionListener listener)`—registers a listener for any network connection events.
- `void close()` throws `javax.mail.MessagingException`—closes the network connection for this store.
- `void connect()` throws `javax.mail.AuthenticationFailedException`, `java.lang.IllegalStateException`, `javax.mail.MessagingExcep tion`—attempts a connection to the network service represented by the mail store object, using details provided by system properties. If a connection could not be established, or was already established, an exception will be thrown.

- void connect(String host, String username, String password) throws javax.mail.AuthenticationFailedException, java.lang. IllegalStateException, javax.mail.MessagingException—attempts a connection to the network service represented by the mail store object, using the specified connection details. If a connection could not be established, or was already established, an exception will be thrown.
- void connect(String host, int port, String username, String pass word) throws javax.mail.AuthenticationFailedException, java. lang.IllegalStateException, javax.mail.MessagingException— attempts a connection to the network service represented by the mail store object, using the specified connection details. This method takes an extra argument, allowing a mail port to be specified. If a connection could not be established, or was already established, an exception will be thrown.
- protected void finalize()—cleans up mail store state before being garbage collected, and terminates event dispatching thread. This method should not normally be overridden, and if it is, should be called from any subclasses.
- URLName getURLName()—returns a URL address for the mail store. The URLName class differs little from a java.net.URL class, and only in as much as it does not support connections to the service represented by the URL.
- boolean isConnected()—returns "true" if the service is connected, "false" if not.
- protected void notifyConnectionListeners (int type)—notifies all registered connection listeners of the specified event type.
- protected protocolConnect(String host, int port, String user, String password) throws javax.mail.MessagingException—is over-ridden by service implementations to provide protocol-specific connec-tion routines.
- protected queueEvent(MailEvent evt, Vector listenerVector)— adds the event to a queue of message events, which will be delivered to the specified listeners.
- void removeConnectionListener( ConnectionListener listener )— deregisters the specified connection listener.
- void setConnected(boolean state)—modifies the connection flag for this object.
- void setURLName(URLName url)—modifies the address representing the service.
- String toString()—returns a string representation of the service, by invoking getURLName.toString().

### 13.4.4 *Store Class*

A mail store represents an external Internet mail service (such as a news server or mail server). Like Message, Store is an abstract class, whose implementation is supplied by mail service providers—it is not instantiated by applications. A Store provides access to individual folders (collections of messages), through which messages may then be read. In some simple systems there will only be a single folder available, the INBOX, and in others a wider variety of folders will be provided. It is extended from the javax.mail.Service class, which provides methods to name a service and to have it connect to the network service it represents. The Store class also provides methods to register and deregister event listeners (discussed later in the chapter).

#### *Methods*

All methods of the Store class are public unless otherwise noted.

- void addFolderListener (FolderListener listener)—registers a listener for any folder events.
- void addStoreListener (StoreListener listener)—registers a listener for any mailstore events.
- Folder getDefaultFolder() throws java.lang.IllegalStateExcep tion, javax.mail.MessagingException—returns the default folder for the mail store. If not connected, an exception may be thrown.
- Folder getFolder (String name) throws java.lang.IllegalState Exception, javax.mail.MessagingException—returns a folder for the specified name, if available.
- Folder getFolder (URLName name) throws java.lang.IllegalState Exception, javax.mail.MessagingException—returns a folder for the specified URL. Note that the URLName is a new class introduced as part of the javax.mail class, and differs only from a URL object in that it does not support methods to open a connection to the resource.
- protected void notifyFolderListeners (int type, Folder folder)— notifies all registered folder listeners of the specified event type, and the folder that is the focus of the event.
- protected void notifyFolderRenamedListeners (Folder original Folder, Folder newFolder)—notifies all registered folder listeners that a folder has been renamed.
- protected void notifyStoreListeners (int type, String message)— notifies all registered store listeners of the specified event type and the event details.

- void removeFolderListener( FolderListener listener )—deregisters the specified folder listener.
- void removeStoreListener( StoreListener listener )—deregisters the specified store listener.

### 13.4.5 Folder Class

A folder represents a collection of messages, such as a mailbox or a newsgroup. Individual messages can be selected from a folder, searched, and deleted. Messages stored in a folder also have an additional property—a set of flags that indicate whether the message has been read, should be deleted, and so on. Folders are accessed through a mail store—each folder is named, and the name associated with the default folder is INBOX.

#### Fields

The following member variables are publicly declared, and are used for identifier folder access permissions.

- Folder.HOLDS_FOLDERS—indicates that a folder can contain subfolders.
- Folder.HOLDS_MESSAGES—indicates that a folder may contain messages.
- Folder.READ_ONLY—indicates that a folder may be read but not modified.
- Folder.READ_WRITE—indicates that a folder may be both read and modified.

#### Methods

- void addConnectionListener (ConnectionListener listener)—registers a listener for any connection events.
- void addFolderListener (FolderListener listener)—registers a listener for any folder events.
- void addMessageChangedListener (MessageChangedListener listener)—registers a listener for any change in messages events.
- void addMessageCountListener (MessageCountListener listener)—registers a listener for any change in the number of messages within a folder.
- void appendMessages(Message[] messages) throws javax.mail. FolderNotFoundException, javax.mail.MessagingException—appends the specified messages to the folder. However, this should not be used to send new messages.
- void close(boolean expungeFlag) throws IllegalStateException, javax.mail.MessagingException—closes an open folder, and if the

expungeFlag is set to "true," any messages marked as deleted will be removed from the folder.

- void copyMessages(Message[] messages, Folder targetFolder) throws java.lang.IllegalStateException, javax.mail.Folder NotFoundException, javax.mail.MessagingException—copies (not moves) the specified messages into the target folder. If the messages are not part of the current folder, or the current folder is not open, an exception will be thrown.
- boolean create(int folderType) throws javax.mail.Messaging Exception—creates this folder on the mail store, and if necessary, any parent folders. Returns "true" if folder was created successfully, "false" if not.
- boolean delete(boolean recurseFlag) throws java.lang.Illegal StateException, javax.mail.FolderNotFoundException, javax. mail.MessagingException—deletes the folder, and any subfolders if the specified recurseFlag parameter is set to "true." If the folder is not already closed, or does not exist, an exception will be thrown.
- boolean exists() throws javax.mail.MessagingException—returns "true" if the folder exists in the mail store, and "false" if it does not.
- Message[] expunge() throws IllegalStateException, javax. mail.FolderNotFoundException, javax.mail.MessagingException— expunges any messages marked as deleted, without closing the folder. A folder must be opened, and exist on the server, or an exception will be thrown. Once messages are expunged, they are gone, and new message numbers will be assigned. This method returns an array of deleted messages.
- void fetch(Message[] messages, FetchProfile profile) throws java.lang.IllegalStateException, javax.mail.MessagingExcep tion—prefetches a group of messages at once, to allow more responsive access at a later point in time.
- protected void finalize()—called by the garbage collector, to allow folder operations to be cleaned up before being disposed of.
- Folder getFolder(String name) throws javax.mail.MessagingExcep tion—returns a folder object associated with the specified pathname. If an absolute path is not specified, the folder name will be interpreted as a subfolder of the current folder.
- String getFullName()—returns the full pathname of a folder.
- Message getMessage(int number) throws java.lang.IndexOut OfBoundsException, java.lang.IllegalStateException, javax. mail.FolderNotFoundException, javax.mail.MessagingException— retrieves the numbered message, and returns a Message object. If an

invalid number is specified, the folder is closed or does not exist, or a
network error occurs, an exception will be thrown.

- `int getMessageCount()` throws `javax.mail.FolderNotFoundExcep`
  `tion, javax.mail.MessagingException`—returns the number of messages stored within a folder.
- `Message[] getMessages()` throws `java.lang.IllegalStateException`
  `javax.mail.FolderNotFoundException, javax.mail.MessagingExcep`
  `tion`—returns an array, composed of all messages stored in the folder.
  If no messages exist, a blank array will be returned.
- `Message[] getMessages(int[] specificNumbers)` throws `java.lang.`
  `IllegalStateException javax.mail.FolderNotFoundException,`
  `javax.mail.MessagingException`—returns an array composed of
  the specified messages.
- `Message[] getMessages(int startRange, int endRange)` throws `java.`
  `lang.IllegalStateException javax.mail.FolderNotFoundException,`
  `javax.mail.MessagingException`—returns an array composed of the
  messages in the specified range (`startRange .. endRange`).
- `int getMode()` throws `IllegalStateException`—returns the access permissions for the folder. A value of `Folder.READ_ONLY`, `Folder.READ_`
  `WRITE` will be returned, or –1 if no permissions could be determined.
- `String getName()`—returns the folder name. An absolute name is not
  returned; for this, use the `getAbsoluteName()` method.
- `int getNewMessageCount()` throws `javax.mail.FolderNotFoundExcep`
  `tion, javax.mail.MessagingException`—returns the number of new
  messages in this folder. A new message is a message whose "recent"
  flag is set to true. Some store providers may not support this functionality, in which case a value of –1 is returned.
- `Folder getParent()` throws `javax.mail.MessagingException`—returns
  the parent folder, if one exists. If not, a value of null is returned.
- `Flags getPermanentFlags()`—returns a `Flags` object, containing all the
  flags supported by the folder, or null if unknown.
- `char getSeparator()` throws `javax.mail.FolderNotFoundException,`
  `javax.mail.MessagingException`—returns the separator character used
  to separate one folder from another in a pathname. For example, on
  Wintel systems the file separator is "\," whereas on Unix systems the
  separator is "/." Mail systems can also have different separators, and
  this information is often needed at runtime to compose pathnames.
- `Store getStore()`—returns the store that is associated with the folder
  object.

- `int getType()` throws `javax.mail.FolderNotFoundException, javax.mail.MessagingException`—returns a folder type int, which is either `Folder.HOLDS_FOLDERS` or `Folder.HOLDS_MESSAGES`.
- `int getUnreadMessageCount()` throws `javax.mail.FolderNotFound Exception, javax.mail.MessagingException`—returns the number of unread messages, determined by the state of the message "seen" flag. If the store provider doesn't support this functionality, a value of –1 will be returned.
- `String getURLName()` throws `javax.mail.MessagingException`—returns a URLName for the folder.
- `boolean hasNewMessages()` throws `javax.mail.FolderNotFoundException, javax.mail.MessagingException`—returns "true" if new messages are available, "false" if not.
- `boolean isOpen()`—returns "true" if the folder is open, "false" if the folder is closed.
- `boolean isSubscribed()`—returns "true" if the folder is a subscribed folder.
- `Folder[] list()` throws `javax.mail.FolderNotFoundException, javax.mail.MessagingException`—lists subfolders underneath the current folder.
- `Folder[] list(String pattern)` throws `javax.mail.FolderNotFound Exception, javax.mail.MessagingException`—returns a list of folders matching the specified pattern (for example "*box" to find "inbox," "outbox," and "personalbox").
- `Folder[] listSubscribed()` throws `javax.mail.FolderNotFound Exception, javax.mail.MessagingException`—returns a list of subscribed folders beneath the current folder.
- `Folder[] listSubscribed(String pattern)` throws `javax.mail. FolderNotFoundException, javax.mail.MessagingException`—returns a list of subscribed folders beneath the current folder, matching the specified pattern. For example, "*java*" might return the newsgroups "comp.lang.java.help" and "comp.lang.java.programmer."
- `protected void notifyConnectionListeners(int type)`—notifies all registered connection listeners of a connection event.
- `protected void notifyFolderListeners(int type)`—notifies all registered folder listeners of a folder event.
- `protected void notifyFolderRenamedListeners(Folder target Folder)`—notifies all registered folder listeners that a folder has been renamed.

- `protected void notifyMessageAddedListeners(Message[] messages)`—notifies all registered `MessageCountListeners` that the specified messages have been added to the folder.
- `protected void notifyMessageChangedListeners(int Message message)`—notifies all registered `MessageChangedListeners` that the specified message has been modified within the folder.
- `protected void notifyMessageRemovedListeners(boolean removal Flag, Message[] messages)`—notifies all registered `MessageCount Listeners` that the specified messages have been removed from the folder.
- `void open (int accessMode)` throws `IllegalStateException, javax. mail.FolderNotFoundException, javax.mail.MessagingException`— opens a folder in the specified access mode, either `Folder.READ_ONLY` or `Folder.READ_WRITE`.
- `protected void removeConnectionListener(ConnectionListener listener)`—deregisters the specified listener.
- `protected void removeFolderListener(FolderListener listener)`— deregisters the specified folder listener.
- `protected void removeMessageChangedListener(MessageChanged Listener listener)`—deregisters the specified message changed listener.
- `protected void removeMessageCountListener(MessageCountListener listener)`—deregisters the specified message count listener.
- `boolean renameTo(Folder folder)` throws `java.lang.IllegalState Exception, javax.mail.FolderNotFoundException, javax.mail. MessagingException`—renames the current folder to the specified folder. Not every folder may be renamed; the success of the operation is returned as a boolean value.
- `Message[] search( javax.mail.search.SearchTerm term)` throws `java.lang.IllegalStateException, javax.mail.search.SeachExcep tion, javax.mail.FolderNotFoundException, javax.mail.Messaging Exception`—searches through all of a folder's messages for the mail matching the specified search term.
- `Message[] search( javax.mail.search.SearchTerm term, Message[])` throws `java.lang.IllegalStateException, javax.mail.search. SeachException, javax.mail.FolderNotFoundException, javax. mail.MessagingException`—searches through a subset of a folder's messages for the mail matching the specified search term. Only the messages specified as a parameter will be searched for a match.
- `void setFlags(int[] numbers, Flags flagSettings, boolean value)` throws `java.lang.IndexOutOfBoundsException, java.lang.`

`IllegalStateException, javax.mail.MessagingException`—modifies the flag settings of the specified message numbers to the specified value.

- `void setFlags(int startRange, int endRange, Flags flagSettings, boolean value) throws java.lang.IndexOutOfBoundsException, java.lang.IllegalStateException, javax.mail.MessagingExcep tion`—modifies the flag settings of messages in the specified range to the specified value.

- `void setFlags(Message[] messages, Flags flagSettings, boolean value) throws java.lang.IndexOutOfBoundsException, java.lang. IllegalStateException, javax.mail.MessagingException`—modifies the flag settings of the specified messages (which must be part of this folder), to the specified value.

- `void setSubscribed(boolean subscribe) throws javax.mail.Folder NotFoundException, javax.mail.MethodNotSupportedException, javax.mail.MessagingException`—subscribes this folder, if subscriptions are supported by the current mail store. For example, a newsgroup may be subscribed to, and a list of subscribed newsgroups could then be listed by invoking the `listSubscribed()` method.

- `String toString()`—returns a string representation of a folder.

### 13.4.6 Transport Class

A `Transport` represents an Internet mail service that allows messages to be sent (as opposed to a store, which is designed for retrieving messages). `Transport` is an abstract class, and may not be instantiated by applications. Static methods are provided, which use the default transport system for each type of recipient address (for example, a newsgroup address type gets sent to a newsgroup, while a mail address gets sent to a mail account). This class extends the `javax. mail.Service` class, and provides several additional methods.

#### Methods

The following methods of the `Transport` class are public unless otherwise noted.

- `void addTransportListener (TransportListener listener)`—adds the specified listener to a list, which will be notified whenever a transport-related event occurs.

- `protected void notifyTransportListeners ( int type, Address[] validSent, Address[] validUnsent, Address[] invalid, Message msg)`—notifies all registered transport listeners of an event, and to which recipients the specified message has been sent, and which recipients were not sent the message.

- `void removeTransportListener (TransportListener listener)`—removes the specified listener from a list, which is notified of transport events.
- `static void send(Message message)` throws `javax.mail.SendFailed Exception, javax.mail.MessagingException`—sends a message using the default transport system for the message's recipient address. If a message could not be sent to one or more recipients, a `SendFailed Exception` will be thrown, and valid recipients may not receive the message.
- `static void send(Message message, Address[] addresses)` throws `javax.mail.SendFailedException, javax.mail.MessagingException`—sends a message, using the default transport system for each recipient address, to all of the specified recipients. This is an overloaded version of the `Transport.send()` method. An easier alternative is to specify the recipients of a message during its construction.
- `static void sendMessage(Message message, Address[] addresses)` throws `javax.mail.SendFailedException, javax.mail.Messaging Exception`—sends a message using the default transport system for each recipient. Unlike the `Transport.send(..)` method, valid recipients are guaranteed to receive the message if there are some invalid recipients and a `SendFailedException` is thrown.

### 13.4.7 Session Class

The `Session` class represents the interface between a mail client and a mail server. This class acts as a factory for `Store` and `Transport` objects. Using a `Session` instance, an application can request a particular type of store or transport, and if an implementation for that protocol is available, it will be returned.

#### Methods

Methods of the `Session` class include:

- `boolean getDebug()`—returns the state of the debug flag, which controls whether debugging messages are displayed.
- `static Session getDefaultInstance( Properties properties, Authenticator authenticator)`—returns an instance of the default session object. As each session can contain sensitive information (such as usernames and passwords), granting access to the default session may be risky if multiple applications are running within the JVM. For this reason, an `Authenticator` object may be passed. In most situations, however, it is safe to pass a null value for the `authenticator`

parameter. Mail session properties may also be specified, to control the actions of the session object.

- `Folder getFolder(URLName location)` throws `javax.mail.NoSuch ProviderException, javax.mail.MessagingException`—returns a folder object for the specified `URLName`. If a folder could not be found, a null value will be returned, and an exception may be thrown.

- `static Session getInstance(Properties properties, Authenti cator authenticator)`—returns a new session object, which will use the specified mail properties and authentication mechanism. The authenticator parameter may be null.

- `PasswordAuthentication getPasswordAuthentication (URLName location)`—returns a `PasswordAuthentication` object for the session.

- `Properties getProperties()`—returns mail properties used by a session.

- `String getProperty(String key)`—returns the value of the specified mail property.

- `Provider getProvider(String protocol)` throws `javax.mail.NoSuch ProviderException`—returns the default implementation provider for the specified protocol.

- `Provider[] getProviders()`—returns an array of protocol implementation providers.

- `Store getStore()` throws `javax.mail.NoSuchProviderException`—returns the default mail store, determined by the `mail.store. protocol` property setting, if one is available.

- `Store getStore(Provider provider)` throws `javax.mail.NoSuch ProviderException`—returns the mail store offered by the specified implementation provider, if one is available.

- `Store getStore(String name)` throws `javax.mail.NoSuchProvider Exception`—returns the mail store representing the specified protocol, if one is available.

- `Store getStore(URLName location)` throws `javax.mail.NoSuch ProviderException`—returns the mail store associated with the specified `URLName` object, if one is available.

- `Transport getTransport()` throws `javax.mail.NoSuchProvider Exception`—returns the default mail transport, determined by the `mail.store.transport` property setting, if one is available.

- `Transport getTransport(Address address)` throws `javax.mail. NoSuchProviderException`—returns the mail transport associated with the specified address's type, if one is available.

- `Transport getTransport(Provider provider) throws javax.mail. NoSuchProviderException`—returns the mail transport offered by the specified provider, if one is available.
- `Transport getTransport(String protocol) throws javax.mail. NoSuchProviderException`—returns the mail transport for the specified transport protocol, if one is available.
- `Transport getTransport(URLName location) throws javax.mail. NoSuchProviderException`—returns the mail transport associated with the specified URLName object, if one is available.
- `PasswordAuthentication requestPasswordAuthentication(Inet Address address, int port, String protocol, String prompt, String username)`— prompts the user for a password and returns a `Password Authentication` object when called. This method is invoked when password details have not been provided.
- `void setDebug (boolean debug)`—sets the state of the `debug` flag, to activate debugging information, and modifies the value of the `mail.debug` system property. This information is irrelevant to users, but can be helpful during debugging.
- `void setPasswordAuthentication (URLName location, Password Authentication authenticator)`—assigns a `PasswordAuthentication` object for the session, which will be associated with the specified URL location. A null value may also be specified, removing any password authentication.
- `void setProvider(Provider provider) throws javax.mail.NoSuch ProviderException`—registers the specified provider as the default provider for its protocol.

### 13.4.8 Using JavaMail to Send Messages

Armed with a basic knowledge of the essential classes in the JavaMail API, we will now take a look at a practical application. Sending messages with the JavaMail API is extremely simple, and a good demonstration of the capabilities of the API. A default implementation of the Simple Mail Transfer Protocol (SMTP) is available, which is used to send e-mail messages to SMTP mail servers. We'll use this implementation to send an electronic message using SMTP and JavaMail.

#### Code for SendMailDemo

```
import javax.mail.*;
import javax.mail.internet.*;
import java.util.Properties;
```

```
// Chapter 13, Listing 2
public class SendMailDemo
{
    public static void main(String args[])
    {
        int argc = args.length;

        // Check for valid number of parameters
        if (argc != 2)
        {
            System.out.println ("Syntax :");
            System.out.println ("java SendMailDemo smtphost to_address");
            return;
        }


        String host = args[0];
        String to   = args[1];

        // Create a properties file, specifying mail
        // settings
        Properties prop = new Properties();
        prop.put ("mail.transport.default", "smtp");
        prop.put ("mail.smtp.host", host);


        try
        {
            // Get a session, with the specified properties
            Session mySession = Session.getInstance (prop, null);

            // Create a message to send, specifying our
            // session
            Message message = new MimeMessage (mySession);
            message.setSubject ("Test message");
            message.setContent ("This is a test message....",
                "text/plain");

            // Create an InternetAddress, for specifying
            // recipient
            InternetAddress toAddr  = new InternetAddress ( to );
            message.setRecipient (Message.RecipientType.TO, toAddr);

            // Create an InternetAddress, for specifying sender
            // address
            InternetAddress fromAddr= new InternetAddress (
                                        "nobody@nowhere.
                                          com", "SendMailDemo" );

            message.setFrom (fromAddr);
```

```
        System.out.println ("Sending message");

        // Send the message
        Transport.send(message);

        System.out.println ("Message sent");
    }
    catch (AddressException    ae)
    {
        System.err.println ("Invalid address " + ae);
    }
    catch (MessagingException me)
    {
        System.err.println ("Messaging failure : " + me);
    }
    catch (Exception ex)
    {
        System.err.println ("Failure : " + ex);
    }

  }
}
```

### How SendMailDemo Works

The first thing our application must do is to import the necessary classes from the JavaMail package, as well as the Properties class from the java.util package.

```
import javax.mail.*;
import javax.mail.internet.*;
import java.util.Properties;
```

The application then checks for the correct number of command-line parameters. To send even the simplest of mail messages, we need to know several pieces of information—including the hostname of the SMTP server, the recipient of the message, and other message details such as the subject and body of the message. Our mail application is fairly simple, and we can provide a default subject and body for the purposes of a demonstration. The application must, however, be informed of the recipient of the message (your e-mail address) and the SMTP server name.

```
public static void main(String args[])
{
    int argc = args.length;

    // Check for valid number of parameters
    if (argc != 2)
    {
        System.out.println ("Syntax :");
        System.out.println ("java SendMailDemo smtphost to_
        address");
```

```
        return;
    }
    String host = args[0];
    String to   = args[1];
    // .....
}
```

Next, we must prepare the settings for sending mail. We start by creating a new `Properties` object, and specifying the mail transport protocol we wish to use, as well as the hostname of the SMTP server.

```
// Create a properties file, specifying mail settings

Properties prop = new Properties();
prop.put ("mail.transport.default", "smtp");
prop.put ("mail.smtp.host", host);
```

**NOTE:** If you'd like to see what is going on behind the scenes, or need further information for debugging purposes, simply set the `mail.debug` property to a `String` value of "true." In this example, you could add the following line here:

```
prop.put ("mail.debug", "true");
```

We pass this information on to JavaMail, when we request an instance of the `Session` class, by using the static method `Session.getInstance()`. It takes as a parameter a Properties object and an `Authenticator` object (which can be set to null).

```
// Get a session, with the specified properties
Session mySession = Session.getInstance (prop, null);
```

Once you have a `Session` object, you can then begin to create a mail message. Remember that the `Message` class is an abstract class, so we need to use a concrete implementation. We create a new instance of a `MimeMessage` (which is used to handle a variety of message types, including plain text), and pass to its constructor our `Session` object (needed later when we want to transmit the messsage). Then we can begin to populate our message with data, such as the subject and message contents.

```
// Create a message to send, specifying our session
Message message = new MimeMessage (mySession);
message.setSubject ("Test message");
message.setContent ("This is a test message....", "text/plain");
```

Addressing the message is slightly more complicated. We can't specify a "To:" or "From:" address simply by passing a String. Instead, an Address instance must be passed. For news messages, we would pass a NewsAddress instance, but for mail messages we pass an InternetAddress instance. You'll notice too that for the "From:" address, two parameters are used. An InternetAddress can take a raw e-mail address, or an e-mail address and a personal name. In this case, we use "nobody@nowhere.com" as the e-mail address, and "SendMailDemo" as the person.

**NOTE:** An InternetAddress is not the same as a java.net.InetAddress. There are also different types of recipient addresses (TO, CC, and BCC). A TO address is sent to the named recipient, while a CC address is sent as a carbon copy. A BCC address is sent as a blind carbon copy; that is, other recipients of the message won't know that it was sent to the address listed as BCC. The address types are represented by constants defined in Message.RecipientType:

```
// Create an InternetAddress, for specifying recipient
InternetAddress toAddr  = new InternetAddress ( to );
message.setRecipient (Message.RecipientType.TO, toAddr);

// Create an InternetAddress, for specifying sender address
InternetAddress fromAddr= new InternetAddress (
"nobody@nowhere.com", "SendMailDemo" );
message.setFrom (fromAddr);
```

Finally, we are able to send the message. Sending the message is the easiest part of all. Simply call the static method Transport.send( Message ), and the message will be sent. Transport knows the correct mail settings, because our message knows the correct Session instance, which was created earlier. If you want finer control over message sending, you can request a Transport instance and open connections yourself. For a single message, however, this is the easiest way of delivery.

```
// Send the message
Transport.send(message);
```

We also need to wrap most of this code in exception handlers, as there are plenty of errors that can occur at runtime. For example, the address specified by the user might not be an actual address (if the user mixed up the order of parameters). The SMTP server might be incorrect, or might be down. These are a few of the many errors that can occur at runtime. For this reason, applications must at least catch a MessagingException.

### Running SendMailDemo

You'll need to specify the hostname for an SMTP server on your local network, or the SMTP server of your Internet service provider. You'll also need to specify your e-mail address, so that you can check whether the message was delivered correctly.

The syntax for the `SendMailDemo` is as follows:

```
java SendMailDemo mysmtpserver myemail@mydomain
```

## 13.4.9 Using JavaMail to Retrieve Messages

While sending messages is useful, it is only part of the functionality of the JavaMail API. Reading messages from an Internet mail server (such as an IMAP/POP3 account or a newsgroup), is also possible, as the next example demonstrates.

### Code for ReadMailDemo

```
import javax.mail.*;
import javax.mail.internet.*;

// Chapter 13, Listing 3
public class ReadMailDemo
{
    public static void main (String args[])
    {
        int argc = args.length;

        // Check for valid number of parameters
        if (argc != 4)
        {
            System.out.println ("Syntax :");
            System.out.println (
            "java ReadMailDemo protocol host username password");
            return;
        }


        String protocol = args[0];
        String host     = args[1];
        String username = args[2];
        String password = args[3];


        try
        {
            // Get a session, with default system properties
            Session mySession = Session.getDefaultInstance
                    (System.getProperties(), null);
```

```
                // Get a specific mail store, such as
                // imap/pop3/news
                Store myStore = mySession.getStore(protocol);
                myStore.connect (host, username, password);

                // Request the INBOX folder for this mail store
                Folder myFolder = myStore.getFolder("INBOX");
                if (myFolder == null)
                {
                    System.err.println ("No default folder available");
                    return;
                }

                System.out.println ("Accessing " +
                    myFolder.getFullName() + " folder");

                // Open in READ_ONLY mode
                myFolder.open(Folder.READ_ONLY);

                int messagecount = myFolder.getMessageCount();
                System.out.println (myFolder.getFullName() + " has "
                    + messagecount +
                " messages.");

                Message[] message = myFolder.getMessages ();

                for (int i = 0; i < message.length; i++)
                {
                    Address[] fromAddr = message[i].getFrom();
                    System.out.println (fromAddr[0] + ":" +
                        message[i].getSubject());
                }

                myFolder.close(false);

            }
            catch (MessagingException me)
            {
                System.err.println ("Messaging failure : " + me);
            }
            catch (Exception ex)
            {
                System.err.println ("Failure : " + ex);
            }
        }
    }
```

### How ReadMailDemo Works

As in the previous example, it is necessary here to import the basic JavaMail
packages. We won't be specifying any properties, however, and the import
statement for java.util.Properties can be omitted.

```
import javax.mail.*;
import javax.mail.internet.*;
```

The next thing that must be done is to check command-line parameters. There are four parameters to this example, which control the protocol used (either IMAP or POP3), the hostname of the mail service, the username, and finally the password. If there are missing or extra parameters, a message showing the correct syntax will be displayed.

```
int argc = args.length;

// Check for valid number of parameters
if (argc != 4)
{
    System.out.println ("Syntax :");
    System.out.println ("java ReadMailDemo protocol host username password");
    return;
}

String protocol = args[0];
String host     = args[1];
String username = args[2];
String password = args[3];
```

Next, we need to get an instance of the Session class, by using the static method System.getInstance(). We don't need to specify any properties, but the method still requires a Properties object. We could create a new Properties instance that is blank, but it is better to select the default system properties, as any existing property settings will be preserved.

```
// Get a session, with default system properties
Session mySession = Session.getDefaultInstance
(System.getProperties(), null);
```

The application can now connect to a mail store. Since the user of the application will specify a protocol as a command-line parameter, we don't need to choose the protocol ourselves. This shows the power of JavaMail—whether you're working with a POP3 server, an IMAP server, or some other type of mail server, the code will remain the same. Before using a mail store, though, it is important that it is actually connected. Here we specify the hostname, username, and password, by using the Store.connect() method.

```
// Get a specific mail store, such as imap/pop3/news
Store myStore = mySession.getStore(protocol);
myStore.connect (host, username, password);
```

Mail systems store messages in folders. Some mail systems may have many folders, whereas others may support just one folder. Generally, the INBOX folder will be the default folder for incoming messages. The application requests the INBOX folder, and opens it in READ_ONLY mode. Before a folder can be used, it must be opened.

```
// Request the INBOX folder for this mail store
Folder myFolder = myStore.getFolder("INBOX");

System.out.println ("Accessing mail account now");

// Open in READ_ONLY mode
myFolder.open(Folder.READ_ONLY);
```

The folder, now open, can be used to retrieve messages. First, the application requests a count of the total number of messages available. Next, it uses this information to select a batch of messages, from the first message to the last. This will be returned as an array of messages.

**NOTE:** Messages are numbered from 1 (1 is the first message). Arrays in Java are zero-indexed, meaning that the first element is element 0.

```
int messagecount = myFolder.getMessageCount();
System.out.println (myFolder.getFullName() + " has " + message-
count + " messages.");

Message[] message = myFolder.getMessages ();
```

The application then traverses through each element of the array (starting with the first message, at element 0). The application displays the sender of the message as well as the message subject. Message has a getFrom() method that returns an array of Address objects. There isn't a simple way to get the sender of the message, so to display the sender, you can usually simply access the first element of this array. The JavaMail API allows for multiple senders, so if the mailing system your application is using supports this facility, then for completeness you may want to have your applications check the length of the "From" array.

Getting the subject of the message is far easier—simply call the getSubject() method.

```
for (int i = 0; i < message.length; i++)
{
    Address[] fromAddr = message[i].getFrom();
    System.out.println (fromAddr[0] + ":" +
    message[i].getSubject());
}
```

Finally, we can clean up open folders and connections to mail services by calling the close method on any open folders or stores. The `Folder.close()` method takes a boolean flag parameter, indicating whether any messages marked "deleted" should be removed. As we're opening the folder in read-only mode anyway, this is unnecessary, so a value of "false" is passed.

```
// Close messages, don't expunge
myFolder.close(false);
// Close connection to store
myStore.close();
```

### Running ReadMailDemo

You'll need to specify four parameters for this demonstration. These are the name of the mail protocol to use, the hostname of the mail service, the username of the account, and finally the password. If you have an IMAP account, use the protocol name of "imap," and for a POP3 account, use the protocol name of "pop3." Remember, too, if you haven't done so already, to install any additional protocol implementations that you require.

**NOTE:** Case sensitivity applies to protocol names. "POP3" is not treated the same way as "pop3."

The syntax for the `ReadMailDemo` is as follows:

```
java ReadMailDemo protocol myserver myusername mypassword
```

For example:

```
java ReadMailDemo pop3 ficticiousemailserver.com johndoe
xxm312ras
```

## 13.5  Advanced Messaging with JavaMail

The examples up until now have been pretty straightforward. They only scratch the surface of JavaMail, however. Simple tasks are easy to perform in JavaMail, but more advanced functionality is available. Let's take a further look at what JavaMail has to offer.

### *13.5.1 JavaMail Event-Handling Model*

The JavaMail API uses the JDK1.1 event-handling model, which readers may already be familiar with from using the Abstract Windowing Toolkit (AWT) and Swing. For those without prior experience with this model, a brief overview is offered. Readers acquainted with this material may choose to skip to Section 13.5.1.2.

### 13.5.1.1   Overview

AWT event handling in JDK1.02 used a clumsy callback mechanism that required developers to extend a `Component` and provide event-handling methods, or to provide these methods in a parent container such as an applet. As of JDK1.1, this model has been replaced with a far superior mechanism.

The new event-handling model requires objects that are interested in observing events to register with the event source as a listener (see Figure 13-2). Each type of listener defines a set of methods that define event handlers. When an event is generated by the event source, one of these handler methods will be called, for every registered listener. This model allows multiple listeners for a given event source, as well as multiple types of event listeners. Other listeners will be notified independently of each other; one listener cannot block the notification of another.

Let's look at a brief example of this event-handling mechanism in action. For example, suppose an application wanted to terminate when a button was pressed. Rather than subclassing the button to provide event methods, the

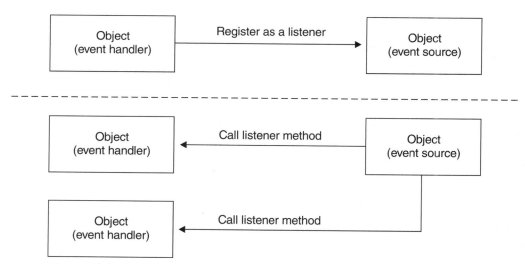

**Figure 13-2**   Event-handling overview

application can implement the appropriate listener interface and register with the button.

```
public class myapp implements ActionListener
{
        public myapp()
        {
            Button b = new Button("Exit");
            b.addActionListener(this)
            .....
        }

        public void actionPerformed(ActionEvent e)
        {
            System.exit(0);
        }
}
```

In this example, which uses `ActionListener`, only one event callback method was required. However, more complex event listeners require many methods. If you only want to implement one or a few of the methods of an event listener, there is usually a listener adapter class provided. An adapter class implements every method you need for a listener interface, and by overriding individual methods you can save yourself a considerable amount of time and effort.

Inner classes are another way of working with short event handlers. An inner class is a class within a class. If you frequently write event listeners that use adapters, you'll find that you often need to create new Java source files, which can become difficult to manage. Inner classes are a language feature of JDK1.1 and higher. A thorough discussion of Java language features is beyond the scope of this book. However, examples using inner classes for event handling can be found later in the chapter.

## 13.5.1.2   JavaMail Events

Several JavaMail events are defined in the javax.mail.event package. The event classname, its corresponding description, and the usual sources of the event are shown in Table 13-1.

Each event can be responded to by implementing the appropriate event listener classes. There are six listener classes, and some support adapters that are useful when a single event action, or a few event actions, must be monitored.

1. `ConnectionListener`—listener interface for `ConnectionEvent`
   - `ConnectionAdapter`—adapter for `ConnectionListener`
2. `FolderListener`—listener interface for `FolderEvent`
   - `FolderAdapter`—adapter for `FolderListener`

3. `MessageChangedListener`—listener interface for `MessageChangedEvent`
   - `MessageChangedAdapter`—adapter for `MessageChangedListener`

4. `MessageCountListener`—listener interface for `MessageCountEvent`

5. `StoreListener`—listener interface for `StoreEvent`

6. `TransportListener`—listener interface for `TransportEvent`
   - `TransportAdapter`—adapter for `TransportListener`

## 13.5.2 Writing JavaMail Event Handlers

Let's look at a practical example of JavaMail event handlers. Earlier in this chapter, we looked at how to send a simple message using the Transport class. However, other than catching exceptions thrown at runtime, there wasn't any strong error-handling code. For example, the message might not have been delivered if the SMTP server rejected the recipient or IP address of the sender. The earlier example has been rewritten to illustrate the JavaMail event-handling mechanism. It registers a `ConnectionListener` and a `TransportListener`, to detect connection and transport events. While some of the code is the same, changed portions are described below.

### Code for SendEventDemo

```
import javax.mail.*;
import javax.mail.event.*;
import javax.mail.internet.*;
import java.util.Properties;

// Chapter 13, Listing 4
public class SendEventDemo
{
```

**Table 13-1**   Events Defined by the javax.mail Package

| Event Class | Event Description | Source |
|---|---|---|
| `MailEvent` | Represents general mail events | Any |
| `ConnectionEvent` | Connection and disconnection events | Store/ Transport |
| `FolderEvent` | Represents a folder-related event | Folder |
| `MessageChanged` | Represents change to messages | Folder |
| `MessageCountEvent` | Represents a change in the number of messages | Folder |
| `StoreEvent` | Represents an event pertaining to a mail service | Store |
| `TransportEvent` | Represents a message transport event | Transport |

```java
public static void main(String args[])
{
    int argc = args.length;

    // Check for valid number of parameters
    if (argc != 2)
    {
        System.out.println ("Syntax :");
        System.out.println ("java SendEventMailDemo smtphost to_address");
        return;
    }


    String host = args[0];
    String to   = args[1];

    // Create a properties file, specifying mail settings
    Properties prop = new Properties();
    prop.put ("mail.transport.default", "smtp");
    prop.put ("mail.smtp.host", host);

    try
    {
        // Get a session, with the specified properties
        Session mySession = Session.getInstance (prop, null);

        // Create a message to send, specifying our session
        Message message = new MimeMessage (mySession);
        message.setSubject ("Test message");
        message.setContent ("This is a test message....", "text/plain");

        // Create an InternetAddress, for specifying recipient
        InternetAddress toAddr  = new InternetAddress ( to );
        message.setRecipient (Message.RecipientType.TO, toAddr);

        // Create an InternetAddress, for specifying sender address
        InternetAddress fromAddr= new InternetAddress (
          "nobody@nowhere.com", "SendEventMailDemo" );
        message.setFrom (fromAddr);

        // Get a transport instance
        Transport transport = mySession.getTransport(toAddr);

        // Create an anonymous inner class for connection listener
                    transport.addConnectionListener( new
                    ConnectionListener()
                    {
                        public void opened(ConnectionEvent e)
                        {
                            System.out.println ("connection opened");
                        }
```

```java
            public void disconnected(ConnectionEvent e)
            {
                System.out.println ("connection disconnected");
            }

            public void closed(ConnectionEvent e)
            {
                System.out.println ("connection closed");
            }
        });

        // Create an anonymous inner class for transport listener
        transport.addTransportListener( new TransportAdapter()
        {
            public void messageDelivered(TransportEvent e)
            {
                System.out.println ("Message delivered");
            }

            public void
            messageNotDelivered(TransportEvent e)
            {
                System.out.println ("Message not delivered");
            }
        });

        // Open the connection
        transport.connect();

        System.out.println ("Attempting to send message");

        // Send the message
        Address[] msgAddr = { toAddr };
        transport.sendMessage(message, msgAddr);

        // Close the connection
        transport.close();
    }
    catch (AddressException   ae)
    {
        System.err.println ("Invalid address " + ae);
    }
    catch (MessagingException me)
    {
        System.err.println ("Messaging failure : " + me);
    }
    catch (Exception ex)
    {
        System.err.println ("Failure : " + ex);
    }

    }
}
```

### How SendEventDemo Works

The first major difference is that we need to get an instance of a `Transport` object. While `Transport` has a static method that allows messages to be sent, you will need an instance of `Transport` to register a `ConnectionListener` or `TransportListener`.

```
// Get a transport instance
Transport transport = mySession.getTransport(toAddr);
```

Next, we have to create a listener and register it with our transport object. In this example, anonymous inner classes are used, though it is also possible to create separate classes for this purpose. An application could implement a `Listener` interface, or extend an `Adapter` class if not every listener method was required. To illustrate the difference, both approaches have been used.

```
// Create an anonymous inner class for connection listener
transport.addConnectionListener( new ConnectionListener()
{
    public void opened(ConnectionEvent e)
    {
        System.out.println ("connection opened");
    }

    public void disconnected(ConnectionEvent e)
    {
        System.out.println ("connection disconnected");
    }

    public void closed(ConnectionEvent e)
    {
        System.out.println ("connection closed");
    }
});

// Create an anonymous inner class for transport listener
transport.addTransportListener( new TransportAdapter()
{
    public void messageDelivered(TransportEvent e)
    {
        System.out.println ("Message delivered");
    }

    public void messageNotDelivered(TransportEvent e)
    {
        System.out.println ("Message not delivered");
    }
});
```

When the listeners are registered, you can then work with the `Trans port` object. The first step is to open a connection to the remote transport, by calling the `Transport.connect()` method. This will trigger the registered `ConnectionListener`, as a connection will be established.

```
// Open the connection
transport.connect();
```

Once connected, the message can be sent. The static `Transport.send()` method can't be used, as our listeners are registered with another `Transport` object instance. Instead, the `sendMessage()` method must be used, which takes as a parameter an array of `Address` objects. This will trigger a `TransportEvent`, which will be passed to the registered listener.

```
// Send the message
Address[] msgAddr = { toAddr };
transport.sendMessage(message, msgAddr);
```

Finally, the transport must be closed down. When closed, a `Connection Event` will be passed to our listener.

```
// Close the connection
transport.close();
```

### Running SendEventDemo

As in the earlier `SendMailDemo`, the hostname of an SMTP server must be specified as a parameter, as well as a valid e-mail address.

The syntax for the `SendEventDemo` is as follows:

```
java SendEventDemo mysmtpserver myemail@mydomain
```

Not only will a message be sent, but you'll also see the application progress, when a connection opens and closes and when a message is delivered to the SMTP server.

## 13.5.3 Sending a File as an Attachment

Previous examples in this chapter have dealt with purely text documents. However, one of the most useful features of e-mail is the ability to send files as an attachment. E-mail makes it easy to get files across to other people on the Internet, such as documents and compressed files archives. JavaMail supports MIME attachments, and makes it easy to compose and transmit a multipart message with a file attachment. This next example is based on a demonstration provided in the JavaMail SDK.

### Code for SendAttachment

```java
import java.util.Properties;
import javax.activation.*;
import javax.mail.*;
import javax.mail.internet.*;
import java.io.File;

// Chapter 13, Listing 5
public class SendAttachment
{
    public static void main(String args[])
    {
        int argc = args.length;

        // Check for valid number of parameters
        if (argc != 3)
        {
            System.out.println ("Syntax :");
            System.out.println (
            "java SendAttachment smtphost to_address filepath");
            return;
        }

        String host = args[0];
        String to   = args[1];
        String file = args[2];

        // Create a properties file, specifying mail settings
        Properties prop = new Properties();
        prop.put ("mail.transport.default", "smtp");
        prop.put ("mail.smtp.host", host);


        try
        {
            // Get a session, with the specified properties
            Session mySession = Session.getInstance (prop, null);

            System.out.println ("Composing message");

            // Create a message to send, specifying our session
            Message message = new MimeMessage (mySession);
            message.setSubject ("File attachment file");

            // Create an InternetAddress, for specifying recipient
            InternetAddress toAddr  = new InternetAddress ( to );
            message.setRecipient (Message.RecipientType.TO, toAddr);

            // Use the same sender address as recipient
            message.setFrom (toAddr);

            // Construct a multipart message
            Multipart part = new MimeMultipart();
```

```
            // Create the message body
            BodyPart  msgBody = new MimeBodyPart ();
            msgBody.setText ("There is a file attached to this message....");

            // Create the message attachment
            BodyPart  attachment = new MimeBodyPart();

            // Use a file data source for reading the file
            FileDataSource fileDataSource = new FileDataSource(file);

            // Set the appropriate data handler
            attachment.setDataHandler ( new DataHandler ( fileDataSource ) );

            // Set the filename of the file (don't include path info)
            if (file.indexOf( File.separator ) != -1)
            {
                String fileName = file.substring
                    (file.lastIndexOf( File.separator)+1, file.length());
                attachment.setFileName(fileName);
            }
            else
            {
                attachment.setFileName(file);
            }

            System.out.println ("Adding attachments");

            // Add msg body and attachment to multipart message
            part.addBodyPart(msgBody);
            part.addBodyPart(attachment);

            // Set our multipart message as the msg contents
            message.setContent (part);

            System.out.println ("Sending message");

            // Send the message
            Transport.send(message);

            System.out.println ("Message sent");
        }
        catch (AddressException    ae)
        {
            System.err.println ("Invalid address " + ae);
        }
        catch (MessagingException me)
        {
            System.err.println ("Messaging failure : " + me);
        }
        catch (Exception ex)
        {
            System.err.println ("Failure : " + ex);
        }

    }
}
```

### How SendAttachment Works

Sending a plain text message is relatively straightforward—simply create a new instance of a `MimeMessage` and pass the text contents of the message to the `MimeMessage.setContent()` method. When a multipart message (one composed of multiple parts) is needed, further work needs to be done. The first step will be to create a new Multipart object.

```
// Construct a multipart message
Multipart part = new MimeMultipart();
```

The `Multipart` object acts as a container for the various components that will make up our message. The first component will be our text body. This is where the normal text of the message goes.

```
// Create the message body
BodyPart  msgBody = new MimeBodyPart ();
msgBody.setText ("There is a file attached to this message....");
```

Next, we need to create a second BodyPart, to hold our attachment. We will also need to specify a data source for the part's contents, using a `FileData Source` object from the JavaBeans Activation Framework (JAF). We must also specify a `DataHandler`, which will use our `FileDataSource` to get the contents of a file.

```
// Create the message attachment
BodyPart  attachment = new MimeBodyPart();

// Use a file data source for reading the file
FileDataSource fileDataSource = new FileDataSource(file);

// Set the appropriate data handler
attachment.setDataHandler ( new DataHandler ( fileDataSource )
);
```

We also need to assign a name to the file that will be stored as an attachment. If an absolute filename (a filename that includes path information) is specified as a command-line parameter, we need to strip this information away using some simple string processing.

```
// Set the filename of the file (don't include path info)
if (file.indexOf( File.separator ) != -1)
{
    String fileName = file.substring
        (file.lastIndexOf( File.separator)+1, file.length());
    attachment.setFileName(fileName);
}
else
{
```

```
       attachment.setFileName(file);
}
```

Finally, we add each individual part to our `Multipart` object, and assign this object as the content of our message.

```
// Add msg body and attachment to multipart message
part.addBodyPart(msgBody);
part.addBodyPart(attachment);

// Set our multipart message as the msg contents
message.setContent (part);
```

### Running SendAttachment

The syntax for `SendAttachment` is as follows:

```
java SendAttachment mysmtpserver myemail@mydomain filename
```

This message will send the specified file as an e-mail attachment. Your mail client must support attachments in order for the file to be read.

## 13.6  Summary

The JavaMail API is a comprehensive framework for sending and retrieving mail messages. Creating your own implementation of a mail protocol is feasible, but involves additional effort and replication of code. The JavaMail API has many benefits as well, including an interface that makes the choice of mail protocol transparent during coding. Whether using IMAP or POP3, the code to access mail folders remains the same, and future mail protocols can be included with little or no changes.

---

**Chapter Highlights**

In this chapter, you have learned:

- How to install the JavaMail API implementation and POP3 provider
- How to determine the available `Store` and `Transport` providers
- How to compose and send a mail message using a `Transport`
- How to retrieve mail messages from a `Folder`, using a `Store`
- How to write JavaMail event handlers
- How to send a file as an attachment

# INDEX

# More books from Addison-Wesley

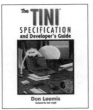

ISBN 0-201-72218-6

ISBN 0-201-70074-3

ISBN 0-201-70244-4

ISBN 0-201-61617-3

ISBN 0-201-70906-6

ISBN 0-201-70921-X

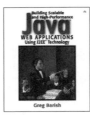

ISBN 0-201-72956-3

ISBN 0-201-70043-3

ISBN 0-201-59614-8

ISBN 0-201-72897-4

ISBN 0-201-72588-6

ISBN 0-201-75880-6

ISBN 0-201-75875-X

ISBN 0-201-70916-3

ISBN 0-201-75306-5

ISBN 0-201-61646-7

ISBN 0-201-70252-5

ISBN 0-201-73410-9

ISBN 0-201-73829-5

ISBN 0-201-71962-2

ISBN 0-201-75044-9

http://www.aw.com/cseng

♦ Addison-Wesley

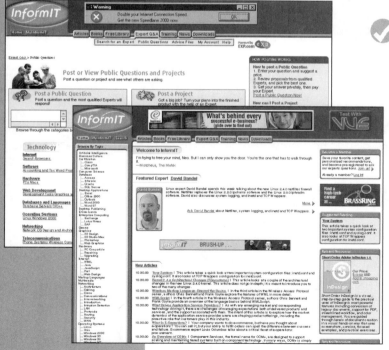

# Register
## Your Book

at www.aw.com/cseng/register

You may be eligible to receive:

- Advance notice of forthcoming editions of the book
- Related book recommendations
- Chapter excerpts and supplements of forthcoming titles
- Information about special contests and promotions throughout the year
- Notices and reminders about author appearances, tradeshows, and online chats with special guests

## Contact us

If you are interested in writing a book or reviewing manuscripts prior to publication, please write to us at:

Editorial Department
Addison-Wesley Professional
75 Arlington Street, Suite 300
Boston, MA 02116 USA
Email: AWPro@aw.com

**Addison-Wesley**

Visit us on the Web: http://www.aw.com/cseng